THE CLASSICS
OF WESTERN
SPIRITUALITY

THE CLASSICS OF WESTERN SPIRITUALITY
A Library of the Great Spiritual Masters

President and Publisher
Kevin A. Lynch, C.S.P.

EDITORIAL BOARD

Devotio Moderna
BASIC WRITINGS

TRANSLATED AND INTRODUCED BY
JOHN VAN ENGEN

PREFACE BY
HEIKO A. OBERMAN

PAULIST PRESS
NEW YORK • MAHWAH

Copyright © 1988
by John Van Engen

Library of Congress Cataloging-in-Publication Data

Devotio moderna.

    (Classics of Western spirituality)
    "About one-quarter of the texts were translated from
Middle Dutch alone . . . one-half exist in both Middle
Dutch and Latin versions, and both were used"—Introd.
    Bibliography: p.
    Includes index.
    1. Devotio moderna—History—Sources. 2. Grote,
Geert, 1340–1384. I. Van Engen, John H. II. Series.
BR270.D48   1988   274'.05   88-5817
ISBN 0-8091-0403-2
ISBN 0-8091-2962-0 (pbk.)

Published by Paulist Press
997 Macarthur Boulevard
Mahwah, New Jersey 07430

Printed and bound in the United States of America

Contents

CONTENTS

Editor of this Volume

JOHN VAN ENGEN is presently director of the Medieval Institute at the University of Notre Dame. He received his undergraduate degree from Calvin College, and his graduate degree from the University of California at Los Angeles. His dissertation and first book dealt with the life and works of a twelfth-century Benedictine monk, *Rupert of Deutz* (University of California Press, 1983). In 1987 this book was awarded the John Nicholas Brown prize by the Medieval Academy of America. With the support of a Guggenheim Fellowship, Van Engen spent the 1985–1986 academic year in Louvain, Belgium, where he pursued research into religious movements in the Lowlands during the Later Middle Ages. Van Engen has been a member of the History Department at the University of Notre Dame since 1977.

Author of the Preface

HEIKO A. OBERMAN is professor for Medieval, Renaissance and Reformation History at the University of Arizona, Tucson. Dr. Oberman was born in Utrecht, Holland, and received his Doctorate in Theology at the University of Utrecht. During his distinguished career he has been Professor of Church History, Harvard University, Director of the Institut für Spätmittelalter und Reformation, University of Tübingen, and Fellow of the Institute for the Humanities, University of Wisconsin. In 1985, he was the recipient of the Historischer Sachbuchpreis for *Luther-Mensch zwischen Gott und Teufel*. Among his many works are *The Harvest of Medieval Theology: Gabriel Biel and Late Medieval Nominalism*, and *Forerunners of the Reformation: The Shape of Late Medieval Thought*.

for
my mother,
Winnie Van Engen,
and for
Abram and Esther Wessels

Preface

This volume is published at an auspicious moment. In an external sense it arrives in time to commemorate the third and most influential foundation by Geert Grote (d.1384): After the sisters of the common life (1379), and in its wake the brethren, the Windesheim Congregation near Zwolle was established in 1387. There is, however, a more substantial reason for welcoming this volume. In religious history it is not uncommon that a considerable period of time is needed to gain a proper perspective on the significance of a movement; in the case of the Modern Devotion, some six hundred years were needed to remove at least some of the major obstacles. An internal reason for regarding this volume as timely is that scholarship in this field is now in the very beginning of what promises to be its most creative phase of research. As often in the history of Western thought, this is the third phase: following the nineteenth-century claims for the significance of the Modern Devotion, climaxing in views that regarded this Dutch movement as the center of the Christian Renaissance or as the forerunner of both the Renaissance and the Reformation north of the Alps, in a much-needed correcting phase, scholarly energy had to be invested in retrieving the solid historical basis of the documents themselves.

At this point in time we are about to move away from a situation in which much space and energy had to be invested in establishing what the Modern Devotion was and what it was not. To get a handle on a movement that for such a long time proved elusive, it is essential to realize that its period of growth and strength stretched over almost one and a half centuries and may not have reached its zenith until the end of the fifteenth century. Since a century lasts one hundred unique years, ten decades of breathtakingly rapid shifts in social conditions and intellectual assumptions, it is mandatory that any characterization of the movement be provided with a time index. Of no less import is the realization that during this period the movement spread from the Ijssel Delta in the Netherlands to northern and southern Germany, Belgium, France, and Switzerland, so that together with the category of time the importance of space and place must also be taken into consideration. However, before the extent of growth and change can be measured, and the glorious but tough questions of the past as to the relation of the Modern Devotion to the Renaissance and the Reformation can be reopened, the principles and ideals of the founding period have to be clarified by concentrating on the work of the three great men—Geert Grote (d. 1384), Gerard Zerbolt of Zutphen (d. 1398), and the charismatic organizer, Florens Radewijns (d. 1400).

In searching for a connection with Renaissance humanism and the Reformation, past studies concentrated on doctrines and on the ideological profile of the Modern Devotion—and it would be wrong to deny that there is indeed a "program," individually developed and shared by the founding fathers of the movement in the fourteenth century. But as our present knowledge of the sources indicates, the best available working definition is a functional description, namely, that the movement had its common thrust in the search for a new meditation technique for the working classes, directed toward the reformation of the soul and the rejuvenation of the spirit as the basis for renewal of the communal life, whether within or outside monastic walls.

This last statement is not without special significance: within *or* outside the monastic walls. The Modern Devotion in its first two historical forms of expression, namely, as the community of the sisters and the brethren of the common life, propagated a life without vows and therefore without the official monastic rules as prescribed by canon law. Even when, after 1387, the movement was regularized under the rule of St. Augustine, this original vision was kept alive in the characteristic interpretation of the vows (1) as the necessary forms of the communal devotion, and (2) as the means by which other monastic houses are not won over and incorporated to strengthen their own organization, but brought to reform from within, in order to have a greater spiritual yield for the world "outside." In the suspicion against vain curiosity and the "hot air" of academic learning—*scientia inflat!*—we should note not merely the undeniable element of anti-intellectualism but also the awareness that the inhibiting rules of classroom logic and textbook dialectic have in common with the *consuetudines* or life-style of the monastic orders that the true *praxis pietatis* (that is, the fertile soil for the tender roots of spiritual experience) will dry out. The movement would never have had such an impact, however, if it had been just a protest movement springing from antimonastic or anticlerical sentiments—

which often explain better the excitement and praise of later interpreters than of the late medieval authors themselves. The reform of
the soul is seen as the road to reform of late medieval monasticism,
and beyond that of the prelates and of the clergy in general—and
thus indirectly as the road to the quickening of the Church at large.

Modern interpreters will be quick to point out that the movement was a failure, soon overshadowed and bypassed by Renaissance humanism and Reformation reorientation. But in one sense,
no movement of rejuvenation of any sort has ever been a long-term
"success," including Christianity itself. In another sense, the Modern Devotion has continued to survive under many other names,
such as Jansenism or Puritanism, and it fed into that resurgence in
vitality which we vaguely call "reform Catholicism," particularly in
its plethora of new monastic foundations. Above all, it performed its
most lasting service as a reminder that the greatest threat to true devotion is the professionalization of religion.

Acknowledgements

In preparing this book, I have incurred a number of debts. John Farina, general editor of the Classics of Western Spirituality, graciously agreed to include this volume and subsequently showed both firmness and understanding when unexpected administrative responsibilities slowed its progress. Most of the work was finally completed at the Groot Begijnhof in Louvain, Belgium. A generous grant from the Onderzoeksraad of the Catholic University of Louvain (KU Leuven) made it possible for the work to be carried out in a setting as close to that of the *devotio moderna* as any to be found in the modern world. Special thanks go to Dirk van den Auweele, who oversaw the arrangements, and to Jack and Joske Dick, our neighbors in the Begijnhof, who helped make it a memorable year. In Louvain I was able to draw on the resources of the university's libraries and to meet other scholars in this field, especially Willem Lourdaux, Marc Haverhals, Werner Verbeke, and A. G. Weiler. My wife, Suzanne, and our four sons adapted quickly and enthusiastically to life in the Begijnhof, while patiently allowing me to go on thinking and writing about the "brothers and sisters of the common life." In the final stage of preparation, Marcia Kopacz took over the typing responsibilities with care and efficiency.

This book is dedicated to my mother and to my parents-in-law, who have been for me over the years exemplary teachers of Christian devotion.

Introduction

Between 1415 and 1420, Henry Pomerius wrote a short history of his religious house, Groenendael (located outside Brussels), together with an account of its most famous resident, the Flemish mystic John of Ruusbroec (d.1381). To highlight Ruusbroec's importance, Pomerius described meetings with several noteworthy contemporaries, including Master Geert Grote (d.1384), identified as the "chief source of that new devotion found today among the canons regular throughout lower Germany."[1] In 1412 Groenendael had formally joined the Windesheim Congregation of canons regular associated with Grote, and that surely lay behind Pomerius's reference to this movement of "new devotion" (*devotio moderna*). Only a generation after Grote's death, therefore, and at a distance greater than one hundred miles from his hometown, he was perceived to have started something that then and now carried the label "modern devotion." Sometime between 1430 and 1450 the prior of Windesheim (located just south of Zwolle and twenty miles north of Grote's hometown at Deventer) wrote a short account of this religious movement for its younger adherents, and his first section bore a similar title, "On the rise of the new devotion in our land."[2] About the same time, Thomas of Kempen, novitiate master at the related house of St. Agnietenberg north of Zwolle, encouraged his charges to persist in their profession and portrayed to them the lives of the "modern fathers," beginning with Geert Grote and his disciple Florens Radewijns.[3] By the 1460s John Busch could write a history of Windesheim, both as a house and as a congregation, together with its most illustrious representatives, and refer without explanation to congregations of the "new (modern) devotion," whose members he labeled simply the New Devout.[4] The title has stuck to this day both in textbooks and in more detailed studies, although controversies about its meaning and import have never ceased.

Readers with any prior knowledge of the Modern Devotion will tend to associate that name either with *The Imitation of Christ* or with a reforming movement in northern Europe active on the eve of the Reformation. Both associations are correct in part, although both are also potentially quite misleading.

The *Imitation of Christ* has undoubtedly proved the most influential devotional book in Western Christian history. Written only a good generation prior to the invention of printing, it exists still in some 750 hand-written copies, and from its first edition in 1472 down to the last century it appeared in some 3,000 editions (50 of them prior to the year 1500). Even today, despite a marked turning away from this kind of spirituality, its attraction holds: A quick glance at a library shelf in Louvain turned up three English, a Dutch, and a French translation, all published within the last decade. Manuscript and other evidence demonstrates, moreover, that this book was frequently copied and read in the circles of the New Devout. The complication, simply put, is that its ascription to Thomas of Kempen (or, à Kempis), one of the most prolific authors among the Modern Devout, has been contested since at least 1500, and the *Imitation* itself should in any case be approached, historically speaking, by way of the New Devotion rather than the other way around. A few brief remarks must suffice on a problem treated in several lengthy books and countless articles.[5]

The *Imitation* initially circulated anonymously, and over time acquired a list of more than forty purported authors. Beyond such ancients as Augustine and Bernard, it was ascribed early on to Jean Gerson (d.1429), probably the most prolific and influential theological author of that age, and then, possibly by scribal error, to a certain "John Gersen," a presumed Italian abbot. For neither, despite a few ardent Italian nationalists, is there any real evidence in support of authorship, although *The Imitation of Christ* was known in Italy and France in the first half of the fifteenth century and exercised some influence there among observant monks and canons. Next there followed a host of unprovable hypotheses, including some more probable ones such as an unidentified Carthusian from Germany or the Lowlands—which would explain its anonymity, its early spread in their houses, the germanic echoes of its language, and its distinctively "cloistered" spiritual tone. The most abiding ascription, however, one made by John Busch at Windesheim in the 1460s and the one still held tentatively by most scholars today, is that to Thomas à Kempis (1379–1471), canon regular at St. Agnietenberg, northeast of Zwolle.

Born in Kempen (now just inside Germany), Thomas spent his teenage years (1392–1399) in Deventer, where he received his schooling and came under the influence of the earliest house of brothers associated with the New Devotion. He spent nearly all of his remaining seventy-odd years at the Agnietenberg priory, making profession there in 1406, receiving ordination in 1413, and serving as subprior and novice master in the years following 1425 and 1448. His connection to the *Imitation* is clear enough: He copied it at least three times, although without ever explicitly claiming authorship; the manuscript he completed in 1441 (Brussels, Royal Library 5855–5861) is now sometimes called the "autograph." Yet there are at least thirty copies scattered across Europe that must be dated to the years between 1424 and 1441 (many with only one of its four books). The oldest copy containing all four books (1427: now Brussels, Royal Library 22084) belonged to another house of Augustinian canons in Nijmegen, and the earliest Middle Dutch translation of Book I dates to 1428. If Thomas was indeed its author or compiler, the *Imitation* must have been essentially finished just after 1420, gained instant attention, and been repeatedly copied, distributed, and translated even while Thomas himself continued to correct and re-copy it. From the "autograph" it is clear, moreover, that its four books originally comprised only the first of some thirteen distinct treatises that often traveled separately and were initially brought together in differing combinations and orders. Only after 1450, when Thomas was in his seventies, did the present four in their present order increasingly become the accepted convention.

What bearing does all this have on the "brothers and sisters of the Modern Devotion"? Caution on the question of authorship seems still in order, but there is a far more fundamental point, as other scholars saw earlier when they tried to uncover a supposed primordial version of the *Imitation* written by Geert Grote himself. In the late medieval Lowlands there existed religious communities that fostered the gathering and propagation of short "sayings" and "teachings." In the *Imitation* these have been organized under four rubrics, "contempt for the vanities of this world," a "call to the inner life," the resultant "inner consolation," and a proper "approach to holy communion." If Thomas in fact compiled, wrote, or refined all these sayings around 1420, he did so originally for brothers and especially novices in the new house of canons regular outside Zwolle. That house in turn had originated as an extension of a religious movement contemporaries referred to as the New Devotion. This book, then, which translates for the first time the sayings and teachings of the Brothers and Sisters of the Modern Devotion, presents the context or "incubator," so to speak, out of which *The Imitation of Christ* almost certainly was born.

The very term *Modern Devotion* (the misleading translation of a Latin word [*moderna*] for "new" with the sense of "renewed" or "present-day") seems inherently to suggest some rejection of the medieval past. Many readers consequently have come to associate the Brothers and Sisters of the New Devotion with movements that in some way looked forward to the Renaissance or the Reformation. That is a long association, attested by more than a century of heated scholarly debate, often invoked still in popular accounts or by scholars with no firsthand knowledge of the source material, and one that has received very few truly convincing or properly nuanced accounts.[6] Broadly speaking, however, scholars are now in agreement that this religious movement, whatever its later influences or permutations, was decidedly "late medieval" and "Catholic" in origin, not somehow an early form of the Renaissance or the Reformation. Yet within the later medieval Church, these brothers and sisters sought to work out institutional structures and devotional forms consonant with their particular vision and pursuit of Christian perfection. That effort sometimes brought changes or confrontations resonant of issues raised later in the Renaissance or Reformation. The relationship between this devotional movement and the later Reforms was, however, rarely a direct one. It would be far better to think in terms of common problems or issues, surfacing ever more obviously in the medieval Church from the late fourteenth century onward, to which each of these movements, and others as well, offered varying responses. Most pertinent were questions as to the good or holy life and how best to achieve it, the place of education in clerical and Christian life generally, and the free organization of voluntary groups with a common spirit and a common religious purpose. The answers provided to these questions by the Brothers and Sisters of the Modern Devotion may have looked and sounded at some points like those proposed by humanists or reformers (and they may even have entered into coalition with them on some particular occasions), but the approach taken by the brothers and sisters was originally and remained distinctively their own. If they were "forerunners" of any later developments at all, the closest links may well be to certain aspects of the Counter-Reformation. For the purposes of this book, however, it will suffice to say that the brothers and sisters should be read for themselves and not with an eye on later developments. Readers would do better to focus on the late medieval Church and to discern how these New Devout attempted quite consciously "to work out their salvation in fear and trembling," within the particular restrictions and difficulties they confronted in the Church and in European society generally around the year 1400.

The aim of this book is to introduce the spirituality of the Modern Devout by translating several of their representative texts. So far as I know, earlier scholars have not brought together texts from the Modern Devotion on any extensive scale either in the original languages or in translation. Selection and organization were therefore important points, and a few explanations are in order. First, the texts chosen here stem overwhelmingly from the original heartland of the movement, the eastern Netherlands, with very few examples from Germany or the southern Netherlands (Belgium), where the movement also spread to become a noteworthy aspect of religious life. Second, the movement remained vital from the 1380s until about 1500, but most of the texts translated here were written during its first and second generations (roughly 1380s to 1430). For these two points space was a major consideration, together with an interest in origins. Third, use of the vernacular was one of the movement's distinctive points. About one-quarter of the texts presented here were translated from Middle Dutch alone; another one-half exist in both Middle Dutch and Latin versions, and both were used. The Middle Dutch material, unfortunately, is still inadequately sorted through and published; indeed most of the Latin material is not to be found in modern critical editions and is scattered throughout publications inacessible outside a major research library. Fourth, this movement flourished among brothers and sisters alike, as reflected in the title, but in the nature of medieval sources far more texts are from and about the brothers, and that is also reflected in this book.

I make no claim to offer a new interpretive synthesis; that would require a fresh historical analysis of religious life in the early fifteenth century. Far too much has already been said about the Modern Devotion without sufficient knowledge of its basic texts, however, and the chief concern of this book is to present those texts. To render them more intelligible, the introduction will provide (1) a historical description of the movement, (2) a summary of its key or distinctive spiritual teachings, and (3) specific introductions to the texts translated, followed by a short conclusion.

CONGREGATIONS OF THE NEW DEVOUT

Around 1375 Master Geert Grote of Deventer, a man of independent means, considerable university education, and every hope of making a successful clerical career, resolved at age thirty-five to rethink his ways. He gave his house over to the use of poor religious women, adopted a penitential way of life, spent time in retreat at a Carthusian house, and read widely in spiritual authors. At the end of four or five years, about the beginning of 1380, he decided on his course of action: He would not enter a religious house but obtain ordination as a deacon, together with a special license to preach, and carry his message of conversion and repentance to all parts of the diocese of Utrecht. This he did for four years, until opposition from the clergy in Utrecht, whose morals he had severely attacked, and sudden death from the plague on August 20, 1384, brought his apostolic activities to a close. What plans for the future he had conceived must remain unknown, but the men and women who had been stirred by his preaching, both clerical and lay, began voluntarily to gather in private houses, where they lived out the devotion he had represented to them as the way of life of the earliest apostles. These gatherings spread from their place of origin in the Ijssel river valley of the eastern Netherlands (Deventer, Diepenveen, Windesheim, Zwolle, and so on) across the entire medieval diocese of Utrecht (roughly equivalent to most of the modern Dutch state except the far south), then east into northern Germany by way of the neighboring dioceses of Münster and Cologne, south into the southern Netherlands (much of present-day Belgium), and finally in a subsequent impulse into the upper Rhine (southwestern Germany). This is not the place to recount that historical development in any detail.[7] But to understand the texts it produced, readers must have some understanding of the way of life found in those gatherings, their main institutional manifestations, the shape they assumed locally, and their personnel, the New Devout themselves.

These new "congregations" or "gatherings," as they were called in Latin and Dutch respectively, took shape more or less spontaneously in response to Master Geert's preaching and the felt need for a more intense religious life. Sisters and brothers are known to have assembled privately by the middle 1380s, some perhaps still with Grote's knowledge and support; by the middle 1390s their houses were a recognized reality, requiring churchmen and town magistrates alike to take a position on such gatherings of the New Devout. Townsmen were suspicious and sometimes sardonic. Even though

the Modern Devout lived in private houses still under civil jurisdiction and showed an unusual openness to lay people, late medieval
magistrates had seen more than enough of tax-exempt religious in-
stitutions, whose personnel lived off the town without producing
wealth of their own, competed with the local parish church, and
sometimes evolved into centers of disorder and immorality rather
than the reverse.[8] Several leaders from among the New Devout,
however, like Geert Grote himself, had close ties to the patrician
classes in these towns, and by cooperating closely on all matters of
property and personnel status and by reaching out to the townspeople in constructive and edifying ways, the devout eventually gained
acceptance and even a measure of acclaim.

Churchmen, by contrast, were more skeptical. The Council of
Vienne in 1311 had banned beguines and beghards, another form of
free gathering dating back to the thirteenth century, and although
this ban was modified the Modern Devout were often viewed with
the same suspicion as these groups. Moreover, beyond a great number of beguines, the Lowlands had already produced more than its
share of "free spirits," mystical writers of doubtful orthodoxy, and
other religious sects charged with the most outlandish carryings-on.
The New Devout had therefore to defend their good intentions and
their way of life against suspicious churchmen, especially inquisitive
Dominicans. In the middle 1390s Brother Gerard Zerbolt of Zutphen produced a one-hundred-page legal defense, which was then
reinforced with opinions from a canon of the cathedral chapter in
Utrecht (Everardus Foec), the abbot of Dickening, and several jurists
from Cologne. Together they carried the day, and in 1402 Bishop
Frederick of Utrecht approved their way of life. The Dominican
Matthew of Grabow continued the struggle against them, but he was
finally reprimanded for it in 1417 at the Council of Constance, where
the brothers and sisters gained the support of no less than Jean Gerson and Pierre d'Ailly.[9]

These legal documents and early charters contain descriptions
of the New Devout that by the early fifteenth century had already
become relatively standardized. Four common points deserve attention here.[10] First, the devout are said to be pious persons who live
together and in common on the basis of their work, their ecclesiastical incomes (where someone already held, for instance, a vicarage),
and their own contributed wealth. From this arose the designation
by which they are probably best known, the "brothers and sisters of
the common life." The heart of the issue, in the charges raised
against them, was their right to pool resources and live in a commune

of their own making within a given city and parish. Propertied townsmen and religious taking vows of poverty were established figures in the Late Middle Ages, but brothers and sisters living a "common life" seemed to violate every known category. How this common life first arose is, interestingly enough, not made clear in the sources, but its reality was crucial to the New Devout. They were determined to be self-sufficient, to live from the work of their own hands. Together with most other laymen and secular clerics in the Late Middle Ages, they resented and criticized the great wealth that monks had accumulated and from which they now lived, often in luxury and increasingly with personal allowances or stipends that in effect re-endowed them with private property. Moreover, these brothers and sisters, like the townsmen from whom they came and among whom they lived, reacted in disgust to the begging and crass fund raising that had come to characterize the mendicant orders. The new devout would neither draw rents nor beg; like St. Paul, the apostles, and the Desert Fathers they would support themselves and live in common. This they did with the work of their own hands, the brothers primarily as copyists supplying books, the sisters as seamstresses supplying textiles and laces. The New Devout took no vow of poverty and unlike the early Franciscans never came to see poverty as a crucial end in itself, but most of them lived in great simplicity, and most of their houses remained relatively poor.

These brothers and sisters were described, second, as planning to found no new religious order or collegiate church but only "to frequent devoutly their (regular) parish churches." Theirs was not to be a new religious order but a voluntary gathering of the devout. They refused to take vows, with all their legal consequences, claiming instead the right to associate freely and to persist willingly in their chosen way of life. They were to be "devout" without becoming professed "religious." Medieval historians, especially Kaspar Elm, have identified this as a recognized "third" or "middle" status between the laity and the orders.[11] Occasionally the sources themselves suggest some practical considerations: This status offered a testing ground for the religious life (and many did become canons or monks), a haven for those lacking the entrance fee still required in most monasteries, a humbler setting for the less physically or mentally fit. The New Devout, however, would have dismissed much of this, or even found it insulting, and insisted that theirs was simply the free choice to live a genuinely religious life in common. The Modern Devout accordingly remained regular members of their local parishes.[12] Although many congregations soon added chapels in which to say the appointed prayers—just as many prelates, lords, and wealthy merchants in the Late Middle Ages added private chapels to their houses—the local parish was where brothers and sisters normally went to hear mass, make confession, and so on. Negotiations with local priests were soon required, therefore, chiefly over confessors (brothers and sisters came to prefer their own) and burial (which was preferred eventually in their own chapels); but the Modern Devout remained in the parish, where they formed cells of devotion, if you like, attesting to the requirements of true piety.

As a movement the New Devout were, third, declared obedient to their prelates and the Roman Church, and not involved in any error. With all the suspicions about "free spirits," "libertines," "mystics," and others in the late medieval Lowlands—often generically and quite unfairly lumped together as "beguines and beghards"—this was a crucial point to make. That the New Devout had no peculiar doctrinal positions to propagate was undoubtedly crucial to their relatively rapid acceptance. In time they were in fact to gain a reputation on the other side. Their zeal to obey the "Roman" pope in the midst of the Great Schism and to observe interdicts in the midst of various wrangles between prelates and cities meant that local townsmen sometimes came to resent their "scrupulous religiosity," forcing them consequently to leave town for a while and thereby inadvertently spreading the movement to another city.

The New Devout, fourth, were said to live together in humility and love and in pursuit of the virtues. This somewhat bland or generic description of what should apply to all Christians—and that was indeed the point, as the brothers and sisters saw it—captured the ascetic and, if you will, somewhat "moralistic" emphasis that was at the heart of their spirituality. Because this will be described at length in the following section, it suffices here to say that this quite particular spirit was already evident and perceived as distinctive from the very beginning.

What the Bishop of Utrecht approved—the right of these men and women to live together in communes, to make regular use of their parish churches, and to pursue all the Christian virtues free of any suspicion of heresy—hardly seems in retrospect any great concession. To have stirred up unrest and even protest these communities must have had something more to them than their newness and the features described thus far. In fact contemporaries perceived, without finding an exact way to formulate it, a whole separate program, a resolution to live religiously apart from the recognized religious orders. In addition to the spiritual aspects of this program, there were contested points, much discussed in the brothers' defense, which the bishop and others chose not to include expressly in their official documents. Although these practices were also to gain acceptance as aspects of the Modern Devotion, they edged closer to the line of what could be officially approved.

From the beginning the brothers and sisters made extensive use of the vernacular in their religious meditations and reading of Scripture. This came, it is worth noting, at exactly the same moment in time when the issue was raised in England by the Lollards and in Bohemia by the followers of Hus (although there is no indication of any direct connection). The Church's position on the vernacular was far more nuanced and *ad hoc* than what might appear from post-Tridentine emphases and from some contentious accounts of the Reformation. While Latin was the only approved language for doctrine, liturgy, and law, the vernacular was permitted for private edifying purposes. Generally speaking, as the threat of heresy seemed to rise among various private groups and sects, the Church's nervousness and rigidity over the use of the vernacular increased correspondingly. In the case of the brothers and sisters, the bishops concerned were persuaded finally that the purposes of the New Devout were indeed private and edifying and therefore within the bounds of what was permitted.[13] This was to prove a crucial point. Geert Grote himself translated a significant portion of the liturgy used daily by sisters and lay brothers; all the devout made extensive use of devotional materials in the vernacular for private reading and readings at meals; the Modern Devout were involved in some of the earliest and most widespread translations of Scripture into Middle Dutch;[14] and their attempts to reach others through moral addresses and spiritual advice took place entirely in the vernacular. It is worth noting, parenthetically, that on this point the brothers and sisters were only keeping pace with the developing culture of their own towns. Exactly fifteen years prior to Grote's conversion and thus about twenty-five years prior to the formation of the earliest congregations, record keeping in Deventer had switched from Latin to Dutch. Grote's father, an active member of the patrician class, had kept the city records of Deventer in Latin in the 1340s; Geert Grote himself, had he followed in his father's footsteps, would have kept them in Middle Dutch. Instead he translated devotional treatises and liturgical prayers into the language of the people.

Another crucial right and practice of the New Devout, equally unmentioned by the bishop, was that of holding "collations" (in effect, sermons) within their gatherings as well as for interested students and townspeople. In part this was done in imitation of much older monastic practice, as when a rector, the chosen leader of a congregation of Devout, addressed the community, much as an abbot would his monks. It could also take the more novel form of brothers or sisters discussing together for their mutual edification passages from Scripture or the Fathers. Moreover, at selected times, usually Sunday afternoons, they invited townspeople to join them, and when they took charge of students those young men were also addressed regularly in a kind of compulsory chapel. For the brothers and sisters the only point was to edify and to win souls; ordination and the authority to preach (many brothers were in time ordained) were entirely secondary considerations and of no real consequence. Once again, a kind of quiet compromise was reached whereby the practice (still under the name of collations, not sermons or homilies) was continued, and local curates and mendicants were mollified: These were no substitutes for sermons or church services, only private sessions meant to encourage devotion. What remains significant is that the brothers in particular ardently defended this practice, and their right to it, as central to their way of life. Indeed, in ways we can only imagine, since the sources largely fail us here, these collations must have given the brothers a very distinct profile in their towns.

A third related practice was that of "fraternal correction." It looked very much like the monastic "chapter of faults," but the brothers and sisters put much emphasis on it as essential to the spirit of their communities. Open confession of faults, continuous admonition of others, and readiness to accept such admonition are virtues steadily advocated by the brothers and sisters. For them such receptiveness to mutual aid and encouragement was a matter of humility and edification and therefore central to developing the spiritual life. To suspicious clergymen it looked very much like a substitute for the canonically required confessional—and it probably functioned partially in that way. Hence the importance of agreements reached with the local curate. So long as he knew that the standard obligations were fulfilled, either with himself or with a rector-confessor whom he agreed to, he could tolerate quietly whatever these brothers and sisters might wish additionally to do—crudely put—to satisfy their own religiosity. Such mutual correction could often prove quite disconcerting for the average layperson, potentially a harrowing personal experience that ran contrary to certain impediments built into human nature. This mutual correction, however, together with the use of the vernacular and of collations, became one of the distinguishing marks of these congregations.

With these seven general characteristics in mind, a word is in order about the main institutional manifestations of the movement that became known as the Modern Devotion.

Sources pertaining to the *Sisters of the Common Life* are not very plentiful, particularly in the Netherlands, and outside a new book on the German houses have never been systematically investigated.[15] The first "gathering" of sisters was in Master Geert's own house. In the early stages of his conversion, in 1375, he seems to have intended little more than a kind of hospice, but by the end of his life in 1384 and then clearly by the 1390s this had become a distinct religious community.[16] Contemporaries considered and sometimes called these sisters "beguines," because like them they formed voluntary communities and lived in private houses under civil jurisdiction according to a set of customs or statutes of their own making. There were nonetheless essential differences from the start.[17] Sisters were to live in common and could not possess individually, as beguines did, houses or personal items; indeed beguines required property and income to set themselves up, whereas nothing was required of a sister but religious resolve and the readiness to give up all personal property. This orientation toward a community rather than an individual effort also affected the tone of life within each house. Sisters living in common not only worked together but also mutually admonished and aided one another in the spiritual life. Bonds eventually were formed among various houses, while pastoral care was normally provided by sympathetic brothers rather than mendicants or parish priests ordered, often against their will, to serve a female community. Few houses were large—Master Geert's house initially had room for eight sisters in the "front" and eight in the "back"— and still fewer houses became at all well-off. Later claims about houses of 150 or even 500 sisters are somewhat dubious; yet they suggest how many women in these late medieval Dutch towns found this an attractive way of life, and the high numbers appear to be borne out in Germany by Rehm's recent study. By 1460 there were, by R. R. Post's conservative reckoning, 34 houses in the Netherlands (this includes 5 in Deventer, 4 in Zwolle, and 3 in Zutphen). An older, less critical list put the number at 106, of which 47 soon became Third-Order Franciscans and another 14 Augustinians. In northwest Germany Rehm has identified some 60 houses.[18] In short, sisters' houses, although often poor and certainly poorly documented, were founded first and consistently outnumbered brothers' houses. The main difficulty was to sustain and protect their precarious position between the world, the parish, and a monastic order. Many of the original communities, perhaps the majority, became Third-Order Franciscans or professed Augustinians, the two alternatives that seemed closest to their original intent. Although a brother normally served as priest and confessor, the gathering itself was governed by a "rectrix" or "mistress" whom the sisters elected from among themselves. By late medieval norms, these female communities were remarkably self-governing, with one or more sisters appointed to look after external affairs (Lubbe Peters for a time, for instance, in Master Geert's house). City magistrates rather than bishops normally had immediate responsibility for good order and fiscal soundness. All sisters were expected to do a minimal amount of reading in the liturgical hours and devotional books; all were to work in support of the house (chiefly in textiles and sewing, but also in brewing, and so on); and many also engaged in copywork like the brothers, but then totally in Middle Dutch, not in Latin. For all the modesty of these houses and for all the emphasis in the sisters' spirituality on humility and self-effacement, these were noteworthy congregations of devout women settled in the heart of late medieval towns, fully self-supporting and capable of sustaining a contemplative way of life outside a cloister and alongside their parish.

The origins of the *Brothers of the Common Life* is still more obscure and disputed.[19] In the wake of Master Geert's preaching, small numbers of like-minded clerics and schoolboys (in effect, young clerics) gathered in private houses at Deventer, Zwolle, Amsterdam, and elsewhere to live a life more in keeping with their new devotion. In Deventer, Florens Radewijns, a vicar for the altar of St. Paul at the main church of St. Lebuinus, opened his vicarage to such a gathering, and he was universally regarded as the father and organizer of the brothers in Deventer. Eventually they secured a house of their own, not the vicarage, and two years after Radewijns's death in 1400 received approval from the bishop. In Zwolle more documents have survived,[20] and the picture is correspondingly more complicated, involving several devout clerics, an important benefactor, and a sympathetic parish priest at the main church of St. Michael's. In time the house at Zwolle became the larger and more dynamic congregation, expanding to occupy the better part of a city block set between the main parish church and the beguines. Its rector, Dirk of Herxen (1410–1457), eventually brought all Dutch houses together once a year for common discussion and decisions. Subject by their very nature to the uncertainties of holding together like-minded persons and the difficulties of raising sufficient support, these congregations came and went, much as the sisters' houses. The most recent studies summarize their development as follows: six houses by 1400, eleven by 1420, twenty by 1460, thirty-nine by 1500, and forty-one on the eve of the Reformation (after which only seven survived into the seventeenth century, mostly in Catholic parts of Germany).[21] That the brothers remained active and even expanded almost to the end of the fifteenth century is borne out by their chronicles and copywork as well, although much of the latest expansion came in Germany, while the number of Dutch houses held steady after about 1460. These houses also remained "gatherings" and never became very large; the largest, that in Zwolle, for instance, numbered only between twenty and thirty persons, and most probably remained closer to fifteen. While statutes for the sisters' houses were often essentially contained in the founding charters approved by city magistrates, most brothers' houses eventually drew up additional constitutional arrangements of their own, and their chosen rector was normally also their father-confessor.

The third branch of this movement was, in numerical and institutional terms, the most successful, and it is now also the best known, owing to a far greater supply of both primary sources and secondary studies. The *Windesheim Congregation of Canons Regular* was to become the legally authorized branch of the Modern Devotion, an established religious order with a rule, constitutions, papal bulls, and all the rest.[22] From the beginning there were those who objected that the "in-between" status of the brothers and sisters could not be maintained and who themselves aspired to a more ordered religious life. Some sources claim that Grote himself recognized and supported this. The origins are slightly confusing with independent efforts made at Eemstein (1382, apparently modeled on Ruusbroec's Groenendael), Windesheim near Zwolle (1387), and what was to become the Agnietenberg (1398/99), also near Zwolle. These and two other houses, Marienborn near Arnhem and Nieuwlicht near Hoorn, were led by people who had come under the influence of Geert Grote. The same held for the first house of canonesses in Diepenveen outside Deventer, which was founded out of Master Geert's own house (1400/1402). Crucial moments in the congregation's development were the union of four houses into a "chapter" under Windesheim in 1395, the adoption of a common set of statutes in 1402,[23] and expansion under John Vos de Heusden (1391–1424), reaching nearly thirty houses by the time of his death. In all there were to be some eighty-four male and thirteen female houses, fifty of them in the Netherlands, although all the later growth came in Germany.

In recent years historians have emphasized the differences between canons and brothers. Certain points are clear. Canons lived in cloisters and behind walls, usually outside cities. They took vows and lived under obedience, their property and persons clearly a part of the "ecclesiastical" world and law rather than the civil. Their writings, moreover, tended to radiate more of that disciplined withdrawal from the world characteristic of monastic spirituality and perhaps too, as some have said, a greater yearning for union, even mystical union, with God. They also sought to make connections with older traditions of Augustinian canons, not only the recent foundations in Brabant (like Ruusbroec's in Groenendael) but also, interestingly, those of the Victorines in Paris.[24] In full accord with all these observations, this volume has concentrated largely on the brothers and sisters rather than the canons and canonesses.

Yet before leaving the Windesheimers altogether, a few points should be made about ways in which they too belonged to the world of the New Devout; indeed, the very designation originated with them. The Windesheimers also looked back to Geert Grote as their founder, and there was distinct continuity in personnel and in houses: Many houses began as congregations before shifting over at a certain point, usually to gain greater stability and discipline, into a priory. So too many of the devout began as brothers and sisters and took vows later in one of the Windesheim houses—Thomas à Kempis, for instance, began at the brothers' house in Deventer—but there is much more. The Windesheimers kept up the interest in the vernacular (despite their more regular clerical status) as well as the practices of collation and fraternal correction. They also tried to support themselves as copyists, worked as confessors in the houses of sisters and canonesses, served as advisers and helpers to brothers' houses, and promoted and elaborated on the same traditions of spirituality. While it is appropriate to make certain distinctions, the lines of continuity in this common movement of New Devotion must never be overlooked.

This movement was and remained essentially local in character, never developing all the organizational uniformity of an order. We must therefore return now to the brothers and sisters to consider how they lived, who they were, and what they did.

The houses in which the brothers and sisters lived were indeed "houses" (always *huis* or *domus* and their equivalents in the sources), not convents or monasteries; they were located in towns or cities on ordinary streets, not set off as a separate complex until late in their development, if ever; and they were owned communally by the New Devout, either through purchase or gift, under city laws and civil jurisdiction. These were larger medieval houses of a kind still to be seen in northern European cities. They had an inner courtyard allowing privacy in work and other business, different wings and floors applied to various purposes, and a fairly severe front on the street with a single door or gate, thus shutting them off from the immediate outside world. If the number of devout required and their income permitted, buildings might be added or annexed, beginning often with a chapel and/or work room (i.e., a library and copy area for the brothers, a sewing area for the sisters). Larger houses might add a separate kitchen, refectory, or dormitory. All remained houses in a city, often near the parish church and rectory or alongside an old beguinage (in Zwolle it was between them). This house was where the New Devout had resolved to spend their lives in prayer and work; once a day or once a week, depending upon the community, they walked out in single file and in silence to hear mass. A few brothers or sisters also went regularly out into the public square to look after external affairs. Yet, for all of them, family, friends, the world and its amusements, even (as some stories make clear) old lovers, were only one door away, with nothing to block them— no walls and no vows—except their own resolve and the internal pressures exercised by their community.

Brothers and sisters came from all social classes, but most frequently from the middle and lower rungs of the urban and nearby rural population.[25] At the beginning there were a few masters, a few noble ladies, and a few wealthy merchants, but in general the devout were suspicious of masters for their learning and of noble ladies for their wealth and manners; both could introduce corruption all too easily. In their own writings and in the references of others to them, the brothers and sisters were generally depicted as a humble and unprepossessing group, in contrast with both urban patricians and lordly monks or mendicants. On the balance between lay and priestly members in their houses, much has been written, mostly of a polemical nature. Those looking for the possible roots of the Reformation have emphasized, rightly, the free inclusion of laypersons and the grumbling this brought from those clergymen who wanted and expected a clearer distinction of estates. In reaction, Post emphasized, also rightly, that

22

many brothers became priests, that priests normally acted as rectors in the houses, and that there was no sign at all of any anticlericalism in the Modern Devotion.[26] In the Late Middle Ages, the Church was fully as class-conscious as the world, with the distance between a prelate and a minor cleric at least as great as that between a lord and a peasant worker. Many monasteries and cathedral chapters, especially in the German Empire, barred non-noble members. By contrast, the gatherings of the New Devout drew primarily from the lower urban clergy, whence their houses were frequently called quite simply "the clerics' house." This ill-defined "lower clergy" represented the great mass of clerics in the Late Middle Ages. They could well hold some minor post in a church or busy themselves with some aspect of the church's work without ever experiencing any inward conversion or satisfying any deeper religious longings, and they were consequently the objects of much talk about ignorant and immoral clergymen. For them, as well as those lay men and women who associated with them or sought in their local parish church some greater expression of piety, these houses offered a devout way of life, rooted in the model of the first apostles, without requiring them to leave town or church and without imposing any of the difficulties and obligations that came with taking vows and joining an order. At a time when all of Europe was calling for the reform of the clergy and the Reformation would be carried forward by a wave of violent anticlericalism, the Modern Devout quietly began living up to the ideals many were preaching. When the Reformation came, the brothers and sisters mostly did not join, in part at least because, with respect to this one point anyway, they did not need to—as Luther also recognized in an oft-cited letter on the exemplary devotion of these "brother clerics."[27]

The New Devout spent their lives in ordered prayer and work. Here the distinction between priests and minor clerics or clerics and laity was minimal: While priests might be obligated to a longer office or laymen to more involvement in external affairs, all essentially lived the same way of life; among sisters there was no distinction excepting those assigned to external offices. Their prayers followed an arrangement of the hours taken from cathedral chapters or collegiate churches rather than from monasteries. Brothers had often first learned the liturgy of the hours as young men in such churches, and many sisters had first followed them there. Whereas late medieval canons often delegated their appointed prayers to vicars or neglected them altogether, the New

Devout said their hours voluntarily, without let, and with inner concentration. The rest of the day was spent in work, partly as an aspect of religious discipline and partly to support the house. The sisters' concentration on textiles and lace was in continuity with the beguines, and was also, very simply, the most logical way for them to earn their keep while working in solitude. Sisters were also able to do some copywork, chiefly in Middle Dutch; unfortunately, little is known about that. The brothers earned their way primarily with their copywork, purchasing their properties and necessities with the fees they collected. Most of their work involved bibles, missals, homiliaries, and standard religious texts, which they prepared for local churches and monasteries. Here their "clerical status" was again in evidence, but now in the double sense of the word: They could at one and the same time earn their keep, work in a disciplined and "literate" way, edify themselves, and quietly spread the Word.

While prayer and work were at the heart of what they did, a few other items deserve brief notice. A certain portion of the day was set aside for edifying reading and self-examination in private. Both of these religious practices, so common in early modern religious life, were already a regular part of the routine urged on these brothers and sisters, only one short step away from the lay life. The reading and discussion of Scripture received particular emphasis as singularly edifying. Second, a fair number of brothers and canons served as confessors in the sisters' houses and also on occasion as confessors to laymen who came for the collations. This was their way of "winning souls," or evangelizing. This was, in its own modest way, a form of taking up the pastoral task much as the early mendicants had conceived it; their later resentment of the brothers comes as no real surprise. Finally, and in keeping with the "clerical" status emphasized earlier, the brothers took a particular interest in young student clerics, fourteen to twenty years of age, who came to study in Deventer, Zwolle, and elsewhere. In medieval schools, intellectual formation had normally been the main point; moral and spiritual formation was left largely unattended. Here the brothers stepped in, eventually building "convicts" or dormitory houses in which to house and care for these young men. Their spiritual formation became the brothers' chief concern; sometimes that came to include their schooling as well. At Louvain, the only university city in the Lowlands, it eventually permitted solid connections to the professors, as it did in Tübingen.[28] The point is that a clerical body whose first interest was religious and devotional could, because it was ultimately a voluntary and local organization, stretch itself to meet needs and opportunities as they arose in various places, including intellectual tasks on some occasions.

THE SPIRITUALITY OF THE NEW DEVOTION

The Modern Devotion was recognized from the outset as a movement of spiritual renewal. Over the years historians have reached broad consensus on several of the most characteristic features of its spirituality.[29]

The person of Jesus Christ stood central to this New Devotion.[30] Here the brothers and sisters inherited a tradition derived ultimately from the Cistercians and Franciscans, which by the Late Middle Ages had spread across nearly all orders and levels of Western Christendom. The works most read by the New Devout included the sermons of Bernard, the life of Christ by Bonaventure, the meditations of Ps-Anselm, the *Book on Divine Wisdom* of the Dominican mystic Henry of Suso, and versions of the life of Christ by the Carthusian Ludolf of Saxony.[31] They appropriated all of this for themselves and in their own way. "Imitation" is probably a misleading term for their outlook. Their emphasis fell neither on imitation in a strict sense, as in works of mercy, nor on "mystic union," as in the teachings of many late medieval authors, but rather on an individual and affective identification with particular moments in Christ's life, chiefly his passion, the result or purpose of which was ideally fourfold: to "relive" with Christ his virtuous life and saving passion, to have him ever present before one's eyes, to manifest his presence to others, and to orchestrate, as it were, all of one's mental and emotional faculties around devotion to him. This emphasis was entirely positive: to have the New Devout live in Christ and Christ in them. There was no proto-Protestant repudiation of Mary or the saints, whose model and intercession were taken entirely for granted and also mentioned. Yet this focus on the person of Jesus Christ was so total, as the works translated here should make abundantly clear, that there was in effect, if not necessarily in conscious intention, something of a shift toward a more exclusively Christocentric form of piety.

To focus on the life and passion of Christ was to read the Gospel and the writings that explained and ordered it. The contemplative reading of holy writings, especially Holy Scripture, was prescribed for all brothers and sisters, who were expected additionally to make up a kind of "notebook" (*rapiaria*) of those passages they found most compelling. Here too the New Devout stood heirs to a long monastic tradition, best exemplified in early medieval *florilegia*, now effectively extended to those outside the orders. Scripture plainly received special emphasis: Brothers and sisters were expected to read it daily in their own rooms, while the formal theology of the schools went almost entirely unread. Consistent with this emphasis was a concern to make Scripture available in the vernacular as well, a right stoutly defended on behalf of sisters and lay brothers. The collations or moral addresses given within their houses, as well as for others, were supposed to have as their point of departure a passage from Scripture, even as nearly all their meditations revolved around some incident or verse taken from Scripture. This focused devotion toward Scripture was, like that toward Jesus Christ, almost entirely positive: As the only certain source of divine wisdom, the Holy Writings needed to be read, absorbed, and distributed. Critical as the Modern Devout could occasionally be of the Church in their time, they never turned Scripture against tradition, as the Protestant Reformers were to do only two or three generations later, and that seems an important distinction sometimes overlooked in earlier literature.

Third, the whole approach of the New Devout toward Christ, Scripture, and meditation has frequently been described as "moralistic" and "antispeculative." Grote's conversion began in part as a reaction to the failure of schools to satisfy, as he saw it, any purpose beyond that of making a career. To believe and act on the truths of the faith was the heart of the matter; to delve into them intellectually was usually, and at best, mere curiosity. This was a theme reiterated in dozens of ways throughout the writings of the Modern Devotion. Progress in the virtues was the central issue, and to it they returned on every page and in every collation; all else, including intellectual activity, was secondary. All that said, the point must not be unduly exaggerated, as it sometimes is, nor understood outside its ecclesiastical and social context. The brothers were, after all, constantly at work copying, reading, writing, and translating books. But the New Devout were mainly the representatives and products of the lower clergy and an early lay literacy in late medieval towns; they were mostly not of the university elite. Learning was for them never an end in itself nor the prerequisite to a career, but rather and quite simply a means to an end, the increasing of personal holiness. The New Devout were certainly moralistic in their constant emphasis on progress in the virtues, and they also evidenced something of an early bourgeois skepticism about any learning devoid of utility. The utility (a word they used themselves) was in this case advancement in sanctity. Yet it would seriously distort their position not to recognize that they entirely presupposed the use of books and of writing in all their religious exercises—and this in a social class where most of their relatives were probably still illiterate.

Every aspect of the brothers' and sisters' religious lives, from their Christocentrism to their private reading and moral progress, turned finally on a deepened "inwardness" or "interiority." For this they drew on the whole contemplative tradition in the West, with the Carthusians and Cistercians as their leading exemplars. Yet they were themselves people who had not taken vows and still lived partially in the world. The interiority toward which they strove was not so much that of the late medieval mystics or related groups, for the Modern Devout said almost nothing about mystical union. The proper point of reference or comparison was rather the perfunctory practice that apparently characterized so much of late medieval religious life: days of obligation, holy days become holidays, pilgrimages become travel tours, shrines become scenes of bedlam, churches become social meeting places, and so on. Without casting all that many aspersions on their fellow townsmen, as so many contemporary reformers did, the New Devout quietly returned to their "houses" and "cells" to develop the inner man, an affectionate devotion to Christ, the subduing of the old nature and all carnal impulses, together with the training of the "heart" in all the virtues. In this exploration of the inner man, there was a good deal of psychology, much of it practical and taken from Cassian or Gregory but some also theoretical and taken from Aristotle and others by way of the schools. They recognized, as both schoolmen and monks (especially Cistercians) had earlier, the need to understand the makeup of the soul, and they set out systematically to exploit that knowledge in behalf of training and disciplining their inner selves.

On these four points—an emphasis among the New Devout on living in Christ, reading Scripture, progressing in moral sanctity, and developing interiority—nearly all scholars agree. The citations in their footnotes, however, refer overwhelmingly to Geert Grote or Thomas à Kempis (as author of *The Imitation of Christ*), both important figures in the Modern Devotion but neither, strictly speaking, one of the brothers. It is the brothers and sisters who must still be heard, and one good approach to their spirituality is to note the words that recurred most frequently in their texts. For all the historical studies of the Modern Devotion, relatively few scholars have analyzed closely the language those communities used to express their newfound piety. The present list of a dozen terms is itself, let me say, essentially subjective, not the product of a computerized count but impressions borne of my own reading.[32] Some points are self-evident. Immersed as they were in the whole Western contemplative tradition, the New Devout produced works containing many echoes of Cassian's collations, Bernard's sermons, Ps-Anselm's meditations, and the Franciscan tradition of treatises on the life of Jesus. Few words probably appeared so frequently as "Jesus" and "Christ," although the New Devout preferred in Middle Dutch "our dear Lord" (*onze lieve Herr*), which paralleled the standard late medieval term for "Our Lady" (*onze lieve vrouw*). "Death" (*dood*), and all the associated terms on heaven, hell, and the last things, were equally common. It must be added that for the New Devout the emotions and anxiety raised by the whole *memento mori* tradition represented only a starting point, that which helped to focus priorities and get the devout started down the path to virtue; it never became an end in itself. Between these two poles, then—fearful anxiety over impending death and judgment and an inward-looking devotion to Jesus Christ—the brothers and sisters developed their devotion. Its contours may be grasped by way of a dozen terms that came up repeatedly in their writings and shaped the tone of their spirituality.

Conversio: Bekeerynge/zich keeren

The "conversion" of Master Geert Grote marked the beginning of this movement, and the decision of each of the New Devout to join one of the congregations of brothers or sisters was regularly referred to as his or her conversion. So too, those, like Master Geert, who brought others into the community by example or preaching were said to have converted them. There was here no fascination with the moment or the means, as in modern revivalist traditions, but only with the reality and its results. It was in essence a "turning toward," a "taking up," of this new way of life, the only one, as they saw it, that marked a sure path to salvation. But "conversion" and "turning toward" were used in overlapping ways. Turning toward the Lord was after all a continuing process, to be lived out in these gatherings: Thus John Brinkerinck could give a talk on conversion that was in effect a description of their whole way of life. The Modern Devotion began and ended in conversion, in turning the self toward the Lord. This conversion they sought to nourish in one another, to effect in those who came to visit their houses and collations, and also to represent to all those still out in the world.

Resolutio/intentio: een goede opzet maaken

"To make a good resolution" was at the heart of that process of conversion. However much the devout conceded the need for divine grace and the reality of providential intervention in their lives, and whatever their theological reflections in this regard, their emphasis fell in practice on a personal resolution to change one's status in life and to start down a surer path to salvation, meaning, in practice, willingly to join this voluntary religious gathering. Grote's own conversion was first evidenced by a set of "resolutions," and in the exercises the brothers and sisters prepared for themselves as well as in the sermons and addresses delivered to them, the New Devout were constantly urged "to make a good resolve" to carry out all that was expected in the way of prayer, work, and training in the virtues. This might well have provoked reflection on the place of the will in relations between the human and the divine, but that line of thought was deflected by greater concern (see below), to "break one's own will." A good resolution required submission of the human to the divine will; this each devout tried to accomplish in exercises and resolutions worked out concretely for himself. In practice, steady encouragement to make a good resolution could generate enormous tension and insecurity, evidenced in the lives of several sisters who suffered anxiety and depression or even left the house. It could also produce great inner strength, a personal will or resolve tried like iron in the fire, when brothers and sisters were constantly urged to turn to the Lord and submit to the divine will.

Exercitium: oefening

For the spirituality of the New Devout, the importance of "exercise" cannot be overstated. They could apply the word at times virtually to their entire way of life, including their prayer and work. More specifically it referred to the "spiritual training" they regularly subjected themselves to. It is most evident in its meditational aspect. When they read in Scripture or a devotional book, when they systematically focused on the life and passion of Christ at certain times of the day and attempted to absorb and relive it, all of that counted as "exercising," as training their spiritual selves. The same held for practice in the virtues. When they put themselves out in a matter of obedience, fasted to counteract wicked imaginations, accepted chastisement from a brother or sister without demur, and so on through a long and nearly endless list, this too came under the category of spiritual exercises. Although the notion of exercise was not original with them, the New Devout gave it an emphasis rarely or never found earlier, and scholars have debated long, and without definitive result, as to whether this marked the beginning of that "methodical meditation" that Jesuits and others would make common in the early modern era.[33] The question of influence aside, this emphasis on constant exercising in the spiritual life arose naturally in a community built essentially on personal resolve rather than vows and institutional ties. Exercises were the practical manifestations of a good resolve, and shared the same strengths and liabilities: They could instill a powerful inner assurance but they could also generate anxiety as to whether someone had exercised enough, whether negligence, laziness, sluggishness, and so on (words also common in their treatises) had not impeded their progress and even threatened their salvation.

Profectus virtutum: in doegeden voert gane

"Progress in the virtues" might well be labeled the "leitmotif" or "basso continuo" of this entire movement. Different words were employed—"advancing," "progressing," "bettering"—but the basic idea held throughout, receiving its most systematic exposition in Gerard Zerbolt's description of a series of spiritual ascents. The concept, although apparently general enough to fit any serious-minded medieval Christian, in reality served to distinguish the Modern Devotion from other movements in the Western contemplative tradition. For these brothers and sisters, the point of focus was not ascesis, although they also undertook a fair measure of self-denial and told stories (like those of the Desert Fathers) about their great rigor; yet poverty, fasting, chastity, and the like were never to become virtual ends in themselves. So too, however widely they read in mystical authors, in Bernard, Suso, and Ruusbroec, they never came to focus on mystical union or extraordinary experience as the endpoint of their religious lives; from the beginning there was a series of warnings against the spiritual errors and abuses introduced by this kind of fascination with and seeking after mystical experience. For them, the point was rather growth in the virtues, and their goal was to have all evil instincts and impulses so purged or subdued within them that a brother or sister could commune with God and his fellow man in perfect love and harmony. The New Devout accepted a relatively sobering view of man as overwhelmed with evil passions—

not much different in practice from that of the Protestant Reformers—but they went on to work so much the harder toward perfect love and harmony as their goal, although one not reached finally and perfectly until after the purgation that followed in the afterlife. This much talk about progress in the virtues could sometimes become, as recent scholars have stressed, wearisomely moralistic. Yet, at its best, their devotion to progressive sanctification could yield a gentle and well-rounded humanity, not marred by the excesses in experience and language that sometimes came with too much emphasis on either ascesis or mystical union.

Scholars have as yet hardly investigated the source of this emphasis on the virtues and vices. At one level, the answer is obvious, for the entire Western tradition, beginning with Cassian and Gregory the Great (two oft-cited authors), had described the religious life in this way. The Modern Devout, however, lived still, strictly speaking, in their local parishes, and there by the Late Middle Ages the virtues and vices had become central to preaching, teaching, and the confessional. This emphasis, therefore, although rooted in traditions stemming from the religious orders, moved the devout closer again to the ordinary parishioners from among whom they had come and with whom they still went to church. When the New Devout addressed students and their fellow townsmen, it was nearly always on the very themes that their lives were to meant to exemplify in the midst of town and parish. In a full study of the Modern Devotion, a paragraph or more could easily be devoted to each of the vices and virtues, as treated and understood by the devout, but only three have been selected here as receiving special emphasis in their circles.

Charitas: liefde

Love or charity was the goal, the endpoint, toward which their whole way of life was directed. Although a principle they held in common with all Christians, theirs was a love that was to arise from the depths of the heart and to reach out to embrace God and all people. The love that bound them to God was almost never described as "ravishing" or "self-annihilating"; it was rather "sweet" and "delightful," bringing "peace." Love for their fellow man was expressed, in practice, primarily within each congregation, and reached out chiefly to those students and "good men" who associated with the houses and came under their influence. These communities were ultimately contemplative, not directed in the first instance to acts of mercy like those that ran hospitals and hospices; as contemplatives voluntarily withdrawn from the world, their love was first for the brothers and sisters who shared their new devotion. Ranked high among acts of love, therefore, were matters of spiritual encouragement and mutual admonishment.

Humilitas: oetmoedichlicheid

However the brothers and sisters may have ranked the virtues and vices in formal lists, nothing received more emphasis in actual practice than humility. There was, first, a theological reason: Pride they counted as the first and greatest of all evils. There were also more practical reasons that touched on both the spiritual and the emotional planes. Arrogance and self-assertion was common enough in the Middle Ages too, and nowhere more so than in the merchant, artisanal, and petty noble circles from which most of the New Devout came. To acquire humility and to break down the mechanisms of self-assertion, of insisting on your own rights and dignity, ran contrary to nearly everything in their social upbringing and setting. Accordingly, one of the most important exercises, normally reserved for superiors, was "humbling," subjecting a person to humiliating work, admonishment, discipline, or other spiritual tasks certain to remove any remaining traces of personal pride. The outcome could also be, ironically, a kind of competition in humility, attempts to outdo others in self-effacing actions. Indeed their whole way of life was humbling and even humiliating, for by voluntarily choosing a state between the world and the cloister they effectively gave up all the privileges attached in the Middle Ages to either way of life.

Obedientia: gehorsamheid

Parallel to this emphasis on humility, and with the same ultimate aim, came a concern with obedience. This was obedience conceived as a virtue. Obedience to the community's way of life was expected and insisted on, but that remained a voluntary commitment, an internalization of the legal and religious requirements that would have come with a religious vow. Obedience was directed to superiors and to God; it was humble submission without demur. Within the community it probably differed little, in function and understanding, from obedience inside a cloister. Toward God it took the added dimension of submission to the divine will, of which all events, good and bad, were seen as a providential expression. In Geert Grote especially, but in many others as well, humble submission in the face of suffering, reproach, and difficulties of all kinds was interpreted as an important part of obedience to Christ and identification with his suffering. Closely related to obedience, and prob-

INTRODUCTION

ably a clear expression of what was ultimately intended, was the mandate to "break your own will," expressed just that graphically. Willfulness was an expression of sin, deeply rooted, and purged only after much exercising. To break that self-will, a lifelong task, was crucial to becoming humble and obedient before the sight of God and in the company of your fellow devout. Breaking your own will in humility was therefore the counterpart to making a good resolve. The New Devout were to turn "willingly" toward Christ and then to submit their wills totally and inwardly to his.

Cor: hert

All that transpired in the remaking of a devout person took place essentially in his or her heart. The devout also spoke of the mind, the "reason" or rational faculty that had to control the passions, but that innermost part of a person to which their new devotion was directed they called the "heart." This was rooted in biblical language, but they insisted on it as a way of addressing the whole person, beyond the mind addressed by the schoolmen or the moral will addressed in sermons or the confessional. All the progress in the virtues, the whole strength of their resolution, that complete inwardness of the truly devout—all of this was to grow out of the heart. The New Devout took over, without developing in any greater detail, the whole accepted vocabulary, Greek in origin and passed through the monks and the schools, concerning the faculties, passions, humors, and so on that made up the soul. While they also spoke often of the "soul" or the "spirit," the most common word, and the one that came closest to their own concerns, was the "heart" as the God-given core of every person, that which needed to be molded in a new devotion.

Affectus (affectio): begheerlichheid

The New Devout thought of the heart or soul as carried along by desires, instincts, and impulses of all kinds. As a result of the fall, the dominant desires in most people were evil or concupiscent, twisting the heart toward all manner of vice. The soul could not, however, be void, without affection or emotional force of any kind. The point therefore was to cultivate the right kinds of affections and impulses, desire for God and delight in the good. Theirs was no quietism, no state beyond passion and being, as in some mystical traditions. Few words were so common in their texts as desire, delight, and affection. A heart purged of carnal affections and evil de-

33

sires but full of godly affections and goodly desire was the goal of their way of life.

Ardent: vuurig

The language of the New Devout has little or no subliminal sexual language, no talk of ravishing union or sweet kisses; there is language from the Song of Songs, but mostly of a purely conventional sort. Yet all their emphasis on inwardness and resolution was not lacking in intensity. By far the most common image, one that appears so often as to become the translator's despair, was that of being "afire" or enflamed, "ardent" in Latin and English. Every brother or sister who had caught the spark, whose inner life was moved with desire toward God and goodness, was described as "ardent" or "kindled" or "fervent." The New Devout looked for that glow, for that inner radiance, that inner light, marking a heart now following down the path of the new devotion with intensity, with "fire."

Puritas cordis: reinigheid des hertes

The ultimate goal of this inwardness, resolution, and moral progress was purity of heart. This could be described—in language now standard and bland for us—as someone "of good conscience" or dying "in good confession." The emphasis on inwardness and moral progress, however, carried additional connotations. This was a person who was directed toward the Lord with resolve and in love, whose passions and affections were in order, whose whole moral and emotional being was focused on what God first intended, love of God and man, without inner conflict, wayward desires, or an unresponsive carnal self. This was a goal, not reachable finally in this life, but it was the ideal toward which all their writings pointed. Behind them lay Jesus' own promise: The pure in heart would see God.

Many more words might be cited, but these twelve, taken together with the most common expressions for Jesus, meditative reading, the last things, and interiority, will serve to signify the inner world of the Modern Devotion. Neither the devout themselves nor their contemporaries, it must be remembered, thought of this devotion as "new" in the sense of novel or extraordinary. The main features of their spirituality had been distilled out of elements common to much of late medieval religious life as practiced in observant orders and preached in parishes. Contemporaries seem to have recognized that and rarely commented on the actual teachings or spirituality of these communities. What struck contemporaries as remarkable, eliciting both scorn and admiration, was the resolve of these individuals to live a devoutly religious life in places and ways of their own choosing, together with the degree of ardent intensity they brought to that resolve and their "methodical" organization of voluntary religious exercises— and this from people, lay men and women and minor clergymen, from whom such "devotion" would hardly have been expected, especially not in this "modern age," when so much else in the Church seemed to suffer from indifference and corruption.

The Translated Texts

THE FOUNDER: GEERT GROTE

The brothers and sisters of the New Devotion looked back on Master Geert Grote of Deventer (1340–1384) as the founder of their movement. Outside the sisters who lived in his house, the cluster of clerics who formed the first brothers' houses in Deventer, Zwolle, and Amsterdam, and those persons who were converted to the new devotion by Grote's own preaching, most never knew him personally. Their view of him and of the New Devotion he preached rested on oral accounts passed along in their houses and written down a generation and more after his death. Two liturgical commemorations and three lives in prose largely fixed the image of him that held into this century.[34] Only in the last generation or two have historians attempted to construct a picture based more on Grote's own writings, some eighty letters and ten treatises.[35]

Geert Grote was born on October 16, 1340. His father, a wealthy merchant, belonged to the inner circle of twenty-four men who governed the city of Deventer. Twice in Geert's childhood, during his third and eighth years, Werner Grote served as city treasurer, from which office he dealt with all the local powers, the representatives of other cities in the Ijssel river valley, the count of Gelders, and the lord bishop of Utrecht. But at age ten, in the summer of 1350, Geert lost both his parents to the black plague and was left in the custody of an uncle. Until age fifteen he attended the distinguished Latin grammar school at the collegiate chapter of St. Lebuinus in his hometown. Then he was sent off to Paris for study, a privilege made possible by the orphan's inherited wealth. He matriculated in the English nation and by age eighteen, an early indication of his zeal and intelligence, he graduated a master in the arts.

The next sixteen years (1358–1374), the crucial time between his eighteenth and thirty-fourth years, are poorly attested in the records. Much of the time was spent in further study, probably at Paris, but he never completed any advanced degrees. Canon law, the best route to advancement in the Church, attracted most of his attention, but he also studied medicine, astrology, natural philosophy, and perhaps a little theology. He pursued the career of a late medieval cleric, putting in bids for at least five benefices or church livings, and gaining two good ones, a seat in Charlemagne's church at Aachen and in the cathedral chapter at Utrecht. He was minimally resident in them (income, not office, was the point) and maintained his contacts in Deventer, early on (1365–1366), for instance, representing the city in a case against the bishop of Utrecht at the papal court in Avignon. In reference to his extended youth, at least one passing use of a strong biblical image (of having "fornicated on every hilltop and under every spreading tree")[36] suggests that his moral life deteriorated in the midst of study, travel, and ambition.

In 1374, at age thirty-four, he experienced a great turn-around or "conversion," as the later lives called it. At the heart of it was a thorough-going crisis over his entire way of life, wondrously evident in his subsequent *Resolutions*. This may have been fostered by warnings from worried friends (of which there are contradictory accounts in the lives). But the immediate circumstance seems to have been an illness, confronting him with fears of death and judgment, and a related crisis over astrology, which had come to fascinate him as a way of understanding the cosmos and his own fate. The result of this crisis was not, however, as so often in the Middle Ages, entry into a religious house. Although he spent at least one lengthy period in retreat with the Carthusians at Monnikhuizen and came to revere them ever afterward as the most exemplary of religious orders, he resolved to pursue the spiritual life in his own way and outside a cloister. He turned his large family home into a hospice for poor women, reserving only a small space for himself. He renounced his church livings, adopted a rigorously penitential way of life, and attended mass regularly at the Franciscan church near his home. He paid a visit to the great Flemish mystic, Jan Ruusbroec, and made a trip to Paris to buy books, presumably to aid in his new study of the religious life.

At the end of five years (late in 1379) he emerged with a call to preach. He did not seek ordination, for which he claimed himself unworthy, but obtained instead a special license to preach as a deacon in the diocese of Utrecht. Over nearly four years, from early 1380 until late 1383, he preached up and down the diocese, especially in his own Ijssel river valley. He took with him a companion to announce his coming and to copy down his words and a barrel full of books to help in his preparations and to defend himself against malcontents. His themes seem to have been the same nearly everywhere, although he preached in Latin to clerics and in Dutch to the people: Repent, for judgment is coming! (Letter 29); Convert, and persevere in the way of devotion, for only such will be saved! (Letter 62). The climax of his short career came in 1383, when he was invited by his bishop to preach before all the clerics of the diocese assembled in synod. Master Geert railed against their shortcomings, above all their incontinence, and took the position that concubinate priests (*focaristi*: those having a female companion at the "hearth") and ordinary folk who knowingly attended their masses were in a state of mortal sin. This brought down the house, and his preaching tours were suspended by way of a general ban on further preaching by anyone except ordained men. Master Geert sought refuge in another town and appealed to Rome, but he died of the plague on August 20, 1384 (St. Bernard's feast day), possibly caught while visiting plague victims.

Geert Grote was a deeply learned and powerfully driven man. His early death prevented him from writing any single mature work summing up his vision of this new devotion. His eighty extant letters and ten treatises, written in less than ten years, convey little of the peace of mind and tranquillity of spirit he wished to nurture in the devotion of his own disciples. His works are crammed with references to authorities, the fruit of wide reading and rigorous canonistic training, and his style is difficult, at times almost tortured, in the worst tradition of so-called scholastic Latin. Yet there shines through it the personality of a man who had disciplined his own willful nature and dedicated himself to a penitential way of life, who was "giving himself over to mortification for Jesus' sake so that his life might be revealed in our mortal body" (2 Cor 4:11, a favorite text), in the conviction that only those who "persevered or stood firm to the end would be saved" (Mt 24:13, another favorite text). He was unrelenting in his attacks on the shortcomings of the Church: the heretics who spread false teachings, the monks and sisters who had destroyed genuine poverty and community by their self-indulgence, the clerics given over to a dissolute way of life and setting such bad examples, and the people lost in indifference and ignorance. Over against all of these—heretics, corrupt religious, fallen clerics, and indifferent people—he had a vision of communities of the "devout" or the "spiritual" or the "converted," terms used almost interchangeably. While he was willing to recommend disciples to good religious houses, where they could still be found, his attention was increasingly directed to these clusters of converts forming communities on a voluntary basis in private dwellings. His own house became such a community for women, and like-minded men (mostly clerics or priests) began to gather at homes in Deventer and Zwolle even before his death. Each community demanded, above all, a genuine commitment to the spiritual life: devotion, and not community of property, was the key issue in the earliest stages, and also later.

Few of Grote's extant writings were directed specifically to these nascent communities, and even those that were invariably addressed quite particular matters. From his own works came therefore, at most, the impulse toward and not the full program of devotion. It should be noted in closing that by far the most influential of all his works (some 800 or more extant manuscripts) supported directly this New Devotion. In the last year of his life, after his preaching was suspended, he translated into Middle Dutch certain liturgical hours (those of the Blessed Virgin, the Holy Ghost, Holy Wisdom, the Holy Cross, and the dead) together with the seven penitential psalms and the litany of the saints.[37] This gave hundreds of men and women with little or no Latin the means to engage in a form of worship that was at once public and private and that could be pursued outside the divine office of some religious order or the Sunday mass at their local church. Such meditational prayer life, centered on Scripture and the hours, was at the heart of the Modern Devotion.

Resolutions and Intentions but Not Vows

Not long after his conversion, presumably late in 1374 or more probably in 1375, Geert Grote wrote out a set of guidelines for his new life.[38] He was manifestly still in the throes of reorientation. The document contains a series of relatively disorganized proposals and resolutions, little more than notes and arguments about the way of life he now proposed to adopt and the reasons for doing so. It is as if we could look over his shoulder and watch him thinking and arguing his way through the changes required by his spiritual conversion. The topics are those that any ambitious and learned cleric would have had to confront in the fourteenth century (here provided with headings to help the reader). Master Geert resided at his house in Deventer, and had probably just resigned his church livings, or was on the verge of doing so. The decisions facing him reveal that he still lived very much in the world, although now as a minor cleric (virtually a layman), and he apparently had not yet made any plans to go into retreat among the Carthusians. This document marked in retrospect the beginnings of the movement called the New Devotion. Later brothers and sisters preserved Grote's *Resolutions*, and several of them imitated it with programs of their own, but they

looked on his as exemplary rather than normative. These were resolutions and intentions, privately drawn up and adhered to; they
were not religious vows publicly professed. Grote and the brothers
and sisters who came after him saw themselves as pledged in conscience and before God to uphold their resolutions, but certainly not
as bound in obedience to any religious rule or superior. This attempt
to find a third way, between the world and the cloister, had prece-
dents particularly, as noted earlier, among the beguines. Yet no beguine or beghard is known to have written out or left behind any
such set of personal resolutions. Other medieval clerics or laymen
may well have made resolutions on some religious subject, but few
or no others are known to have set out to draw up their own religious
guidelines.

Noteworthy Sayings of Master Geert
The aim of Geert Grote, as of the sisters and brothers, was not
to produce anything "new" as such, but to make the devotion of the
apostolic community and the Desert Fathers live "today," in the
"modern" world. They did not set out therefore to write new devotional works, but to recover the great works of the past, beginning
with the Scriptures themselves, followed by the teachings of the
Desert Fathers (Cassian's *Collations*) and then especially the masters
of the twelfth-century revival (Anselm, Bernard, William of St.
Thierry, Hugh of St. Victor, and so on). But there soon developed
within their houses, in a kind of genuine revitalization of the Desert
Fathers, a tradition of sayings that had originated within the community and were passed down by word of mouth. This likewise began with Geert Grote himself, of whom two or three different
collections were written down and preserved; this translation is of
the largest and most widely distributed collection of his sayings.[39]
So close is the resemblance between some of Master Geert's sayings
and some of those found in the *Imitation* that more than one scholar
has been tempted, almost certainly incorrectly, to make Grote the
original author of the *Imitation*.

Letter 29
Grote's work as a religious teacher and preacher is most readily
accessible through his letters. Many circulated independently as religious discourses, and two have been selected for translation here.
Letter 29 was addressed to a certain Johannes ten Water, a young
man associated with the earliest house of the devout in Zwolle, who
had been encouraged by the magistrates in that city to pursue a uni-

versity education in Cologne.⁴⁰ Grote had only recently made the
opposite move, from universities and cities to a simple religious life,
and he regarded this as none other than the devil's own ploy to lure
away one of the new devout. This letter reveals to us what Grote's
many "conversion" sermons must have sounded like as well as the
high value he placed on associating with one of these new gatherings
of the devout. By instructing his disciple to read Ruusbroec and
Suso, Grote placed himself and his followers in the tradition of the
greatest masters of spirituality in the fourteenth century. Above all,
the letter signals a trait found in Grote himself, in much of the Modern Devotion, and beyond that in ever more of late medieval spiritual
literature. Religious renewal was to begin with a powerful and fearful sense of the imminence of death and judgment, as a spur to take
up and persist in a new life of devotion. Grote, by the way, was successful. Johannes eventually became a much respected canon at Windesheim, and this letter may have been preserved partly as a means
of recruiting other potential "devout."

Letter 62 on Patience

A second letter, one of Geert Grote's best known and most frequently copied, illustrates another aspect of his spirituality: the
humble bearing of suffering, trials, and temptation as a necessary
part of becoming Christlike. Grote saw the world as deeply corrupted by evil, but he was not a fatalist. All evil occurred under the
providence of God and was meant to teach and exercise the devout
in the virtues that would make them ever more like Christ. This letter also casts light on the circumstances that fostered the sisters' and
brothers' resolution to live religious lives outside cloisters. As had
apparently become very common in the Late Middle Ages, a certain
unworthy person had gained entrance (possibly by simony) to a
monastic house, where his abusive character was expected to disrupt
the spiritual life. On behalf of a devout friend in that house,⁴¹ Master
Geert had attempted to block the man's entrance through legal mea-
sures taken at the bishopric in Utrecht, but to no avail. Grote's disciple now wanted to break his vow of stability and transfer to another
house. Master Geert counseled him to remain in the house, to suffer
through this trial, and thereby to grow spiritually, even in the face
of untoward circumstances within a religious house. To this end,
Grote outlined the centrality of imitating Christ and meditating on
Scripture in any truly devout life, even or especially in the worst of
circumstances.

INTRODUCTION

A Sermon Addressed to the Laity

Between 1380 and late 1383 Master Geert Grote preached regularly to the laity in their own language, and one of his companions reportedly wrote his words down; but only one sermon has come down to us in the original Middle Dutch. In this sermon, however, all the traits characteristic of the New Devotion are already evident, especially an emphasis on interiority rather than external exercises and the expectation that this devotion could be developed outside the cloister as well, even by married folk. The vices he castigated here were those most evident in the expanding commercial centers of the northern Lowlands, where urbanization and social instability subjected people to all forms of avarice and low life. According to a much later and doubtless apocryphal or exaggerated story, Grote once told of a vision in which he saw all the magistrates who had served with his father on Deventer's city council condemned to hell for their avarice and abuse of the church.[42] In such a setting, which Grote knew all too well from Deventer and Zwolle, he encouraged the nurturing of an interior devotion expressed in straightforward (rather than exaggeratedly ascetic) virtues, meaning in this case uprightness in commercial transactions and fidelity in the marriage bond. While poverty and celibacy were not the point here, a genuine spirituality, coming from within, was very much the point, and married folk could learn too from the image of Christ's marriage with receptive souls.

On Four Classes of Subjects Suitable for Meditation: A Sermon on the Lord's Nativity

Master Geert was a man of great learning with an insatiable appetite for books. However deep his experience of conversion and however trenchant his repudiation of vain and false learning, he never undid or attempted to undo habits acquired during fifteen years as a student in nearly all branches of human learning at the University of Paris. As a preacher he continued to write legal opinions, and his single most important sermon, his attack on clerical concubinage in the diocese of Utrecht, underwent expansion into a major treatise arguing his position through twenty-four points. While several treatises and many letters betray his canonistic expertise, his philosophical learning stands revealed almost uniquely in this document, a sermon expanded into a treatise on the birth of Christ. At first glance it might seem more a philosophical than a devotional work, but it reveals Master Geert using philosophical analysis to understand and purify devotional practice.

42

INTRODUCTION

The date and occasion of this sermon-treatise is not known,[43] but its general setting is clear enough. In the later fourteenth century, as attested by hundreds of extant manuscript illuminations, paintings, sculptures, and devotional manuals, meditation on and through images had become crucial to the fostering of the spiritual life, and the danger was great—especially, it was thought, in circles of unlettered women—that forms of collective fantasizing could gain the upper hand and seriously mislead the faithful. Grote recognized this danger and addressed it on two levels, both evidently informed by his own spiritual experience. For the ordinary devout (in the original sermon?) he provided sensible advice on the use and abuse of images in meditating on Christ, the center, as he repeatedly said, of all devotional life. For more learned readers (the presumed recipients of the expanded treatise) he offered a philosophical analysis of the cognitive processes involved, demonstrating the need for such images as well as the necessity ultimately of transcending them.

Grote clearly knew about abuses firsthand, such as meditating on the poverty and passion of a "nude Christ," allowing mental images to assume an almost palpable reality, fantasizing on matters of Christ and the saints outside the authorized sources, and so on. Grote warned against them, and stressed that meditation on images should always be tested against the scriptural record, its interpretation, and its application in a life of holiness. The inherent difficulty in all this, however, was of another kind and received its best treatment at the philosophical level.

Grote was a "realist," converted from the "nominalism" he had learned as a student in Paris. He believed that the essence of things, that which lay behind and went beyond image and sensation, was the only true reality, and its apprehension offered the only genuine knowledge of God. Yet he took for granted the indispensability of sensible images both in the cognitive process and in spiritual meditation. His problem was to rectify the two. While treating other "classes" of images, Grote rested his case mainly on the nature of scriptural images and the practice of meditating on them in such a way as to have them vividly represented to the mind and affections. Building on Aristotle's outline of the senses and sensation, he explained how God had provided that spiritual desire and knowledge should come by way of sensation, including the sensations generated by meditation. This therefore was good and necessary, within certain scriptural bounds. But the faith that constituted true knowledge had ultimately to be purified of all image and sensation in order to grasp the transcendent. This too was right and necessary, although not easily attained. He reflected on the way in which it seemed to come most nearly through hearing, particularly the "hearing of the Word," but he then went on to show—thereby defending meditation again—that even hearing required visual delineation to represent the heard realities to the mind. Moreover, while transcendence was the aim, it could come only through the long and careful process of purifying the images and sensations aroused in meditation. He warned against "short cuts"—probably meaning the kind of spiritual techniques of which groups like the so-called free spirits were suspected.

The result is a position strikingly close to that which would come to characterize the Modern Devotion: an emphasis on constant meditation, especially meditation on Scripture or scriptural images, but with an end that was neither sensational nor mystical but rather a deepened interiority expressed in holy conduct. Grote's treatise may be read in retrospect, therefore, as a kind of philosophical and psychological exposition of the spiritual way of life that most brothers and sisters of the New Devotion would be concerned to exemplify in practice. This document also helps correct a certain imbalance produced in most secondary literature by a one-sided emphasis on the "anti-intellectualism" of this movement. In its first generation, and also subsequently in appropriate settings (such as St. Martin's in the university town of Louvain), its adherents were quite capable of applying learning to the defense and exposition of what they understood to be the practice of the true spiritual life.

THE DEVOUT

The devotion that Master Geert Grote sought to instill by way of example, preaching, and the gift of his house spread after his death among the New Devout, the brothers and sisters of the common life. This New Devotion was propagated in the first instance, as was to be expected of such a self-styled community, by the brothers and sisters themselves, not by any institutional or constitutional arrangements. Through their lives they bore witness to their conversion and devotion, and thus attracted others to join them—also, incidentally, drew criticism and even cynical rebuffs, as from the man who reportedly quipped that Master Geert should cut out this nonsense and allow his fellow townsmen to go down to hell in peace. The very lives these brothers and sisters lived in their houses and towns, not the prescriptions of any theoretical program drawn from the past or outlined by a founder, shaped the spiritual dynamic of the new devotion. There was evident here a certain reaching down, if you like, of the higher ideals of the medieval Church into the lives of ordinary men and women.

The stories of the New Devout were initially told and retold inside each house. Master Geert's own life underwent a certain idealization as the founder and first exemplar of the New Devotion.[44] The members of the movement always remembered that, following Grote's early death, others had played a key role in organizing these houses, Florens Radewijns for the men and John Brinckerinck for the women, and the stories of their lives were accordingly also told and eventually written down.[45] In roughly the second generation of this movement, when those who had known the founders were also beginning to die, the stories of the more "ordinary" New Devout were first put into writing. The purpose was clear: It was a way of remembering and celebrating the development of their movement; but it was also, and in the first instance, a means of teaching the New Devotion as evidenced in the lives of its devout practitioners. The first of these written accounts came from none other than Thomas à Kempis and grew out of his work with novices, his efforts to teach new recruits at the St. Agnietenberg in the 1420s.[46] Such works soon came to be written for all the main houses, for the brothers at Deventer and Zwolle,[47] the sisters of Master Geert's House in Deventer,[48] the canons at Windesheim,[49] the canonesses at Diepenveen,[50] and for many other houses of greater or lesser importance. For the most part these were not chronicles, but collected lives of brothers and sisters, often written up shortly after their deaths in a kind of religious commemoration.

All these written lives share characteristics common to the spiritual teachings of the Modern Devotion. The virtue or virtues fostered and acquired by a brother or sister tended to dominate the entire story. Inevitably there was some idealization and repetition, but almost nothing of miracle or prophecy. Indeed, John Busch specifically declared that these people were to be seen as holy and even as saints despite the fact that no miracles and no cults were attested of them.[51] The spiritual testament of holy lives was their most important legacy. Their virtues were built, moreover, on discipline and persistence, and were generally not of heroic proportions. The accounts of their lives betray a certain "ordinariness" not found in most legends of medieval saints. In the best of them the love and humility on which the brothers and sisters put so much emphasis has issued in a gentleness and a sense of humanity that appealed in their own day and may perhaps still in ours. These stories were meant to teach what they represented to their audience, and there breathed through them a remarkable spirit of peace, of goodwill, and of compassion for the condition of sinful humanity.

Master Geert's house was, strictly speaking, the first gathering of the New Devout and, appropriately enough, its sisters were among the first to write up, in Middle Dutch, "some edifying points from the lives of the older sisters."[52] This work treats the lives of sixty-seven sisters, chronologically arranged according to the dates of their deaths, from 1398 to 1456. The work appears to have come, in its present form at least, from the hand of a single sister. She drew on oral traditions, the memories of older sisters, and possibly some lost written accounts; but she saw it all as a single tradition, her tradition, and noted occasionally what she had herself witnessed. The only extant manuscript (Deventer, Gemeentelijke Archief) belonged to the canonesses of the house at Frenswegen and dates to about 1480, but the original must have been completed not long after 1456. The Middle Dutch original is repetitious at times, particularly in its parallel structures, which undoubtedly proved useful for driving points home in an oral reading; but the whole is perceptive and has about it an air of authenticity. Since any selection is arbitrary and risks overemphasizing certain points or choosing only the "best" examples, I have decided to translate the introduction, the first seven lives (followed by a chapter on the rigor of the early sisters), and the last four lives. These are fully representative of the style and the spiritual teachings found in the whole.

For the brothers I have chosen a house founded out of Deventer, but not until 1467 and on the far eastern edge of the diocese. Emmerich lay in the county of Cleve (and therefore today in Germany), but in the Middle Ages belonged ecclesiastically to Utrecht and culturally to the Lowlands. This house, although it has not received quite the attention accorded to some others, has a particularly rich chronicle, also organized around lives. There is a single manuscript again, from about 1500, recently edited together with the customs of the house, making plain the link between the lives and the guide for those lives found in the customary.[53] The work opens with a chapter on the founding of the house and then proceeds to treat fourteen departed brothers, beginning with the first rector. The last of these died in 1494 and 1495 (the first in 1472), and the work apparently came from a single hand in the late 1490s. In this case, a selection was made for translation, partly to draw attention to an important aspect of the Modern Devotion not otherwise treated in this volume, the pastoral care and instruction of young boys. This was love, the highest virtue, demonstrated through care and hospitality, whereby the brothers significantly deepened the lives of many a young cleric. The virtues described are those prized both in the house and in the running of the schools.

THE DEVOTION

The brothers and sisters described in the collections of lives maintained in their various houses thought of their devotion as "renewed" but not as "new." They saw themselves restoring ancient spiritual traditions going back to the apostles, the Desert Fathers, and the Church's greatest teachers. They learned about the apostles through the New Testament, about the Desert Fathers chiefly through John Cassian, and about the saints of the medieval Church chiefly through the works of such twelfth-century figures as Bernard of Clairvaux, Anselm of Canterbury, Hugh of St. Victor, and the like. These texts, together with the whole Bible and various books of hours, were what the New Devout spent most of their time copying, studying, and meditating on. The brothers and sisters never set out to write anything themselves in the way of new or distinctive spiritual treatises, and a search for innovative or "new" texts will initially yield little. One of their earliest and most abiding genres of literature took the form of *rapiaria* (literally, "snatchings" or "grab-bags"), collections of excerpts from the spiritual tradition compiled individually and then sometimes passed around. Whether Master Geert produced such a copybook of favorite sayings is unknown, but one of two prepared by Florens Radewijns has been preserved (and well edited) under the title "A little devout treatise on the uprooting of the vices and passions and the acquisition of the true virtues, especially love of and union with God and our fellow man." Dirc of Herxen translated into Dutch teachings of the Fathers that fill two good-sized codices, and Gerard Zerbolt, whose influential treatise on the spiritual ascents is translated in Part IV below, prepared for it by gathering the teachings of the Fathers into a large volume on the reformation of the soul. Beyond these there were any number of anonymous collections.[54]

The search for original texts becomes much more rewarding when it is remembered that the brothers and sisters never looked on themselves as a mystical movement or a learned sect, but simply as a devout way of life. That way of life they tried repeatedly to explain and to propagate, partly, as we have seen, by telling the stories of their departed brothers and sisters. They set out their intentions most plainly, however, in a series of texts I have distinguished as customaries, exercises, and collations.

A Customary for Brothers

The brothers met in free and voluntary gatherings, but as their households increased in size and number they recognized the need for order and discipline. The result was a "customary," a guide to the structure and purpose of their way of life, or, put another way, something like Master Geert's "Resolutions" extended to encompass a whole community. These customaries had, strictly speaking, no legal status in the Church and therefore must have varied widely in content and especially in application from house to house. Yet brothers in one house learned from those in another, and there was clearly a kind of common fund of wisdom, especially after 1431 when the rectors of all the Dutch houses met annually to "talk" and to make common decisions (Zwolse Colloquium). Six such customaries for brothers have come down to us, but the question of their exact origins, dates, interrelationships, and use are still not entirely resolved.[55]

Translated here is the better part of a customary that originated in Zwolle in the early fifteenth century (1415–1424) and that parallels another thought to have come from the Lord Florens house in Deventer.[56] Dirk of Herxen, rector for many years at Zwolle (1410–1457), reportedly wrote up its customs, and this text may therefore stem in part from his hand. The most important point about this document, however, is that it was not seen as a legally binding rule or constitution but rather as a guide to a devout way of life. While the omission of a few of its more administrative sections may enhance that impression here, what has been translated is characteristic of the whole. In the customary from Herford, almost two decades later, the "religious" and the "administrative" materials were separated into two distinct books, with the religious coming first, but the actual texts remained over long stretches virtually identical with those translated here. The section on the rector was included here to show both the organization of the house and its spiritual concerns, and that on the librarian because books and copywork were at the heart of the brothers' ways of life. (This section also has great historical interest in its own right.) The emphasis throughout is on advancement in the virtues, the only real rationale for the house's existence and thus for a guide to its usages: Charity, obedience, chastity, sobriety, and community of life were the chief end of the brothers and sisters who freely gathered here to cultivate the devout life.

INTRODUCTION

An Exhortation to Sisters Founding a New House

Outside the regulations established for Master Geert's own house in Deventer, little is known about the customs practiced in the sisters' houses. Often their way of life was regulated by the statutes or charter granted by the city magistrates.[57] An exhortation written by one sister to others planning a new foundation has been preserved. Salome Sticken (1369–1449) was experienced in every phase of the movement of Modern Devotion. Her noble father was converted by one of Geert Grote's own sermons, although she joined Master Geert's house only at age twenty, after she was persuaded that this represented a better way of doing penance for earlier excesses than making a pilgrimage to Rome. Her noble bearing and religious sincerity were both challenged initially by the humbler sisters, but she soon emerged as rectress of Master Geert's house. In 1409 she took formal vows as a canoness in the related Augustinian foundation of Diepenveen outside Deventer, where the rector was still John Brinckerinck (d. 1419), himself resident in the Lord Florens house. She was subsequently elected the first prioress there (1412) and served almost until her death in 1449. By then she had become celebrated as probably the best known of all the sisters of the New Devotion, a model of discipline and piety whose life was written up in both Dutch and Latin.[58]

Henry of Loder, rector of the Augustinian canons at Frenswegen (1414–1436) and reformer of several women's houses, asked her advice. This "formula" represents a kind of summary of her views on the devout way of life, dating probably from near the end of her active life (mid-1430s). A certain firmness, one of her trademarks, is evident, but so too is the unrelenting intensity of her devotion. Particularly noteworthy, and applicable to nearly all sisters' houses, is the emphasis on work as essential and occupying most of the day. Experiential grace was, moreover, no end in itself but only a possible result of constancy in this devout way of life. This more "sober" approach quite clearly set off the sisters from other late medieval women's groups, for whom extraordinary religious experiences had often become virtually the whole point. For the sisters, devotion meant humility and steady advancement in the virtuous life, and this came through constancy in work and prayer.

The Life and Passion of Our Lord Jesus Christ and Other Devout Exercises

Customaries guided the communal life of the New Devout, exercises their individual religious lives. The distinction was not a rigid one, and many exercises read like customaries adjusted to individual

49

usage. Or, perhaps more accurately put, customaries probably grew out of exercises, such as the one ascribed to Florens Radewijns himself: They were resolutions and exercises applicable to the whole congregation. Within the general framework for gatherings provided by the customaries, it was the exercises that most significantly shaped the religious lives of the brothers and sisters. From a large number of preserved examples, three have been selected here as representative and especially influential.

Exercises were not an invention of the brothers and sisters, although they were to become one of their distinctive trademarks. The New Devout, moreover, almost surely gave their use an added impetus that carried over into the famous exercises of the sixteenth century. The notion of exercises, originally a military term, was applied to spiritual matters by the Church Fathers and especially the early monks, but the notion was first fostered by Franciscan devotional authors, and only came into widespread usage during the fourteenth century.[59] For such influential authors as Henry Suso and Richard Hampole the term was self-evident in meaning, and in the fifteenth century, partly owing to the influence of the New Devout, it became standard everywhere. In origin it embraced fasting, prayer, meditation, and all the focused devotional activities of religious persons. With the Franciscans and their heirs it took on the additional meaning of empathetic meditation upon the life and passion of Christ. The New Devout assumed and developed both, adding an emphasis of their own on steady progress in battling the vices and acquiring the virtues.

The most influential of these exercises among the Modern Devout was undoubtedly that known as the "Letter on the Life and Passion of Our Lord."[60] Johannes Busch, who provided a Latin translation of the Middle Dutch original in his *Windesheim Chronicle*, claimed that it was assiduously used by brothers in their gatherings and by lay brothers in the Windesheim Congregation.[61] In the Middle Dutch original, moreover, the audience was addressed as "sisters," meaning it was also employed in their circles.[62] The question of authorship remains unresolved. Busch reports only that it was scrupulously used and promoted by John Vos of Heusden, the second (but first significant) prior of Windesheim (1391–1424). This work dated therefore to the earliest days of the movement of New Devotion. The work is effectively in two parts. The first, on meditative devotion to the life and passion of Christ, has many parallels in earlier literature, although no one direct source. Hedlund found its scheme closest to Bonaventure's *Tree of Life*, Ps-Bonaventure's

Meditations on the Life of Christ, Ubertino da Casale's *Tree of Life of the Crucified Jesus,* and *The Monastic Exercizer* of Henry Egher of Calcar, a Carthusian and former friend of Geert Grote. More truly original is the second part, on the cultivation of the virtues. Here there is a characteristic concern with persevering to the end as well as with breaking the individual will in humility in order to reform it in a pattern of devotion. Matters that a superior might be expected to teach have here taken the form of personal admonishment and exercise.

The Exercises of John Kessel

How many brothers followed a general pattern of exercises, such as that outlined in the foregoing example, and how many prepared exercises of their own, is not known, but a large number of exercises are to be found in extant manuscripts. That from John Kessel (d. 1398) has been translated here. It became known through its inclusion in Thomas à Kempis's *Dialogue for Novices.* Written by a layman, it comes from the earliest days of the Lord Florens House in Deventer.

John Kessel was born in Doesburg and became a successful merchant in Holland and Flanders, with an office for overseas trade in Dordrecht. As an adult he resolved to become a priest, went to the chapter school at Deventer to begin studying Latin letters, and there became so impressed with the brothers' way of life that, as Thomas à Kempis (who knew him well) put it, "he left the rules of Alexander and Donatus and entered the school of heavenly training [literally: exercises] to learn the will of the Lord in the house of Lord Florens." At his own request, he served as the house's cook, and word quickly spread among Dutch merchant circles that "this rich businessman had now been made a poor little cook and humble brother." Humbling himself, "like Christ assuming the form of a servant," he never aspired again to the dignity of the priesthood. He sold off the rich clerical garb he had ordered in anticipation while still a rich merchant, and in the brothers' house became one of their strongest spokesmen for poverty. Alexius, Francis, and the widow Elizabeth were his preferred saints. As Thomas à Kempis summarized it, "He made an oratory of the kitchen, knowing that God was everywhere, and from its hearth he stirred up a spiritual flame." Of the learning that enabled him to draw up his own exercises, Thomas says only, "Although he was not a greatly learned man, he had a good mind for understanding the writings; he could discern between the virtues and vices and provide effective remedies for those suffering trouble and temptation."[63]

INTRODUCTION

The Exercises of Dirc of Herxen

Just as there is no absolute line between customs and exercises, so there is none between exercises and collations. While those parts of the exercises that focused on meditative empathy with the life and suffering of Christ had built on earlier traditions, as noted above, the parts that attempted to inculcate the virtues by way of short sayings and reflections were more distinctive to the brothers, and achieved their greatest influence through *The Imitation of Christ*. What the brothers sought to impress on themselves in these exercises, however, differed hardly at all from what they communicated to others in the form of collations.

Dirc of Herxen (1381–1457) was probably the most influential figure in the second generation of the movement.[64] Born in a small village near Zwolle, where his family held some land from the bishop, he obtained special permission to give up his secular responsibilities and to pursue a religious career. He too studied at Deventer and there came to know the brothers' way of life (probably between 1395 and 1405). He struggled with a religious vocation among the canons regular at Windesheim and the Carthusians at Monnikhuizen near Arnhem, but resolved in the end to become a brother in Zwolle. He ruled that house as rector for nearly fifty years (1410–1457), and during that time became the "father of all the New Devout," defending their status against attacks from city magistrates and mendicants alike, founding new houses, drawing up customaries, organizing a common "colloquium," and writing a number of religious exercises and treatises in both Latin and Dutch for both brothers and sisters. These exercises show him applying to himself the same spiritual standards he presumably applied to the brothers in Zwolle and taught outside his house to interested sisters, students, and laymen.

Collations

Beyond the customaries that guided communal spiritual life and the exercises that shaped individual spiritual lives, collations were the most important source of the brothers' and sisters' spirituality.[65] Exercises were common to many groups in the Late Middle Ages, but were given special emphasis in the Modern Devotion. Customaries raised more problems, for they placed the New Devout somewhere between the lay and the monastic world, as persons trying to live ordered religious lives outside religious orders. Collations were probably the most controversial of all, for they seemed to threaten directly the monopoly on teaching and preaching enjoyed by local

52

priests and the mendicant orders (especially the Dominicans) and to raise the specter of religious instruction in the Scriptures done within small circles and outside the oversight of Church authorities.

There were four identifiable audiences: the brothers themselves; the sisters over whom they had charge as confessors; the students and young people they attracted to their houses and eventually housed and cared for in "convicts"; and any good men and women who chose to come, especially on Sunday afternoons, to hear their admonitions. In the extant lives and sources many brothers are noted for the fine and effective collations they delivered, thereby winning many souls, but very few of their "sermons" seem to have been written down, and still fewer edited and published. It is generally said that these addresses were essentially hortatory and moralistic, urging repentance and teaching the virtues. This may well be true, but it is a judgment passed without much careful examination of the extant sources. Four texts have been selected for translation here.

Gerlach Peter's First Letter to His Sister Lubbe

This text takes the form of a letter, although its contents fall somewhere between the categories of an exercise and a collation. It encourages and teaches spiritual discipline in much the same way as an exercise, but it reads more like the kind of moral address brothers delivered among themselves as well as to sisters and interested lay folk. The specific situation is that Lubbe Peters, one of the early sisters in Master Geert's house and a person remembered for her exacting standards (see below Part II, 1), has taken on the position of "procuratrix," making her responsible for all the house's external affairs. The brothers and sisters looked on this as humble service but also as a considerable threat to devotion, or in the scheme of Gerard Zerbolt, the lowest (*Spiritual Ascensions* c. 70) of the descents made back down the mount for the sake of other brothers and sisters. Lubbe's zeal and determination to do everything right only increased the danger that her spiritual life would suffer grave damage from her anxiety over the house's external affairs. In this situation, her brother Gerlach drafted a letter outlining the priorities of the devout life. This "letter" soon gained notoriety among the sisters—it was written for them in Middle Dutch—as an outstanding description of the goals of the New Devout.

Gerlach Peters (1378–1411) is generally counted among the most able of the first generation of spiritual writers among the New Devout.[66] Like so many other brothers before and after him, he first went to school at Deventer, then was attracted into the circle of the

New Devout at the time of Florens Radewijns (the later 1390s), and finally became a canon at Windesheim (1403–1411). He died very young and also had difficulty with his eyes, so his works, as we now have them, were probably compiled after his death. His *Breviloquium* is clearly related to the genre of "resolutions" and "sayings" that originated with Grote and Radewijns. This "First Letter," although written in Middle Dutch, has many parallels to the *Breviloquium*. His *Soliloquium*, by contrast, is a more sustained contemplative treatise, which exercised influence down to the time of Port Royal. Distinctive to Gerlach in all these works is a greater focus on union with God than was generally found in the spirituality of the brothers and sisters. While he took over all their themes—humility, obedience, love, and progress in the virtues—he went a step further to speak as well of union with God, of the lover and the beloved, and of the joys that flow from such union, but still always in terms of "sweetness" and "delight" rather than of some transcendent rapture. To describe Gerlach as more "mystical," as is sometimes done, is somewhat misleading; he simply placed greater emphasis on the endpoint of the New Devotion, the sweet delight that comes from ultimate union with God.

John Brinckerinck on Conversion and on the Sacrament

John Brinckerinck (d.1419) belonged to the earliest generation of the New Devout, someone converted by Geert Grote himself, a lifelong resident of Florens Radewijns's house in Deventer, and the rector and organizer of the first successful house of canonesses at Diepenveen.[67] Nine of his collations have been preserved. They were almost certainly delivered to the sisters at Diepenveen, but the language is in fact general enough, at least in the preserved texts, that they could have been delivered and later read almost anywhere in the circles of the Modern Devout. Central to this New Devotion was conversion to the Lord and lifelong advancement in the spiritual life. What was understood by that notion is well represented in Brinckerinck's collation "on conversion," which also happens to be the first in his collection. Many of these collations must have been quite spontaneously conceived—thoughts on a certain subject suggested by Scripture rather than any outlined argument. This too is no model of organization, and is best read as several different approaches to what was understood as conversion in the circles of the New Devout. Readers should note especially the importance of the will, the resolve to turn to the Lord and ever to be about the business of bettering their spiritual lives. Related, and yet distinctive, is the importance of intention as carrying the sister or brother forward and toward peace even when faults and failures are still plentifully in evidence. The purpose of these collations was to be bracing and challenging, always calling for a deeper and purer spiritual life, without generating utter despair—for which there is also some evidence in the lives. Will and intention, if directed rightly and exercised regularly, would eventually issue in sweet desire, a kind of reward to be enjoyed but never sought in itself.

The second of Brinckerinck's collations chosen for translation concerns the sacrament of holy communion. One of the oldest generalizations about the New Devotion holds that its emphasis on interiority sprang from or eventually produced a certain deemphasis with respect to the sacraments. Insofar as scholars have understood this to mean that the sacraments were less central to the New Devout than to other medieval Christians and that movement had started down the road to the Reformation, this thesis is surely wrong. As Brinckerinck's sermon clearly shows, the New Devout may well have held too high rather than too low a view of the eucharist, and Brinckerinck himself fully intended to instill such a fearful and reverential view if it were not already there: Awe and trembling before its dignity were essential, and anything less could bring disaster. Yet there was another side, and this legitimately deserves attention too. Thorough spiritual preparation, conceived of as itself spiritual communion, was where all Brinckerinck's emphasis lay, and it, more than the sacrament itself, made all the difference in the reception of grace, thus potentially—and in one sentence literally—rendering reception of the sacrament virtually unnecessary. Thus the life of devotion, of constant conversion, of deepening and improvement, became the heart as well of a gracious and grace-bringing approach to the sacrament, and one that at least equaled it in providing grace.

Rector Peter of Dieburg on the Schism of 1443

The fourth text carries this theme and problematic a step farther. Peter of Dieburg wrote the chronicle of the house of brothers at Hildesheim.[68] He interspersed his chronicle, already an important and informative source, with digressions, and the first of these was in effect a collation. It presents a text that was, or could have been, delivered on the occasion of an interdict, when for political and ecclesiastical reasons regular divine service had been suspended, raising all kinds of fears and anxieties about Christian burial, and so on. Dieburg took the sacramental system of the late medieval Church altogether for granted, and his only criticism was of excess and—

again—of unworthy priests. Yet an occasion like this (an interdict) can remind us, he says, that Christ is the only true temple, the only source of grace and Christian burial, and that we ourselves must be spiritual temples from within, thereby removing virtually all anxieties about the sacramental ministrations themselves. Here again, in a text written in the 1490s, that emphasis on spiritual interiority characteristic of the Modern Devotion returns full force, and comes within a breath of challenging the whole sacramental system, even while still presupposing it.

GERARD ZERBOLT OF ZUTPHEN'S
SPIRITUAL ASCENSIONS

All that has gone before—Master Geert's call for a new devotion and a new resolve, the brothers and sisters who followed in their gatherings, the customaries that guided their devout way of life, the exercises that nourished and trained it, and the collations that propagated it—all this finds a kind of natural summary in Gerard Zerbolt of Zutphen's *Spiritual Ascensions*. Many of the items translated thus far exist in relatively few manuscript copies, reflecting the modest character of the brothers' and sisters' houses. But the *Spiritual Ascensions* has come down to us in at least one hundred handwritten copies and twenty-nine printed editions (a dozen of those between 1483/1486 and 1500) as well as early translations into Middle Dutch and Middle High German. This was the one devotional work probably common to nearly every house of the Modern Devout, who regularly recommended it; beyond their circle it entered many of the reformed contemplative orders of northern Europe in the Late Middle Ages, where Luther, as an observant Augustinian hermit, also read it. It was thought useful still in the early twentieth century to republish it in Dutch and English versions.[69]

Gerard Zerbolt of Zutphen (1367–1398) was, after Master Geert himself, the most learned and intellectually influential figure among the first generation of brothers.[70] Little is known about him, although he was among the first to make the transition from the famous chapter school in Deventer to the gathering of devout men in Florens Radewijns's vicarage. He then earned a master's degree at Prague, returned to write several significant treatises defending the New Devout, and died of the plague at age thirty-one in 1398. Drawing on much the same materials as Florens Radewijns, he compiled his own *rapiaria*, a book of spiritual gleanings, but this a far more systematically organized treatise entitled "The Reformation of the

Soul," itself widely dispersed in manuscript and print. Then, so to speak, leaning back and presupposing all the texts gathered earlier from the fathers, he sketched out his own view of that progress in virtue, that spiritual ascent, which was at the heart of the brothers' and sisters' New Devotion.

Gerard Zerbolt's conception of a "spiritual ascent" successfully combined a number of traditional elements in medieval spirituality into one overarching scheme. Each individual section or chapter spoke quite clearly for itself, and the chapter headings, almost certainly from Zerbolt himself, set out their themes. In many of the original fifteenth-century manuscripts, small duodecimo volumes that fit comfortably into an adult hand, those chapter titles were in red. The devout could thereby select a suitable topic without reading through the entire treatise. Yet when all the individual sections are combined, they make up a distinctive whole, and that whole reflected the spirit of the Modern Devotion. A summary of that larger scheme should render intelligible its essential spiritual framework.

The point of devotion is to return to mankind's original state of rectitude. This requires an understanding of that original state (2), recognition of the natural powers of the soul lost at the first fall into original sin (3), of the resultant impurity of heart or inclination to lower things (4), and consequent fall into mortal sin (5). Only severe self-examination of past sins, of all faculties of the soul, and of their present inclinations, together with a firm plan for setting matters right (6–9), will prepare a man for return or ascent, this explained in terms of methods for self-examination with warnings against confusing the means and the ends. To turn back from mortal sin, the final and farthest step downward from natural rectitude, requires, in the first ascent, the sincere practice of penance, complete with a full description of contrition, confession, and satisfaction (11–14). The second ascent, toward restoring purity of heart (one of the chief goals of the New Devout), is a much longer and more complicated process, which takes up roughly half the treatise. Fear, working together with compunction or remorse, must first drive out impurity (15–18); to this end Gerard provided an excursus on methods of meditating on death, judgment and the pains of hell (19–21). This was to be balanced by hope and desire for things celestial, born of meditating on the goodness and benefits of God (22–25); in this way a person may expect to acquire in reality all the virtues and genuine purity of heart. Innate inability to stir up such desire and hope is to be overcome by systematic meditation on the life of Christ (27–41), the perfect source of and exemplar for our ultimate purity, although this will never be completely perfected in this life (42). For those ascending toward this purity of heart and perfect virtue, refreshment is necessary along the way, and provided chiefly by holy reading, meditation, and prayer, each explained at some length (43–46).

In the third ascent, it is the fallen powers or faculties of the soul—that which was affected by original sin—that must be reformed. This can take place only by way of a steady battle against the assembled vices (48). There is no shortcut by way of extraordinary desire (49), a dangerous illusion, and a person must be armed with persistence, a spiritual guide, and the wisdom to battle all eight individually and according to their own natures (50–54). In combating each, the devout person is to employ fear and then hope in the expectation of thereby moving toward purity (55). There follows a lengthy treatment of the eight principle vices: gluttony, lust, avarice, anger, envy, tedium, vainglory, and pride (56–63).

Finally, those who have ascended must also descend in discipline of the self and service to others. The devout may at times find they can better discipline the inner self by returning to one of the lower exercises, or putting the outer self in order (this includes a discussion of friendship), or engaging in manual labor if the inner man has become problematic (65–67). Service of others is another form of descent that occurs when someone is ordered to cease contemplation to help a neighbor, to support others (especially in the winning of souls), or to bend down to take up administrative burdens for the sake of lesser brothers (68–70).

With this Gerard Zerbolt's *Spiritual Ascensions* abruptly ends. There is no summary, and no final exhortation or description of the joys of ultimate union. What interests him, and what inspired the New Devotion, was the process of sanctification, the continuous straining toward ascent and descent in a steady movement toward an ultimate purity of heart.

CONCLUSIONS

This introduction has concentrated on describing the texts of the Modern Devotion together with the communities that produced them and the distinctive spiritual themes they fostered. Many questions pertinent to the origin of that New Devotion, its setting in the Late Middle Ages, and its possible influence remain entirely untreated. The New Devout themselves saw their teachings and way of life in timeless terms, as recovered from Scripture and the early Fathers and as having a continuing universal claim. In this series dedicated to the history of spirituality, it is appropriate that the New Devout be read first as they wanted to be read, as issuing a general call to truth, devotion, and virtue. In looking back, historians and general readers will invariably raise questions about the original cultural and social milieu of those texts. At the risk of considerable reductionism, but with a certain appreciable insight nonetheless, many scholars have seen at work in these brothers and sisters the spirit of mercantile towns in the Late Middle Ages: the individual resolve, the planning, the systematic upbuilding, the somewhat limited horizon, the sobriety, and the determination. Some have even spoken of a "Dutch sobriety and frugality" already in evidence, but all of this cannot really be accepted until more systematic comparisons have been made with religious movements elsewhere in Europe during the Late Middle Ages.

A few simple points may be made here in summary. As Kaspar Elm has recently emphasized, the medieval church had a long tradition of "middle-ground" groups such as the beguines, of persons who were neither married and propertied laymen nor professed religious under vows. These were people who gathered voluntarily and under their own arrangements to pursue a more intensely religious life, sometimes constructing wholly new forms, sometimes borrowing a great deal (as the brothers and sisters did) from various existing orders, sometimes orienting themselves more to the active life of mercy (as with those who kept hospitals and hospices), other times more to the contemplative (as did the brothers and sisters). The irony in this instance is that the core of this voluntary group came mainly from among the secular clergy and the lay men and women who chose to associate with them.

There were, in addition, a number of significant contemporary movements that shared the concerns of the brothers and sisters. At the very same moment that the New Devout went their own way, the religious orders they found so corrupt also underwent a major process of internal reform known as the "observant movement."[71] The prayer life of the brothers and sisters, centered in the reading of the hours and systematic meditation on the life of Christ, found support and sustenance as well among the ever larger number of pious laymen and clerics in the Late Middle Ages who owned and observed their own "hours"—as attested by the success of Grote's own translations, extant still in more than eight hundred manuscripts, many of them illuminated. So, too, the core of their New Devotion, an affective piety focused on the life and passion of Jesus and a disciplined appropriation of the virtues, was rooted in long-standing traditions, the first especially from the Franciscans and the second from both monastic spirituality and the practice of the confessional. In this instance these materials were not prescribed by a superior or imposed by a confessor; they were willingly, even ardently, taken up by "converted" individuals. Likewise the concerns for pastoral care evident in their collations and mutual correction as well as in their convicts for students fit in with a European-wide effort to revitalize the care of souls, seen in hundreds of pastoral manuals and especially in an ever greater emphasis on effective preaching and confessing. Even the reform of the clergy, so endlessly discussed in the era of the councils and on the eve of the Reformation, had in effect taken place in the houses of these brothers and canons. Many more parallels could be cited, especially in the devotional literature written and favored then in Carthusian circles, but the point is clear enough. The Modern Devout seemed both "modern" or "present-day" and "devout" precisely because they shared so many of the concerns and aspirations of other religious individuals in the period of the Great Schism and the councils.

What finally about their "modernity"? How are we to explain the influence of *The Imitation of Christ?* What about Luther's interest? The contacts of Erasmus, Calvin, and Loyola? In any strict sense, continuity with or anticipation of the Reformation is excluded. With one or two exceptions, wherever the Reformation took hold, the houses of these brothers and sisters closed or were closed, and their magnificent libraries sadly dispersed and often largely lost. Any close reading of these works, with all their emphasis on the will and disciplined training in the virtues together with merit and reward, could only bring horror to some Reformer with a radically Pauline and Augustinian theology of grace. Yet, there is still another way of approaching this question of influence and continuity.

What the Modern Devout represented better than most others was a religious outlook that nearly all spiritual thinkers in the fifteenth century discovered for themselves or took for granted. So also Luther, the product of an observant cloister, admired the brothers and read their literature, including *The Spiritual Ascensions.* He absorbed this outlook with his unique energy and thoroughness, and he worked to sustain it for a good decade or longer. In the end, his "liberating" doctrine of justification by faith alone appears to have "short-circuited" the whole system in the most fundamental way thinkable: He declared himself "sinner" and "saved" at the same time. His teaching on justification by faith alone is misunderstood, however, when it is not linked to his continued preaching of a reform in life consonant with the monastic maxim "Not to progress is to regress." The ideals in this New Devotion—its sobering view of the natural man, its emphasis on discipline, sobriety, and humility, its vision always of greater glory in the future—he largely took for granted still in his own life and preaching. So too Calvin's famous book on the Christian life in what is now the third book of his *Institutes* took up these same themes—contempt of the world, the virtues, the future life, the benefits of God—and sometimes almost in the same language, but now as the work of the Holy Spirit and as an act of gratitude rather than of a disciplined will. The continuity seems greater still with the so-called left-wing groups, with their emphasis on the imitation of Christ, the inculcation of the virtues, and even in some instances of a common life. The continuity is greatest, in my view, embracing both the religious ideal and in large measure the theological principles, in the Catholic or Counter-Reformation. Scholars have repeatedly pointed toward the parallels and even possible connections to Ignatius Loyola. The same holds, however, for the general pattern of renewal after Trent: its disciplined reforming of the clergy in the new seminaries (of which the brothers' houses, with their combination of religious formation and intellectual training, seem to me an anticipation and, more striking still, in which the use of the physical building is direct in some places in Germany); its evangelization of the people with methodical exercises, hours, and programs in the virtues; and its combination of building up a true Christian life with maintaining some uncertainty still about the ultimate outcome, the fearful last stage of the ascent. It is little wonder that both Protestants and Catholics could read the literature generated by the Modern Devotion and, each in their own way, find it altogether appropriate and edifying. The real question, historically speaking, it seems to me, is how and why all this took shape in the years between 1375 and 1450, persisted in one form or another for so many centuries, and then fell so suddenly and completely out of favor over the last generation. A presentation of the texts of the Modern Devotion may help in a small way to begin sorting through some of these questions.

PART ONE

The Founder:
Geert Grote

CHAPTER ONE

Resolutions and Intentions, But Not Vows

Written Out by Master Geert in the Name of the Lord[1]

I intend to order my life to the glory, honor, and service of God and to the salvation of my soul; to put no temporal good of body, position, fortune, or learning ahead of my soul's salvation; and to pursue the imitation of God in every way consonant with learning and discernment and with my own body and estate, which predispose certain forms of imitation.

[PURSUIT OF GAIN]

The first thing is to desire no further office or income [lit. "benefice"], and in future to place neither hope nor desire in any temporal gain:

¶ The more I had, the more doubtless I would want.

¶ In keeping with the early Church, you are not allowed several benefices.

¶ At death you would be full of remorse, as it is commonly said: "No one has died holding several benefices without repenting of it."

¶ The more benefices and goods I had, the more I would have to serve. But this is to become all the more burdened down, and that is contrary to liberty of spirit, which is the principle good of the spiritual life. For the affections then become bound to all sorts of things, and remain held in bondage to them. Such affections infect the soul, driving out peace of heart and tranquillity of mind, and the cares that come with them pollute and disturb the mind again and again.

¶ The hunger for more must be cut away, then the possessions themselves discerningly reduced to a minimum.

¶ If I want to give generously of my own, why engage myself for more? It is all the same in God's eyes if I give moderately from moderate means or much from great. For God considers the heart and not the amount: The Lord preferred the widow who gave two mites (Mk 12:42) above all the rich.

65

¶ I see too that the things I have already bind me well enough. How much more if things yet to be acquired were added to it!

¶ I have enough for the ordinary needs of life and dignity. I will serve no cardinal or churchman with a view to gaining benefices or temporal goods, for such service is prone to many lapses and back-slidings.

¶ You are frail and should not expose yourself to danger except in the service of God.

¶ You are very near to death and would not be able to sustain any great banqueting.

¶ Serve no temporal lord in pursuit of gain.

¶ Never serve as astrologer to any lord.

[ASTROLOGY]

Practice none of the forbidden sciences for any man of the world because these things are for the most part superstitious, suspect, and forbidden.

¶ Remove all such superstitions and curiosities from men's minds so much as you are able while preserving your own tranquillity of mind, purity, and liberty of will; thus in the very thing I once displeased God I might now please him according to his will.

¶ Never make forecasts [elections] for journeys or bloodlettings or any other such thing, except perhaps very approximately as suggested by the climate. Forecasts of this kind are prohibited in the decretals and by the holy fathers.

¶ Whatever I begin I should begin in the name of the Lord, and place my hope in him to direct me in all matters into the way of salvation. My hope should not rest in the least on fate or the celestial orbs, but rather on nothing other than hope in God, prayer, the good spirits, and their keeping.

¶ Indeed how is it useful for me to know if I will prosper on some journey or undertaking? Most often in fact it is not useful, because anxiety or tribulation is often more useful. I will therefore subject myself to the ordination of God, for blessed is the man who hopes in God. "Cast all your care upon him, because he will take care of you" (1 Pt 5:7). Yea, with what great mercy he has recalled me, even with blows and against my will. We are not to be anxious about what we will eat (Mt 6:25): How much less about the stars and other superstitions? For every Christian with a pure heart must abandon himself and commit himself instead to God.

¶ I will make no judgments for the future, and in general I will con-

cern myself only moderately with the future, since I have given myself and all my things to God.

[PURSUIT OF LEARNING AND ADVANCEMENT]

Man is corrupted by the honors, favors, and especially the greed that
drives everyone. Through the lucrative arts he becomes so tainted
and enflamed that his natural uprightness is forgotten and his appetites infected; he no longer looks to the things of God, of virtue,
or of bodily good. Whence it is the rarest thing for someone given
over to one of the lucrative disciplines—medicine, civil law, or canon
law—to be found upright, or balanced in reason, or just, or tranquil,
or of genuine insight.

¶ Spend no time at geometry, arithmetic, rhetoric, dialectic, grammar, lyric poetry, civil law, or astrology. For Seneca already reproached all these things as something the good man should look on
with a wary eye: How much more ought they to be repudiated by
the spiritual man and the Christian!

¶ It is all a useless waste of time, and of no profit for life.

¶ Among all the pagan disciplines moral philosophy is the least rep-
rehensible, often very useful and beneficial for both your own self
and for teaching others. The wiser men, such as Socrates and Plato,
accordingly reduced all philosophy to ethics. And if they did speak
of high things, they would present them lightly moralized and figuratively, as is clear from St. Augustine and your own experience,
so that morals could always be discovered through thinking. Seneca,
therefore, following this, liberally included ethical matters in his
Natural Questions. For whatever does not make us better or restrain
us from evil is harmful.

¶ The secrets of nature are not to be studiously sought out either in
the books of the pagans or in the law of our own Old and New Testaments. But when you happen upon such things, praise and glorify
God for them so that natural learning may become meritorious and,
as with the righteous Abel, offered up as a sacrifice to God on high
in thanksgiving, something good conceived to the honor of God.
Take care at all times because these things corrupt and never satisfy,
and you will, I hope, by the grace of the Most High find them only
nauseous.

¶ Never take a degree in medicine, because you intend to acquire
from it neither gain nor profit. Similarly, no degree in civil or canon
law because the purpose of these degrees is only gain, benefices,
empty boasting, or worldly fame. When these things are not directed

to gain or benefices, they are simply useless, superfluous, and most foolish, contrary to God and to all freedom and purity. And when a man seeks them, he falls into greater evils, worse still than gain and benefices.

¶ Study no liberal art, write no book, undertake no journey or work, and practice no applied science to spread your own fame and the renown of your own learning or to gain honor and gratitude from anyone whatsoever or to have yourself remembered afterward. For if you should do such things or any other act for this reason, by expecting a reward from them you would not be rendered one by your Father who is in heaven (cf. Mt 6:1). If ever I do such things, then always only for the good and for an eternal reward. And so making a name for yourself is to be avoided in every way.

¶ Such empty glory, renown, and fame have been so thoroughly repudiated even by philosophers that anyone worthy of praise would hardly accept them. And if praise should come from a work done for God, in which the intention remained hidden but the work itself radiated outward, render that praise and glory to the Most High.

¶ Bernard teaches you to utter not a single word to make yourself appear religious or learned.

¶ Avoid and abhor every public disputation held simply to score a triumph or to make a good appearance, such as all those disputations of the theologians and artists in Paris. Do not be present even to learn. Clearly they disturb tranquillity; they sink to quarrels and disputes; they are useless, ever inquisitive, and what is worse, superstitious, bestial, diabolical, and earthly, so that their teaching is rotten, harmful, and never useful, making them a waste of time. You could during that same time acquire spiritual profit either in prayer of a meritorious sort or in study of a devotional author.

¶ Nor will I ever dispute with any person in private, unless a certain good end be in prospect and it be a person who wishes to hear me and with whom I can debate modestly and without contention, or unless some evil requires rigorous argument to attain a good end—and this never unless it has already been well considered. Clearly everything having a good end ought to be ordered to the praise of God; for instance, always to pray. So do not argue with someone who will not in the end concede the truth.

¶ Never study to take a degree in theology, or strive toward this, because you do not want to pursue gain or benefices or fame, and you can have the learning just as well without the degree.

¶ In general it is a carnal subject, and all of them think very carnally.

¶ In large part it would draw you away from the salvation of your neighbor.

¶ Also away from prayer, purity of mind and contemplation.

¶ You would have to be present at many vain lectures and among a multitude of men, where a person becomes corrupted and distracted.

¶ You will not study civil law or medicine, unless it should happen that you could do something good with them. For they are not in the least nourishing in themselves, but rather divert the mind. Out of love for peace or in an unusual or necessary instance, however, you could have a look at the law books, or for the sake of your own body or a companion's, at the medical books. These are secular matters in which it is more fitting to suffer someone else's counsel than to give it yourself.

¶ Law and medicine are forbidden to theologians, monks, and all those desiring the law of God.

[WORLDLY ACTIVITY]

You will not give doubtful medicines, or medicine at all where the illness is unknown or to just any sick person, unless you prescribe a little in a case of grave necessity where it could not otherwise be had. But otherwise do not intervene.

¶ Note how many good men rejoice to be freed of its practice.

¶ You will not give counsel or intervene in any controversies or court cases, unless it is clear to you that it was an obvious case of calumny, or of a person very much in need, or a godly cause, or the repression of very obvious evil men, or the uplifting of poor men, and you are able to intervene while retaining tranquillity of mind. After your intervention, pull back lest leftover concerns persist. Take careful note here that you are not moved by ties of friendship or kinship or hatred. And if it is a friend or relative or former enemy, examine yourself as to whether you would do the same if he were unknown or not hateful to you. It is clear that the peasant's bliss arises from the fact, as Vergil puts it, that he does not see the "iron laws and the insane court."[2]

¶ Make no appearances before any officials or judges spiritual in behalf of friend, kin, or anyone else, unless the absolute necessity of piety requires it, and even then you ought to send another procurator, if there is such a need, and not go yourself. For peace of mind is disturbed if you go and interject yourself in the turmoil and shipwreck of this world. In all other things send the dead to bury their own dead (Mt 6:22).

¶ Do not appear before magistrates or judges secular in Deventer, unless compelled by similar necessities, for your friends handle quite enough of these matters before magistrates. Never intervene in any human quarrels, unless as above, to restore peace if it can be restored quickly and without great commotion. Even where a composition ought to be arranged, do not intervene if it can be done just as well by someone else. And always be mindful of this: For the tranquillity of your own soul do not dismiss any peace you are able truly to establish.

¶ Whenever one of your kin is whipped, killed, or beaten, do not trouble the aggressor, or take counsel to do him evil, or assault him verbally, or avoid him. Rather warn him in a consolatory manner and bring him to peace. And if friends wish to take vengeance, use peace-making words to keep them from vengeance, and from inflicting injury. You should forgive all and offer such an example as will serve to admonish others.

¶ I will never handle the affairs of friends or kinfolk or lords—unless they are entirely godly and inclined toward mercy, piety, and justice and are not matters others could handle just as well. For it is evil to forsake, even for contemplation, any godly usefulness to your neighbor and especially the piety and justice another cannot do.

SACRED BOOKS TO STUDY

I return to learning. The root of all your study and the mirror of life is, first, the Gospel of Christ because there is found the life of Christ; then

¶ The lives and collations of the Fathers [= John Cassian's Collations].

¶ The epistles of Paul, the Pastorals and the Acts of the Apostles.

¶ Devotional books, such as the *Meditations* of Bernard and Anselm, the *Horologium* [of Henry Suso], Bernard's *On Consideration*, Augustine's *Soliloquy*, and other similar books.[3]

¶ Legends and excerpts concerning the saints.

¶ Instructions of the Fathers in morality such as Gregory's *Pastoral Rule*, St. Augustine's *On the Monastic Life*, Gregory's *On Job*, and so on.

¶ Homilies on the Gospels by the holy Fathers and the four doctors.

¶ Commentaries of the holy Fathers, and postils on the epistles of Paul contained in the readings of the Church.

¶ Studies of the sayings of Solomon, both Ecclesiastes and Ecclesiasticus, contained in the readings of the Church, for I will pray in the spirit, and also in the mind (cf. 1 Cor 14:15).
¶ Study and understanding of the Psalter because it is contained in the Church of the holy Fathers, and I will sing the Psalter in the spirit, and also in the mind (1 Cor 14:15).
¶ Study of the books of Moses, of the histories (Joshua, Judges, and Kings), and of the prophets, and the Fathers' exposition of them.
¶ Skim through the decretals to know what the ancient authorities and the Church have established, not to take them entirely in, but only to skim them: lest by ignorance of the law you turn piety into disobedience; so too that you may see the great fruit of the early Church; and that you may know what to look out for and what to warn others against.

ON MASS

Every day you can, hear mass read to the end, as [Gratian's] *De consecratione* D.1 c.64 prescribes every Sunday for the laity, and as the gloss on the same, every day for the clergy.
¶ Stay in church on feast days until the celebration of mass is completed.
¶ The chant, as you know from experience, helps our carnal nature toward devotion.
¶ Always rise at the reading of the Gospel and remain standing, whence it says in the decretum, "We decree by apostolic authority that . . . we should not sit but stand with a respectful bow in the presence of the Gospel." Included in the word *respectful* is the idea that we should pay honor to the Gospel. So also it says, "Listen attentively to its words, and worship in faith." Which is to say, the words are venerated by the body's attitude. Such corporal acts of veneration are: to bow; second, to remove hats as is customary; third, to bow at the words *Jesus* and *Mary* because the devout so conduct themselves.
¶ When the Gospel is read, the mind should not substitute some other prayer or direct its attention to some other reading. A mind intent upon many things is less attentive to particulars. The *De consecratione* also orders that the words of the Gospel and the writings of the Apostle be attended to in worship services. It is senseless to listen if we do not pay attention.
¶ These exterior exercises are meant to induce their mental counterparts, and are therefore in vain if there is no correspondence.

¶ To meditate with the mouth and the mind is much more than with the mouth and head alone. Whence I should hear with the head and the ear, and also the mind, otherwise I am as a clanging symbol or a sounding brass. I will have no part of words or talk whose meaning I do not perceive.

¶ After the consecration of the Sacrament, if you are not able to see it or the chalice, remain with a bared head, bent knees, and a bowed back. Such humbling adoration and inclination of the body, honorable to God and fitting for the mind, aids devotion in every way. The best, as you know, is to bow the head over the lower arm. For servants must especially show reverence to their Lord in his presence. Bowing is marvelously suited to the devotion of the mind, because of the analogous movement of the imagination. When you are distant or not able to see, recline with your head bent and pray in secret to your God from the *Sanctus* to the *Pacem*, and then, whether you receive [communion] or not, up to the Gospel of Saint John.

¶ Take up the Pax[4] reverently and devoutly because you are in contact with the body of the Lord through the mouth of the priest. Did Veronica not venerate it? Is not an image of Christ, even an unconsecrated host of Christ, also venerated? For all the faithful used to communicate in the early Church, and now the Pax is given in its place as a kind of communication with the body of Christ. The reason the body is not given commonly to all, I judge, is that they were better in the early Church, warmed still by the blood of Christ, and religion which has now grown decrepit was then in its vigor and at its peak. Christ therefore withdrew himself bodily, as he has spiritually. When the Pax comes, be prepared to receive it as the body of Christ, and then lift up your desire and prepare yourself so that even though you are not up to eating the sacrament carnally you may yet eat it spiritually.

¶ After communion your desire must remain fixed as it was in the Pax, and must persist inwardly for a long time. If you begin to become distracted, as often happens to you when your thoughts begin to wander, direct yourself to the passion of Christ.

¶ From the *Sanctus Sanctus*, prepare to see the Sacrament. Do not all customarily prepare to see the King, by whom they are also seen? After seeing him, prepare to partake of him, and do nothing else because at that moment the presence of Christ is at work, aiding your infirmity, and so will inspire you to a love of the Sacrament. This is evident from what is said: "Lift up your hearts," and "We have lifted them up to the Lord."

¶ Always draw near to the priest, as decorum permits, so as to hear the mass and see the Sacrament and stand in his presence.

¶ Never advise or tell or help anyone (unless he be a most devout person) to take holy orders. First, because of the teachings pertinent to the office, on what they must be, and would not be, as in the fourth book of the *Sentences* and in the *Decretals;* second, because of simony, which commonly interjects itself; and third, because of the sorry state of the Church.

ON ABSTINENCE

[Resolutions] that seem good, though not vowed.

¶ First, keep the prescribed fasts.

¶ Second, never eat flesh, for which you have reasons given in the marginal gloss of the *Decretum, De consecratione* D.5 c.32.

¶ Third, always fast in advent and septuagesima, never giving this up without cause.

¶ Fourth, fast daily, never quite filling up unless the cold requires it. All philosophers argue for this, especially Seneca and Aristotle. While there is still appetite, pull back your hand. But it is hard to know when you are full, so consider how much you would eat if you could take as much as you liked and then hold back a little, whatever seems reasonable, while you still have an appetite.

¶ Fifth, at the end of your meal or with your last dish, consider how much you ate and how much you would eat if you were to continue, and cut back from this (which follows from or precedes the preceeding point).

¶ Sixth, at the outset, when you begin to prepare your meal, consider it and the amount.

¶ Seventh, beware of more than one cooked pear after the meal, or of a very large one, or three very small ones.

¶ Eighth, always eat in the evening between the fourth and fifth hours, unless guests, infirmity, some other matter, a journey, or something of the sort prevents you. This is founded upon twelve reasons. First, it is better for digestion that food not be digested in your stomach during vigils because there is insufficient heat then. Second, because study or something else may impede digestion during vigils, such as anxiety or unhappiness. Third, lest too much drinking impede digestion. Fourth, lest too much drinking weigh on your conscience, as often happens. Fifth, lest you be tempted during the day to take a raw apple, spices, or something else. Sixth, because your sleep will be sounder, since a full stomach sleeps more soundly. Seventh, because then study and prayers during the day will be less hindrance to sleep. Eighth, because a man will then go quickly to sleep, always within an hour. Ninth, because there will then be one continuous rest owing to falling asleep on time. Tenth, the delights of study will then tempt you less at night. Eleventh, you will then have the whole day for work and prayer. Twelfth, your vigils will then be completely sober and abstemious, delicate and suitable to God and to work.

¶ A man who eats desires more food than one who fasts, just as a man is unable to abstain when he is in or near the kitchen.

¶ Eat only once in the day from the Exaltation of the Holy Cross until Easter, which is the practice of the Carthusians, the Cistercians, and others.

¶ This should begin in September around the equinox and last almost until the spring equinox. In extreme cold it is permissible to eat more, but still only once, which is the teaching of Hippocrates.

¶ This will also help you to resist colds which you can otherwise hardly resist. You may therefore also sleep an hour or a half longer.

¶ When you must eat twice, do so moderately of easily digestable foods, as, for instance, one egg, not more, or else something drier like bread and wine, or herbs with a little bread, or else wine, and so forth. For these reasons apply to the digestion as well as to eating at night, as above.

¶ I wish never to drink wine without due cause, as long as I am healthy, lest I go against the teaching of Paul. For wine drinking is too excessive (Eph 5:18). Also too expensive.

¶ Never drink before, after, or during a meal, unless required by illness or some major and reasonable cause. Never drink during or after work until the heat has subsided; this is healthy for both body and soul. Let no conviviality draw you to drink between hours or to break fast. It is good to place your feet in the shackles of wisdom (Sir 6:25).

¶ There should be a set hour to read through the things you have written in this book, because they order your estate. It seems to me that the Desert Fathers offered brief and frequent prayers so that their hearts might ever and continuously be lifted up to the Lord and not grounded in things but rather withdrawn from things—and so it must be.

¶ I resolve in the name of the Lord always to fast on Wednesday unless illness or some reasonable cause prevents it so that I may not hold this up as fixed but rather as that toward which I should strive; likewise on the Sabbath and on Friday. For on Wednesday Judas

betrayed the Lord, and on Friday he was crucified, and whoever refuses to fast seems to betray and crucify Christ with his crucifiers,
with no cause. I am bound to this all the more because I am a cleric,
one of the Lord's elect.

¶ Health is also better preserved, and I sense that my soul is better
with God. Even if it should do a little harm to the body, pay no attention, for you will always be better off when you fast. Always render something to your God, and you will always be more mindful
of his claims.

¶ Look out for greedy, or gluttonous eating. For such haste comes
from an inordinate love of the object. And such inordinate appetite
is tainted with desire and vice. As Gregory says in his exposition on
Job, "It excites talkativeness, or rather it inebriates, heats up, and
disorients, just as intoxication or too much talking kindles and encourages lust."

¶ It cuts short and chokes off all thoughts of God. One act done well
with much deliberation is better than an aberrant one done with little. As for the body's well-being, the more decently and properly
food is taken in, the more easily and more beneficially digested.

[GENERAL CONDUCT]

So also in writing, speaking, and acting, you ought to make it a point
not to hurry. You are, moreover, not able to seek the glory of God
in these things when you are carried into them with such force that
all your strength is extended. Learn therefore to wait and to hold
back from action. Do no good thing in such a way that you hasten
into disobedience.

¶ In temporal affairs, money, revenue, and books, conduct yourself
as a steward, and see to it that you find yourself faithful and prudent.
Allot yourself therefore a frugal portion of clothing and food, more
to the poor and the deserving, and more still for the salvation of
souls. Never give anything to someone not in need, because you can
find many poverty-striken people. And if you give to someone with
more than enough, you have not dispensed faithfully nor prudently
as regards your salvation.

¶ In giving do not become carnally puffed up.

¶ I will accept no temporal goods from anyone so long as more needy
folk can be found, because I will not ask of others what I do not wish
them to do.

Noteworthy Sayings of Master Geert[5]

A man ought never to become anxious over any worldly thing. He who acts upon what he knows deserves to know much more, and he who does not act even upon what he knows deserves to become blinder still.

It is a great thing when a man proves obedient in matters that are contrary and difficult: This is true obedience.

In all things and before all people, seek to humble yourself, especially in the heart but also outwardly before the brothers.

It is the highest of all learning to know that one knows nothing.

The more a man perceives how far short he is of perfection, the closer he is to it.

The beginning of vainglory is to please one's self.

A man never stands better revealed than when he receives praise.

Seek ever to observe and conceive something good about another.

So often as we inordinately desire something beyond God himself, we become unfaithful fornicators, whence the Prophet says: *It is good for me to cling to God* (Ps 72/73:28).

We ought to be vigorous in prayer and not easily brought to a halt. Nor should we imagine that God does not want to hear us; rather, even when we feel put off, we should not despair. The weak-spirited ought to pray as a son to a pious father, just as it says in the Gospel: "Which of you asks bread of a father; will he give him a stone?" (Lk 11:11).

Temptation lurks in everything in this world, even if a man does not perceive it.

The greatest temptation is not to be tempted: When a man discovers in himself something that needs to be cut off, then he is in good standing. When an evil suggestion comes upon you, think what you would ask your companions, and then the devil will stand confused.

Always put more hope in eternal glory than fear in hell.

Let every person beware lest his behavior scandalize others, and so let him study to correct his ways and to conduct himself uprightly everywhere that others may be edified.

With whatever thoughts a man goes to sleep, he will also rise, so it is useful to pray and to read a few psalms on retiring.

Moderate confusion suffered here forestalls eternal confusion before God and all the saints.

Study to please and to fear him alone who truly knows you and all that you are.

Suppose you were to please all and displease God; to what end? Turn your heart therefore away from all creaturely things, even with great force. Turn it so that you may perfectly vanquish yourself, and raise your heart ever on high to God, as the Prophet says: "My eyes are ever upon the Lord" (Ps 122:2).

CHAPTER THREE

Letter 29⁶

Chosen one, once highly loved and still much loved in Christ, whom I strive to win singularly and especially for the greater glory of God and your own salvation, with a zeal granted, I believe, from on high! Would that you might cease singing and walking in the way of iniquity and of worldly deception! Do not proceed in the way of anxiety, sorrow, fear, labor and grief, of which the world is full, but in the way of sincerity, exaltation, certainty, and uprightness; in spiritual joy and in an abundance of things good and true, not false and transient and quickly corrupted, but eternal and lasting. O my beloved soul, yet my very own soul, O Israel, what will be your reward, how great will be your glory and the place of your habitation, if through all this transience you cling permanently and persistently to your Lord! For he who stands firm to the end will be saved (Mt 24:13)—not he who begins, but he who finishes, not he who wavers but he who keeps the Word of God he has received; he will gain the reward. For, as the Apostle says, only he who has truly fought the battle will receive the crown (2 Tm 2:5).

Who enticed you to come so near to a fall? Who drew you away from all good and from Him who is the source of all good, O my beloved, my beloved in the Lord, and led you to the precipice? O treacherous enemy, how many are your spears, how great your force, that you could lead such a devout young man, our John, into such a whirlpool. But you will not, I hope, drown him, suck him under. You have deployed a thousand tricks, but there will be one to free him, I hope, from the fowlers' snare and your deadly word (Ps 90/91:3). Lord O Lord, heavenly king, our most blessed guardian Mary, together with all the saints and angels of God, come to his aid! Help me to drag him, to drag my most beloved back from the jaws and snares of the abyss that are about to overwhelm him, so that the adversary may not gloat over him because his feet have slipped (Ps 37/38:17/16).

See the treachery of the enemy. How forcefully he draws you away from your good intentions under the guise of study so that you turn your face away from the Lord and your own good resolutions and then descend into all manner of carnal, worldly, and vain desires. You sense it, I fear, yourself. I perceive the testimony of your own conscience, which knows that it is being buffeted by all kinds of desires, vacillations, and useless things. Watch out lest you assume the face of a whore and refuse to blush (Jer 3:3); lest you become hardened in evil, if you once begin; lest you slide even further if you are pushed. For the impious, as the wise man said (cf. Prv 18:3), when he reaches the depths of evil, becomes contemptuous. Take care lest your heart become hardened, lest you become calloused and insensitive.

Return, return, my beloved. The wound is recent and deep, still curable and responsive to medicine; *resist beginnings*.[7] We all await you, your God and all his saints, your own angel, and also poor me, I who grieve—God alone knows how much—over all the innumerable evils that will overtake you if you turn away from God. Hear the word of the apostle Peter (2 Pt 2:20–22): "Those who have escaped the corruption of the world by knowing our Lord and Savior Jesus Christ and again become entangled in it are defeated, and they are worse off at the end than they were at the beginning. It would have been better for them not to have known the way of righteousness than to have known it and to turn away from the sacred commandment that was passed on to them. Of them the proverbs are true, 'A dog returns to its vomit,' and 'A washed sow goes back to wallowing in the mud.' " So too Paul (Heb 6:6): "Such crucify the Son of God for themselves again and hold him up as a spectacle." Think too, most beloved, of how difficult the same Apostle says your return would be if you were to become hardened in evil, much more difficult than if you had never tasted the sweet goodness of Christ. This is particularly so if you persevere until evil is turned into custom or an excuse, or again until many evil spirits make their way into the paths of your soul, spirits who are much worse for you and seven times more devious in keeping you in evil than they were before your conversion. For according to the Gospel (Lk 11:26), they take seven spirits worse than themselves and enter the house which had formerly been in some sense cleaned and set right, and the latter state of the man, according to Christ, is worse than the former. Those adversaries will keep guard over you so much more forcefully because earlier, by adhering to Christ, you grieved and burdened them. And there is greater joy among the evil angels over one good man turned away than over ninety-nine hardening in their wickedness, just as the Gospel (Lk 15:7) says by contrast that there is greater joy among the angels over one man converted than over ninety-nine righteous.

But I hope that you are not totally turned away. I hope you are still curable, and near to salvation, however sharply and forcefully, yes much too forcefully, tempted. Place before your eyes and remember your coming end. Look out: What would it profit you to win the whole world and suffer the loss of your soul (Mt 16:26)? Would, my beloved, that you would become wise, come to understanding, and discern what your end will be (Dt 32:29). Would that you would come to your senses and grieve over yourself the way you once grieved over your father. How you wondered then at your father's blindness and indifference to future dangers. It is indeed unbelievable how much evil can occur when once the will has been turned to evil, for nothing truly and lastingly green remains on the tree once the root of good will is excised.

See now how your eyes wander about, how distracted your heart is, how brazen your face, how laborious the way you have started down. If only you would observe how many evils threaten, how many instruments have been fashioned by diabolic powers to advance your evil and punishment. I ask you to turn your eyes a little toward me, and read the chapter in the *Horologium of Eternal Wisdom* on death and the art of dying.[8] Read it, I ask you, twice or three times. Would that you read it through in a month and by the grace of God were restored to health. Fear, most beloved of my prayers, fear to offend the infinite majesty of God. Do not soothe yourself with thoughts of his mercy as you persist in your sin, for just as he is the father of all mercy and of all consolation (2 Cor 1:3), so he is also a just judge, strong and fearful to the sons of men. As the Psalmist says (Ps 89/90:11), who knows the power of his anger and who can tell his anger for fear? For the God of vengeance, just as he gives abundantly of his goodness and does not spare (Jas 1:5), so, because he gives all to his glory and to that end, requires his honor be upheld in all inner or outer gifts he makes to men. For the honor of the King, as the Psalmist said (Ps 98/99:4), loves justice. Fear this especially: He will extract everything from us down to the last penny.

Stand in horror, as I said before, of a hard heart through which infinite evil enters a man. Shun the inner darkness that follows upon sin, continuously becoming deeper and denser until at noon you are groping about as in the shadows. Consider how short and transient the time we spend here, and how many of your companions, kin, and forefathers died in sin to receive their just deserts. Against them the whole earth and everything in it now wars and will war into eternity. They say and will say into eternity in effect what is found in Wisdom (5:7–9). "We have grown weary in the way of iniquity, we have walked in difficult ways and do not know the way of the Lord. What use to us is pride and the boasting of riches? All these things pass away as a shadow and a fleeting messenger" and many other such things found in that same passage. A little later (Wis 6:14–15) the following is added: "Such things they say in hell who sin, since the hope of the ungodly is like dust driven away by the wind or a thin froth blown away by the wind or the memory of a guest passing through for one day." If you consider these things in the depths of your heart, you will certainly return.

Once again, dearest, tremble before an evil will, since your life is so unsure, your death and its hour so uncertain, since the day of the Lord is like a thief that comes in the night (1 Thes 5:2). When people live in indulgence and vanity, the calamity of death overtakes them in an instant; they die without warning and in a moment go down into hell (cf. Jb 21:13). Then Christ, the eternal wisdom, will say to those who refused to heed the warnings in the time of salvation: "I in turn will laugh at your destruction and I will mock when what you feared comes about, when sudden calamity and destruction overtakes you like a storm, when distress and anxiety come upon you; then they will call upon me and I will not hear; in the morning they will arise and not find me" (Prv 1:26–28). There are many other such things in that passage which ought truly to instill an awesome fear.

Consider well, my beloved, and tremble before the last hour of your life lest perhaps you seek an opportunity for repentance and find none—"That day, [dies irae] the day of wrath, calamity, and misery," and so on. Who then will free you from those infernal claws and fearful faces coming to devour you? What then of riches, learning, male or female friends will be able to help you when—God forbid—a lion comes to snatch your soul and there is none to rescue it (Ps 7:3/2)? What of all these things will you be able to bring with you? Everything will suddenly desert you. In an instant your friends and your things will forget you entirely. Only your merits according to your labors and your good or bad conscience will follow you down. Alas, how much fear then in the face of evil! What trembling and tension then! Oh, how they will seek death and not find it (Rv 9:6)! How good for them if they had never been born (Mt 26:24)! Tremble, most beloved, before the infinite duration of infernal punishment. What consolation for the damned if such punishment lasted only some countable or conceivable length of time. That fear of the abyss seems to me unspeakable and unimaginable, an infinity of infinite punishment. Consider the variety and bitterness of the punishments, the prick to the conscience, the gnawing worm and a soul near bursting, exceeding all combustion or solidification, and the pain of divine absence which afflicts a soul removed from the body and earthly comforts with unthinkable pains.

Read, I ask you, Ruusbroec's little book *On the Faith*,[9] in which he sets before you the infinite glory of the saints in both body and soul and the punishments and evils of the wicked. Note there what punishments the wicked are exposed to in their sight, their hearing, their touch, their smell, and their taste; what horror, foul corruption, strife, quarrels, remorse, envy, and disturbance will be there; what cold and what heat; what appearance of worms and that deepest of all whirlpools. Tremble before that severe judge, the coming Christ, who was so often mild to you in your prayers. Fear this awful face, fear the sound of the trump calling to judgment, fear the fall and ruin and conflagration of the whole world. Take fright at the dissolving of all things. And especially stand in horror of that irrevocable sentence, that voice saying, "Depart, you who are cursed into the eternal fire" and so on (Mt 25:41).

Open your eyes, my beloved. See all this lest you remain in eternal blindness. Learn these things: These things are more necessary for you than any worldly learning, to which the devil spurs you on even though you are not up to it. For how could you learn great things when you grasped lesser and boyish things only with difficulty? The adversary says: A priest must know and learn many things. You will know much if you recognize that you are not up to it. I write to you what I know from my own experience: All who come to studies without a good foundation will remain crude asses forever even if they study for a hundred years. Charity is the thing necessary for you; it is never superfluous even if knowledge and learning should cease. For if you do not have charity, which does not exist apart from a good will and a good resolution, you are nothing even if you speak with the tongues of men and of angels and you have all faith, learning, and prophecy with an evil will (1 Cor 13:1–2, 8). What is knowledge except armed injustice, as it says in the "Politics"? The worst of men is a learned man with an evil will, much worse than a drunk or unfaithful man. Such learning is therefore an impediment for those who possess it. The devil could care less that a man is learned, for he knows that learning puffs up (1 Cor 8:1). But he takes care, indeed much industry and zeal, to corrupt a good will. It is often to be observed that, through the Adversary and with God's permission, men who were formerly lazy and ignorant suddenly acquire such learning for themselves as far to excel all others in studies.

My beloved, my whole inner being calls out to you. You know that I do not seek anything of yours, which with God's help I regard as dung (Phil 3:8), but I seek you. Come therefore, beloved, to your lover, who truly loves you and nothing of you except God in you. I ask that you deign to come to me and seek consolation with me, or rather to console me, for I grieve no small amount over you. I lay an oath upon you to come. I swear before heaven and earth and all that is in them that you should come to me, for your sake, for your salvation, and for the glory of God. And I exhort you again to read frequently that chapter on death as well as from Ruusbroec.

My heart, as God gives, nearly bursts for you. Would that it would burst over in true charity for you, and that I dying might have you with me alive in Christ, for Christ, and following Christ. Farewell and may you fare well, be strong and may you become strong in Christ, our sweetest and richest Lord in whom all good and all divinity resides in the flesh (Col 2:9).

Geert, your servant and humble messenger, most joyously and sweetly acting as a legate to you from Christ.

CHAPTER FOUR

Letter [62]:
On Patience and the
Imitation of Christ[10]

Most Beloved in Christ Jesus,

You know that I could not receive the account of your anxieties and difficulties without becoming distressed myself. How much I grieve with you and your companions, he alone knows who bore in his body all our labors and sorrows. Oh, how I wish I could console, how I wish I could offer succor. But it has not been granted from on high, and it is not in a man's power to raise up a man, unless the consoler of the poor, the helper in times of trouble (Ps 9:10) himself offers consolation and succor.

Would that my words, or rather and more truly the words of Scripture, might offer some solace. Rejoice, rejoice, my beloved, when you fall into various temptations and trials because after you have stood the test you will receive the crown of life (Jas 1:2, 12). God is faithful, and he promised not to permit man to be tempted beyond his strength (cf. 1 Cor 10:13). But just as in proving someone, he permits him to be tempted, troubled, and distressed, so he also gives the ability to bear up and resist. But in this, alas, many of us ourselves give offense, either by not learning his ways and our own abilities or by not working and resisting vigilantly and vigorously. We must therefore be constant in prayer that we not be led into temptation, constant and studious in reading that we withstand the subversion of ignorance and foolishness, the seedbed of many evils. We ought also to have frequent experience in adversity so as to deepen concretely the knowledge and testing of ourselves, and through our blessed Lord God to train our hands for warfare and our fingers for battle (Ps 143/144:1). You know that by warfare we mean one whole long war and by battle a single encounter at arms. So it is by the blessing of our Lord that in a massive confrontation we may have our hands, that is, the operative virtues, trained and strong; so also in an extended war we may conserve the fingers, that is, distinct and discrete considerations of prudence.

Frequent reading and meditation upon Holy Scripture offers succor to the distressed in three ways: It drives away sadness, teaches fortitude, and promises a crown. For all Scripture is divinely inspired (2 Tm 3:16) and although it does not teach us to fight, it fortifies the heart, even as it gilds, illumines, and gladdens minds laboring in holy meditation. All of Holy Scripture, in sum, is divinely effective and of unique service, as Augustine made plain when he was so troubled at the death of his mother, "I confess it to be my daily solace and the antidote to my grief."[11] For the grief-stricken, solitude combined with contemplative leisure or contemplative leisure itself becomes especially difficult, for all the sorrows press in upon someone in seclusion and overwhelm his imagination. For that reason any kind of work, but especially the reading of Scripture, proves in most cases an effective refuge and consolation for the despairing, the melancholy, the tempted, the faint-hearted, and the troubled. But for those with poor minds manual labor combined with pleasant meditation profits more than frequent reading.

We are most particularly comforted and aided by Scripture when it not only gladdens us, but gives us an image and a promise of an end to battle, a hunger for victory, and the hope of glory. For according to the Apostle, "All that was written was written for our instruction so that through patience and the consolation of the Scriptures we might have hope" (Rom 15:4). Those teachings of Scripture which gladden us in our present troubles or draw out our desire for the promised future are especially to be chewed over and reflected upon. For instance: "The sufferings of the present time are not worth comparing to the future glory that will be revealed in us" (Rom 8:18) and "What at present is light and momentary in our troubles works in us an eternal weight of glory beyond measure in its sublimity— when we meditate not on what is seen—that is, on our trials—but upon that which is not seen"—that is, the promise (2 Cor 4:17–18). There are many such places in Scripture, particularly useful for meditation when the sinner sits over against us and we are silent and hold our peace even from the good and our grief is renewed (cf. Ps 38/39:2–3).

There was in our time a certain master of theology, a virtuous man, who, whenever he suffered the pricks of this present vexation, would reflect on the shortness of this tribulation and say to himself repeatedly this psalm verse: "Of everything, I have seen an end" (Ps 118/119:96). All the trials I have suffered previously came to an end;

so too this will have its end. Trials, moreover, increase virtue and merit, just as they add to the amount of reward, though reward comes through merit. For just as study precedes learning, so humiliation, or being downcast, goes before humility, which in Christ is the one and true foundation of all virtues; and just as the morning star precedes the sun, so patience in adversity goes before peace of heart and gentleness of spirit. And again just as through grace we are made just and temperate by acting justly and temperately, so by suffering we are made patient and peaceable and by being brought low we are made humble, strong, and gentle, proven in bearing up under temptation, prudent, cautious, experienced, and forthright—especially when we come to see God's oversight in our various trials and the utility, or rather necessity, for us of temptations according to divine ordinance. Would that with the Apostle we could freely "rejoice in our sufferings, knowing that suffering produces patience, patience character, character hope, which does not disappoint those hoping, in whose hearts charity has been poured out through the Holy Spirit, who has been given to us" (Rom 5:3–5). Let us take care not to become wholly devoured by grief. Take care, too, that disturbances not make us confused or downcast, or that the pit not close its mouth over us or that the floodwaters of tribulation not engulf us (Ps 68/69:16/15) or that the apostolic progression from tribulation to hope be turned by tribulation into despair.

May it never be that tribulation produce in us a faint heart; a faint heart, confusion; and confusion, the desperation that destroys. It is certain that when the devil sees a distraught person he attacks vigorously, boldly, and cruelly, frequently overthrowing him. But when he sees someone who awaits battle with confidence in the Lord, pouring contempt so far as possible upon the arrows sent against him and showing impatience with him and all his little ploys, then the hostile plotter falls back and a vigilant man will see at once the fruit and harvest of his temptation. The issue here is mental vigilance, so that a man will come to see for himself the careful oversight of God who watches over the troubled closely and circumspectly. "Is not God our strong arm in the morning and our salvation in time of trouble" (Is 33:2)? "Is the Lord not near to those who are troubled in heart" (Ps 33/34:19/18)? "He is our refuge, and our help in trouble, even when it is too near. Therefore we should not fear, though the earth be shaken and mountains be cast into the heart of the sea" (Ps 45/46:2–3/1–2). But what should we say? Is not trouble a sign from the Lord of his love and keeping, because those whom he loves he chastises and those whom he receives he punishes (cf Heb 12:6)? "Blessed is the man, it was said to Job, who is corrected by the Lord. Do not despise his discipline, because he wounds and will bind up, he strikes and his hands will heal" (Jb 5:17–18).

I trust confidently in the Lord that if all of you persevere and look forward in the manner of a farmer to the precious fruit of a plant sown in tears and trouble, waiting patiently, you will receive that fruit in its time and season (cf Jas 5:7), that is, you will reap with exultation (Ps 125/126:5) what came late or delayed. Would that I were found worthy to participate in the harvest, as I do now in the sowing!

What more? Does not the right and necessary way to the kingdom lead through distress? Does not Scripture say "Many are the tribulations of the righteous" (Ps 33/34:20/19) and we must "go through many trials to enter the kingdom of God" (Acts 14:21)? And again: "All who want to live piously in Christ Jesus will suffer persecution" (2 Tm 3:12). "So if they persecuted Christ, will they not also persecute you" (Jn 15:20)? "The disciple is not superior to his master" (Mt 10:24). Was it not "necessary for Christ to suffer and thus to enter into his glory" (Lk 24:26)? Is it not necessary for us Christians, for whom Christ suffered, "also to suffer and continuously to bear about in these our mortal bodies the mortification of Christ, so that the life of Jesus may be made manifest in our bodies?" For at all times, the Apostle says, "we who live are given over to death, so that the life of Jesus Christ may be revealed in our bodies, in our mortal flesh" (2 Cor 4:10–11). For this reason, the Prince of the Apostles says, "Christ suffered for us leaving us an example, that we might follow in his steps" (1 Pt 2:21), so that we might be made "heirs of God and coheirs of Christ, for if we suffer with Him," the Apostle told the Romans, "we will also be glorified with him" (Rom 8:17).

For this reason I always and nearly everywhere teach that the passion of our Lord Jesus Christ is ever to be before our minds. Reflect upon it as often as possible, for in this way no adversity can strike that will not be borne with an even-tempered soul. Nor should we grasp it in our minds only through meditation but even more through the desire of our affections. By imitating his suffering, abuse, and labors we may come to be configured to Christ in work and in effect. For through desire and affection the mind is moved, as it finds opportunity, toward Christ's crucifixion, suffering, and rejection. And this is the end to which meditation upon Christ's passion is finally and principally directed; remembrance of the passion alone avails little, if it is not accompanied by an overpowering desire to imitate Christ.

Therefore whenever we meditate upon some aspect of Christ's passion, we ought always to hear, as from above, the voice of Christ: "Do this and you will live" (Lk 10:28) and for this reason I suffered for you and on your account, that you might follow my steps (1 Pt 2:21). When a holy mind begins to love the humanity of Christ powerfully, even beyond every delight in this world, and to suck upon the wounds of Christ, as oil from a rock and honey from the hardest crag (Dt 32:13), and to draw near the inner acts of Christ—oh, how much then he will yearn to be vexed, tried, and reproached so as to be made both like and pleasing to his lover. Although perhaps one still tender, a fresh novice, is not yet up to so much pressure and especially not yet able to reach what he desires, he should propose nonetheless to suffer with Christ; he should arrange, order, plead, and seek it from the Lord. Sometimes he fails and is humiliated; sometimes he sees it through, gives thanks, and presses on vigorously to what lies ahead (cf. Phil 3:13). In this way a man denies himself, takes up his cross and follows Christ (Mt 16:24). For the cross of Christ is every voluntary assumption of the labors, pains, and reproaches by which the world is crucified to man, that is, the things of the world held in contempt by a man, and he to the world (Gal 6:14), that is, he despised and afflicted by worldly men. This is the cross of the Lord Jesus Christ, this is conformity to the cross, and from it, as a stream from a fount, as rays from the sun, it flows into us.

Alas, many of us freely take up a cross which we have made for ourselves, such as a hair-shirt or private prayers or extraordinary fasts, but that which God makes for us, also truly ours to be borne and embraced, we not only fail to take up voluntarily but cast from us in horror. For truly whatever pain we suffer at the hands of some greater, equal, or lesser power, and with whatever intention, just or unjust, on the part of the doers, they also come upon us justly and piously from the hand of God, even as they were ordained to come, as in that saying, "Nothing happens on earth without cause." It is therefore all the more meritorious and salvation-bringing, indeed all the more necessary, that we bear such crosses without resistance or murmuring and hold for naught by comparison all those things others subject us to, however laudable in their own time. For what is more forceful than to break your own will? What more divine, what richer than to conform to the will of God? There is nothing in heaven above or hell below that is able to overthrow us if we deny our own will and commit ourselves entirely into the hands of God.

This cross of Christ should therefore ever be raised before us in meditation; his passion, his contumely, derision, injury, and sorrow should ever move our affections. And this for three principle reasons. First, out of loving desire to honor and imitate Christ Jesus with no thought of merit or reward. For the merit and reward will be even richer if our trials have no mercenary intent but are rather configured to Christ, humbly offered with him and through him to the Father, and so begun, pursued, and brought to fruition on the merit of Christ and not on our own strength. Second, they are to be borne out of love for the divine fruits, merits, and rewards that so richly flow from trials and tribulations, as was already said. Third, out of love and fervor to satisfy divine justice, which we so gravely offend in so many ways and which allows no evil to go unpunished. We ought therefore freely and patiently, so long as we live, to accept all labors and pains as salutary penance. This profits wonderfully toward removing punishment, for a moderate penalty, particularly one permitted or sent by God, will remove great pain in purgatory where we will suffer against our will. But pains freely borne will profit more as complements to divine justice and the divine will than any applied simply to removing penalties.

I wrote all this on consolation in distress for your admonition and my own instruction, just as it occurred to me. For the rest, beloved, beware of a forceful grief that injures the heart, as Proverbs says, as the moth does clothing or a worm wood (Prv 25:20). It will corrode the splendor of those virtues with which the soul is innerly clothed and from which the inner spiritual edifice is built. Rejoice in the Lord, and again I say rejoice: Let your prudence be known (Phil 4:5) in your entire house. Pour out and restore the oil of gladness in your conscience, and your testimony will ever be a joy to you. When you do all things well and the proud reproach you, leaving you no external witness to your virtue, then in the manner of the prudent virgins gather the oil in your jars along with the lamps (cf Mt 25:3–4). For the jars carried by the prudent virgins contained that which would not give light in the sight of men: that is, to be scorned when someone does well; or to do well to our neighbors without favor, acquaintance, or any hope of return; or never to take vengeance upon enemies or persecutors, not even with face or tongue; or to appear as if you cannot, when you are able to bear every grief and pain and infirmity without complaint or making a show or murmuring; to hide your gifts; publicly to confess your faults; to make yourself vile and ignominious, even in those things where you might be able to show off.

But alas, how frequently I fall short in the very things I teach. May God grant it to both you and me to gain perfection in the things whereof I have spoken to you all. But you, beloved of my prayers (Prv 31:2), know very well that it does us no harm if we are derided as simple and foolish—would that we were such in the Lord!—particularly if we are found simple as doves and wise as serpents (cf. Mt 10:16). In evil let us be simple and in malice babes.

I say all this because of him who sought to enter your community. Against the law and on his own initiative he obtained letters from the lord bishop. He set forth his own basic pleas, which allege as usual some things that are less than true and which I did not want, even if I could, to express in plain words or my own letters. Are not such pleas violent and abominable and worse than carnal? Far be it from me that I should do evil so that good might result. I knew I could do nothing in this matter other than to state the order he would enter and draw the superiors toward benevolence. I did not wish myself to strike out with the sword of letters. Nor was this displeasing to me: Let God have the honor and we the shame, as we well deserve from other things. Let the sons of this world, who are shrewder than the sons of light (Lk 16:8), have it for themselves. It is enough for me to have done what I could, in keeping the honor of God and to the honor of God.

Moreover, my beloved, I remained in Utrecht one whole day beyond what I expected, but because I had no way to help you at once, I was not able to see clearly what more could be done. Uncertain therefore, I committed you to the Lord Jesus Christ and his Spirit. May your saving profession profit you into eternity. You know, beloved, that I now have no power of transferring you. The Lord knows that I did at the time what I could and that I will always do for you what I can. But I wish, beloved, that you would lodge this firmly in your own mind. Never desire to leave or to transfer elsewhere. The mere desire of transferring disquiets and disturbs a man unbelievably, distracting and upsetting him; therefore determine in your mind the certainty of staying and impossibility of leaving. I do not say that you should vow, but you should most firmly resolve. There is no peace for a man out of harmony with those around him. You will see, as a dawning day: Something of peace will arise if you become firm in this, and then you will more patiently bear with adversities. A forewarning about that man in Utrecht, though I mean not to judge him in any way nor, I hope, ought he to be judged, nor should you judge him. Rumor often lies about a man, and men are quick to abuse; hence fidelity is rarely ascribed to us. Let it be as it is, so long as there is fidelity in Christ. I know your good will toward me from your sincere and faithful warning beforehand.

Do not be adverse that I single you out individually, for this is the custom in letters written for the utility of others beyond those to whom they are addressed, even when they are supported by the dignity of a superior. To all your companions, my own most beloved, wish well-being with your mouth in my spirit. Farewell and be strong in every strength of Christ Jesus our Lord. Thanks be ever to God.

CHAPTER FIVE

A Sermon Addressed
to the Laity[12]

The holy teacher St. Paul says that God's heavenly kingdom consists of righteousness, peace, and joy in the Holy Spirit (see Gal 5:32). Whoever desires to reign eternally with God, or to come to God, or to have God come and dwell in him, must sense these three in himself, or else reach out and study to acquire them with all his strength. In seeking these three, a man should let every external religious exercise go. For all external exercises, whether fasting, scourging, keeping vigil, much psalm-singing, many Our Father's, manual labor, hard beds, or hair shirts, have only so much good and profit as they bring righteousness, peace, and joy in the Holy Spirit. Men should do such works only in order to acquire those three and measure accordingly whether to do more or less. Any exercise that gets in the way of righteousness, peace, and joy in the Holy Spirit, or any one of the three, is harmful, burdensome, and improper for a man. It comes rather from man's enemy, the devil, and from man's own perverse conceit and self-absorption. The devil sets men to doing many such exercises that look good on the outside—and could also be good if they were done righteously and for the right reasons. But the devil leads men into such an ascetic life that—as he knows well it will—it makes them sick in the head, quick to anger, ill-natured, and arrogant, or he brings a man to think he is doing something good so that his own works become pleasing to him. The devil knows very well that exterior works, without the interior, are not of God, and that without interior righteousness such works are in fact more harmful than helpful. The devil drives some persons to such an austere life that they lose the kingdom of heaven by neglecting their interior life and the things that are more needful.

And so it is little wonder that there are many people who are much in prayer and who lead very austere lives, and yet are unrighteous within and covetous still of temporal good. Goods earned unjustly they have not returned, and indeed cannot, though they may at times want to, because such goods have grown so near their hearts that wickedness, miserly practices, and the devil's pleasures are now closer to their hearts than God himself, his love, and his commandments. Through their religious exercises these people make a good appearance on the outside among simple people, but that is of as little profit to them, in Christ's own words, as the external gleam of sepulchres which on the inside are full of worms and stench—and so it is with these people. We should know, as St. Paul said, that though these people could speak with angelic tongues and do all things and understand all mysteries and practice all the arts and do such miracles as to move mountains and live so ascetically as to give their bodies to be burned, yet it would be worth nothing if they had not a godly love which outweighed all temporal things (see 1 Cor 13:13).

No godly love or power resides in the man who knowingly clings to or desires unjust goods. Justice and judgment must prepare the way in a man before God or love, which is God, will enter into him, as David says in the Psalter: *iusticia et iudicium, praeparatio sedis tuae* (Ps 89:15). Which is to say, justice and judgment are a preparation for the throne of God in us, presupposing that we prepare ourselves to become fit places for God to come in and take his seat. This, I repeat, is the first thing: God will have judgment from us according to the justice that is within. We should so judge ourselves that, so far as we can, we render full restitution to our fellow Christians for all misdeeds done to them and for all that we have taken from them unjustly—even if we ourselves must suffer in order to make sure that we do not see them forced to beg for their bread. So much at least the command of God and holy love ought to move us to give.

Love encompasses justice and wants to praise her beyond all speaking. A righteous Christian should not bring his sacrifice to the altar until he has done justice; until then, in fact, his sacrifice, whether interior or exterior, is not pleasing to God. It should be recognized that St. Thomas spoke truly in the *Secunda Secundae:*[13] A man can, may, and should restore what he has taken unjustly; but if he withholds and increases it, doing nothing else, the withholding and increasing is a mortal sin bringing death to the soul. The love of God cannot dwell in a man during the time that some temporal good so stirs him that he desires unjustly and against God to have or get it, and takes it at any hour that he can, with might or with cunning, in secret or in public. And all confessors and others who keep him in this business are nothing but advocates and helpers of the devil. For so long as a man possesses goods of other people that are pleasing to him, or goods that he has to produce, prepare, or preserve in an underhanded way, or takes of them as it suits him without the people's concurrence, or exchanges them to suit himself, or advises people in a way harmful to them but profitable to himself—for all that time the love of temporal goods possesses a man's heart more than the love of God. This is contrary to God's command and makes a man blind, inclining him toward himself and, still more, toward the devil and the advice of false confessors. And so he is ever finding things he wants, always managing to excuse his covetousness, and thus deceives himself horribly, indeed all the way to hell and death, because all such false pretensions allow a man to remain in his foolishness.

If such men would reflect on their lives and not abandon them at once to gathering and a blindly ascetic life-style, they would discover that their lives actually stand outside of love. For they would discover the degree to which little temporal things, no matter how small they might be, move them against God and against justice. A small word, for instance, may easily unsettle their hearts and loosen their mouths. They quickly become wretched over some one little thing that has escaped their grasp. This is entirely contrary to joy in the Holy Spirit which renders men so much the less grieved over worldly things as they come to love ever more things that are truly godly. And for that reason such people eventually become quick to anger, quarrelsome, murmurers, gossips, obstinate, and out to please themselves. Nor have they any peace within, as shown by their words and works. But wherever there is no outer peace, not God but the devil is present. For the Prophet says that God's city enjoys peace, and the Lord says that his spirit comes to rest only in restful men.

Peace was the first gift the angels announced to all men of goodwill at Christ's birth. A good will is to be measured by peace: You have much goodwill if you have genuine peace, and you will also have genuine peace if you have goodwill. What then is goodwill except that a man conform his will to God's so that he wills nothing other than what God wills? Now since all things that happen come from the will of God, working and disposing things according to his holy peace, the good man should be at peace with all things that God arranges in pain or difficulty and sends against sin. The just man of goodwill can always make peace within and without, keeping himself from slanderous talk, rebellious action, or anything that might unsettle others. The apostles spoke peace to all the houses they entered, and David said in the Psalter, God spoke peace to his people, and turns around the hearts that are dead within. Christ, in coming and going, spoke peace to his people inwardly and outwardly. Inwardly he spoke of a peace that passes all understanding for those who are perfect, and so the more impure a man in heart, the less he has of genuine peace. For purity of heart cannot exist without interiority of heart and interiority and kindness are practically the same. A distraught heart cannot withhold itself from complaint and lashing out, and thence come externally unrest and lack of peace.

External suffering and dissatisfaction come especially when a man wants things to be other than the way they have turned out, and cannot and will not accept what has happened, whether pleasure or loss, good or evil, as coming from the hand of God. The just man makes an effort to bear these things equitably, along with all that God sends, and those who cannot do this perfectly should strive for it more and more. It is much better for a man to suffer through the pain and difficulties that God sends or arranges in his eternal wisdom and goodness than to attempt to deal with these things with his own strength and never know whether they are pleasing to God or not. But a man should know that God wills all that he disposes for a man to suffer, and should know that more surely than if the holy angels themselves had said it with their own mouths. Indeed God speaks it to him with his own mouth, for God's speech is nothing other than his works, and therefore his works are the most authentic testimony on earth to God's will that all things should fit together. And for that reason the just and kindly man represses all evil-speaking and all injustice because for him all is at peace.

All too distant from these men are those who cry out dreadfully within and without over one little unworthy thing, and thus destroy the peace of everyone around them. In truth they ought to know that their tongues and hearts are enflamed with the fires of hell, like those tongues whereof St. James spoke. These men desecrate not only their hearts but also their bodies and set them afire with the flames of hell (see Jas 3:6). Oh, poor souls! How many a husband is enflamed with hell-fire, in heart, tongue, and body, horribly festering and boiling within over one little word spoken by his wife. And oh, poor souls! How many a wife, who ought to be subject to her husband, is enflamed with hell-fire over one little word, heard from her maid or husband, which so unsettled her that she set up a great clamor, scolding without ceasing and destroying the peace of all about her. What more can one say than that these are hellish beasts, and yet they do not repent. Yea, in my own mind, they are spiritually burdened in this state with the hellish beast himself.

And so this ends up concerning much more than one little thing. It is much worse than if they simply mistreated someone to whom by God's command they ought to be subject, as a child his father or a wife her husband or a servant his lord, and worse too than if a lord thus mistreated his servant or a father his child or a husband his wife. For God willed and foresaw that they should be subject and also arranged it so, but, contrary to God, they have set themselves above, against his wisdom and law to their own great loss of peace. It frequently happens that elderly folk become ruined in body, goods, or wisdom, or that a husband cannot earn enough or becomes old and lame, and then along comes the evil child or nasty wife to set themselves above their father or husband, wishing them subject instead to child or wife and thus breaking God's law simply to gain a little earthly advantage.

Speak, wife, is that why you have disturbed and broken the ordinances that God has set and no man can trim? Just because your husband or father can no longer earn enough? Because, dear wife, it is God's holy law that you neither can nor should be without a head: Your husband should be your head and Christ should be the head of your husband. You should come to Christ in this way, and in no other than with your husband as your head. That is, he should be above you in all governance and in all things concerning your household and body. You have no power over your own body; indeed if you were to earn anything by your own work, it would come under the power of your husband. On the other hand, if you earn nothing, your husband should still provide for you with tenderness and as best he can. Whatever you earn is your husband's, as if he had earned it with his own hands, and in this way your hands are more your husband's than your own.

A man likewise should look upon his wife, as St. Paul said (Eph 5:22–33), even as Christ looks upon his holy Church, that is, as a communion of marital love. He should love her and protect her with all his strength, while a wife should be subject so that all she brings is held in common. Each should love the other spiritually, and so all that he earns and possesses he should pour out and set afire and offer up in the same love as does God himself. Oh, if husband and wife would only reflect on the love and ordinances that prevail between Christ and his communion of souls! For married love is an image and sign of that love. Both man and wife should see in the heavenly wedding feast their own mutual belonging to each other and should take their ordinances from it. Meditate on it, all you wives who serve God! Let the heavenly marriage take root within you. Learn from it many wonders and special things which you should do for your husbands. And you husbands, likewise, learn from it what you owe your wives. Out of it should grow unity, peace, and tranquillity so that you love to be together, preferably more in spirit than in the flesh. And you wives too: Out of it you should grow to prefer your husband's rule and instruction to doing your own will. And so you will become very careful not to wreck this peace or to spread abroad your mutual secrets and burdens, but rather quietly to bear together both good and evil and happily to remain together in your home. You, wife, will think you see Christ in your husband, and you, husband, will think you see the loving soul in your wife.

Yea, those who taste of this will care little about going into taverns and clubs, as do so many now who spend much time abroad and little at home. One should not say this of wives, for no good wife goes, nor may go, abroad to eat or out into society without her husband's permission according to the command of God and the saints—just as Christ says to the soul: Without me you may not do anything that depends on our mutual unity. I would rather, says Christ, have a wife who was extraordinarily subject to her husband in peace and tranquillity, but who did not lead a very ascetic life, than a wife who in penance led the most austere life ever known among women but who was not subject to her husband or lacked kindness or chattered useless things ceaselessly. An ascetic life is an extraordinary good and one necessary for us and for all men—if, that is, it is done in righteousness and obedience. For an ascetic life finds all of its goodness in justice and obedience and peace, in quietness and joy in the Holy Spirit. Without them an austere life is dead; it is as chaff and dust, and will be without the fruit of eternal life.

CHAPTER SIX

A Treatise on
Four Classes of Subjects
Suitable for Meditation:
A Sermon on the Lord's Nativity[14]

"For to us a child is born" (Is 9:6). Who is born an adult? It hardly seems necessary to say that someone was born a child. But this was said for us, to make it understood that he was born and made a child for us, and thus to show that we must also be born and become children with him. "Unless you become children like unto this child, he said, you will not enter the kingdom of heaven" (Mt 18:3). "Like unto" is a comparative adverb, for just as we have borne in our flesh the likeness of an earthly child, so we are to bear that of a heavenly child (see 1 Cor 15:49). The birth of Christ teaches us in this way to become like him in humility and stature. No one can be born with Christ unless, as Christ, he becomes like unto a child. Let us therefore be children with the Child, not thinking ourselves superior: Let us speak as children, think as children, and reason as children (see 1 Cor 13:11). Milk and drink ought to suffice for us who cannot yet bear solid food. Are we not still carnal, sold under sin? For there is still strife and contention among us and we walk still as men do (see 1 Cor 3:2; Rom 7:14). Let us walk therefore in the pathways of the Church, fortified by sharing in the holy sacraments and the Scriptures. Who knows but that God will forgive and send mercy from on high, and by putting away childish milk and nourishing us with more solid food bring us to a measure of manhood? What discretion it shows in him not to keep us too long on milk nor to wean us too quickly, not to raise us too rapidly from soup to solids, from emptiness to fullness, from poverty to riches, from the debased to the exalted. In all things the most pure birth, righteous life, and holy death of Christ are the only true antidotes to our impure birth, perverse life, and fearful death. Let us therefore bear them about in our thoughts, words, and deeds, so that this spiritual rebirth may radiate through our lives and the life of Christ may be made manifest in our souls and bodies through the mortification of our flesh.

If we wish to rise with Him and ascend into the heavens, three things are necessary by which, with God's help, we may be conformed and made like unto the birth, life, and passion of Christ: preparation of the mind, expression with the mouth, and completion of the work. Of the three, Christ's birth preceded his life and passion, just as among our three exercise of the mind comes before that of the mouth and the deed. Yet exercise of the mind is pointless, devoid of all honor and purpose, if it does not lead and compel us to labor in the things of Christ and to bring them to completion with confession of the mouth and imitation in deed. Exercise of the mind in meditation on the birth of Christ is prior in order, sweeter for us children, simpler in its meaning, and easier than all the others.

Since every exercise of the mind arises from meditation and finds its completion there, I judge it necessary first in this sermon or treatise to discuss certain common matters that justify and guide our affections with respect to the life and passion as well as the birth of Christ: The end of the commandment and of every exercise is love, and all should arise from a pure heart, a good conscience, and a true faith (1 Tm 1:5), so that we might act as the mouth of the Lord, separating as the Prophet says, the precious from the vile (see Jer 15:19). The reason I speak to this matter is that I have observed many devout folk err in these things and I thought it might prove useful to offer some reflections on them. Those things which aid us in meditational exercises on the aforesaid matters are and ought to be divided four ways, assigned to four different classes of material suitable for meditation, from which the child may form his meditations. In the first class are things concerning the birth, life, and passion of Christ contained in canonical Scripture; they may not be considered other than as they are. In the second class come matters treating the same themes but revealed or said to be revealed at a later time to certain saints. In the third class are those matters that arise from the teachings of the doctors as likely conjectures, probable arguments, or convincing reasons; they are called respectively likely, probable, or reasonable.

[THE FOURTH CLASS]

In the fourth class, however, are many imagined and fictive things, received in some lesser manner as aids to our childishness. They are to be accepted not because they are believed true as such but rather

99

because our feeble imaginations are thereby helped, our childish minds more potently and suitably nourished with the milk of Christ and more surely brought to his love. It is not at all silly to the accomplished if we as babes adjust such little things to our stature and later leave them altogether behind. For even the Most High, condescending to human frailty, employed corporeal forms and figures far removed from God, the angels, and spiritual things for his own external appearances and addresses to men, as well as for inner visions and inspirations. Moreover, all of Holy Scripture generously employs such holy figures lest our darkened eyes be ruined by too much light, and then too, lest those unable to imagine anything other than corporeal realities be shut out from the Scriptures. Thus Holy Scripture humbly favors children, leading even the great from small things to larger, accommodating itself to all and averse to none, profound for the great and yet open to little children. Scripture is exactly like its Writer, gentle and humble of heart (see Mt 11:29) and yet exalted and sublime.

Note, if you will, the forms taken by angels: lions, cattle, sheep, eagles, beaks, wings, chariots, thrones, incensors. And again the forms and fictions by which the Almighty has expressed himself to us: fire, air, water, earth, gold, human, and animal. Indeed he sometimes even took the form of indecent acts: God as drunk, gluttonous, angry, confused, desirous. Scripture describes him with a stomach, head, and other members, and as using various tools; and throughout it imposes the corporeal upon the spiritual, form upon the formless. Thus it portrays churches, faculties of the soul, or vices and virtues with human members and parts of buildings. And why this? Most certainly and most beneficently to nourish us children in our inner sight and minds with his milk.

Nor is this a form of falsehood, any more than the poetic figures which instruct us in morality. No one is so childish as to think there are talking trees or animals. The literal sense of poetry and of scriptural poems and figures is its figural sense, and the words are not what they might first seem or sound. Frequently indeed the further removed the mere ring of a word is from its truth, the less a mind is allowed to dally over its litero-historical sense. Who would think literally, as it says in the book of Judges, that trees wanted to elect a king over themselves and the fig, vine, olive, and branch spoke thus and such of his election (see Jgs 9:8–15)? So also Christ used various figures in his teaching; indeed, according to the evangelist (Mt 13:34), he never spoke to them without figures. He also used certain parables which in some instances I do not believe are to be understood as having literally occurred. Indeed sometimes he represented morally good things through the morally evil, so that the figure (type) was transferred from sons of this world to sons of light (see Lk 16:8), from an iniquitous to an equitable judge. Thus the Apostle transfigured the dissensions of the Corinthians in order to apply them to himself and Apollo (see 1 Cor 4:6). In this way Nathan set David against himself by rendering judgment on the rich man who stole the only sheep of the poor man (2 Sm 12:1–4). Thus Joab ordered a story put to Absalom's father in his behalf in the mouth of the woman of Tekoa.

What is the point of all these trifles if not that things refer more fully to other things than do words to things? Difficult matters, not easily impressed upon our senses or understanding as such, are communicated to us by way of other corporeal and sensible things, that is, to men themselves corporeal and animal, who are thus enabled in some way to ascend from the visible to the invisible. Whence Dennis says in the second chapter of his *Celestial Hierarchy:* For theology has quite artificially made use of sacred poetic figures for nonfigurative mental abstractions, disclosing them to our soul, supplying it according to its own nature, and adjusting to it the anagogical Holy Scriptures.[15] Note this too: Just as negations are truer of God than affirmations, so dissimilar and disjoined similitudes about God and spiritual things are more useful. Since they contain in themselves nothing worthy of God or spiritual matters, they compel the mind to turn away from them and to seek higher things. So also in the ways we most commonly treat of Christ, things farther removed from reality can often, so long as we do not cling to them, profit us more.

But when a person places himself imaginatively in the presence of Christ and his deeds, it is good at times to juxtapose something contrary to Christ's presence that may serve to recall us mentally for a moment, lest we become deceived in our actual sight by some image. For just as we endow Christ's divinity with forms and figures, deeds and instruments, so we need not fear to ascribe to his humanity and human deeds in our minds things more and other than, though never anything contrary to, what has been written. Indeed we should dare to bring it all into our own presence and time, as though we saw him and his deeds and heard him speaking. This is the teaching of the blessed Bernard, Bonaventure, and several other saints and devout men for us children. For thus we are always in a position to place ourselves before him and to construe his face as well as the figure and stature of the saints; to take up conversation, seek counsel, and put questions to him and the saints; to offer ourselves to him and them as obedient domestic servants; and while faithful in this our service and obedience also to seek help and our desires; indeed almost to live in the same house with Christ and Mary, and to go on pilgrimage with the pilgrims, to weep with the weeping and to rejoice with the rejoicing (Rom 12:15), and to suffer with the suffering.

All this I said about the fourth class of objects suitable for meditation. Nor is there any falsehood in them so long as the mind does not cling to them but rather presumes them to be only something helpful and imagined—much as we take up wooden images to further our meditations, using them to render the deeds more present. It does not matter how or by what means something is signified so long as what is signified is true. Such images should be taken for nothing other than signs and directed toward the signification of past events, so that the past might be represented to and more forcefully impressed upon the present. Nor is it so unusual to have the present signify the past, which is very common. Indeed the past only enters the mind through something present, since opposites sometimes signified each other, as when Jesus said of John "What did you go into the desert to see? Sand blown around by the wind? But what did you think to see? A man dressed in skins?" (Mt 11:7). So too people indignant about something said or done will often say, "You are some good man!"—thus, in fact, accusing him of evil by their address, even though that is not found in the words themselves. Similarly, in the life of St. Nicholas, he who handed his adversary a baton in which the silver was hidden and then swore he had given more silver than he owed, was in actuality lying.[16]

I said all this so that no infant would shrink back from this fourth class of objects suitable for meditation, which is in fact most useful, however childish and in the end to be put wholly away. Yet a person should take great care in this kind of exercise lest the mind become transfixed and hold something to be truly present that in reality is not. For it is in the nature of images and species firmly pressed upon the mind, especially when they are consciously projected as present, to return to their origins in the external senses. Then the visualized image is made real, as if it were in our very presence, and the phantasy is taken up by our external sense organs. Thus a simple man will believe that he can sense the very corporeal presence of Christ, or seem to see him with his eyes or hear with his ears, or touch some saint he has imagined. Such deceptions are not without danger. Indeed here signs are employed as things, just as when someone believes an image of Christ to be Christ himself. Far be it from us to worship such a strange or newly invented God. Never! This is to offer honor to your own imagination, as is clear from many teachings of Saint Augustine, especially in his *Confessions* and his *On True Religion*.[17] Therefore the simple, who sin less in this, are ever to be counseled to discuss their meditations with a wise and discrete person.

Then too this form of imagination, with its apparent presence of Christ or a saint, can puff up the mind, which may begin to believe itself worthy of an appearance from Christ or one of the saints. This happens particularly with the sense of sight—it can happen also to the other senses, but more rarely—since through it we grasp the distinction and certitude of things. Infants find it difficult to distinguish between the real presence of Christ, shown to many, and their own imagination. A certain devout religious told me that happened to him in his exercises; that when he entered into profound reflection upon Christ, he seemed to stand before him. I hold it for certain that people who are subsequently neither illuminated by the visual presence of Christ nor filled with a more ardent charity have rather been deceived by imaginations of this kind, particularly if they should offend against the command of charity. A certain woman told me that Christ was frequently present to her but that she received no spiritual profit, as was indeed evident from her words and life, even though she appeared to be of goodwill; indeed she finally fell from the way of life to which she had solemnly bound herself. For the firm foundation stands, sealed with this sign: "The Lord knows who are his," and "Every man who calls upon the name of the Lord must depart from iniquity" (2 Tm 2:19).

These things were said by way of caution in this matter, particularly lest we spend too long in pursuit of a simple image of a nude Christ, without clothes or attire, with no garment of splendor or fortitude or righteousness or light. "The spirit gives life; the flesh profits nothing" (Jn 6:63)—strictly speaking it profits nothing to the formation of true life or of inner righteousness. Therefore the flesh is to be clothed and permeated with divine forms. When he comes in his glory what will it profit the damned to have seen the flesh of Christ and been transfixed? What did it profit Herod or Pilate or the Jews to have seen Christ with their eyes when they did not follow his precepts? Or what would it have profited the apostles to have continuous communication with Christ, if they had turned a deaf ear to the counsel of poverty, especially since the Holy Spirit would not come to the apostles unless Christ departed corporeally? As Christ said, "Unless I depart" (Jn 16:7), and so forth. Thus what would it profit an evil man if Christ appeared to him in his human form? The corporeal image as such therefore profits far less, as will be demonstrated more firmly below.

[THE FIRST CLASS]

The first class of material for reflection, that to which we should cling, comes from the canonical Scriptures and is itself capable of division. Things from the New Testament that preach Christ and his deeds are to be taken purely and simply according to the letter, piously and firmly to be believed, and in believing meditated upon. But things from the Old Testament—to which, I think, should be added certain things from Revelations—are to be meditated upon as treating of Christ and his deeds. For these are such that it is sometimes doubtful whether they should be taken literally or figuratively, as verified or to be verified concerning Christ. Of these I think that nothing from the prophets or the Mosaic law concerning Christ needs to be held necessarily on faith as done or to be done unless the Gospel, the canonical Scriptures, or the whole Church has so approved them, or unless they follow from tested, certain, and inevitable deductions. But all the other things that might be conjectured or tested or proved from Old Testament Scripture are most useful in meditation and more necessary for us than we can know or construe for ourselves, since through them we are led into the anagogies and tropologies of the Old Testament Scriptures and thus immersed in their fullness. Or rather from them we gain a certain fuller understanding of Christ and his deeds, and in turn from our consideration of Christ and his deeds an inner spiritual grasp of these matters.

I do not think it worth spending time on the question as to whether certain events from the Old Testament can be calculated or asserted absolutely as happening to Christ or around him. For instance, whether according to Isaiah both a cow and a donkey, as is thought likely, were present at the manger because it says, "The cow knows his owner and the donkey his lord's manger" (Is 1:3). Or whether according to Habakkuk, "The Lord was placed between two animals" (Hb 3:2, *Vulg.*). So I think it was and hold it to be, not on faith, however, but as an opinion or argument arising from the Scriptures, holding it not for necessary but probable. And what difference does it make whether it was or was not so? If it were not so, it would still hardly contradict the law or the prophets, which in many and nearly all places we hold for true in the spirit and apart from the letter. If it was so, then the reality itself indicates spiritually, though more fully and plainly, what the prophet expressed verbally in the same spirit, only more obscurely and indirectly. What difference does it make so long as we understand and hold to the end for which in reality the Prophet spoke and the Lord revealed? For if it was really done so by Christ, its reference is to the deeds of Christ and not to its meaning for us. If he did it, he did it for us and for the end addressed by the Prophet. If he did not do it, we grasp through the Prophet the same end Christ would have signified if he had done it in fact.

For example, to give a straightforward instance, I am quite sure that on Christ's entry into Egypt the idols fell over, according to the testimony of Isaiah (19:1): "The Lord will ascend on a swift cloud and will enter Egypt and the idols of Egypt will be shaken." Yet I do not hold it on faith but rather by argument from Scripture and the narrative. It is certain that idols fell spiritually throughout the world, that is, the veneration of idols from the mind of man, and that they still fall spiritually in any man Christ enters; this, undoubtedly, was the Prophet's true spiritual intent. If material idols also fell upon his entry into Egypt, this figured their spiritual fall. I have therefore an understanding of the Prophet's principle intent, to which a deed of Christ is ordered as to its end, even as a sign to that which is signified. I freely accept this probable sign from Scripture; I have persuaded myself that it was so and will debate anyone disputing or denying it; I forgive anyone sticking stubbornly to his view; indeed sometimes I ignore it altogether because it is not a point contrary to the faith. Let us hold therefore to the true and spiritual sense, and if we sail thus to the shore, it is not for us to look back from our present habitation and to point out how or with which ship we made the passage. On this there is no point in disputing long or tenaciously.

Similarly I will not willingly dispute the question as to whether Christ performed miracles between his twelfth and thirtieth years, though I am myself persuaded he did not. If he did none, as I quite firmly think, he abstained, in my view, for our sakes, as an example of humility, lest we take up preaching too quickly: We must show ourselves vile and contemptible to men before we become wondrous. If it was so, his minority must have rattled and confounded all the minds and deeds of men—in comparison with all that was said and done earlier concerning him and through him—as if only a silly mouse had been born when from the fame of his birth and other signs it seemed the mountains would give birth. But if in fact he performed miracles during the time about which the Gospel narrative is silent, I have no doubt that those miracles were passed over for the very same reason that, if he had not done them, Christ abstained. What difference then does it make if we arrive by one route or the other, so long as we come to the point to which either the written Gospel writings or Christ's deeds are leading? For if we only employ the deed of Christ or the word of the Gospel toward humility without vainglory, it makes little difference whether or not it happened in just that way.

This then is what we accept from the Old Testament writings in meditating upon matters pertaining to Christ but not contained in the New Testament: All that we can reasonably conjecture, prove, or deduct. It is fitting and useful always to turn such matters toward the spiritual sense, that our faith be more certain and not feigned, that our charity be purer, fuller, and more confident, and that pure faith may work purely toward pure love of the truth (see 1 Tm 1:5). By this application there comes a great separation of the precious from the vile (Jer 15:19) so that strange or unbelievable things may not enter in. Indeed the entire Old Testament Scripture becomes a kind of Gospel narrative when the pure grain is gleaned from the harvest, when the Gospel gleaners purify and repurify, purge and repurge the gleanings, so that it becomes a word of the Lord, a chaste word, and our meditations become pure and chaste meditation, silver tested, tried, and purged seven times over with the fire of love (Ps 11/12:7/6).

[A PHILOSOPHICAL TREATMENT OF PERCEPTION IN MEDITATION]

Gospel meditations drawn from the New Testament with a firm faith are not always preserved inwardly in purity and without falsehood, as Augustine asserts at length in his *On Trinity*.[18] . . . He says the same of meditation on the Apostle or the Virgin, namely that meditations useful to the faith are gathered from both specific and general knowledge and from those things we know and believe. He says there, however, "For we believe the Lord was born of a Virgin called Mary, but what a virgin is, what a birth, what the proper names—all that we do not believe but simply know." As if to say: These things we have from a universal knowledge of species, from the definition of their very natures. But he added of Mary, "With due respect to the faith we can say 'perhaps she had such and such a face, or perhaps not'; but it is not permissible to say 'perhaps he was born of a virgin.' " From the foregoing words of Augustine it seems quite clear that sincere meditations and devotions, founded upon belief and faith and through which we hope, desire, and love things believed and hoped, ought to be purged of all corporeal lines and forms. The soul should concentrate upon the genera and species and upon their very essences, so that from them the understanding may compose, hope, and love what is believed.

For faith does not reside in any of the internal sensing faculties of the soul, in its imaginative or judging faculties, but rather in its intellectual faculty, far removed from images of sensible forms. Faith accepts abstractions which have been distanced and abstracted from sensible forms without deception and thus comprehends things according to their universal or original reasons and their eternal causes. So that these things might thereby take form in us, we have been provided for in a marvelous way: We are taught that faith comes only through hearing (Rom 10:17). Nor does faith assume, import, or signify to itself anything seen, anything endowed with form or lines, just as hearing is not received simply as hearing. An individual visible form or single figure as such, or any single visible thing insofar as it is visible and singular, is not and cannot be signified or described with the voice. And even though proper names are signs of individual and single things, intellectual apprehension nonetheless perceives singular things only through the universal. Thus since I have never seen Plato, when he is spoken of I understand a certain wise Greek man called by this name and the teacher of a certain other man called Aristotle. These things are all universals, even if quantity and similitude are added together with whatever other things represent universals to the understanding—even if they signify in another way to the senses and the imagination, there reducing them to sensible images.

Whenever something is heard, therefore, out of infirmity and habit our soul immediately turns in upon itself in search of visible things, that is, visible singular forms or images, or to things seen individually, or to something formed out of things seen. Why this? Because sight is more certain than any of the other senses and shows the properties of things in greater plurality than any of the others. Hence the imaginative faculty, desirous of certitude, by its own natural force turns more quickly to images of visible things, both because there both more knowable objects and greater certitude are to be had. Indeed only sight takes in the form of a thing as such. What is hearing other than the repercussion of things? What is smell other than the scent of things? What does taste discern other than the agreeability or not of things chewed up and mixed with saliva? What does touch take in other than a first impression of the first qualities of things? In this touch is more powerful than the rest because it agreeably joins to itself many other sense perceptions, even common ones, but not unless it joins itself to the thing and moves either itself or the thing.[19] Sight, however, from a distance without any movement of the thing, and almost at once, takes in the whole figure, place, order, light, color, and much more of a thing; and therefore, as closer to the common sense of it, it is the source of all learning and argumentation. It is little wonder then that the faculty for learning and understanding, lacking an image of something, turns very quickly, even in matters heard, to sight itself and things seen.

I also think, I might add, that just as the external eye cannot fix upon or see anything but solid and delineated objects, so the inner imagination requires something placed before it that is solid and delineated. Thus hearing, formed from little more than empty air, does not shape the imagination, but rather that which comes from something solid and is expressed as a solid. A mental exercise that employs images, therefore, does injury to the persons meditating only in that they require for themselves the formation of certain solid species, which cannot be effected without some treatment and transformation of blood and spirit. I have said these things by way of my philosophy so that a person who understands the origin of these things may be better able to direct himself in them when he perceives that his experience will conform to reason.

It should be noted, therefore, that when we hear a matter of faith expressed in corporeal figures, we are diverted in three ways toward things visible. First, because the same things we hear we sometimes read, and we often represent them to ourselves as letters and syllables. When those things are said to us, therefore, particularly if they concern the invisible essences of things or genera and species or things spiritual and eternal which lack images, we are diverted by memory to books and the places in books where we read those things or indeed to the very forms of words, syllables, and letters. When however someone is diverted to letters in this way—at least someone who has examined himself fully and completely in some matter—it is as to something known, for the images of letters and syllables often aid us in retaining something in our memory. But once it has aided our memory, then the intrusion of these things, now received into the memory, should, I think, be avoided and as a raven or some other great and unclean bird be driven from our thoughts. But in meditating upon eternal and spiritual matters or on the essences, causes, genera and species, and definitions of things, it is most difficult to drive out altogether the forms of the letters and never to return to them, except for some person truly elevated and abstracted toward things higher. Indeed it is not for the slow and lazy to determine and discern in certain matters if and when and how letters intervene, however gently.

Such forms of letters disturb the literate and the learned more than the illiterate who, knowing no letters whatsoever, are wholly free of such interference—and in this they have something over the learned. When a learned man, for instance, hears something sacred expressed in his mother tongue, he seems to conceive in his mind something new or fresh by way of that mother tongue, first impressed on his mind when he was still a boy ignorant of all letters; indeed it seems newer and fresher than if the same thing were said to him in the accustomed Latin way to which his lettered mind would normally turn. But the less the minds of such laymen are cluttered with letters, in my judgment, the more firmly, lastingly, and deeply they are bent toward and seized upon by other images. For there is a certain fixed impression and reflection made of people speaking or preaching or of other such circumstances, so that when they hear or recall this or that again the memory immediately adds what was heard from that person or in that place. Therefore in the stage of purgation all images of places or persons speaking or other such circumstances must be removed. For this is like some great bird—or if it is some very holy and endearing person, some fine-feathered creature that may be less harmful—and it must finally be purged and wiped clean from the imagination.

The memory of a person is sometimes wondrously helpful, and sometimes quite obstructive; specifically, it helps to think upon and receive the word from some holy and sublime person as somehow sweeter, more endearing, more sublime, and thus also more sacred and lasting—and the contrary from a vile and despised person. Who does not receive and embrace more sweetly and firmly a word from Christ than from some philosopher, from a saint than from some clever man? No small part, indeed a very large part, of eloquence, as is known from rhetoric, comes down to the person speaking. Alas, how many misled young people of today, for this very reason, convince and persuade themselves of many things which they have hardly or in fact not yet truly understood at all, solely because it was Aristotle or some other philosopher who said it. This is today one great impediment to philosophy, which arises from ascribing matters of true understanding to the reputation of the person speaking and

109

various other such circumstances. Still another greater and more common impediment is that when they treat basic matters such as the essence, nature, substance, matter, form, genus, or species of things, they reflect upon them only in the primary mode, not as they are in themselves but largely as a set of words. I confess that I philosophized in this manner for a long time, and I know many whose minds have drowned in thinking about these verbal forms. But if anything of substance and understanding ever does emerge in this way from the mind, it is mighty little and wholly hemmed in by the remaining darkness. And when we philosophize so, we think to be philosophizing with our intellect, but in fact we are imagining things and are stuck still in sensible reality.

Third, we are diverted to the visual signifiers of words by which we "see" the thing, or we form the shape of things not seen, both visible and invisible, shaped according to things already seen. Thus in our inner perception a visible species is added to what we hear, and it is not therefore purely a matter of auditory sense. For a heard voice is something sensible, but the signifying word that forms faith is not something seen nor conjoined to visible forms but accessible only to the intellect.[20] In this way the word is a pure sign, carrying with it nothing visible from the speaker or the place, having no admixture of diction or syllable, and bearing nothing of visible accidents in what it predicates essentially and communicates substantially. For if in some matter of faith reference is made to a particular color or light or other such thing in a general way, it takes shape in the mind, insofar as it becomes subsumed under knowledge or faith, without visible likenesses but rather according to the appropriate definitions, actions, genera, and species—and this despite the fact that we are more naturally inclined to take from what is signified visible things to meditate upon.

But if Scripture or the faith makes mention expressly of some particular color, light, or figure, the individuality of that color or light as such, according to the mass of its extension or accidents, is not in itself describable in any determinate matter, and thus it is conceived and considered generically, as it might be by some unknown man. Yet the species of light, colors, figures, and places cling tenaciously to the mind, for they are fundamental to all spiritual and intellectual cognition, preparing and leading the way, because nearly all intellectual and spiritual cognition arises out of an earlier sensible cognition. But these must be left behind as we approach our end, like ships coming into shore.

Of all the visible forms it is most difficult to imagine distinctions in color without visible forms, for instance, to think of green or red generically; it is much easier to reflect upon color itself generically and apart from any visible image. But the differences and definitions, actions and properties, of specific colors are so inherent in things that they can hardly be conceived in some universal way by any but the most accomplished of persons. Thus when reference is made to colors or colored things, to figures or figured things, the mind must focus on those colored or figured things as if they were without color or figure, or rather upon the spiritual significations of those colors and figures, which are most evident, as anyone may easily experience in meditation by moving from purple and deep red to the blood of Christ. And the more tenaciously and pointedly the words force us to focus upon the visible forms of things as such, the more quickly a person ought to have ready to hand their mystical signification.

Ascent to such mystical significations is easy for those who take up the moral or anagogic sense. But it is difficult to focus the intellect upon the particular species or genus or essence of these colors and figures, which truly have no image. Nor should anyone employing images be deceived in this, thinking he has the very species of all redness or greenness when he hears green or red. I believe that all images are signs of particular things and have in themselves nothing universal. He is deceived who believes there is anything of the truly universal in some image. He is like someone who is shown an egg and then while his back is turned and he is unaware, someone replaces it with a similar egg and he thinks it is the same one.[21]

The image of an individual green thing is then referred to the memory or imagination of various green or other things seen or imagined, just as that same individual green thing in the external world calls forth by its likeness various other green things to be remembered or reflected upon. What it calls forth is common to all those various green things and perhaps even to the image of greenness. Neither the senses nor the imagination can perceive this in its common or universal nature, although the senses perceive things wherein that universal nature is found, by which, for instance, brute animals are often moved and aroused. And this is the fundamental reason why a particular sensible object is neither knowable nor describable as such. Indeed no knowledge consists in images, and only those persons have knowledge who are able—and they are very few—to transcend images.

Even they, however, are not able to have pure faith without some admixture, for faith is a light that raises us above natural objects and thus all the more above images. Indeed intellectual knowledge or faith, though of a particular thing, is gained through a universal composed from some other universal and thus rendered appropriate only to some particular thing. Thus we meditate mentally upon the Virgin Mary by way of the universal notions of virginity and giving birth because to her alone applies both virginity and childbearing, or as that woman who bore the God-man and savior of the world, and that too through those universals. For there would be no proper meditation if it were said to be only of a virgin called Mary because this might apply to any number of women named Mary and might be commonly predicated of several women. But according to the faith a virgin giving birth can apply to no one but her.

Many notions concerning Christ are formed in this way: A man who is united to God, or a man who was born thus, or lived thus, or died thus. These things concerning Christ are believed in their manifold particulars and grasped in the intellect through universal conceptions concerning particulars. For these universals are fully drawn or abstracted from the effects of particulars, from their original causes or their limiters, according to genus and species. This is to have a purified faith or intellect, just as contamination arises when genera, species, distinctions, and universal properties, not to speak of incorporeal or spiritual substances and essences signified directly by words, are referred back to something sensible or corporeal or imaginable. By "directly" I mean an absolute reference to a man, an angel, God, or something similar, capable of being meditated upon directly in its original and common reasons through the very terms themselves and without any images.

It is not purely an auditory matter when, upon hearing that the man Christ was tall, you form for yourself an image, for this is a necessary sign for someone's particular quantity; and hearing alone did not express this to you. Thus on hearing of Christ's bitter passion, if you were to visualize in an image a certain degree of bitterness, the heard word would not have said this because it spoke to you only of bitterness in general. No particular sensible thing, in sum, is heard or expressed merely according to the individualizing aspects of sensibility, and pure hearing is called faith, an adherence to something not seen in its primal verity.

With respect to genus and species, therefore, color, redness, light, or triangles, however much more difficult to perceive, lack images. Just as color is not easily retained in the intellect by those not accustomed to extended meditation except by sinking to some species of color, so redness is even more difficult to think about apart from some specific red thing. For when someone says "redness," he thinks of something more or less red variously according to the images he forms, even though "redness" in species is capable of neither greater nor lesser intensity. The most difficult to remove is the image of light; so that in thinking of God we can hardly abstain from some image of light, however attenuated. Among the images imposed upon spiritual abstractions this is the last to be removed. Nor is it any less difficult to meditate at length on specific or particular colors without images, but in the manner of those eating the passover, that is, of those in transit, it needs to be consumed quickly (see Ex 12:11), at least at the beginning.

For just as when someone begins to be illuminated and receives occasional bright flashes even before he is illuminated more lastingly, so also in transit the very sound of the words *species, genus, specific properties, specific causal definitions,* and *the essence of things* pass quickly through the mind, as if accustomed to hurrying and with the transience of images. The more a person is able to withdraw himself from such images and to persist in this abstraction and to place his hope and love in these abstract things, the more truly and purely— short of a full understanding of things—he meditates upon the birth, life, and death of Christ and upon the Holy Scripture, and the more nearly he approaches the eternal.

For it is necessary to make extended use of external writings, signs, and images for a long time in our meditations, and they are not to be left behind until faith and love have been wholly purified, so that, for instance, the sense of Scripture can be reflected upon as if not even written and as if signifying without signs. This is what I call leaving the Scriptures and external signs behind. So also we should not withdraw from images and the imagined in our new birth until Christ and spiritual understanding have again taken shape within us, until we are spiritual beings judging all things spiritually (1 Cor 2:15) and discerning between one day and the next and all days (Rom 14:5). Thus Dennis said to the first of the angelic hierarchies: "It is not possible for a divine ray to illumine us unless it is veiled anagogically in a variety of sacred images and prepared for by those things divine providence disposes for us."[22] Indeed in a fatherly way these elements are first given over to us because if someone falls from a knowledge of them prior to perfection, he rarely returns to an easy reading of them. On the contrary, those images that stick more tenaciously to the mind also imprint all the more forcefully the spiritual realities signified through them. Thus Scripture frequently employs such images, using more difficult ones for more difficult realities, so much so that it describes the most excellent realities and the farthest removed from sensibility by way of things, qualities, and properties of the sense of touch, which is the crudest of the senses with respect to its own object, especially where it concerns the most bestial act. What after all is more spiritual than the unions of God and the soul, of Christ and the Church, of Christ and his own flesh in oneness of spirit? And yet what is known to be cruder than the oneness of a woman and a man commingled in the flesh?

So also the taste, the hunger and thirst, for things sensible can by analogy wondrously draw a sensible man to things divine, to a hunger, thirst, and taste for things spiritual. So too our chief antidote, the sacrament of the body and blood of Christ, was most beneficently and thoughtfully provided for us in the species of wine and bread that can be tasted. Thus all sensible sacraments contain spiritual signs proportionate to the invisible grace operative in them. For that reason, words and signs of things touched, tasted, or smelled make strong impressions (especially those of taste and touch because they are conjoined to the things themselves), and they thus compel the soul to join itself and to adhere to spiritual realities all the more firmly. Indeed all spiritual taste, it seems to me, has its origin and comes from corporeal taste, from which it arises when spiritual and corporeal taste are properly conjoined. That transpires above all in the sacrament of the altar. Taste therefore, as Bernard said in his book *On the Love of God*, inwardly directs, rectifies, judges, and purifies all the other senses.[23]

Similarly the qualities peculiar to touch teach us to ascend to the heights of all love and peace. Spiritual touch is found in love of God and your neighbor, especially when you gain the one you desire and love and then rest in peace in that lover. The love of neighbor is usually and appropriately assigned to touch for two reasons: first, because warmth is the positive and originating principle of all touch, while cold is its privative or secondary principle; second, because we touch each other in expressing and communicating love, indeed with a closer application and conjoining of touch than what people would normally exercise.

Sweet-smelling scent infuses an inspiring and yearning soul with something like the very substance of the beloved, whence angels, even after their departure, often leave behind a fragrance almost corporeal. Therefore the lover in the Song described the limbs of his beloved not simply as fragrant but as very fragrant and sweet-smelling. Sometimes he likened the quality of her fragrance to the scent of wine: "Smelling of cinnamon and balsamon, as a select myrrh, I gave off a sweet scent" (Ecclus 24:20). So also of many others, and again frequently by way of sweet-smelling things such as flowers, roses, aromas, unguents, vines, pigments, and so on [terms drawn mostly from the Song of Songs]. But taste requires touch as well because taste is, according to the Philosopher, a kind of touch, and it also requires smell; so taste in effect includes both senses. Distinctions in smells are identified by the names of the tastes principally and fully found in them. Therefore Dennis said in the first chapter of his *Angelic Hierarchy:* "A sensible sweetness is the figure of an invisible source."[24] Thus the images of those three senses—which are to name them truly and properly, motion, the residue of things moved or moving, and the words and signs signifying them—all order the spiritual appetite, even while drawing and inducing it toward its beloved object.

The signs of visible images, however, purging more properly the intellect, illuminate particularly those things which are above. And when words signifying beauty or beautiful and proportionate things or attractiveness are joined beautifully to these signs of visible things, then they draw the affections still more, as it often says in the Song of Songs: "Your cheeks are beautiful" (Sg 1:10) or "My lover is beautiful" (Sg 6:3/4) or "You are wholly beautiful and there is no flaw in you" (Sg 4:7). So too in the love song when sweetness or sweet singing is added to the voice, it draws the affections even more than the voice signifying alone, as in "Your voice is sweet, the voice of a dove heard in our land" (Sg 2:14). Something attractive has been added to the merely auditory sensation. For in this way the hearing, though once plainly formed, draws the affections still more, but only as the signifying voice draws differently according to the diverse modes of what is signified, either in the intellect or the affections. But such hearing is directed especially and mostly to the forming of knowledge and faith, or, second, to forming the intellect, particularly in genus and species, the definition of things and their inherent reasons, which is the work of abstraction.

So too the sacraments have a certain audible visuality, that is, the sign is seen and yet nothing of that visually signified is signified as if it were visible through the sign. It is signified in quite another way, as if gained and perceived through hearing, almost as if it were heard to be within. Thus what words are to learning, all the sacraments and the sacramentalia together with the substance, ornamentation, and offices of these sacraments are to matters of faith. In a sacrament those qualities of the sign which have no signifying value are to be avoided, as for instance the whiteness of the species in the bread, which has no signifying value. Focus rather on those aspects by which the sacraments have a likeness to what they signify, thus in the sacrament of the eucharist the tastiness, the nutritional value, the drink, and the food. In the other sacraments, likewise, always turn to that which in its own way reflects and bends toward what is signified. In the sacrament of the altar, for instance, there is a certain mixture of spiritual and material taste, or rather a certain ascent from the material to the spiritual. Solomon indeed specifically made use of words signifying colors or figures by way of objects themselves extraordinarily colorful, things rarely inherent in the common apart from images, and all this so that we might be more singularly, deeply, and compellingly drawn with desire for the beloved object. Thus he freely polluted the feet of the intellect to reach the height of affection—as when he spoke of the redness of a pomegranate and of burnished arms (Sg 4:3, 5:14).

From all this it is clear that sensible things and images are necessary for us, especially in the first class of objects for meditation, but also in the fourth which consists almost entirely of images; indeed it represents a kind of sensible conversation and direct communication with the saints. And just as this fourth class of objects for meditation in the end simply disappears, so also these images of sensible things are to disappear by elimination, not precipitously, not of their own will or strength, and not suddenly; yet gradually they recede or rather are transformed into a certain spiritual harmony, so that the interior man as well as the exterior, the one coming in as well as the one going out, as Christ says, will find pasture (Jn 10:9). Animals too, that is, animalic motions and senses, will follow; as in the vision of Ezekiel (chap. 1), they will stand and be elevated together with the intellectual wheels, that is, the motions of the soul, which Dennis calls circular in the fourth chapter of his book *On Divine Names*. According to the teaching of that same Dennis in his Letter to Titus, "It is fitting for human life, being both divisible and indivisible, to be illuminated with divine cognition according to its own proper nature, that is, in both forms of life: the impassible aspect of the soul, that is, the intellect, to distinguish the simple and intimate visions of the divine forms; the passible aspect, the sensible, to run naturally with and extend itself to the divine intuitively by way of the composite forms of signifying figures, which are for it natural veils to the known."[25]

This conformity between the sensible and intellectual powers renders and holds men fixed under the cross of Christ so that they glory in nothing else (Gal 6:14). They seek with their every desire to conform themselves within and without to that cross so that, as the Apostle says, "they are always giving themselves over in their bodies to mortification, so the life of Jesus may be revealed in their bodies and their mortal flesh" (2 Cor 4:11–12). Thus "for those deeply loving the law of Christ and God, there is great peace within and without and there is no scandal" (Ps 118/119:165). For there is in them a spiritual abundance owing to an infusion and plenitude of forces from on high, like the precious oil pouring down from the head to the beard [the beard of Aaron] and all the way down to the last limb of our carnal garment.

But this is to make present in some way the future and glorious resurrection, as St. Bernard says in his book *On the Love of God*.[26] It is very difficult to achieve such perfection, though we must be striving toward it. And to walk that royal way of conformity to Christ seems to me the most desirable, humble, and secure. Thus Jerome in his third book on the Epistle to the Galatians says, "It is not an easy matter to live in this present age such that the life of Christ is revealed now in our flesh. For it is thus that we are justified, including even our mortal bodies, through his Spirit coming to dwell in us."[27] Those who ascend suddenly and through another way, who do not take care to direct themselves earlier or later into that royal way, should look out lest they fall into the snares of thieves. But this should suffice for now on the use and abstraction of images in meditating on Christ by way of the Old and the New Testaments.

[THE SECOND AND THIRD CLASSES]

We do not have to take much time on the second class of objects suitable for meditation [special revelations to saints]. Such revelations of particular things are of little use, except when they are to be mystically understood and foster higher ascent; these are found in nearly all those revelations, full of mysteries, vouchsafed to the extraordinary. Most other revelations are proportioned to those who see them, since they are meant primarily for their utility. A certain mother who wept excessively over the death of her son, for instance, as it is told in the *Book of the Bees*, saw him carrying her tears and weighed down by them.[28] So also the visions and forms of angels and of God himself take a shape appropriate to the acts they are to do or to the bearing of those they are to meet, even when they are saints. But those revelations are especially to be accepted which were revealed generally to the saints and are not at odds with Holy Scripture

117

and good reason, particularly if they are in accord with the visions of the saints recorded in Scripture.

About the third class of objects suitable for meditation [conjectures from the doctors] I say only this: They are to be purged and received according to their differences and gravity. At the outset there should always be some hesitation present, a certain measured reticence and no sudden adherence. There should persist something of the academic temperament with its "perhaps," "maybe," "probably," "likely," "reasonably," and so on. Afterward it will suffice to maintain an engrained, if not constant, attitude of distrust and skepticism. So much, then, on hesitancy and temperament. For the rest this class and the second are to be purged from error, just like the fourth, though generally it is not mixed with as many errors. But look out for stubborn persistence in your own understanding, which is to be feared here. Always take up the more reasonable and obvious view of the saints. These two are likewise to be purged of images, just as was explained concerning the first class, so that pure truth in accord with faith and knowledge may descend directly through the means of the Almighty into the faithful soul according to the reasons inherent in those images. May this pure truth, purified of all falseness, be preserved, hoped in, and loved to the glory of Almighty God who is blessed throughout the ages. Amen.

PART TWO

The Devout

CHAPTER ONE

Edifying Points of the Older Sisters[1]

Here follow some of the edifying points of our older sisters. It is good to hold their lives before our eyes, for their ways were truly like a candle on a candlestick, casting light upon all those in the house. The light fell not only upon those in this house but also upon all who saw their ways and with whom they spoke. It was evident at once that God ruled them from within, for all their external manners and morals attested to a devout piety. These were truly notable women, rich in virtue, and, as the wise man said, zealous for beauty (Eccl 44:6), though, as the Apostle said, not many were noble according to the flesh, nor wise, nor rich as the world judges such things (1 Cor 1:26). Yet they so perfectly possessed and attested to the true virtues that they never lacked for inner nobility and godly wisdom and true wealth. They were poor by birth, but made rich in virtue. And what they were in the eyes of God was evident from the fruits they produced, for from its fruit is the tree known (see Mt 12:33). Just as our dear Lord Jesus Christ converted the rich and the wise and the noble through his poor disciples and not the poor through the rich, so through these humble and simple children of God he drew many rich and noble together with innumerable other virgins and women into his service, thus establishing these poor sisters as their original root and lineage. We let it to others to tell about the coming of the rich and the noble, their true conversion and their progress in the virtues. We like to tell about the virtues of our poor and humble sisters, so much more the amazing because such are not often to be found among these poor and partly rural folk. Yet they possessed the right and true virtues, so purely indeed as if they had seen and read them right out of Holy Scripture and the saints' lives. But it was the Holy Spirit, who filled them, who had also taught and illumined them; and just as they were illumined, so they continued to illumine others, one in obedience, another in humility, a third in resignation, and a fourth in sisterly love, while the others seemed devoured by

121

the earnestness of the house of God (see Ps 68/69:10). They were thus so decorated that each seemed to have something special with which God had endowed her above all others.

Since we cannot have their presence among us in the body and it is most important to have their edifying lives present in our memory, we have written down some of their most noteworthy points, as we could hear and learn about them from the older sisters who were blessed enough to see and rejoice in their ways. Because some of them lived in our house so early that we could learn nothing for certain about them from those still living, and because some others died so early on, we have not been able to write everything about all of them that might have been edifying. Some were also so secretive and hidden in their virtuous ways that they seemed almost to "steal" virtues. At times they did all they could of humble and lowly work without sinning, even while they kept hidden and secret to themselves their grace and good works, so it could be said of them, "The beauty of the daughter of the king is already within them" (Ps 44/45:14). Others were like a candle on a candlestick and a hill that cannot remain hidden (Mt 5:14–15), and like, so to speak, the columns which helped to hold up this house. They were so edifying and godly in their ways and so wondrous to others that each tried not to be seen doing anything contrary to true virtue. They held their superiors in great respect; what they ordered or established, they took as ordered or established by God himself. They were poor in their own wills but rich in the virtues, simple in obedience but wise in counsel. And the Holy Spirit, simple and yet manifold, endowed each according to his good pleasure and their own natures and according to the degree that each in her youth had applied force and piously resisted evil desire. For you can be sure that those who were outstanding in virtue in their later years had brought considerable force to bear upon themselves in their youth: that is, that they had not given themselves over to rough joking, laughing, idle talk, and other kinds of flippancy—which, unfortunately, so many people who appear religious now yield themselves to, thus raising obstacles and resistance to the inflowing of the Holy Spirit, more even than people realize. For this very reason, alas, we also remain stranded and do not increase in virtues as they did who lived only a short time before us. Let us then sew up our old clothes so that the shame of our nakedness will not appear in public. Let us listen with inner desire to how these devout maidens of Christ, our fellow sisters, did their exercises, and not imagine it impossible to imitate what they did before us in this same place and at nearly the same time. Moreover, when we describe

and take in the lives and morals of good people, they seem in a certain
sense to go on living after death, and they awaken many from living
death to true life.

1. SISTER KUNNE GINNEKINS (d.1398)

Good sister Kunne was among the first to live here, not long after
our venerable father, Master Geert Grote. It happened that in her
time a great death broke out in Deventer so that on one occasion more
than fifty died on a single day. Since sister Kunne was ardent and
devout and her wealth was not of this world, she desired to be freed
and to be with Christ. And so whenever she went out into the city
to hear mass, she used to say with desire: "Dear Lord Jesus, when
will you come to my house?" This or something like it she said time
and again. After she had thus called out with desire for a while, she
gave herself to our dear Lord as one of the plague victims. Then Jesus
came and visited her too, and so she died, departing hence with Jesus
as she had long desired.

2. OLD GESE, OUR SISTER (d.1402)

Good sister Gese excelled particularly in this virtue, that she confessed her faults whenever someone spoke with her, as it is written:
"The just accuse themselves first of all" (Prv 17:17). It happened once
that a cleric came and spoke to her and as was her custom, she lamented to him her faults, saying that she was dull and failing, also
blinded, and did not confess her faults enough. The good father answered, "Well, sister Gese, I too have heard quite a little about that."
When this man had gone away, she said, "And who might have told
the good father about my faults that he should have heard about
them in Zwolle?" In her goodness and simplicity she failed to note
that she had herself told him.

When good sister Gese lay in her last illness, our worthy father
John Brinckerinck came to her and wanted to hear her confession;
after she had confessed, she wanted very much to partake of our dear
Lord. It was then Lent and the vigil of the Annunciation, when the
angel brought the news to our Lady, and since it was so near to
Easter, our father appeared somewhat hesitant. When sister Gese
heard that, she cried out of the great burning within her heart, "My
lord, is not this also the day the Lord has made?"[2] And he answered
warmly, "Yes Gese, this is the day the Lord has made." Then he
had our dear Lord brought to her from the church, and he gave him

to her. She became so ardent during this last illness that whenever she thought no one was looking she would get up on her knees in bed to pray. She did not live long after her communion.

3. SISTER GESE BROEKELANTS (d. 1407)

When good sister Gese Broekelants died, our worthy father John Brinckerinck said of her that she had set an example for all her fellow sisters in devotion, thoughtfulness, humility, modesty, sobriety, chastity, and tranquillity. While still living with her parents and not yet very old, she was promised to a man. When she heard about it, she was extraordinarily grieved and wept a good deal. Since she knew no person who could help her, she turned to our dear Lord. She went to church, prostrated herself before the holy sacrament, and prayed to our Lord that if he would remove this burden from her, she would be his serving maid forever. As she lay there and offered herself to our Lord, she thought she heard it said to her that she should leave for Deventer and ask for a place in Master Geert's house. Before she even rose from that place where she was praying, she dedicated her purity to God. How ardent and devout her ways were once she came here, that we have heard from Father John Brinckerinck in his witness to her. She was especially devoted to the passion of our dear Lord so that at times she would burst out into many tears, like a person no longer in control of herself, and she had sometimes to leave the other sisters. Once it was asked her in secret what she spent most of her time thinking about. She answered, "The passion of our dear Lord." She was amazed at the love he had shown to us, and this appeared to be her daily exercise, especially on Thursday evenings and throughout Fridays. On Sundays she used to think about the resurrection, as if each one were Easter morning. She was also so filled within with eternal life that the whole expanse of time was much too short for her and she could not restrain herself from rejoicing. Thus she once said to the sister who worked alongside her, "Can there be anyone in the world with so much wealth and so much pleasure that at just one moment they are as well off as some poor little beguine united from time to time with her dear Lord?" She went around with her head bowed and so turned in upon herself that it was if as she could see our Lord standing before her very eyes. She used often to say, "If I am conscious at death, I will surely rue the fact that in youth I did not give myself over more to denying and mortifying myself." At work, if she had a little time, she sat with folded hands. She was kindly, patient, and never sharp. She took careful note of her faults, and often confessed at the feet of our dear Lord. She used often to lament that she was a liar before him because she thought that she was never getting better. She observed silence so carefully that when she was about to tell something good she would say, "I feel inclined to talk, but let us for God's sake keep silent." When someone came to her while she was at work and told her something that was not necessary or not useful or that weighed upon her heart, this would prove very hard for her and she listened to it most unwillingly. She was very loving and drew others to the virtues, being herself exceptionally obedient, modest, and thoughtful. If she was sick, she remained so lovingly cheerful that no one else seemed to suffer from her sadness. When she lay in the illness from which she died, something happened that caused her considerable suffering. Then, one of the sisters said that she should run with it to our dear Lord, offering it and herself up, and that she should not turn herself much anymore toward other people—and then she would sense peace. She answered with such a happy heart and friendly face that the sisters there rejoiced in her words: "My trust lies in our dear Lord." As her death drew nearer, she got a kind of stroke or paralysis so that it seemed as if she had died. But when she came back to herself, she said warmly with a loving face and folded hands, "O good Jesus, where have you been so long?" And when death came over her, she seemed so joyful that it was as if she was laughing at it. That arose from her good conscience which she felt within her, for the Holy Spirit was bearing witness to her spirit that she was a child of God. When they reported all this to our father, John Brinckerinck, he answered and said, "Let her laugh freely, so that she may pass into eternity full of laughter."

4. SISTER NYESE FELIX (d.1411)

Good sister Nyese excelled in this virtue, that she liked especially to go to church and to hear the Word of God, or else to hear something narrated out of Holy Scripture. One time, after she had been to church and heard the preaching, she was so on fire from hearing the Word of God that it was as if she was literally burning. When another sister heard she was so kindled by hearing the Word of God, she also began to rejoice in our dear Lord and said, "All the sisters who become so ardent and devout over the Word and produce such fruit from it should be allowed to go to church." She was indeed a very ardent and devout person, and gave herself wholly to our dear Lord and to all the virtues. She had no external responsibilities or activities, but she sat humbly and spun a certain kind of cloth (*celicie*) and in this way gave herself to the Lord. She was an older person who had lived here along with almost the very first sisters, in the time still of John van den Grond [d.1392, first rector], so that she had suffered through much poverty and misery.

5. SISTER KATHERINE HUGHEN (d.1411)

Good sister Katherine was far along in years when she came to the sisters, for she was already over fifty years old. She was an ardent and devout person and took pains—because she had entered the Lord's vineyard in her eleventh hour—to give herself all the more ardently to the virtues, for she had spent her time in the world foolishly. She tried now therefore to retrieve twice as much: Just as earlier she had served the world with everything that was in her, so now she served our dear Lord with everything that was in her. She had once lived with people who were great in the world's eyes, and there she had grown accustomed to much worldliness and done all to serve her own pleasure. But when she came to join the sisters, she converted herself wholly to God and gave herself over to great humility and lowliness, as if she neither had nor had ever had great possessions in the world. For she saw what she had done and therefore counted as nothing what she now did in turn. Because she had joined fully in the idle pleasures of this world, she possessed all kinds of beautiful jewelry; this she brought along and gave to our dear Lady or elsewhere, as there was need. She was very loyal to our house. Because she wanted so very much that the sisters should receive her earthly possessions, she held on so powerfully in her final illness that she nearly died without the holy sacrament.

6. SISTER WIBBE ARNTS (d.1412)

Good sister Wibbe used to take care of the inner courtyard of our house, and this was her office. She did this humbly; it was her way of turning herself to our dear Lord. She was an elderly sister and had lived here a long time, but she walked about simply and plainly as if she were a very young sister. She was a plain and simple creature by nature, and she turned to our dear Lord in this same way. She was never sharp or complaining, and was never heard talking or murmuring about the things her superiors had charged or ordered. She did the work charged to her very devoutly and was at peace with it, allowing things to go up and down just as God and her superiors wished. She also spurred others on, according to their abilities.

7. SISTER LUBBE PETERS (d. 1413)

Good sister Lubbe was very ardent in admonishing when she saw sisters transgressing our good customs or doing other things contrary to good morals or conducive to further liberties. She was an ardent and upright woman, faithful in the things committed to her, for she used to keep watch over external affairs [procuratrix] so that she had many things in hand, producing a great deal of busyness. She had often to suffer from it, for she sometimes did not know where the means were to come from with which to buy the things that were necessary. It was in addition often humbling or even sharp for her when she had done something to the best of her ability—and it was as if she had done badly in it.

This same sister Lubbe Peters had a brother in Windesheim named Gerlach [There follows a long digression on this man, perhaps the most famous of Windesheim's authors, which concludes thus] . . . and because he was so outstandingly ardent and devout he wanted very much that his sister should give herself over to the true virtues. Therefore he used to send her writings from time to time, wherein he taught her how she should give herself over to suffering and dying and that she should not pour herself out excessively on those external affairs that she had in hand. In particular he wrote her a high and fine letter teaching her how to conduct and rule herself in all this busyness. [translated, III, 6]

8. ON SOBRIETY IN ALL OUR NECESSITIES

When this sister Lubbe was procuratrix and had to keep watch over external matters, as well as say her hours, there reigned such poverty and need in these external necessities that whoever had resolved to persist here to the end needed a very ardent spirit, with her foundations and resolutions firmly set upon our dear Lord. She had to trust to commit her flesh and blood and all else, for God's sake, or she would certainly not have been able to stand fast. When, for instance, someone was sent outside the house, she might well be so poor in clothing that she had to borrow from a sister, because she herself had nothing appropriate. There was a sister named Gese Brandes who had patched her best gray skirt with a bit of animal skin, as they were accustomed to do then; on holy days this was her best skirt, and on workdays she worked in it. Then she had no need to sew an additional strip over the front because the skin she had sewed on her skirt served to cover the whole bosom. When it happened that out of necessity a sister acquired something new, she conducted herself humbly and modestly as if it were the roughest kind of garment. Two of our sisters here had each one skirt from white wool with bits of gray woven in. They wore these skirts humbly and with more joy than many in the world who wear purple or silk.

One of these was that Gese Brandes, an old, ardent, and devout person, rightly called "afire" (Brant). She was at times so devout and turned inward at mass and also at table that the devotion she felt within she could not keep hidden without. Therefore she would have to leave the sisters and be by herself until the devotion had passed. The other sister was called Mette of Almelo, and she was also an elderly and especially humble person who walked in the fear of God. For whatever she did or thought, she had our dear Lord before her eyes and thought how she should guard against doing what might offend God. She was so humble of heart that whatever she did she considered as nothing. How she had given herself in her youth to mortification and self-denial, and how that was attested in works at the end of her life, is written up elsewhere.

At that time whatever anyone had necessary for ordinary use she had completely to use up before she received anything new. It was patched so many times that eventually you could see the cap and the undergarments and whether the cloth from which it was first made was rough or small. No one was to have more than one cap, and if anyone lost it, she was to go without a whole year for taking such poor care of it. And if anyone lost her pen she had to write for one year with a stick before she was given another.

The same was true in drinking, eating, and all the other human necessities, a rigor so great that we would think it impossible now to suffer something they regarded as great superfluity; but they were all content and no one complained as if they were subjected to some terrible judgment. One sister used to say that she lived here probably six years and had never seen salmon [then a relatively common item] on their table. Another sister used to say that she did not know how long she had lived here but had never eaten buttered fish from a stock pond. The younger sisters, who were thirteen years old, were to fast on Fridays as if we were in Lent. The sisters were often given watery shellfish on which they sometimes put oil and mustard; to get that was something special. For a long time they ate a spiced dish that was thin and of poor quality, for they made it with a thin beer, roasted onions, and oil and vinegar. One time there was a good sister in the kitchen named Griete te Baerle. She took compassion on the community, and secretly fetched some better beer from the tapped barrel, wanting to put that in the spicy dish in place of the thin beer. Just then Mother Bertha came in the kitchen and saw what was happening. She heartily scolded her and said, "Do you think you should serve up things you did not find here and which are not the custom here?" After she had been scolded, Griete had to take the beer away and might not put it in the dish. The sisters were also sometimes given a bree made with crumbs from heavy rye bread; there was nothing else in it than the large yellow roots people call carrots, to which was added a little fish, but not much. Sometimes a little watery shellfish was also scattered over that. This bree tasted so bad that some sisters dreaded eating it for a whole week in advance. Because they could not use various costly and heavy spices, some became quite frightened that their natures simply would not be able to hold out. Even those accustomed only to cruder things and who knew nothing of the fine found it a hard job to hold out.

But they had nourishment within that people could not see from the outside: the holy and humble life and passion of our dear Lord Jesus Christ. They made every effort to take that in, and took it up with their whole hearts. That made everything sweet, and they accepted with joy whatever they were given, happy to suffer want in the name of Jesus. One sister used to say that she went away from the table so hungry that if she had had a piece of black bacon (or pork fat) she would gladly have eaten it. The sisters were often weak and sick; it would doubtless have gone better for them if they had had more to put in their mouths. Never or very seldom did they eat "raisin meat" [a special dish associated with holidays] except maybe on a Sunday, and that was then made from pickled meat left over from a previous meal—though if that were not enough, they would buy a little fresh meat in addition. On those days when they ate meat in the evenings they were allowed no butter on it, for that would have seemed extravagant. The sisters were given such great dishes of vegetables (chiefly kraut) and porridge at table that one old sister named Sweene Hoetyncks, an extraordinarily devout and religious person, used to say that she was initially so put off by these great dishes that she nearly left the sisters. Sisters who had been lying in the infirmary and had just returned to the dining room received at first such little dishes that if they were to receive the small dishes now given the common sisters they would have accepted them with thanks and thought it some great privilege and kindness shown to them. For at that time the sick did not receive half of what the healthy receive now.

They could also bear what we could hardly suffer now. Once a sister was very ill, and she wanted to eat grapes. She asked Mother Barten ter Clocken therefore to give her "discipline" and permit her to break some grapes off the grapebranch. This was denied her so she had to suffer through it. This same sister was once sent out under obedience. When she returned to the house and sat down at table to eat, she had no desire to eat because she was still tired from traveling. Another good sister went up in mercy and wanted to offer her an egg from the kitchen. This was also denied her and she had to bear with what was put before her. When such things happened to the sisters they were not reduced to bitterness or turned away, nor did they condemn their superiors as unfeeling or without compassion, but they turned themselves warmly to our dear Lord who enters and draws nearest to a troubled heart. They had therefore no evil passions within and showed no unworthy behavior outward toward others, for they did not take it as from a person but as ordained by our dear Lord in all eternity for their best and as something that had to be. They found peace thus in all things, and afterward encouraged others who had suffering and mortification to bear.

At that time as well, four sisters shared one beer mug [lit. can] at a table, for no sister as yet had her own mug. There was so little beer in the mugs that each sister could hardly get two good swallows of beer at a meal. Otherwise they had to drink the thin beer at every meal, a beer so thin that a young sister just arrived once drank her beer and did not recognize it as beer.

Such was the sobriety in eating and drinking and the other necessities at that time. In the same way our superiors sought in the people they accepted only and purely our dear Lord. They looked not upon coins or the blessing of wealth or worldly profit and pleasure, but only the honor of God and the house's spiritual progress in the virtues. They observed only the person, and considered whether an inner fire and devotion would work in them, looking not at all upon the coins as to whether they were rich or poor. In fact they were much more favorable to a poor young woman and much more helpful in bringing her here, for they felt she would give herself over to the virtues and would conduct herself right humbly and modestly among the sisters—more so than a rich young woman, about whom they had other feelings. Indeed it once happened that a wealthy young woman truly wanted to come here, but she could not gain acceptance despite the best of intentions. And the main reason was

the sisters' fear that the true virtues and the first principles on which
this house was founded and on which it stood should become less-
ened and even put to sleep by way of temporal goods. But they were
so kindly and good-willed that some of this kind were allowed to live
here, if they wanted humbly to do so and would give themselves over
to the true virtues, since these women had themselves received their
wealth for nothing and another [the community] was therefore permitted in turn to receive it for nothing.

* * *

SISTER FYE VREYSEN (d. 1454)

Good sister Fye did not work long for the penny of eternal life, because she was quite young when she died and lived here about six
years. By nature she was friendly and personable. She put herself
out remarkably to serve the sisters where she could, and used often
to take work out of the hands of the older sisters—and so quickly that
when one thought to do it she already had it done. Yet she used to
think she was the laziest of all and to lament that. Because she was
so loving and ever ready to serve, she was loved by all the sisters.
She spent most of her time in the workhouse, where she proved herself so well suited that everyone was glad to work alongside her. If
she was next to someone who seemed not so strong, she often did
much of the work for her, and then acted so kind and friendly as if
someone had done it all rather for her. No one ever heard her complain or grumble that she thought something was too much or anything of that sort.

Once it happened that she went out to a friend to see about some
matters there. Because she was friendly and pleasant, her friends
were also kindly and good mannered. But she was still young and
had not visited much in the world, and the flesh and the devil and
the world can prove very distracting from the good. She would probably have gladly been something in the world, which also distracts
from a good will and a firm resolution. The result was that after she
returned to the house she never again had the same love for this way
of life. She became progressively sick in the body and declined from
day to day until she finally died.

We have said this to point out that we should be very careful
and anxious about going often to spend time with our worldly
friends, who have no taste for the things that belong to the spirit of
God. We should not fall into a passion or displeasure if on occasion

a superior denies us the right to go off somewhere to please our nature. They often perceive things unknown to us, and see that almost nothing is so harmful to us as frequent visits with our worldly friends, especially those who have sunk the roots of their hearts into the love of this world and hold nothing greater than temporal well-being. To go around much with such people when you are still young and inexperienced and not yet firmly rooted in the good virtues is nothing other than a kind of sweet poison or drink of death, for it often brings on the death of the soul and a return to things once spit out, and thus such people become unworthy of the kingdom of God. And if by the mercy of God they are bound in their bodies to some religious state, they will eventually develop such a distaste for the good virtues that they can never or for a long time again win them, and begin thus to go bad in their souls. For the spiritual things in which they should be enveloped have no taste for them, and that which would give them pleasure according to the flesh they cannot get. They are therefore like those who sit uncertainly between two tables and fail to get enough from either.

SISTER HEYLEWICH VAN GROLLE (d. 1454)

Good sister Heylewich was especially conscientious about her work and always ready to take up something humbling, heavy, or rejected. She lived here in the house from early on, at the time the convent in Diepenveen was first founded. In the beginning she did very heavy work there such as digging, carrying sand, and other heavy work better handled by a man than by her. She did the same here, for whenever there was something heavy or filthy she was always the first and the last one at it. One summer she sat and combed out wool for fourteen weeks straight and was never replaced. She paid such close attention to her work and was so faithful at it that she always knew in the midst of it exactly what time of day it was. She was so industrious that no one ever saw her idle at work, and yet she remained so compassionate and sensitive toward others who could not do their work so well that it appeared she would gladly have done some of theirs if they could thereby be relieved. She was so sensitive toward others that she could never think or judge them as doing anything other than their best. Her outward manner was so lowly and humble that it almost seemed right that she should have the heaviest work to the end. Moreover, she was careful to maintain silence during her work. If anyone asked something she answered decently, but if it was nothing she simply kept silent. During work she was anxious and desirous to say her prayers, because afterward she read or thought something good about our dear Lord or the Holy Scriptures. In this she was so conscientious as to set a good example for the sisters who worked alongside her. She was most humble and unpretentious in her clothing, satisfied with the most basic necessities. For all that she possessed was, as it were, the good virtues; her external manner said clearly that her riches were not of this world. She was modest and humble in her morals and so self-effacing about things she needed that she might have been one of the young sisters.

By nature a kindly and merciful person, she could not easily bear to see someone suffer need or difficulty and would have rather suffered it herself, letting the other have her possessions and necessities. She was merciful and compassionate toward the poor and held those sisters in especially high esteem who showed kindness and favor toward the poor. This mercy and sensitivity was not limited to people but extended as well to nonrational animals. When snow lay on the ground in the winter and the birds could not get what they needed, in her compassion she would become so miserable herself that she could hardly hide it. Feigning thirst or when she thought no one was looking, she would bring the little birds something to eat in the public square. Because she was so kindly to them, she knew each of the little birds as if they were people. Whenever therefore she walked over the square or any other place outside the house, the birds came flying to her so totally unafraid as if she were another St. Francis. And when it was said that she should do this no more, she replied emphatically, "Please, dear God, be kindly to them, for this is their heavenly kingdom and they will have no other." As if she meant to say: Because they were created by the Good Lord like us, and are to have nothing more than their daily necessities, so they should always be granted as much as they needed in order to maintain their livelihood. For it was by nothing other than the goodness of the Creator that we were made rational creatures, without any foregoing merit, and it was by his will and goodness that each creature was created and shaped according to his good pleasure.

SISTER TRUDE VAN BREDA (d. 1454)

Good sister Trude was most faithful and careful in watching over our common goods, taking great pains to see that nothing should be neglected through her guilt. She was so conscientious about this that if she ever found so much as a feather she would have snatched it up and found a good place for it. She was very humble and frugal in all things she used, trying to give no opening or cause for superfluity. She patched up her clothing in the plainest manner and humbly wore it so long as she thought there was anything left of it. The same carried over into her books and all her other possessions, humble and cast-off things decorated with the virtue of poverty. She was industrious at work and never seen to be idle during work time. She loved work together with the profit it brought herself and others: She knew that working monks confronted but a single devil while the idle were attacked by innumerable demons. She was quiet and of few words, with little to say, especially during work; she tried to carry on in religious solitude, for she noted that where there are many words there will also be no lack of sin. As St. Augustine said: "Where there is much silence, there is much spiritual strength; and where there is much talking and chatting, there is often much quarreling and a lack of peace." Since good sister Trude saw this for herself, she was very careful to preserve silence in herself and also with others. When she heard useless talk, therefore, she would faithfully admonish about it.

SISTER FENNE WILLMYNCK (d. 1456)

Good Sister Fenne was still very young when she came to Master Geert's house, but she tried to overcome her youth with the morals of the elderly and the mature. She gave herself over to our dear Lord and to all the virtues so ardently that no childishness was to be seen in her. When she was still young and had not lived here long, she often made a good resolution with other sisters to admonish one another faithfully if any did something contrary to our good customs. They also concentrated on other good points so as to grow in the virtues. When they learned something good or were admonished for some fault, they would make a pact together zealously to receive this good point and persist in it or to improve themselves in that point over which they were admonished. In these particular good points sister Fenne, sister Ysentrut of Mekeren, and sister Marie of Tiele and a few other devout seemed nearly like elderly and experienced sisters. Even as sister Fenne laid these foundations for the upbuilding of her spiritual edifice, so she persisted to the end, zealous and determined to bring it all to completion. She was particularly modest and self-effacing about all ordinary necessities so that sometimes people had to press upon her the things she required. Moreover, the house of Master Geert was no little better off through her, for our claims to the property at Willmynck came by way of her.

At one time she had a very poor outer fur garment, which she wore humbly and without murmuring; she actually thought it was much too good to have another. When she was told under obedience to ask for a new one, she was so ashamed that she burst out crying. She was most industrious and conscientious about her work. She sat on her stool and worked until she was an old woman, indeed almost to the very end of her life. Friendly and warm with others so that the other sisters liked to work alongside her, she was always modest and self-effacing, difficult to no one insofar as it depended upon her. She was very plain in her clothing and all she used, especially in her books. She had a book of hours made from sheepskin rather than from parchment, and all her other books were plain and unpretentious in the old style. Even though she was humble and lowly in the things she used herself, she was right generous to others. No one ever heard in anything, small or great, that she grumbled because some had or did more than she. She was a good, sweet, and openhearted person, never nasty to anyone behind her back and to her face. She had a practice that if she heard anything likely to belittle someone she would express something else in praise of the person apparently belittled so as to raise her up in another's heart. She was loving and modest in admonishment, almost as if she were asking someone to make amends. She was just as modest in admonishing younger sisters, though she was herself one of the oldest and most venerable, from the time still of Father John Brinckerinck. If someone was publicly humiliated or shamed, she had such compassion and was herself so sad about it that it seemed she would cry. She would then seek to speak and bring peace, so far as possible, and to minimize the fault, for another's humbling affected her as if she had herself been shamed. She so avoided selfishness in her eating that she sometimes humbled others, because whenever she could she took the most undesirable things and was so generous to others sitting next to her that it seemed she could not bear to see them having anything other than the best. In this she acted the same toward the very youngest as toward the oldest sisters, to the point where it was often said of her as a fault that she made too much fuss at the table. But then she conducted herself so humbly and modestly that it seemed a great injustice to say any such thing about her, for she thought that she had only the most basic necessities coming to her. When the sisters were together—for instance, when they said the hours—she often went to sit with the youngest. There she was altogether common, friendly, and kindly, as if it truly pleased her to be with them. When the sisters first began to sleep above the dining room and the places were newly assigned, one sister asked her, "Sister Fenne, in which place would you prefer to sleep? It is your choice." She replied, "Dear sister, the places are all good, and I do not want to choose any particular one nor to make any difficulty for the superiors about this. Wherever they think I can best be, I will gladly go and be content." She was thus a poor and unusually friendly and helpful maiden, who asked for a place where she would be no hindrance and where our house would receive no disadvantage from it. In this way she was always very loyal to the superiors and to all the sisters in the house. She had charge over the books, and there she proved especially mild and kindly, giving each one what she wanted and what might be useful to her, so that no one, young or old, was afraid to go and ask her for what she preferred. She was herself so able in Holy Scripture and read with such zeal that our superiors said of her: She sits and reads Holy Scripture like someone picking apples and putting them in a basket. When she read at mealtime, she sat and read as if she had the whole of Holy Scripture by heart. After she had provided us with this good example of the virtues, she became sick with jaundice. As she speedily and quite unexpectedly came to her end, she said, "How short a person's life seems when the end comes."

The Chronicle of the Brothers' House at Emmerich[3]

JOHN OF MUNSTEREIFEL

In the year of our Lord 1481 our beloved brother John died. He was the son of John Plesh, a priest from Munstereifel, a town in the land of Julich formerly called the minster of St. Chrysantus because in the collegial church there the head and greater part of her body together with the holy virgin Caria lay honorably buried. From childhood brother John received many gracious gifts from the Lord. By nature he was lively and light [lit. "airy"] with a good memory and a bright mind. But as a youth in his paternal home, not yet knowledgeable in the ways of the Lord, he trained that nature to horsing around and trickery. He so applied himself in boyish games that he had hardly any second in playing, in pushing his weight around, or in deceiving simpler playmates. He was made a choirboy in the local collegiate church, and because of his quick and lively nature he proved most pleasing to its canons and lords. When he reached sixteen years of age, his parents sent him to Deventer to pursue his studies. There he began to associate with our brothers, in whose company he rejoiced, and was so reined in by them that he suddenly became another young man. Virtue and truth came to please and gratify him in a way for which his worldly and, so to speak, natural vanity formerly had no taste. He began to cling heartily to the virtues, so that all his liveliness and quickness, which once hung upon the vanities of this world, were now bound over fervently to divine teachings. On completing his studies he requested most affectionately that the brothers in the house of Lord Florens grant him a place there, asserting that their way of life greatly pleased him inwardly. And what he expressed in word he demonstrated in deed to the end of his life. He continued to love and to commend this way of life, even when in the course of time a number of less favorable developments occurred.

When, for instance, rumor of this decision reached his parents

and relatives, they were no little disturbed and tried first by letter
and then by messenger openly and in secret to influence the spirit of
this young man and to recall him to his homeland. He had a certain
uncle who held a canon's post in the church of Munstereifel; a venerable and industrious man, he loved his nephew most tenderly.
From the chapter he now sought a certain parochial church not far
from Munstereifel called Kirspenich for the use of his nephew John,
promising even to see him promoted in due course to a seat in the
collegiate chapter if only he would return home within a year—and
more in this same mode. But John persisted in the work he had taken
up without the least wavering, and seems hardly to have taken any
notice of such things. Nor did he become upset, dejected, or perplexed, as young men and novices sometimes do in such cases. He
leaped over all the snares set for him with his innate energy and good
spirit.

He was also very open-hearted. He never received any letters
or messengers in secret but immediately disclosed all without any
falsehood or duplicity to the rector of the house or some other superior. He completed his year of novitiate during Christmas 1468
and was received into the brotherhood of the Lord Florens house.
Since at that time our house in Emmerich was just begun and it was
necessary to provide it with many people, the venerable Father Peter
of Utrecht was sent from Deventer to serve as rector, and John of
Munstereifel was appointed to accompany him on the journey because of his industry and ability as a copyist. He had also a capacious
spirit, equipped above others to bear the miseries and discomforts of
this our new plantation. And though he left Deventer most unwillingly and sadly, preferring entirely to live and die among the brothers who had first received him, he humbly obeyed our venerable
Father Egbert and all the other brothers who insisted upon this decision.

When he arrived at the new place, he took great care to preserve
in himself and others all that he had heard and seen in Deventer. He
kept most carefully the time prescribed for work [that is, copywork]
for he had a good and agile way and wrote most willingly. Since we
were few, the office of brewing was also assigned to him. As time
required, he sought to carry out that work with great quickness but
also with decorum and religious good cheer, as indeed he did all his
work, so that the brothers who came to help him found the burden
of labor lightened by his pleasant ways and talk. Even though he was
most able in this kind of work and most useful to our house, because
we had still only two priests John was soon ordained to the priest-

hood by the common consent of our father and brothers. He then began to agitate vigorously with the fathers and brothers in Deventer as well as with those in our own house that we look to procuring a great gathering of young clerics and to promoting our school. We could thereby persist in our calling according to the institution of our venerable forefathers and become littles ones among the little ones, for the attraction of the young in this way lay greatly upon his heart. He was gracious in speech, and both the clerics and the people liked to hear him when he gave addresses [collations] in our church because he was wholly unintimidated on such occasions and spoke most openly and effectively.

He had a certain inclination or rather a natural disorder in the early morning hours so that often when he went to church to say the hours with the brothers, as is our custom, he would suddenly be overcome with such sleepiness and such heaviness in the head that he could hardly read or sing or even hear what was being read by others. But he resisted that passion so manfully, or at least tried to, that sometimes, between reading and falling asleep, he nearly fell prostrate out of his chair into the choir. He rubbed his ears, exercised his legs, bared his head, and shook his whole body almost like a rooster in an effort to drive the sleep out of him.

Over time, as he grew to enjoy this way of life to which he had been called, he took ever more delight in our daily routines, especially in the material prescribed for each day's meditation and the exercising of the Lord's passion during mass, as well as in the loving and humble conduct of the brothers toward one another. The more he preferred this life for its simple attraction of the young and the simple, the less he could bear in good spirit the irrational attacks on our way of life that used sometimes to occur. It was wondrous and commendable how he remained firm to the end in his resolution and his love of our way of life, without any wavering, even though he had been endowed by God with so many and such rich gifts and possessed a special grace in nearly all things. He was a good writer in every aspect of the copyist's work, he was a good singer, he was apt at giving addresses [collations], he was gracious in all conversation, and most intelligent in all matters spiritual or temporal.

Indeed he used to read and memorize the writings that approved our common way of life, so that at opportune times he would have something with which to contradict those disparaging it. I remember a certain time when we went together to the diocese of Cologne on business for our house and we came to a certain prelate, a man renowned throughout Germany for his letters, who was also a canon of the churches of St. Mary's and St. Andrew's in Cologne as well as of saints Chrysantus and Dari in Munstereifel. Because he knew both our parents he began in a teasing way to say many things about our way of life, asserting that we were less than wise to get side-tracked into such a way of life when there were so many royal monasteries to be found wondrously provided with revenue, fields, buildings, and all other temporal necessities. If, he said, you wanted simply to provide your food and clothing by the work of your own hands, as it is now necessary for you daily to do, what was the point of your parents giving up so much expense and wealth to send you to school all those years? Would it not have been better for you to remain in your parents' home from childhood and there to have extended them a helping hand as they earned their bread by the sweat of their brows? And still more things along this line. To everything that popped into this canon's mind and fell from his mouth, our beloved brother John responded so rationally and effectively and with so few words that the man stood astonished, just looking at John. Though he could discover nothing with which to respond by way of counter-argument, he never totally ceased arguing while we were still present, lest the students standing around judge him vanquished. But once we went away—as I afterward heard from those there—he began in the presence of all to extol the genius of our brother, saying that he never would have thought that such things as he had now discovered lay hidden in his heart. Indeed from this discussion the man so progressed himself that our way of life, which he had formerly disparaged, he began now to extol and recommend.

John was moreover full of love for his fellowman, which he showed particularly in this way: Whenever work or a journey gave opportunity to talk with young students, he immediately turned the conversation to some edifying or admonishing word. This by his natural ability he did so discreetly, choosing all his words so appropriately, that he edified those around him while relieving the tedium of time, work, or travel.

So far as was evident on the outside, he also carried out all his abject, humbling, and filthy work with great good cheer. Thus when Theodore de Wiel, our founder, began to live with the brothers near the end of his life, our brother John was assigned to minister to him, and each morning before the first mass he had to carry out the pot full of excrement and fluid accumulated during the whole night. What could provoke nausea in some of us only by sight, John carefully and faithfully handled as if he paid it no mind and it were something else.

John used to complain most humbly and sadly about his impatience, claiming that by his natural makeup he was too easily moved to anger and aroused emotions, but he manfully worked to resist such impulses. If on some occasion he had words with someone—which even in congregations like ours, according to St. Bernard, it is difficult to avoid—he did not defend himself at once by aiming some sharp reply at the other or, as others do, wrinkling up his forehead and drawing up his nostrils; but conscious of his own frailty and natural inclination, he bowed his head and sought refuge in silence and flight, thus, as a man having no arguments in his mouth (see Ps 37/38:15/14) refusing to make more words when he sensed himself upset. Departing from the scene of the battle as one conquered, he returned to his room and rejoiced in having gained the victory. But when in the nature of human frailty he was on occasion hard or stubborn toward someone, he would rise up wondrously within himself and, as if he had himself suffered violence, would try in turn to inflict force upon himself. Never long dejected, perplexed, or bitter, he would then, without any lengthy deliberation, approach the brother whom he had perhaps offended and on bended knee seek forgiveness, as our customs require. And then, with a resolution to do better, he would at once be restored to peace. He used to say, therefore, that it is good sometimes for a spiritual man to knock his head against the wall and to come back to his senses, thus gaining a better knowledge of himself and greater caution. But in all cases and adversities, he seemed to have a certain natural magnanimity so that just as quickly as by an infirmity he transgressed in some human passion he would strive, without perplexity or dejection, to reconcile himself through reason to God, his neighbor, and himself by repenting of his evil action and making a firm resolution to do better in the future. All bitterness of soul thus driven out, he regained his balance, as if nothing had happened, whence with a happy face and a light heart he often quoted that saying of a certain one of the devout: Man is a rational and noble creature, endowed with a great spirit, and therefore with a natural love for ascent and the heights.[4]

I have often marveled that a person so lively and light in nature and so gracious in conduct should nonetheless also be so pure and chaste in his ways and life. I knew him from earliest days when he was still greatly inclined as a youth to horsing around, but I never was able to discover any impurity in him in word or deed nor any inclination to the flesh. And even though by reason of his office as brewer he had to confer sometimes with the sisters, he did so with few words and a disciplined visage.

In his free time he also cultivated and delighted in his cell; he was dedicated to the study of Holy Scripture; and during work time very assiduous in his copy work. But he used to say that as much as he liked to read Holy Scripture he could not stay at it very long, that is, at one time, without burdening his head. Yet at intervals he committed himself to attentive study.

In the course of time John was frequently assigned to minister to the brothers in the infirmary, which he did with all care and alacrity, sparing himself neither by day nor by night. For it was he who watched over John of Wiel, the natural son of our founder, when he became sick with the plague, and our beloved brother, the cleric Bruno of Weda, afflicted with the same disease. He ministered faithfully to both up to the last days of their lives. With our venerable and beloved father, Peter of Utrecht, he remained through the night from the feast of St. Michael until the vigil of St. Nicholas while he suffered badly from the stone and other ailments so that, indeed, through that whole time I thought I never saw John undress but always simply sleeping in his clothes.

After his laborious and praiseworthy sojourn among the brothers, in the year of our Lord 1481, his thirty-third year and just the point when he began to reach a manly maturity, he fell into a grave illness, the occasion of which will be described here. At that time war broke out between the people of Cleve on the one hand and the Gelders together with the lord of Gemen on the other so that we could not use our pastures above the river Reka for our cows as we normally would, nor could we cultivate the land because no one from Emmerich dared go far from the city with horse and plow in fear of incursions from soldiers. We were forced therefore to have that pasture enclosed with fences. Because there was much hay and few of us, nearly all stayed out in the field from morning to night working at drying the hay. And though it was summer time, around the feast of Mary Magdalene [July 22], the instability of the air and frequent rain showers made it seem cold as autumn. Our beloved brother John went out to work one day in his usual way with the brothers. He dressed himself in a simple tunic with another light garment because it was handier for work. The air was serene from morning until the ninth hour, but then a heavy rain shower began to fall, and the brothers, wet from within with sweat, were drenched without from the rain. They rested for a short time in the pasture under a hedge in the hope that good weather would return, but the air became heavier and heavier as if it would prove a long shower and so the brothers were forced to give up their work and return home. That very day, indeed that very hour, our brother John began to feel very poorly in his body, and from that hour—which was and is deeply to be lamented—to the end of his life he became sickly and his whole body infected. We gave medicines and consulted doctors, but nothing helped. John remained of good spirit and very content, giving thanks in the midst of this infirmity and visitation. Though he held on until around Christmas he was never again totally well. Because he was an intelligent man, he himself sensed that his body was becoming steadily weaker. He made every effort therefore to reform and to compose his inner man, as one who was to appear shortly before the face of his Lord God and Creator. He did not stay lying in bed, but so far as strength allowed he performed all our spiritual and corporeal exercises day and night. And when he became less able to manage heavy external labors, he became all the more solicitous about the work of his room and about keeping up still his copy work. For he had in hand a fine and beautiful missal for the diocese of Utrecht, which he had begun earlier and now very nearly finished with his own hand. He conceived a great desire to finish this book entirely before the end of his life, and he was not denied his desire. On the vigil of St. Thomas the apostle [December 19] he finished that book in complete rejoicing.

Though he was sick, little thought was given to his approaching death because he continued to walk among the brothers in his usual way, carefully observing the hours, the mensa, and other communal exercises. Indeed, on the very day he finished the missal, when the common brothers had been called together in the father's room to examine their faults, as was customary, John wanted also to be present. He humbly listened to the faults charged him by the brothers, confessed his guilt devoutly, and begged forgiveness. The examination finished in due course and the hour being late, each returned to his cell to settle in quietly. That same night around the twelfth hour our beloved brother John began to feel powerful cramps and pains in his chest, as if pulled and shaken by terrible weights. Rising with what strength he could muster, he dressed himself, roused one of the brothers who stirred up the fire, and they sat together around it until the hour when all arose. Once the matin praises had been sung, a rumor circulated among the brothers of John's serious and sudden illness. They went to him, still sitting by the fire in the kitchen, and found him laboring with great tightness in his chest. He turned to the brothers, and though he could hardly articulate his words properly owing to his short and labored breath, he said to them: "Until now, dearest brothers, I had no fear of death because

I did not know what it was, but during this past night I suffered such cramps in my chest that I am now terribly frightened in the face of death. If such grave pain was only its prelude, what shall I do when it swells to full strength and opens its mouth wide to devour me entirely?" All this he expressed, breathing laboriously at times and interrupted with great sobs and sighs. He received consolation from the brothers and was brought at once, on the vigil of St. Thomas [December 20], to the infirmary. When he entered it, he cried out in a raucous voice but with a heart moved and seemingly restored, "Thanks be to God, thanks be to God! This place is surely holy where all our devout and holy men have died!" He meant our venerable fathers Peter of Utrecht and John Medenblick, who in this same place and indeed in that same bed had passed to their eternal peace with John present and in fact himself holding the candle in their hands.

When therefore hour after hour without any surcease he twisted in agony from ever stronger cramps in his chest, all things were put in order and toward vespers he received the last anointing with all of us present. He humbly begged forgiveness from the father and brothers for all things done amiss or left undone. During the anointing he had laid back on the bed, but that done he immediately asked his brothers to help him climb out of bed and take his seat, for he was no longer able to lie down or stretch out owing to the terrible cramps that gripped his chest. Seated and with his head resting on the lap of a brother next to him, he spent the whole night and following day, tortured by incredible pains in his chest. On the morrow of the blessed Thomas the Apostle, because he had now endured these pressures and cramps for two or nearly three nights without rest and with no food and little drink, he began noticeably to weaken and very nearly sank into death. With wild gestures and words when he could no longer articulate properly, he asked that something good be said to him or something read to him from Holy Scripture.

Toward the ninth hour the keeper of the church of Zeddam came to our house. A few days earlier he had brought a missal for preparation and illumination. Since no one could deal with him on the book or its price—for so long as John held the office of scriptor none of the brothers interfered in any way—we were forced quite unwillingly to disturb our brother in his hour of utter need with this other business. We were discussing this very quietly among ourselves, when John himself—whether he overheard us or sensed it in some other way, I do not know—suddenly ordered the register brought from his cell. Raising his head from the lap of his brother and taking the register in both hands, he opened it and without delay pointed to the place with his finger, saying: "This is the agreement reached earlier between us." All rose in astonishment at his strength and his magnanimity, that so near to death and oppressed by such sorrow he was still perfectly clear in his mind.

Then toward the eleventh hour, when it was thought he would give up the spirit any moment, John himself raised his left hand and took his pulse in his right. When we asked what he was doing, he responded: "Oh, that this pulse would cease and the end might come." But we admonished him that he should not bear bitterly this scourge of the Lord and that death itself should not be so onerous and unbearable to him since he had already suffered and died with the Lord Jesus Christ on the cross. He responded, in broken and interrupted words, with the saying of Job: "Even if he should slay me a thousand times over, I will still hope in him" (see Jb 13:15). Finally then, between the first and second hour after the meal, after a truly agonizing struggle, he came to rest in peace, in good confession and sitting in his seat, not lying in his bed.

Some of us thought he must have had an abscessed ulcer in his abdomen that the agony of death should have taken him with continuous cramps and pains in the chest that lasted without break from the vigil of the Blessed Thomas until the hour of his death, which was in the year of our Lord 1481, on the morrow of St. Thomas the Apostle around the second hour after the meal. He was buried the next day in our church, in the fourth gravesite, nearly in the nave.

* * *

HENRY EUSKIRCHEN

In the year of our Lord 1494 Henry Ryck died, our beloved brother from Euskirchen, a town in the land of Julich. This brother was the first procurator of our house for clerics and students [also called a "convict"]. He was a young man of a most lively nature, wonderfully agile and able in everything he chanced to take up and very intelligent and clear-headed for his years. He was received among us in all charity already in his early years, sent here by his brother, the venerable Nicholas Euskirchen, from the house of Lord Florens and the schools in Deventer. John Medenblick, our father at that time and a man most devout and discreet, saw his liveliness, aptitude, and suitability, and he feared lest the abundance and wealth of gifts God had bestowed on him should become the occasion for his ruin—if, as we see so often in such cases, they were to be turned rather to arrogance, presumption, audacity, and liberty. Like a good shepherd, our father fixed his eye upon that young man and took the extra care that seemed necessary, frequently admonishing, humbling, and correcting him and carefully instilling the fear of the Lord. But so as not to burden a spirit still so tender or to cast it into bitterness and despair by too much restriction, too sudden a reining-in of his lively nature, our discreet and venerable father gave him responsibilities in the bakery and the brewery and in turning over the grain laid out in the sun room. In these he soon took principle charge, for our beloved brother Theodore Everhard, who had held responsibility for those offices for many years, was now required by various events to make frequent trips outside the house and even outside the town, looking after sundry external matters, and he was therefore not in a position to maintain both. Henry took up these responsibilities with alacrity and care. He set everything in order, adjusted his time to his work, and not only completed what was expected but did it all expeditiously and well. The tools, vessels, and places assigned to his offices were kept in order as well as clean and decorous. He was cheerful at work and kindly toward the brothers assigned to help him. He was most faithful and hard-working, not sparing himself, and he was often wet with sweat over his whole body from his zeal and quickness at work. But he seemed hardly to notice and to care even less, for he would simply wipe his face with his bare hand and stick to his work in all happiness and good cheer.

He was, nonetheless, devoted to his cell, and as quickly as he finished his exterior work he returned there and applied himself to prayer, sacred reading, and other spiritual exercises in complete quiet, as if he had never been away or had no concerns or responsibilities outside his cell. He was thus completely ambidexterous, endowed by God with so many rich gifts that he was no less devout and attentive in spiritual things than he was lively and quick in exterior work. He had a certain exercise in the life of our Lord Jesus Christ, compiled himself, which ran from the beginning of his most gracious incarnation down through his most bitter passion and death, and he fitted to it each of the psalms said for our Lady. Though he had found none of these psalms so interpreted and used by the doctors of the church, it was not contrary to the faith and in my judgment it seemed well organized for simpler folks, good for avoiding wandering thoughts and loss of attention during prayer.

In time, under the care of our venerable fathers John and then

Theodoric, and after the natural impulses and liveliness of his spirit had become suitably tamed by long mortification and humble exercise, our father and brothers decided to establish a new house in the manner of our fathers in Deventer and Zwolle. They wanted to provide a place where young people coming to attend school could be taken in and brought up under our care, an institution, in short, where young men could at a tender age receive training in the fear of the Lord as well as in the sciences and in good morals.

In the year 1482 an area was cleared near the convent of St. Agnes away from our house, since the old domicile built there was wholly inadequate for meeting the needs of these youths. At the instance of our venerable father Theodoric and with the consent of the brothers, our beloved brother Henry was placed in charge of all the work and responsibilities for the new house ["convict"]. I think that if in our whole house we could have found anyone better suited we would not have spared ourselves or that person. For this particular exercise, this zeal and labor to work with youth and little ones, seems to excel all our other works in bringing honor to God and salvation to souls—if, that is, it is done rightly, in all simplicity and humility, in the manner of our venerable forefathers. For though still young, these souls are no less profited by training from childhood in the fear of the Lord and the knowledge of good and evil. That year, the first in Henry's priesthood, he assumed his new task between Easter and Pentecost, and collecting all the little packs he went off to the new house. Then the liveliness and quickness of his nature really became evident and expressed itself in action. He took up such an amount of work and showed such diligence and care for the young men together with their needs and progress that without his most singular and extraordinary mixture of natures and complexions, he would surely have succumbed to the burden. In a short time clerics and youths from various lands, cities, and towns were streaming to him, and he alone was their procurator, their instructor, and their provider in all things. Beyond the hours to which he was bound daily as a priest, each morning and night he also said the hours of the holy cross with supplements in the chapel. Each day he worked through three different exercises or examinations with the young people, not in an improvised or customary way but most effectively. For this he had indeed a most suitable and instructive manner. Hardly a day went by that he did not deliver a short but devout and ardent exhortation to the youth in the chapel, instructing them in the fear of the Lord. He had a telling way of instilling remorse, speaking first of death, then the severe judgment of God, then of hell and eternal damnation and all the rest, so that under him the youth began to advance notably in the fear of God as well as in learning and good morals.

The edifice or domicile which he first found was old and vile and inadequate to meet the youths' needs, and the area around it was still largely open and not bounded with walls or fences. Our purse, however, was still empty, providing no means to erect the walls necessary for keeping watch over these young men. But brother Henry came up with an idea. Once free time in the schools was finished and prior to the self-examination, he went to work. Dressed himself in light garb for labor and joined by all of his students, he took up spades and pikes. They dug a great ditch in the land and raised up a kind of earthen works fortified on top with a hedge full of thorns and prickers so no one could easily get out. He never spared himself in these or any other labors but persisted amazingly so that all he took in hand was not only finished but rightly and in good order. Our venerable father Theoderic would go there upon intervals, and though all that he found was simple and poor he took delight in its convenience, its right disposition, and good order. He rarely or never found Henry idle. Now he was digging wells and cisterns, then a pool in which the filth of the house and the rooms could be disposed, now he was piling up the earthen works and some other hills; he was ever planting and rooting up, building and taking down, so that even though his whole body was drenched in sweat he remained unwearied and happy. He was so happy in this kind of work among the youth that sometimes I felt bound to forewarn him against too great familiarity lest it breed contempt in their hearts. But he seems to have received such grace from God that to the end he always showed himself cheerful and yet edifying. He was therefore sincerely loved by the youth and still no less revered. He had a good mind for the Holy Scriptures, and he found much grist in them especially suitable for the exhortation and instruction of his little ones. He was wonderfully able to mold the youth toward conversion and instruction. Indeed he was untiringly in search of that which he thought might serve for their improvement, and he was ever very watchful over them. He excelled in genius and understanding so that he prospered, and seemingly without effort, in whatever he applied himself to.

In the course of time, owing to the ever greater assembly of youth coming to him, he began to extend the old home out both sides and to put extra rooms there so as to bring under one roof this notable multitude of young men. This house, to the front and back as well as to the right and left, seemed like an overflowing fish pond. More notably still, despite such a multitude of youths and such a limited and modest capacity in the house itself, everything in the house and around it remained so clean and well ordered that in appearance some rich people might have been living there from the proceeds of their wealth.

When our affairs in the school and in the new house seemed to be in the best possible shape from the viewpoint of human judgment and progress, and our brother Henry had been rendered all the more able and suited to his office through exercise and experience, in the year of our Lord 1493 between Easter and Pentecost, the plague began to rage in Emmerich. Fearing for his young men, Henry collected his things and put them and their beds on a ship and with the whole lot departed for Griethausen. Hiring a certain barn there for the modest and poor, he and certain others with independent means were taken in by that venerable and devout man, John of Haldern, then confessor to the sisters there. This father confessor had first been a brother in Harderwijk, a man altogether religious, simple, and just, who received our brother and his young men in all charity and who together with the whole convent faithfully supported the youth in their poverty. The Lord soon gave grace, however, so that the plague seemed to be under control in Emmerich, and Henry, who had departed so unhappily with his young men, returned happily. Then there came such a multitude of young men to us from all around that we were forced to provide another domicile with places to receive them.

In the fall of that same year Henry began to make provision for building by gathering mortar, beams, and other necessities, and so in May of the following year, on the day following the feast of our most blessed patron Gregory, we began to lay the foundations of the new house in both its width and depth, an area it seemed would be large enough. We were all lighthearted and joyful, especially Henry who as procurator had the business principally upon his heart. We proceeded so well in the erection of walls that toward the beginning of May nearly the whole foundation was raised all around. And then there came another change in things, as sudden as it was unexpected, and yet also to be revered as a judgment of God. Before May had ended, our brother Steven ter Beeck contracted plague and came to rest in the Lord on the day of Saint Urban. We were then all in great fear lest the young men should again be dispersed, and so far as possible we persuaded them to stay and to stand firm with us, hoping that God would spare and take this scourge from us. Nearly all were

content and stayed. In his customary way Henry continued diligently morning and night to do his exercises, his readings in the
chapel, and all the rest, sparing himself nothing and never fearing
lest in the summer heat he too should become infected in the midst
of such a crowd of young men. The chapel in which the young men
gathered was a narrow place without any breeze blowing through it.
In such times that seemed dangerous, and in the event, alas, those
fears were confirmed. For not many days later, the seventh or eighth
of June, our beloved brother Henry also contracted the plague. Grief
and sadness gripped us all, especially however our venerable father
Lord Theodoric and the honorable master Arnold of Hildesheim,
then rector at the school of Emmerich, both of whom loved Henry
dearly and were very concerned about the progress and promotion
of our school.

But Henry, like the great spirit he was, asserted that he was not
much indisposed and did not feel all that badly. Both he and we began to hope that it was not the plague but some other chance infirmity of the body. Seduced by that judgment, Henry continued to walk
about still for two days among the youth and among us, twice or
three times delivering readings to the youth. He also calculated,
computed, and signed for the greater part of the youth in his register,
as was clearly to be seen after his death. From there it is clear that
he certainly foreknew his death since he signed here and there in his
register with his own hand thus: Such and such a young man on the
day of my death owes so much. Though infection with the plague
was feared, he still seemed strong and able in body, whether in walking, standing, sitting, or doing things about the house in his usual
manner. He confessed however to a certain dullness in the head
which only increased from day to day. On the third day, finally,
there began to appear open signs and symptoms of the plague. From
that day he was brought from the new house to our house and placed
in the infirmary. There he remained, animated, content, and wholly
resigned. All of the responsibilities assigned to him he stripped totally from his heart from that moment, as if he had spent his whole
life in his cell and without any pastoral responsibilities. He converted himself devoutly to the Lord, to the blessed and glorious Virgin Mary, and to the saints, invoking and sweetly naming off our
patrons in particular. As the illness worsened, he devoutly received
the last anointing, and in full consciousness persevered in confession
of the Lord's name; he completed the days of his life on the eleventh
of June in 1494, the day of St. Barnabas the Apostle, around the
eighth hour in the morning.

At that same hour and moment our venerable Father Theodoric was standing at the altar in the convent of St. Agnes saying mass, carrying out the final exequies for that venerable man Cornelius of Mechelen, confessor and rector of that same convent, who had passed to the Lord on the evening of the preceding day. As he began to read the Gospel, we began in our church to ring the bell, as it was our custom whenever any of our brothers died. Since he was singing mass alone, he could easily hear the strokes, and he understood that our dear brother had passed. His voice began to break then and he wept bitterly, so he could no longer sing another note. Finally, gathering up his spirit, he proceeded to the end, not singing but reading the mass, and thus carrying out the office of burial and death for our venerable Father Cornelius.

Permit me to take a moment here to allude to the wondrous and secret judgments of our Lord God, not as if scrutinizing them in a reproachful way but rather as humbly venerating the inscrutable. It is quite amazing that our fathers and brothers had set out with a single will and labored at their own expense, to the honor of God and for the salvation of souls, to erect a school here in Emmerich to do exercises with boys and clerics just as our venerable fathers in Deventer and Zwolle had done. And now after much care and trouble, everything had been brought to a good state: We had a learned and suitable man for rector, the venerable Master Arnold of Hildesheim mentioned above; the city magistrates and townspeople began to look favorably on it; in our house we had in Henry a man truly so well suited to this work that, in my judgment, in a thousand people hardly his second could have been found; and in addition we had begun to prepare and erect a new house, longer and wider, in which to gather the youths streaming in to us. Then, behold, that zealous shepherd of our souls, our Lord God, as if totally unconcerned with all that we had in hand, which had just begun to flower, suddenly and unexpectedly threw it all into confusion and decline, nearly reducing it to nothing. For just as the sheep are dispersed when the shepherd is struck down, so when our beloved brother died the whole school was thrown into confusion. The youths left in swarms and almost immediately, each one turning into his own way, not it is to be feared, without some danger to their souls and damage to their progress. For we had among us then many very well suited youths, so that in all these years I think there were never before at one time so many and especially such good young men. Nonetheless, to him be the honor and the glory now and through the ages, to him whose judgments, though hidden, are yet never unjust. May he grant us in these and similar trials so to conduct ourselves that his scourge not repel or drive us away but only teach us. If this vexation was necessary, may he grant understanding to those hearing it in this present time, and may he not preserve our evils accumulating to the end lest we be found in the number of those whom he reproached through the Prophet saying, "I struck you down and you did not grieve." Let him who bore a most punishing death out of love for souls turn that away from us. May he who first made the soul of our beloved, now returning to him, restore him to eternal peace for his faithful service and the great labors he expended. He was buried before the altar of the apostles in our church in the second gravesite.

PART THREE

The Devotion

CHAPTER ONE

A Customary for Brothers[1]

These are the customs of our house, the practices kept there and diligently observed by our predecessors, so as to promote peace, harmony, and progress in the spiritual life among ourselves and our successors. We have decided to gather them in an orderly way into these few pages [lit. this quire], lest they fall into oblivion among ourselves and our successors or through declining fervor cease to be practiced. By constant renewal they are meant to preserve our discipline and good morals. For as Hugh of St. Victor said, "Virtue is only grasped when its discipline is kept without negligence." And even though we do not bind ourselves to the observance of these customs or those of any religious order by vows or public profession, someone found negligent or disobedient in these matters, thereby disturbing the peace of the house and giving occasion for a relaxed life, is nonetheless not without guilt.

[There follows the summary of a legal argument on the need for "customs" in any "house."]

The Foundation of a House for Persons Living in Common and Its Purpose
Faithful people founded and endowed our house so that devout men, priests, and clerics might live in common, leading a modest life supported by the work of their own hands [that is, as copyists] and their own revenues and ecclesiastical incomes; that they might together devoutly frequent churches, reverently obey their prelates and curates, wear humble and simple garb suitable to the clerical estate, diligently observe the canons and decrees of the holy fathers, zealously persist in the exercise of the virtues and of devotion, and show themselves examples to others beyond reproof. We seek in this way to offer God a pleasing and acceptable service, not only through our own upright way of life but also by the conversion and salvation of others whose hearts are moved to remorse by our warnings and example. True progress in the spiritual life requires purity of heart; lacking that, we strive in vain for perfection, which consists in love.

Let our greatest zeal and daily exercise be to progress in purity of heart. We should learn therefore to know ourselves first of all, to see without self-deception the vices and passions of our soul and to try with all our strength to root them out, to check gluttony, to restrain concupiscence, to overcome pride, to despise temporal things, to break our own wills, and to fight against any other seemingly invincible vices. Through it all we are to apply all our effort toward acquiring the true virtues, the humility, love, chastity, patience, obedience, and all else by which we become pleasing to God. This is the truer way and safer means of progressing in the spiritual life, just as the holy fathers already determined. You may read this most notably in the first collation of abbot Moses in the *Collations of the Fathers* and also in the *Progress of the Religious*, where it is said of the "Caathicis" whom it judges the best of the three kinds of religious[2]. To this way of progressing we must direct all our exercises: our prayer, meditation, reading, manual labor, vigils, fasts, exercises, and the composing of our inner as well as our outer man. Thus we may come to direct our way to the love of God and acquire a taste for eternal wisdom.

Materials For Meditation

Since the fear of the Lord is indispensable for those wishing to make progress—for he who is without fear will not be able to be justified (Eccl 1:28)—it is expeditious for each of us to reflect untiringly on those matters which provoke a man to the fear of God, namely, on sin, death, judgment, and hell. But lest constant fear, unrelieved by the hope of divine mercy, render a mind dejected and desperate, it is expeditious to intersperse other matters provoking hope and love of God such as the kingdom of heaven, the divine benefits, the life and passion of Jesus Christ. All these matters we are accustomed so to alternate that we meditate on sin on Saturday, the kingdom of heaven on Sunday, death on Monday, the benefits of God on Tuesday, judgment on Wednesday, the pains of hell on Thursday, and the passion of our Lord on Friday. It is also good to meditate on the passion each day during mass, beginning with the life of our Lord on Sunday and subsequently taking up some aspect of the passion each day, as we have mentioned. On major feast days, however, we conform ourselves to the Church Catholic, shaping our meditations and exercises around the matter of the feast day. To stir our memory on such days we are accustomed to read through some pertinent point at morning, evening, and night.

THE DEVOTION

The Hour of Rising and Preparation for Prayer

In the morning we rise together at the sound of the bell midway between the third and fourth hour. This we should do in a quick and lively way, shaking the sleep out of our eyes and remembering Jeremiah's words in Lamentations: "Arise, sing praises in the night at the beginning of your vigils, pour out your heart like water before the face of the Lord, lift up your hands to him" (Lam 2:19). We should offer the firstfruits of our thoughts to the Lord God in some upright thought, turning the intention of our hearts to the Lord. So composed and prepared, we are in a position to begin saying the customary hours and prayers, for that which we wish to find in prayer we must make preparation for before prayer.

Reading the Hours

On feast days the priests and clerics gather in the chapel to say the canonical hours of the Blessed Virgin. On ordinary days the priests read together, and all the clerics two by two, the hours of the holy cross together with those of the Blessed Virgin, saying the psalms for the dead at matins and the appointed prayers for vespers. We should read moderately and modestly, not too quickly or out of unison, but careful always to read uniformly and without confusion. And we should have ourselves composed in our members and movements, sitting down in a lively way, erect, avoiding clamor and noise as much as possible, so that we may complete the office of our prayers and hours devoutly and decently. We read matins and prime together, the rest until vespers separately, except that on feast days we also read nones together.

The Study of Holy Writings

The holy writings, written by the holy doctors, instruct us in the way of salvation and how we ought to walk in the path of God. They also move our affections and will to love virtue and flee vice as well as our memory to put away vain and harmful thoughts and be occupied in fruitful and useful reflections. We should therefore be diligent and constant in the study of the sacred writings, each of us having nearly at all times before us some canonical or otherwise authentic and approved writing. We should choose that book with the counsel of our confessor, and each day read in it some passage that will serve the spiritual nourishment of our soul. To this end we have specially set aside one hour each morning after the reading of the hours. During that hour we should avoid useless wandering about

157

and obstructive business which might draw us away from our study, unless some great utility requires it or obedience enjoins it.

Mass

We are accustomed to hear mass daily. To maintain good order we all go out and return afterward at the same time, though not necessarily together. On feast days we attend high mass in the church, and also on such feasts as those of Gregory, Jerome, Mark and the rogation days because of the procession held then. But on ordinary days we go to the first mass. In church we do not usually stand or sit with the other people lest we become distracted in our minds, but freeing our minds from impediments so far as we are able, we seek out a place where we can prostrate ourselves and thus direct our hearts the more intently toward God. This is especially appropriate during mass. For then through devout meditation, suffering with the Lord's passion, and holy affections we are to prepare ourselves as if for spiritual communion. For if according to Bernard everyone ought to be ready at all times and places, then especially at that time and place, to treat and receive to himself the substance of that mystery unto salvation, just as it was given, that is, to do it with a suitable and godly affection.

Labor

Because human frailty does not permit a man to be totally occupied in mental exercises at all times (as we have time and again proven to ourselves), we engage daily in some work with our hands. He who is not content to work daily with his hands will not be able to remain indefinitely in his cell, as it says in the institutes of the holy fathers. The blessed Bernard spoke of this in his *Letter to the Brothers of Mont-Dieu.*[3] Our fathers in Egypt and the Thebiad, the most ardent representatives of this holy life, worked with their hands, and from their labors fed the poor, living from and dwelling in the work of their hands. Manual labor also renders us free, lest we need to pant after others for gifts. For which reason the blessed Paul wrote to the Thessalonians, "We did not eat anyone's bread without paying for it but labored and toiled so as not to burden any of you" (2 Thes 3:8). Of the various kinds of manual labor, those are particularly recommended that seem to have a greater likeness to things spiritual, such as the work of copying, as the blessed Bernard says, "The serious and prudent soul adjusts itself to its labor," and so on. We generally divide our time so that on ordinary days clerics are engaged for three hours and priests for two before the meal, all then ceasing just before the meal at the tenth hour. After the meal, from the twelfth hour to the third, we are again engaged in manual labor, and at the fourth hour we return to it. On fast days, however, we work before the meal to the eleventh hour and begin again after the meal at the first hour. In our manual labor we ought to be faithful and fervent, for "he is cursed who is lax in the work of the Lord" (Jer 48:10). And though we should be constant, we should not be excessive or impetuous lest we extinguish the spirit. Indeed we should strive to maintain ourselves, if not in constant focused meditation, at least in good affection, frequently lifting up our hearts to God in brief prayers which the blessed Augustine calls ejaculatory. We should also work in silence, dealing expeditiously with those who come to us, unless usefulness patently requires a longer time be spent with them in conversation.

Dining

We should all come to the table orderly, together, and at once when the bell is rung so that everyone is present when the "Benedicite" is read. We usually maintain silence while sitting at table so that we may listen the more quietly and attentively to the sacred writings read to us there. We ought also to keep a check on our eyes, not looking about to see what is happening at table, except for the person who is charged to do so. We ought also to watch out for the exquisite or the singular either in the measure or the means of taking our food and drink. If plenty was served us, we should receive it with thanks; if too little, we ought still to keep our temper and be content, remembering the poverty and frugality of many, including secular folk, who are content with much less and much viler fare.

Rest after Mealtime

In the summer, from the octave of Easter to the feast of the Exaltation of the Cross [September 14], we generally rest after the meal in our beds until the reader at table has finished his own meal and rouses us. During that time the house should be closed, and each should be careful of commotion lest he disturb those resting. In the winter, however, if we feel heavy with sleep after the meal, we generally remain sitting with slightly drooping heads through one or two "Miserereis."

After the Evening Meal

After the evening meal is completed and complines said, each one may do in his room what suits him until the eighth hour, be it washing up or scrubbing clothes or studying or conversing with someone to the edification of his soul. At the sound of the eighth hour we must dismiss at once any strangers present; the house is then closed and each one is to spend time in meditation and silence. Particularly appropriate here is the saying of St. Bernard: "He is a faithful servant of Jesus who each day after compline holds chapter with himself, gathering his thoughts and reviewing each of them," and so on. And so at half past the eighth hour we normally all go to sleep at the same time.

Collations

Mutual collations, whereby we discuss something from Scripture in a charitable exchange, not only instructs us in knowledge but also kindles our fervor, and thus specially nurtures brotherly love. For the holy Anthony considered it best if the brothers mutually consoled one another with their words. Therefore on feast days we are accustomed to gather for an hour after the meal and to discuss in common some edifying material, taking as our point of departure a passage of Scripture read to us by the person delegated as the "overseer of the collation." He should be careful to admonish the brothers that they treat the proposed matters suitably, not bringing in any vain or extraneous material. There should be no disputations or fruitless arguments among us, but each should modestly say what seems appropriate to the material. On Sundays and special solemnities we generally also gather evenings after the evening meal, and after reading compline we treat the material set forth after the meal. On those Sundays we also take counsel concerning the schoolboys and other men of goodwill who come to us for instruction, so that we may get to know them better and prove more diligent toward those who seem to be of good hope.[4]

Admonition

There is a fine custom, on feast days after vespers has finished in the church, that students and other good men come to our house for spiritual instruction. We read to them some passage of Scripture in Dutch, one that is not too difficult and will provoke them to improvement of their lives, something therefore on the vices, the virtues, contempt for the world, fear of God, and the like. Once that is completed, each of us, as he is given the grace, strives to speak with several of them, addressing them on the same subject in edifying words, not indeed as in a sermon but as in a simple exhortation. And this we should do fervently and tellingly, since there is no sacrifice more pleasing to God than the winning of souls. In this we should not seek to employ ornate phrases and magisterial arguments which please only the ears, but rather moving and pricking words that might touch and admonish the hearts and wills of both them and ourselves. Since a private and friendly talk usually moves men more, it is good if now one and then another of us addresses each of them in private, provoking them to improvement according to the status and needs of each. And if any should seek counsel from us, we can suggest to him humbly and maturely what seems good; in difficult cases and ones that require the confessional we should direct them to the person in charge of our house. When someone comes to talk with us in our rooms, we ought not to keep him there long, certainly no longer than a half hour, nor should we make conversation about the nonsense and rumors circulating in the world but rather on matters necessary for the salvation of souls. Thus we should instruct them with urgency, exhorting them in particular to become open about disclosing their temptations and passions as well as ready and willing to acquiesce in good counsel.

Correction

Since correction, insofar as it is an act of brotherly love, seems necessary for the preservation of discipline—for Chrysostom said, "A good man, unless he is corrected, will perish"—we propose to correct one another in love in the way set out by our Savior: "If your brother knowingly sins against you, correct him between you and him alone," and so on (Mt 18:15). In correction we must attend to three things pointed out by Bernard: an affection of compassion, a zeal for uprightness, and a spirit of discretion. We must also correct one another in matters of patent neglect or excess that stand contrary to good morals and pious custom, especially matters pertinent to our copyist work; likewise on loud, jocular, or harsh words, on bursting out laughing, idle words, talking too much during work, discussing matters among ourselves or with guests pertaining to war and rumors of this world that have nothing to do with us, the silence to be maintained after the evening meal and in the kitchen (so far as it can be kept), neglect in duties committed to us, stubbornness in excusing or defending our own counsel or will, behavior and deeds that are undisciplined or out of line; and the like. This seems very important lest if minor matters go uncorrected vice subsequently increase throughout the house and fervor gradually decrease. To render ourselves freer in correcting one another, one brother should approach another once every fortnight begging him to have no fear of correcting him if he is caught in some excess.

The Rector

Since in any republic great or small it is necessary, if it is to be maintained, for there to be one person presiding—for Jerome said, "no city, no kingdom, not the least home will remain long if it has no one whose will is to be obeyed"—on the common counsel of the brothers and of other devout friends and faithful servants of God, we are accustomed to assign one priest to this task who as a kind of head of the household bears principle responsibility for it together with all the persons and possessions that belong to it. He has no jurisdictional authority over the brothers, but they—for the sake of their own progress, the merit of obedience, peace in the house, and the preservation of our holdings and status—find it no burden to subject themselves to him in love. For his part he must correct and admonish the brothers on their excesses, hear the confessions of persons in the house (with permission from their rightful prelates), and by word and example incite them toward improvement. Toward him the brothers seek to maintain charity in their hearts, fidelity in their words, and reverence in their conduct; and especially in his presence, though also elsewhere, they should conduct themselves modestly and respectfully. Without his knowledge and permission no one should presume to send anyone a letter or to open and read messages. Nor should anyone leave the house without his permission except to visit church at the required and customary time, unless he has received a general license for some mission; and even then, should he meet the rector on his way out, let him say in reverence why he is traveling. Without the rector's knowledge none of the priests should serve as confessor to new persons, but if he is absent a priest is free to do so if he thinks he could prove useful. No brother should invite guests in without his permission, and if he is absent invitations should be checked with the procurator. If there are any major affairs or other serious business to be treated in the house, he should call the brothers together, invite each to say freely what he thinks about the matter, and then himself conclude what seemed best to the larger and wiser group. In minor affairs requiring the counsel and deliberation of the brothers, he can, however, without dissent or resistance, quietly settle it in cooperation with the procurator and two or three senior brothers. And if it turns out to be a matter—God forbid—which they cannot expedite among themselves because of disagreement, it should be referred to all the brothers and determined according to what seems good to the larger and wiser group, with no possibility of appeal. The rector of our house should, moreover, remain as nearly as possible like the other brothers in food and drink, in the quality of his garb, and in all our other customs. He should not abuse the office bestowed upon him but know to bear himself toward both outsiders and the members of our house in a manner as far above reproach as human frailty will permit; let him see to it that he seeks not his own but the things of Jesus Christ. He should so chastise vices among the brothers as not to flatter his own, nor should he be taken with his rule: If he truly wants to be found a superior to the brothers, let him study to show himself a servant to them all and truly think himself the least. He should especially strive to be affable, sweetly serious, fervent in admonition, prudent in counsel, and concerned to promote all that is good. He should flee the confusion and distraction of worldly affairs and especially, whenever he can reasonably do so, the execution of wills. The brothers for their part should not be quick to judge or to put a sinister interpretation on his deeds or pronouncements, even when they note in them something all too human; if it should seem useful to forewarn or admonish him, let it be done in a way that preserves proper humility and respect. And because it can happen that something about himself or others will escape him, he should assign one of the brothers to forewarn and admonish him on such matters. But at the same time any brother who so chooses ought freely to open his heart to him.

[There follows an equally long chapter on the "procurator," the manager of external affairs. The emphasis here falls on keeping such matters to the necessary minimum so that he can remain an honest member of the devotional community and not become unduly occupied with worldly affairs.]

The Librarian

To one of the brothers we commit the care of our books, responsibility for the copying and preparation of books, and custody of the parchment. He should see that the books not be ill treated or poorly placed and that those requiring correction, lining, or whatever be so mended. He should have each book separately listed in a register; he should carefully consider to whom he lends them, and note their names and the date due. If any book is found missing, he should say it to the rector; and if he is himself at fault, he should humbly seek forgiveness. So that the schoolboys pursuing their studies not have daily access, he should establish a certain hour on feast days which is free for serving them. Once a year in the summer he should collect all our books, and at some stated hour in the presence of the rector call upon the brothers to examine, clean, and care for them. He should be assigned an assistant for the books in the great library, who will watch over registering them and also provide for the readings at mealtime; but the assistant may not allow any book to go outside the house without the knowledge of the librarian and none of the more valuable books without the consent of the rector, nor for more than a single day. Likewise, another whom the rector assigns will sit next to the reader at mealtime and help him with corrections if necessary. Brothers in our house may take one book from the library assigned to them for study by the rector, after signing their names on the list; they should not take more than one to their rooms except with the permission of the librarian or his assistant. Once at the beginning of each month the librarian's assistant should look over the register and the list of books, gather all books from everywhere (except those being used by the brothers in their private study), and put them back in order in the library.

The librarian is responsible for the copywork done in our house and should see to it that all brothers have enough to copy. So far as possible, he should procure for each of them a Latin work to do in our house. Therefore he should not lightly send away anyone requesting that some good book be copied, even if no brother is free at the moment, but persuade the man to expect it in a reasonable amount of time. When someone asks that a book be copied and there is a copyist free, he should show him a specimen of the writer's hand and reach an agreement on the price of the quires, unless he is content with our customary rate. But for the more valuable books he should come to no agreement with anyone apart from the consent of the rector or whomever he designated for advice. Then he should make a contract with them, especially unknown persons, to avoid an altercation later; to that end he should estimate the value and ask for a deposit. Where prompt payment cannot be expected, he should not hand the book over prior to payment or a suitable pledge. He should also prearrange, if necessary, that if the copyist cannot complete the book owing to illness or some other reasonable cause, he be content to have it completed in a similar hand. He should also be very careful to procure correct exemplars for the copyists, lest we burden our consciences by writing incorrect books. From time to time he should admonish the brothers to do their work faithfully, and oversee our writings, especially those of us who are less able at copying or have begun something new, providing, if necessary, a line or two of model writing. Before the books are bound, he should check whether they have been well corrected and whether the corrections have been written in without any notable dirtying or deformation of the book—about which he should have warned the brothers in advance. He should also provide our copyists with the necessary instruments, that is, pen-knives, quills, pens, chalk, and the like. He should also provide the illuminators and binders with what they need for their work. They should say well in advance what they will need, so he can obtain it for them at a good price and then entrust it to them. He should also take responsibility with an assistant for concocting the ink so that it will always be good ink, for good books are easily lost because of bad ink. He also has charge of the parchment and should procure it and paper in good time so that he will have a plenteous supply and can distribute it when needed. It seems good to prepare a large supply at once with his assistant, lest he be occupied with that daily. In preparing parchment he should watch out for blemishes, corners, ruptures, and sutures so far as possible. A suitable sum should be assigned the librarian for procuring parchment, and each year what remains after the computation should be given the procurator. [There follow concluding details on the annual reckoning of supplies and profits and the annual reassignment of offices.]

[There follow shorter sections on offices connected to the vestiary, the infirmary, and the like.]

Visitors

It seems good for our house that once a year we call out two priests, themselves rectors of congregations, who may be presumed to have a particular loyalty to our house and way of life; at least one should be the prior or another regular from Windesheim. They should discuss with the rector and our brothers that which concerns our peace, concord, and progress. We should also take counsel with them if there are any particularly difficult matters in which we need advice. For instance, if the rector of the house is to be deposed, it should be done with their counsel; and in the election of another it is good to call upon still another, or rather to call in several devout fathers. On their visits they should first call together all the brothers, indicating the reason for their coming, namely, that they have been called out and come in love, ready to do what they can for the utility and progress of the brothers. And when the rector explains why he has called them out, he should admonish the brothers to open their hearts and speak freely about whatever they are asked, so far as they are able. The visitors should speak first with the rector about his peace of mind, the state of the house and the brothers, and as to whether he is burdened by excessive insolence or rebellion from any-one or the house itself by serious debts. Next they should speak with each of the brothers individually beginning with the oldest, exam-ining whether they are at peace with themselves, the rector, and the other brothers, whether they suffer unusual stubbornness or inso-lence from anyone or any discord in the house, whether the daily round and the exercises are too rigorous, and so on. Each should be permitted to say freely what seems to him necessary and useful, nor should anyone be questioned much about his possible motives except in plenary session where the motive of some individual might be noted if it has a bearing. But the brothers should look out lest they charge something in passion, lest their concerns incite more distur-bance than real progress. Those fathers should be carefully discern-ing in this matter; otherwise it could happen that vice be favored rather than destroyed. In the presence of all they should then single out those who seem to need individual admonition and correction. After this they should call all together and make some kind of edi-fying admonition on matters that will spur progress among the brothers, so that after this charitable visitation great peace and con-cord may persist still among the brothers together with great readi-ness and willingness on the part of each to look after his progress.

The Monthly Colloquies

At the beginning of each month, at our earliest convenience, we are accustomed to gather at some hour set by the rector and to discuss those matters which pertain to our way of life. At that time each should consider for himself what is useful to our house and worthy of our estate. Here are some possible considerations: whether any of the brothers is negligent in observing any custom of our house and therefore to be admonished; whether any schoolboys or others who come to our house for confession conduct themselves reprehensibly before men, contrary to what is edifying, and therefore to be spe-cifically approached; whether any possessions of our house seem to be neglected or lost and therefore to be looked after; whether the rec-tor of our house is not vigilant enough in the exercises, for example, in humbling people or breaking their wills or chastising their defects or some other such exercise through which they could make progress in uprooting the vices. If he has not acted on some such matter, it should be their will and desire that he be freer and more diligent in undertaking these and similar exercises—proper discipline and mod-

esty being preserved all the while lest dissensions arise, and each one taking care not to abound in his own good pleasure or to incur the vice of stubbornness and self-will, lest the colloquy, meant to serve our progress, give way to something damaging instead. In that colloquy the rector of the house can respond directly to the inquiries of the brothers in a way he deems fit, unless a matter is raised again and then he must examine the will of the brothers to learn what they in their counsel deem fit. If at that time something is raised pertinent to the principle affairs of our house, that is to be done which seems best to the larger and wiser group.
[There follows a section on specific matters requiring the rector to take counsel with the brothers]

The Quality of the Brothers

Good counsel suggests that our house have four priests, or more if required by utility or charity, and the rest should be clerics, with a smaller number of laymen. When a place comes free in our house and someone wishes to live with us, the circumstances of the person should be carefully considered first, his homeland, his social status, his physical condition, his fervor, and his conduct in his previous life; then whether he is willing, ready, and also suited for the customary exercises in our house. If he is a cleric, whether he understands and is able to write, whether trained in letters, or at least suited for it. Then, whether he is healthy in head and chest, and whether burdened with the care of poor or frail parents. If we come to a reasonably positive conclusion on these matters, we can receive him as a guest and try him out for two or three months. If within that time, after reflecting on his conduct, we truly believe him not suited to us nor this life to him, he should be sent back at once to his own place, or if he is already among us, transferred to a more suitable place, because it is more useful and less disturbing for him and for us that he should withdraw and return to his original place. Therefore anyone thought difficult to remove from the hospice should not be lightly admitted. But if his conduct pleases the brothers, he should still not be received into our common life until he has lived with us and conducted himself in a praiseworthy manner over ten or twelve months. During that time the brothers must consider him carefully: He should be tested as to whether his intention is firm or still inclined to his previous life, whether he can bear correction and humbling, whether he is quick to obey however humble or vile the matter, whether he is open about disclosing his passions and temptations. After he has been found acceptable to our brothers in all this, he can, with the common consent of the brothers or of the wiser and larger group, be received from the hospice as a fellow and brother of our house. In the presence of the brothers the rector should deliver some admonition that will prove profitable to his future improvement. Whoever is so received into our house is accustomed to bring forward and present in common anything he might have and thereafter to live without personal possessions. Within a month of his reception he should therefore make it known before notaries and witnesses that he has nothing of property or ownership in the house or its possessions; that if he should leave the house, he would not seek back or make demands upon anything which he had for his part given to it; and that if he should be ordered by the rector or the brothers to leave because of his bad conduct, he would do so in peace, taking nothing with him and demanding nothing except his everyday clothes. And he should make such a testament of his donation that his heirs would have no right to vex the brothers after his death.

Grounds for Removing Someone
The shepherd who would expose his whole flock to infection rather than separate out one diseased sheep can hardly be called prudent, nor can he be called merciful who would bear with some evil brother to the detriment of the whole congregation. For we should be, as Gregory says, severe with vices and compassionate to nature. For this reason we deliberate among ourselves when some brother of our house—God forbid—has so turned from his good intention and grown lukewarm as to become wholly negligent of improving his life and keeping the customs of our house, or when he has shown himself so rebellious and stubborn toward the rector and the brothers as, with no noteworthy correction, to harden in this: If someone stains our fellowship with the infidelity of private property, he should be warned and seriously admonished by the rector in the presence of the brothers a second and third time, and if he promises no effective improvement he can be cast out of our fellowship by the rector and the brothers. If anyone—God forbid—should fall into some sin of the flesh, or even make a conscious effort to do such a thing, or perpetrate some other manifest and scandalous evil from which our whole congregation could suffer confusion and slander, or burden himself and our house with personal debts and pledges without the knowledge and consent of our procurator (especially apart from an office), or desert our fellowship for another place, he should lose at once all rights within our house and fellowship.

Charity, Peace, and Harmony

We are supposed to keep peace and charity with all men, so far as we are able, but we should try especially among ourselves and toward each other to have one heart and one spirit, one will toward the good. So that charity, peace, and harmony may remain inviolate among us, we should strive especially toward all that will nurture and preserve the harmony of love. We should seek to excel in honoring one another, to bear each other's burdens, to weep with the weeping and rejoice with the rejoicing, to bear patiently with one another's infirmities in conduct as well as in health, and to avoid mutual offense, mockery, slander, and stubborn contrariness. If anyone offends another in such things, he should humbly seek forgiveness. For only humility, as the blessed Bernard says, repairs damaged charity. It is also good to avoid constant familiarity with individuals and particular friendships, which sometimes are not above the suspicion of carnal affection. A common love should rather thrive and be preserved among us, which on occasion may show toward someone thinking himself at odds with us on some point an even greater friendliness and courtesy.

Humility

Of humility the blessed Bernard said, "This is the way and there is no other beside it. He who walks in another way falls rather than climbs because it is only humility that uplifts; it alone leads to life." Because humbling is the way to humility, as reading is to learning, we propose to lead lives humble in dress, deeds, conduct, buildings, and in the furnishing of our house, so much so that even if we should have something decorous and attractive, it should never be anything curious or ornate. Our brothers, so much as they can, should always choose the humbler status as the safer, knowing that the kingdom of God is gained by purity of mind rather than loftiness of status. Not only in our status, but in all else as well, in our rooms, our vessels, our offices, each should choose and request what is humbler and viler so that humility of heart may be inculcated through humbling of the body. Toward such humbling we also have some exercises in humility, such as to wash the dishes and pots, or to seek forgiveness whenever through your negligence something is lost or broken exceeding the value of one Brabant coin, or you have been negligent in keeping some good custom laid upon you under pain of penalty.

THE DEVOTION

Obedience

We propose to observe carefully the law of obedience, lest we should happen to defraud ourselves of the merit and reward of that virtue whose form the Only-Begotten of God displayed to the faithful when he was made obedient, even unto death and said, "I did not come to do my own will but the will of him who sent me" (Jn 6:38). We intend humbly to obey, in the first place, the commandments of God and the Church as well as of our prelates and of the sacred canons so far as we know them and are able; additionally, to acquiesce willingly in the admonishments and counsel of our priest (to whom in the governing of our house has been committed the place of the head of the household), according to the counsel of the blessed Peter, "Chastening our hearts in the obedience of charity" (1 Pt 1:22). Each of us should hang the ordering of his life upon his counsel, listening freely to his admonitions and suffering patiently his reproaches. We should wish to keep nothing secret from him that happens among us whether great or small. We should continuously have recourse to him in temptation, perplexity, and adversity. And even though nothing special has happened, each brother should have an individual colloquy with the rector four times a year concerning the passions of his soul, asking him to be free in reproaching or even exercising him, as seems good for his spiritual progress.

The Common Life and Poverty

Since, as Augustine says, among close friends there should be a common experience—for there should not be a difference in experience when there is a common affection, nor a different fortune when there is a common spirit—we propose in our house to give up all personal property and to possess nothing of our own but to hold everything in common among us, thus to display and to preserve mutual love, to relieve daily cares, and to fulfill the evangelical counsel on giving up all things. There should be a common purse, a common chest, and a common table and provisions, except when someone is specially provided to meet a particular need. That outside religious orders a common life is not only licit but also meritorious and expedient for those wishing to progress in the way of God, for this we have more than enough writings from various doctors who prove it by law, reason, and the authority of the saints, particularly in the case where priests and clerics live in common according to the ancient laws.[5] We therefore intend now and henceforth to observe this fully and freely, to place our temporal possessions in common and be content with the provision made for us, and not to murmur

170

if we do not have everything to our complete satisfaction, lest we be like those pledged to poverty of whom Bernard said: "There are some who wish to be poor, but in such a way that nothing is lacking to them; and they so love poverty that they tolerate no scarcity." We should also take care that we not become bound with a stubborn affection to those things whose use is still permitted us. We should so seek to suspend our affection from all domestic things that if anyone is ordered by the rector to change his room he does so at once, carrying nothing with him except what the rector has designated. For this reason the rector is accustomed once a year, at the beginning of Lent, to go round the brothers' rooms to see what we have in the way of books, utensils, and the like. We are to bring everything out before him so that if he wishes to remove something, he can take it, and also to leave what he wishes to leave. In this same connection, no brother should let any money in his room overnight, unless required to do so by his office. If money should come into anyone's hands, he should bring it to those charged with caring for it. Our frail and miserable condition requires as well a suitable provision of victuals and other necessities, but we propose for ourselves and our posterity a sum of one hundred coins [*scudae*] in annual fixed revenue for the persons of this house, lest we or our posterity exceed the measure of sufficiency and accumulate so much revenue that it is no longer necessary to gain our victuals with labor from our own hands and we thus run the risk of falling into idleness and vagrancy. But if some goods should afterward devolve upon us, we can assign a third part to our library, and give the rest to the poor. If we should become burdened with serious debts through the reception of many guests or by some blow of fortune, it should be left to the advice of those fathers whom we call in annually for counsel to assign some portion of any goods devolving upon us toward meeting that debt.

Chastity

That we may always maintain inviolate the perpetual chastity required of us and so that no sinister suspicions may ever arise about any of us, we propose—as we have and ever shall—to keep all women away from our house and not permit them to come among us. If it is necessary to speak with some woman, then only in an appropriate place [*locotorium*] with a partition carefully closed to prevent mutual access or sight. And if some woman should address us outside the gate or elsewhere, we should take care not to look at her intently or enter into conversation with her, for following the saying of Augustine, "With women our words are to be short and direct."

As an added caution we propose and will that no one converse with any woman in the assigned place or before the gate without the rector's permission. And if a woman should address any brother while he is outside the house, he should answer her appropriately with few words, and then go to the rector and tell him that she addressed him; and if the rector asks what they talked about, he should keep nothing secret. But if it is a matter that concerns only the office of a particular brother, it would suffice to tell him alone. When the rector is absent, the procurator or senior priest of our house takes his place in this regard. In the assigned place, the brothers should not sit while talking with some woman but stand to talk unless it is a mother or a sister or he has special permission from the rector. Brothers with offices should seek general permission to speak with women when necessary.

Sobriety

He who desires to be chaste should be diligent in sobriety, always careful lest we exceed the measure of sobriety and thus become slaves to carnal desire. Even more, when strength permits, we should discreetly castigate our bodies and reduce them to subjection. We should therefore abstain from wine and as well from the exquisite and sumptuous spicing of food. We may drink however on the great feast days, after being bled, or if someone offers us wine as a favor. For guests we provide the same as for the brothers because this is very edifying, and if it seems useful to provide something else, this should be done with the knowledge of the rector, always preserving the proper simplicity appropriate to us. For those feast days when we take communion, we prepare by way of abstinence so that we take no meat for at least three days, unless perhaps the feast of Epiphany or of Mary Magdalene should fall on Wednesday; then we can eat flesh because of the Lord's day, as around the feast of the Visitation we eat meat on St. Peter's day for his feast. So too, beyond the vigil of the day we take communion, on at least one of the three preceding days we go without an evening meal, unless conceded for some good reason. We will also go without meat at Pentecost from Wednesday to the holy day; so too on the feasts of the Assumption and of All Saints we abstain for four days. On ember days and the vigils of saints' days we eat no butter. During Advent we eat no meat and fast with no evening meal three days a week. On Friday we never forgo to fast unless moved by some very worthy cause, for instance, at the rector's permission to taste something in place of the species. But because it is easy to deviate from the mean of virtue, a brother who has become too hard on himself and too sparing in taking food ought to be admonished by the brother who observes it. And if he does not make amends, it should be indicated to the rector so that he can admonish him, lest the brother go to ruin by making himself powerless to perform both spiritual and corporeal exercises.

Silence

It befits us always and everywhere to maintain silence from useless and idle words and especially from the rumors, distractions, and mockery of this world. And if something about worldly matters is heard or said we should try to refer it to piety but should not waste idle time on such things. For the rest, in certain times and places we propose to refrain even from useful words, namely, in the morning for a half-hour after saying the hours and in the evening for a half-hour before going to sleep. In the hall we should also avoid unnecessary conversation, and before and after eating we should avoid telling stories. We should also avoid conversation especially in the kitchen, which we will not enter without permission from the rector, procurator or cook, if present.

Prayer

We should always have ready at hand the most secure refuge of prayer, and pour out prayers not only for our own but also for others' needs. And therefore whenever it is requested that we pray for some pious cause, say, for some poor person who is ill, tempted, or dying, or some other such urgent or pressing cause, we ought not allow this negligently to slip from our memory or do it perfunctorily and superficially. We should rather diligently, with urgency, efficacy, the whole heart, and our whole strength, beseech God with our prayers on behalf of those troubled in heart, concerning ourselves with the needs of anyone so burdened just as we would wish it for ourselves in similar anxiety. When one of our brothers is so weakened that he can no longer go to church, we are daily to read for him at matins and vespers the collect "God of human infirmity, and so forth." Then at the time of his anointing and daily afterward the seven psalms. But if his infirmity should persist for a long time without hope of convalescence, we can read the psalms on one day and the litany on the other. In the final agony of our brother we should read constantly the seven psalms and the litany. After his death we should read at once the vigils of the nine lessons, continuing that daily through eight days, the vigil of three lessons up to thirty days after his death, and then daily for up to a year a collect for our departed brother at the end of matins and vespers. Each brother should also read one whole psalter for the departed brother, and each priest a month of masses. On the first anniversary of our departed brother we should read the vigil of nine lessons and on the following anniversaries that of three lessons. On the death of anyone's parents we should read the vigil of nine lessons, and through eight days that of three lessons, and one of the priests should say one mass; on the first anniversary of one of our parents the vigil of three lessons. For the brothers in Windesheim, on the Mount, and in Bethlehem, for the sisters in the congregation in our parish, and for the brothers confessing in our house, we should read once a vigil of nine lessons. For the brothers in the house of Lord Florens and on the Mount of St. Jerome and in Alberghen, we should do something more, that is, at least a collect through eight days at matins and vespers.[6] For our domestics and benefactors and the devout in other places, we should do whatever seems right to him in charge of the house.

Communion

When we take communion on feast days we wish to prepare ourselves through abstinence, as noted above. So far as possible we arrange it so that in preparation for such feast days we withdraw a day or two from all major tasks and distractions that can conveniently be put off. These are the feast days on which we normally take communion: Easter, Ascension, Pentecost, Corpus Christi, the Visitation, Mary Magdalen, the Assumption, the Nativity of Mary, St. Michael's or the dedication, All Saints, the Conception of Mary, Christmas, Epiphany, the Purification, the Enthronement of St. Peter (if it occurs during Lent, otherwise the first Sunday of Lent), and the Annunciation. On those feast days no one should neglect to take communion without the knowledge and permission of the rector. On these feast days, or at least once a month, we should persuade the clerics and other men of goodwill who come to us for counsel to make confessions, and those who are suitable should prepare themselves for communion, especially on the major feast days.

Vagrancy

The source of all evil is useless wandering about. We propose therefore to make trips difficult, especially back to home regions, except when necessity or some notable utility requires. If it seems necessary and worthwhile to the rector that someone make a certain journey a mile or more from the city, he should arrange to have one of our brothers travel with him. But if it seems to the rector or to two or three senior brothers that a companion from outside the house will suffice or be better, this should be left to their discretion. If it seems expedient to send someone one horse owing to the nature of the business, the rector should do this on the counsel of two or three discreet brothers, but that man should not spend a night in the home of worldly people; and if it is thought that this cannot be avoided, he should not be sent without a companion. Above all we should look out while abroad lest we conduct ourselves in a worldly and unedifying manner: that is, lest we request exquisite food and drink, poke into things here and there that have nothing to do with our business, loosen the rein on our eyes, ears, and tongue, become boisterous, vain, and silly, or in some other way burden our consciences and therefore return home less joyful. Whenever it is possible to be received at the houses of devout or religious, we should go there. He who must remain abroad for a time can, with permission, confess there to a suitable priest. But it seems expedient that on returning he confess to the rector everything that happened from the time of departure, unless he is content with the confession made abroad. On returning, brothers should go first to the rector and tell him the details of their trip, and if any money is left over return it at once to the rector or procurator. When we are sent into the city on business, we should go about it expeditiously and return without looking about in the square or peering into homes and greeting the women. Nor should we enter a home where we have not been specifically sent for some reason, and this we should say when we return. When we return, we should go to him who sent us and report on the business. We should not eat too little or too much in the homes we visit in the city without the permission of him who is in charge, nor should we drink more than once. And if we are not able to observe this for a time without offense to our friends, afterward we should seek permission from the rector on this score.

CHAPTER TWO

Salome Sticken:
A Way of Life for Sisters[7]

At the instance and repeated request of the venerable prior at Nordhorn, brother Henry Loder, Mother Salome Sticken, once prioress at Diepenveen, provided this formulation to serve as the foundation for a spiritual edifice in some new congregation.

In the name of our most beloved Lord Jesus Christ, amen. Beloved sisters in Christ, when you hear the sound of the bell in the morning, rise quickly from your beds with so much fervor of devotion and gratitude as if you were in the very presence of our most beloved Lord Jesus Christ and his holy angels. Humbly prostrate yourselves in devout prayer before his feet and ask that he deign to give you a whole day to spend in his praise and glory, and that in the peace and quiet conducive to your own and your sisters' salvation. Then lift your heart ardently and affectionately to the Lord with meditation on some article of his passion, and beginning to read matins proffer them to the Lord with an alert heart and affectionate desire. You should imagine yourself standing in the presence of the Lord Savior and his holy angels, because the holy angels look with great interest to see how devoutly and ardently we read and offer our hours to the Lord God, so they in turn may offer our prayers and pious desires to their and our most beloved Lord. But alas if we read the hours with vain, distracted, or lukewarm hearts, the demons quickly and joyously appear to offer them instead to their prince. When the hours are finished, you can begin your exterior labors in silence and with such desire and affection that some should inwardly wish, will, and say: "O Lord Jesus, would that I alone could finish everything to be done here because I am less suited to things spiritual, and the other sisters, freed from these matters, might then turn themselves to you more freely and devoutly." You also know, dearest sisters, that before prayer it is important to prepare ourselves with ardent desire if we wish to be found devout and affectionate in prayer before the Lord.

At the beginning of mass humbly prostrate yourselves before the face of our beloved Lord Jesus, and with affectionate sighs and desires confess to him all your faults, especially that vice which is your worst. During mass place before your eyes the dear passion of the Lord Jesus. Pour out to our most beloved Lord Jesus your every wish and whole heart in ardent desire and great gratitude, giving thanks to him with all your strength, for he, who is so incomprehensibly great, deigned to undergo and suffer such awful and repeated torment for you. With heartfelt desire, then, offer up to the heavenly Father the unspeakable and dear passion of our sweet Lord Jesus as a most pleasing sacrifice, adding the superb and most worthy merits of the glorious Virgin Mary, the merits of all the saints, and the common prayer of the entire holy Catholic Church together with the humility, love, and pious desires of all good men as an acceptable and pleasing oblation to God for all your sins. With that oblation offer the Lord God as well the complete mortification and self-denial of your own hearts and souls, together with a sure and perfect will never to depart from his service. Moreover, beloved sisters, if we are fervent and diligent, we can by the grace of our Lord so unfold before us his dear passion, impress it on our minds, and affectionately unite ourselves to it that we are made ready to do and suffer all that he permits to come over us, be it chastisement, humiliation, temptation, or even the condemnation and rejection of all men. Unless we have undertaken to bear patiently such mortifying things, meditating upon the Lord's passion with only lukewarm hearts will be of little moment and bring us little good. But if through such mortification and self-denial you convert yourself to the Lord, he will flood your minds with his generous and overflowing grace, teaching and instructing you more in one moment than any mortal could ever accomplish in much writing or teaching.

When mealtime approaches, I wish that you would make your way to the refectory in silence and without clamor and there read the blessing on the meal with a devout mind. Those in the kitchen and serving the table should prepare the food in great reverence with piety and dignity, placing it before the sisters as if they were doing so before the most loving Lord Jesus, his beloved mother, and all the saints. And those who sit at table should similarly receive the food in great reverence with bowed heads as if they were being served by angels. I wish as well that while eating you would frequently lift your hearts up to the Lord. Those of you blessed with an affectionate heart and great yearning should seek out that in the dish which looks vilest and least appetizing. And if any food or drink should be served that is contrary to your nature or taste, call to mind that the king of all sweetness, the most loving Lord Jesus, drank hyssop and vinegar on the cross for you. While eating, take care to lower your eyes and carefully keep watch that you not try to learn what those sitting near you have or are eating. Instead, with fervent desire convert your heart, and not just your ears, to what is being read, so that your souls may be nourished by the Word of God no less than your bodies by the food of the earth. I know that many of our sisters so turn themselves inward toward the Lord God and are so watchful over their eyes while eating that they hardly know who sits next to them or what has been placed before them. Nor is there any murmuring heard from our sisters over what is placed before them, but by the working of grace they humbly and simply eat what they are served. I heard from our confessor that during the time he has lived with us he has never heard any complaint about the food. But I have frequently heard our sisters complain that foods have been placed before them finer in quality and greater in quantity than necessary, even though what is served them is only crude and common. I also know some sisters who never know what they have before them because during mealtime they unite themselves totally and wholeheartedly with the Lord Jesus.

I write these things to your charity, dearest sisters, because I wish your hearts to be occupied with nothing other than affectionate meditation on the Lord. When you rise from the meal, read the grace with fervent gratitude, making request to the Lord God in behalf of your benefactors and for the remission of your sins in case you transgressed any way in gluttony or the like. I also ask that after the meal you maintain silence for at least one hour, though it is best to spend the whole day or what remains of it in silence and wholehearted devotion to the things of God, that is, [to meditate] on your sins of commision and omission, the uncertain day of your death, the awful day of judgment, the pains of hell and reward of the righteous which is eternal life, the benefits of the Lord, the life and passion of the Lord Jesus—all of which things, I suppose, you already practice and have written out in greater detail in your books. At all times and places, moreover, lift your hearts up frequently to our most loving Lord Jesus Christ in brief prayers poured out with groans and sighs; for instance, in the psalm "Create in me a clean heart, O God" or the hymn "Come Holy Spirit" or something similar. Each hour you should also look into yourself to examine your progress or decline, carefully reflecting on what gladdens or saddens you, what you love, what you hope in. Each evening as you sit before your bed, carefully scrutinize how you spent the preceding day, confessing to the Lord and humbly bemoaning your faults and failures and making a firm and strong resolution to make amends.

When it happens that you leave the convent for some work, I deeply desire that you devoutly pray to the Lord that he watch over your coming and going. So conduct yourself in all things, in your manners and deeds especially, that whoever sees or hears you will be improved and edified. I know some sisters so watchful over their eyes when they go out into public squares that they would have been run over if the Lord had not been watching over them, and on finishing their business they return so quickly to the house that it is as if they were gazing upon an earthly paradise. When people of the world come to you, I beg each of you to flee from them and avoid their conversation, always showing reluctance to accept them as guests. And even those assigned to talk with them, I exhort and admonish to be on your guard against asking about the rumors of this world or talking about vain and useless matters. If such people of the world begin to discuss vain and worldly stuff, interrupt their talk, if you can, with good matter concerning the Lord Jesus and his saints.

I heartily desire, dearest sisters, that you submit yourselves wholly to your mother and to those with charge over you. Do not do, do not even think, anything you know or suspect to be displeasing to them or contrary to their will. Be affectionate toward your mother; think nothing ill or malicious of what she orders. Try so to put off your own will and to put on your mother's that there comes between you a single will and complete agreement, with you doing whatever she wills. Those, too, who help the mother in keeping watch over the house should subject themselves to her so humbly that she can freely and confidently proceed with what she thinks best and most useful—just as I can with my helpers and sisters, though I am much too unworthy and useless for the office imposed on me. Indeed I bear the burden of office almost without burden when I consider the humble submission of the sisters, how they humbly yield and incline their wills, how they interject themselves into nothing and speak only on that which pertains to their care, how they are intent only upon preserving pure and unsullied consciences and pleasing the Lord alone. I see all this and more each day and I rejoice in them. For I know that some of the sisters are so obedient that if I ordered them to set fire to the house or to rip off the roof tiles they would do so without objection. Likewise if I charged them to make a journey of more than a hundred miles, they would be found ready to depart at once and without objection. Therefore I must often think things through in advance before I command, for I recognize that there have been among us a number of indiscretions owing to obedience. Moreover, I also freely afflict, exercise, and chastise them; the more I do so, the more they love me, opening their hearts and coming to me with even freer hearts. Indeed it requires effort for me to think out something whereby I can humble and lower them. But they would be sad if I did not do it, fearing that I was less content because I served up less than the usual dish. All that I impose and they suffer from my hand they seem to count as nothing; this only they hold for important, that I be content and free with them. I insert and write all this that you may know how much I desire you to humble and submit yourselves to your superiors. I heard that our venerable father, Master Geert Grote, used to say that if the superiors set fire to the house their subjects should be so converted to obedience that they would not once ask why. Lord John Brincker-inck, our venerable father, also said to us once, "If the devil were ordained our superior or rector, he could not persuade or advise us to do evil if we humbly submitted ourselves to him in true obedience for the sake of our Lord Jesus Christ."

I also wish with all my heart that you seek in every way to conduct yourselves toward one another in love and peace. This you will not achieve very easily unless each of you strives to humble yourself and to become the least of all, abandoning your own will and hastening to do in all virtue whatever pleases the other. Each sister should freely allow another's fault to be charged to her, even if she was not herself guilty.

I ask further that you vie with each other to be first in taking up humbling and vile work, competing with one another in this regard in a loving contest. Similarly when you gather for work, each should compete to grab the poorest tool. I heard once from a very devout priest that the grace of God is nowhere more plainly evident than in our humble and vile works, if they are done faithfully out of love for God and to counteract sensuality. This is the custom we have observed until now among our sisters. When we gather for work, each without regard for personal comfort fervently seizes work from the hands of others who often discover their work done by another before they have an opportunity to put a hand to it themselves. Often sisters come to me with weeping eyes such that I can hardly comfort them, and all they want is that I permit them to take up, as they wish, all the vile work themselves. There are others whose main complaint is that they are not able to join the rest in this vile work owing to the frailty of their natures. Our sisters go out to work dressed so poorly and commonly that when seen by some person of the world with little understanding of the things of God he usually mocks rather than honors them. I also know many in our house who care nothing about how they are dressed outwardly, but only that they please the Lord God inwardly. They are so inward in their ways and guarded with their eyes even at work that they do not know who is assisting or sitting near or passing them. This they observe not only at work but also in choir: Standing for two or three hours, they do not once open their eyes to look around, which I have observed with my own most careful scrutiny. O beloved sisters, to describe the virtues of all our sisters would take too long, and I am the least worthy to do it.

When the sisters gather with the mother, I greatly desire that their conversation be about our Lord Jesus Christ and the loving-kindness he showed us, the most loving passion he bore for us, and the life, virtue, and ways of his most holy mother as also over the life and teachings of the saints, so that by such pious discussions the sisters might be roused to mortify themselves in imitation. When they gather, they should also mutually admonish one another in love on faults they have observed. But each should be careful not to express something out of passion. When a sister feels herself provoked to say something out of passion, she should choose rather to keep silent or, if it is something worth saying, ask the mother and say, "I would like to say something to that sister, but I feel myself moved by passion and not by love." If the mother then orders her to say it, she should say in all humility and modesty, "This or that seems to me true of that sister, and if such happened to me I would do thus and so, but perhaps there was another intention or another way to see it." Make every effort to see that this mutual admonition and correction proceeds with such goodwill and charity that it arouses mutual love and not mutual indignation. And if you see faults or infirmities in another, try always to excuse them in your own heart, reflecting in humble submission on your own infirmity and countless defects. I beg those of you who are well practiced to look upon and honor one another as thrones of the most holy Trinity and temples in whom the Holy Spirit resides, each one thinking herself unworthy to kiss the very footsteps of the other. I especially beg you not to say things to one another that are unedifying, such as "She is weak," or "We have to suffer much from her," or "She is a burden to the community," and the like. The conscience becomes burdened by such words, and much unrest arises in the congregation together with mutual indignation. Take care, too, not to pour out among the sisters some vain and worldly business you happened to hear outside the house, and also that one young sister not converse with another without the knowledge and permission of the rectress. Moreover, in admonishing others' faults, use very gentle language so that even on the least matters you can warn one another faithfully and in love. For as the glorious Jerome said, the greatest sign of fraternal charity is that we admonish one another even on the smallest matters. Therefore beg the rectress to cut you down freely, to humble, exercise, and correct you, always conducting yourself such that she will be free in dealing with you at any time or place. Try with all your strength not to do anything, even the least thing, without her permission, such as to leave work, wash something, mend clothing, or even to drink without her consent. In all troubles, temptation, and the like, moreover, be entirely open in revealing everything to her, lest the devil find a place to nest in you if you keep it hidden. There is no easier way to conquer the devil than to bring all his counsel out into the open. But be careful as well that when you reveal or confess your defects to her it not be done out of mere custom but with true contrition and a resolve to make amends. Take care not to speak too long and pointlessly with the rectress, especially before the evening meal, because she, already much bothered with the cares of the house, should have at least a little time to return to her heart and be busy with spiritual exercises.

If you wish to achieve a truly spiritual life, you must refrain from too much talking, especially during manual labor, because work is a kind of medicinal plaster for the wound of our sins. If we are concerned to salve our wounds and apply medicine, we must be very careful lest through much talking we instead add wound to wound, which comes when we act unfaithfully and seek our own comfort in labor. It is said of the brothers of St. Bernard that when they were all engaged in serious work they proceeded in such silence that only the sound of the picks, axes, and other tools could be heard. May it be common among you to pray devoutly and lift your hearts up to the Lord God during your labor, because the Lord God is to be sought and found not only in churches, through the prayers poured out there, but in every place and as present to everyone, at least to everyone who by grace desires him. Indeed a greater measure of grace is to be found in humble, vile, and abject labors done in love with a desire to please him. And to express for your edification what work did for me, let me tell you that in all my life I never felt so affected toward the Lord as what I sensed when, still strong in body, I went out to the common labor with the convent, there to knead, to brew, to card, pick, or wash the wool, and all the other heavy or vile things that must be done in our house. It seems to me that if I could still do it as I once could I would find the Lord Jesus nowhere more delightfully and lovingly than in such labor, even though entering the church is also very precious to me.

In all good congregations the custom is that from morning to evening on ordinary days the sisters work in a lively and faithful way, except when they go to hear mass. The exceptions are those sisters whom this does not suit because of business they cannot put off, ministry in the kitchen, or the like. They remain in their places without murmuring, seeking and calling upon the most loving and sweet Lord Jesus in their heart since they cannot go to church. It is also the custom in our house that after prime each sister goes vigorously to work, be it to card the wool, to weave, to sew, or the like, except during the time when they go to hear mass or when they read and sing the hours in choir. The rest who do not visit choir, however, work continuously from prime to vespers, except during the time of mass. Our sisters think they suffer a great loss in divine love if they do not persist faithfully and alertly in manual labor. I know too that in the early days of our house's founding even some of the novices who had just come carried out hard labor from morning to evening, carrying rocks, filling carts with earth, providing lime, and preparing the foundations for the supports and beams. In this hard and continuous labor they were suffused with such a grace from the Lord that they paid almost no attention to externals. And when, for instance, they carried rocks with some companion they were so filled with grace that they walked inwardly absorbed, knowing not where they were going but simply following the file of carriers. Our regulations put first that we concentrate vigorously for God's sake on manual labor. Whoever therefore thinks that the grace of God and inner sweetness is to be found only in leisure and contemplation errs badly. As Bernard says, work of the hands frequently expresses remorse of the heart and makes devotion purer. For this and many other reasons, the holy fathers in Egypt were constant in labor, and therefore magnificently lauded by the holy fathers.

Dearest sisters, I ask as well that you wear humble and plain garb and that its cloth be crude and plain, as it is among our sisters in the house of Master Geert Grote, for external shapelessness and ugliness covers the Lord Jesus within. I specially desire, beloved sisters in Christ, that you submit yourselves in all humility to your confessor, and that you receive whatever he says or counsels as if it came from the Lord God.

Most beloved sisters, to sense and to taste the sweetness of the Lord God is highly delightful, but the foundation of all sanctity lies rather in complete self-denial, mortification of the evil affections in our corrupt natures, and the conversion of our will to the Lord in an effort to conform it totally to his will. Master Geert Grote, our venerable father, wrote in a certain place that "I am abandoned inwardly by the Lord, outwardly I am of no consequence and looked down upon by all men, and to bear this patiently exceeds in merit all contemplation." Because, when the Lord gives us sweetness and solace, he is ministering to us, but when we cling to him faithfully through temptation and trouble, then we are serving him, which is of greater merit. I do not say these things to make you lukewarm and lazy in your prayers or to have you spend the time set aside for prayer uselessly, for we and all mankind must seek the grace of God with great diligence and with vigilant souls. If consolation and internal sweetness is proffered us from the Lord, we should receive it with an expression of great gratitude. But if he sometimes withdraws that which he gives, we should strive to cling to the Lord nonetheless with devout desire and pious affection just as in previous times and places.

Dearest sisters, I write these simple and crude things to you as if you did not know them. I hope however, that you know many more and greater things than I am able to write.

To the Rectress:

Dearest sister, because you have been charged with the care of the house, I exhort and warn you, insofar as the frailty of your nature permits, to treat all sisters the same in food and drink and in the common labor, for this pertains to you as it does to me and all who have charge over others. I ask that you conduct yourself sweetly, lovingly, and devoutly among your sisters so as to bring all to love and fear you. But I do not mean you should take up their vices in a fawning way, but try faithfully at all times to chastise and correct their faults and failures. Whenever you can obtain something from the sisters with kindness, however, do not use severity or austerity, except with the advice and consent of the confessor. Beloved sister, I ask that you yourself strive to maintain discipline with your sisters and to advance from day to day in the virtues, because the advance of the house and the keeping of discipline along with all its other good institutes pertains mostly to you and rests on you. Work diligently therefore in the vineyard of the Lord in which you have been placed so that through good customs and the exercise of the virtues with the counsel of the venerable prior of Nordhorn, you may make it to bear fruit. When sisters come to you who are in trouble, console, instruct, and admonish them lovingly and sweetly. When good cause requires, you can then reproach and chastise them, and that without any distinction of persons. For if one is drawn to you more familiarly and treated more piously, while another corrected with a full measure of justice, unity and harmony will be damaged. But it is not beside the point or unbecoming to love the more virtuous more than the others. If any are in trouble or temptation, faithfully aid and succor them, I beg of you, so far as you able. And if you cannot suffice on your own or the matter is very delicate, take counsel with the confessor over what is to be done.

I desire as well, dearest sister, that you take care to receive guests with love and friendliness, as if it were the Lord Jesus himself. Show them all humanity and charity, so those who come to you may be edified. The reception of guests should be charged not to just any sisters but only the more notable, by whom those coming may be instructed and edified. The other sisters should not be busy with the guests, nor even talk with them without permission, especially the younger ones, because in our house no one approaches the windows for speaking except the two charged with this or someone else I might specifically designate. See to it as well that worldly folk not come within the walls of your place in increasing frequency, especially the unsuitable types, excepting only those who come to be edified and formed in the good. I beg of you, do not permit the sisters to visit friends and relatives outside except in cases of great urgency, especially the younger ones, but also not those you know it not to suit.

Dearest sister, I ask as well that after noon on feastdays you call the sisters together for an hour or two, and confer together on the faults and failures that have crept up among you so that these evil ways and customs might be corrected and improved. But always look out that your admonitions and chastisements proceed in and out of love. To gather in this way also greatly nourishes mutual charity and renders the sisters one in heart; it is much better to spend time so than to wander about and tell stories. Dearest sister, on whom the charge of this house rests, I humbly beg of you to watch out for useless story-telling and frequent wandering about to no purpose. Time free from work is better spent in recollection of yourself and in pleading with the dear Lord so to be united with him as not to become occupied with external things and thus to separate yourself from Him. For a sister falls back easily and the heart becomes dry unless she takes great care not to be busy with external and temporal affairs. I heartily desire that you take special care that your sisters strive to maintain silence, especially on the day they receive the sacrament of our Lord's body, nor should any then presume to speak except out of necessity until the hour of vespers has passed. Strive with all your might to see your sisters advance in the virtues, in mutual love, humility, obedience, and all the rest, just as I hope you do yourself by the grace of God and thus offer them an example. May your charity receive with gratitude this little gift which my little self composed and wrote. May God fill and perfect you according to the measure of your desire.

CHAPTER THREE

On the Life and Passion of Our Lord Jesus Christ, and Other Devotional Exercises[8]

"He who stands firm to the end will be saved" (Mt 10:22). Dear brother, most beloved in the heart of our Lord Jesus Christ, may you hold these words before the eyes of your heart and stand firm to the end. May you be saved in eternity with all the saints, with all those who not only began well but persevered to salvation bearing the holy cross of penance for the love of God. What they displayed outwardly in their habit, they also completed within and without in very truth, in true penance, that castigation of nature and cultivation of virtue in which our Lord and his saints first exercised themselves by way of example for us. In these they persevered and held constant to death, and after a little time and a little labor they acquired and now possess that eternal good which they will hold and enjoy through all ages. In this age and in the future their names will never be consigned to oblivion. They died in the natural world, but more honor is now shown to their dead remains than to living princes of this world, whence we can reflect on the reward they received in eternal life.

But, alas, there are now many men who by the grace of our Lord Jesus Christ begin wisely in the way of perfection but do not persevere; they look back and consume themselves in the flesh as beasts. They are said to be alive, but in their souls they are spiritually dead. Putting off through genuine contrition of heart and pure confession of mouth the whole sinful way of life they once spent so badly in the world, they had prepared in themselves a temple for the Holy Spirit and in receiving him within had sealed a perfect friendship with God himself as their spouse. But, sadly, they did not persevere in his friendship; leaving their first love and their faith, they looked back. Because they have bound themselves with the chain of profession, they cannot return bodily to the unhappy world, but they return in their hearts and continuously run after every delight they can acquire there, like someone starved for temporal food. Yet they do not

187

want to be labeled as such; they wish to seem what they are not, but by their fruits they are known. It is greatly to be grieved and lamented that there are so many of these in religious habits, inside and outside the orders, who are not exercised and remain unknown even to themselves, and—what is worse—rest easy in the judgment of men, which is most deceptive. Whence it is written, "If we judge ourselves, we will never be judged" (1 Cor 11:13).

This lack of exercise and self-knowledge can be recognized in their behavior, their empty and silly words, in which there is neither life nor spirit. Would that they were cold or hot but because they are lukewarm they will be vomited out of the mouth of God (see Rv 3:15). They begin to run after the desires of their own nature, seeking to satisfy their bestial appetites; thus goodwill, the fear of God, and diligence all disappear. Then they grow weary of all spiritual exercises. And because they taste nothing of the good, in themselves they disparage anything unlike them, spending day and night instead with whatever delights their nature, in eating, drinking, sleeping, joking, laughing, and chatting. When they are in conversation, their tongue brings forth that of which their heart is full. And when it is necessary for them to do or to hear something contrary to their will, or when something displeasing is asked of them, it becomes quite apparent what they exercise when they are alone. They are disobedient, unspeakable, stubborn, indignant, not given to peace or patience, not composed in their manner or exemplary in their words. They dislike solitude and prefer to be in public, ever happy to hear and inquire about the state of the world. Idle in their cells and solitude, unfruitful in spiritual exercise, they are yet ever busy, when nature has nothing better to do, with useless things, in which they expend their time without any fruit. During the hours, their hearts are more occupied within with the bestial vanity of this world than their mouths without in chant and reading. Now this and now that, now here and now there, now something in the past or now something present keeps them talking and busy, often things that will never in fact take place. They love to come to table but they are late for prayer, quick to complain and murmur when food or drink or something else falls short of what suits them.

Dearest brother, I plead with you to look out for these things when you transgress in some such way; may it displease your heart, and may you fervently seek to mend your ways and to show it in your deeds. Many good men frequently err on these points, but let them imitate David and say in their heart, "I have sinned before the Lord" (2 Kgs 12:13), and show that this was displeasing by making a real change. Hardened men, however, who make little amends and rarely return to their hearts, are like King Saul who excused his sin, refusing to recognize or correct it, and who, although he showed outward contrition, in fact thought nothing of it.

Be advised, therefore, dearest brother, and watch yourself. Carefully consider that where God is not exercised, these things will necessarily happen, for it is necessary that the nature and heart of man exercise themselves in one thing or another and therefore those who come to such indifference will decline further. How lamentably and bestially the devil will play with them and they with the devil, all because they do not labor manfully toward knowledge of themselves and victory over their shortcomings, and they do not exercise the holy life of our Lord Jesus Christ, neglecting to imitate him so far as they can. May our pious Lord grant you never to know and experience this.

So that, dearest brother, you may ever remainful watchful, increase in virtue, and persevere to salvation in that holy state which you have assumed, know that you must abstain and separate yourself from all occasions that might lead to such things and from all men who offer such an example. You must also exercise yourself constantly in the following points of the life of our Lord Jesus Christ until such time as you are taught by the spirit of truth, who will reveal the will of Our Lord to you inwardly, without any such medium, if you persevere zealously in these things.

The life of our Lord Jesus Christ, in which he preceded us, is the source of all virtue and exemplar of all holiness, the medium by which to arrive most quickly at all the virtues, and indeed apart from which we are unable to gain either the true virtues or his love. And because exercise and knowledge bring forth love, it needs first to be exercised if it is to be known. When the exercise is thus continuously held before the eyes of the heart and borne in the heart, a person comes through knowledge of this kind to his love, upon which all depends. To know these things and perfectly to imitate them is the end to which everything in holy Church is ordained and every sacred page written. Whoever neglects these things, though he know every law and writing ever decreed or written down, will never find them sufficient.

Set yourself therefore to exercise yourself in these things, to hold the works of Jesus Christ before your eyes, and to assimilate yourself to them in true charity, deep humility, ready obedience, and complete denial of yourself, in modesty, piety, peace, and patience, in contempt of all temporal matters and in modification of your own nature. At all times have your heart lifted up to God because he is the way that leads to all these virtues and apart from that way you will never arrive at God. And although, dearest brother, you often find yourself far astray and your nature too weak, do not despair or give up your devotional exercises. Labor all the more and plead for help, without which you can do nothing. I say to you and promise in the faith of our Lord Jesus Christ, if you will but bear up and persevere for a short time, these things and others even greater than can be written to you will be added so quietly that even if you wished to unburden yourself of them you could not.

First of all then, I wish and urgently beg you to put behind you all useless thoughts and all dreams as soon as you rise, whether at night or at dawn, and to put the Lord God before the eyes of your mind. In a loud voice attentively plead for some devout thing so that you may the more quickly and easily be affected by it, your heart become occupied first of all with God, and you may persist in meaningful meditations. Woe is me, a slave to sin on this point! I am myself so miserably distracted and disturbed at that hour that I can hardly hear myself crying out.

But since, dearest brother, you asked me to set forth some rules for good exercises, I write to you what holy and well-exercised men have left me, not what I myself have invented. If you were to have only what I myself had experienced, you would be little instructed, for my exercises, alas, amount still to little or nothing. For although my bestial senses are not bound still like beasts in the stable of my heart, they are nonetheless not anointed with the rich oil of the Spirit. So long as my heart dwells in Egypt, it does not cease to be plagued with flies. Ask God that my heart be fitted for his inspiration so that I be enabled to teach and write from a perfect and experienced heart.

Because I have already extensively praised devotional exercise in the life of the Lord and your time is short owing to many labors, I will describe three points for each day, first on the early life of our Lord, second on the passion and end of his life, and third on your conversion to the saints. Thus are set out three dishes for each day, as the custom is with the infirm. If you are not able to digest the first, then taste the second or third so that you may not be left without nourishment from the true food for your soul, the most holy life of our Lord Jesus Christ, who is himself it.

MONDAY. Dear and most beloved brother, after you rise on Monday and collect yourself, put these three points before your mind as devoutly as possible. First, God created you in his own image in the innermost part of your soul, a rational creature superior to all others and equal to the angels. He gave you five senses and an intellect and he made you able to come to the supreme good, that is, to himself, to enjoy it perpetually, and to possess it and his eternal kingdom with the good angels and all his saints in eternity if you keep his commandments, just as he promised. Again, he created heaven and earth and all that is in them for you, for your ministry and use, that is, the sun, moon, stars, day and night, water and air, birds, fishes, the beasts and all animals, flowers, plants, trees and herbs, and all fruits of the land, silver, gold, and in short all being under heaven on earth, whose multitude is beyond counting and beyond telling. With gratitude, therefore, you can rightly exclaim, "I will bless the Lord at all times" (Ps 33/34:2).

Again, think about the early life of Jesus, his incarnation: how that uncreated eternal truth, that omnipotent God whom all heaven and earth could not contain, took flesh and blood from the most holy Virgin Mary; how humbly she responded and remained within even though she knew and firmly believed the great miracle God had worked within her by which she had conceived and was about to bring forth her Creator and God and yet was to remain a virgin. Sing with jubilation the Ave Maria and devoutly reflect on the Gospel text, "In the sixth month God sent the angel Gabriel" and so on (Lk 1:26).

The second point you are to think about is the beginning of his passion, that is, the last supper which our Lord had with his disciples: how humbly he washed their feet, how after eating that paschal lamb he consecrated his own most holy body and blood, how he gave and instituted the sacrament for his disciples, that meal as a singular testament and his most holy blood in the cup as a memorial to him, and finally how with his words he instructed and consoled them most lovingly. Here you should call to memory some of the special and most loving words from that meal so as to grasp in your heart how much love he showed them there. For instance, "I have eagerly desired to eat this passover with you before I die" (Lk 22:15); or "You will know that you are my disciples if you love one another" (Jn 13:35); or "You will weep and mourn while the world rejoices; you will grieve, but your grief turn to joy" (Jn 16:20); or "I will not leave you as orphans; I will come to see you" (Jn 14:18). You ought to understand, to break and to chew upon those words with all your strength, and with great sobs you should observe how far you are from them yourself. Then consider the prayer he uttered in agony and his resignation of himself into the hands of his heavenly Father even to bitter death and also that bloody sweat he sweat in fear of the death he was about to suffer. Now throw yourself to the ground and with the loud voice of your heart and folded hands cry out and say, "O grieving Lord, how shall I repay you for all you have given me. I will accept the cup of salvation" (Ps 115:12/116:12–13).

The third point is to turn yourself to the holy angels. For on this day, Monday, put before your eyes all the holy angels, their continuous and fervent love of God, their great and admirable purity. Ask them for continuous help and oversight because they were ordained by God to this end. Turn to them with great reverence, knowing that always and everywhere they are watching you and all your works are manifest to them.

On TUESDAY, the first point of meditation follows that from Monday. First, how God created from nothing the heaven and earth and all that in them is together with the angels and every other creature and preserves each in being, how he was made man because of you, indeed the poorest and most abject of all men ever to come forth from the womb of a woman. Consider, brother, how that sweet and holy little boy was wrapped in vile rags, laid upon straw in a manger, announced by angels to shepherds, and how they came with haste to Bethlehem testifying about the boy that he was the savior of the world. Raise your voice now in praise and sing with the angels, "Glory in the highest to God" (Lk 2:14).

Then meditate upon the arrest of the Lord, how humbly and freely he who created the heaven and the earth allowed himself to be bound for your sake, how his loving face was struck and spit upon, and how he was treated by them, bruised, thrown upon the ground, punished throughout the night, and made sport of, and then finally how he was led to Pilate and sent from Pilate to Herod and how he sent him back rejected, bruised, and dressed in white as a fool.

On this same day, when you have a chance, turn to all the holy apostles of God who were made princes of eternal life for their singular holiness and on the last day will judge the world with God. Devoutly implore them to deign to intercede with the Lord for you. And if you love any one of the apostles specially, plead with him so much the more fervently, doing the same on every other day with any of the holy martyrs, confessors, monks, and virgins whom you especially prefer and for whom you can read one Our Father or some other special prayer.

On WEDNESDAY, meditate upon how the boy Jesus was circumcised on the eighth day and how while still so young his holy blood was poured out for you, whereupon he was called Jesus. To this holy name all spirits, in heaven, on earth, and in hell, bend their knees. When therefore you hear or sing this sweet name of Jesus, reverently bow your head because it is by virtue of this name that you will be saved. Always do the same when you hear the sweet name of Mary. Here further exercise yourself in the point of this day, as devoutly as possible.

Next contemplate how our Lord Jesus was stripped of his clothes, stretched out against a pillar and bound there, wounded and scourged from head to foot, and then how he poured out his holy blood so copiously that those punishing him were able to wash their feet in it, the very blood he had once received from the Virgin, and how he alone, man and God, was born without spot or sin from the pure Virgin Mary and yet willed to be so bitterly wounded and punished for your sake. Thinking upon this punishment and all the other points of his passion, lament deeply and continuously that you are able to suffer so little for him, and ardently ask that you be ever grateful for all his pain and suffering so that his precious blood may not be lost on you.

On this same day place before your eyes the faith and righteousness of the patriarchs and prophets and their great desire that Christ should come. Ask that by their intervention they might deign to grant you from Christ perfectly to imitate them and to persevere in every virtue.

On THURSDAY, meditate as devoutly as you can upon how he showed himself to those three wise men and was recognized by them as the true king of heaven and earth, as they demonstrated by their gifts. Consider here with a sweet and loving heart the great faith they had: In the presence of a poor virgin and of Joseph, a miserable old man, they discovered an exiled little boy wrapped in vile rags, whom they nevertheless reverently adored upon their knees. And then meditate further upon such a solemn occasion in the way any sweet and well-disposed heart ought profitably to think on it.

Next consider how our Lord was wounded by the impious. Feel in your heart, alas, how cruelly they pressed that sharp crown of thorns upon his head and how they spit upon him, genuflecting before him, and hit him and hung a despicable robe on his shoulders in derision. O daughter of Jerusalem, my beloved soul, may that glorious King, crowned and so despised, never pass from your heart, and may it forget all other worldly riches, all vain glory, and all the delights of this world for the love of him who for your sake was so scandalously led out and put on display. Finally grasp in your heart the word of Pilate to the Jews, "Here is the man" (Jn 9:14).

Next on that same day turn your attention to the holy martyrs who so lovingly poured out their blood for the love of God and so willingly gave themselves over to death for eternal life. Call upon them also for patience and in every tribulation plead with them for victory, particularly those, as mentioned earlier, for whom you have a special devotion.

On FRIDAY, observe how in the temple over the altar he was offered to his heavenly father in the holy virgin hands of his beloved mother and then redeemed from it just like all other infants, how Simeon and Anna recognized him and how with great desire they fulfilled with him their holy oblation. In all these points our faith and hope are greatly strengthened.

Then with your whole strength exercise yourself in the way your most beloved Creator and Redeemer was whipped, crowned, weighed down with the cross and led away to death like a robber, stripped of all his clothing before all those men on the mount of Calvary, fixed to and stretched out over the holy cross, and abandoned by all men, how bitterly for your sake he died on that cross, he the immortal and almighty God from whom everything that lives receives and preserves its life, who is alone the beginning and end of all creatures and the cause of all causes, and of whose death you are the cause. Think and see what you owe to this holy death, how much voluntary suffering and mortification of all the delights of your nature, how much humility, obedience, and patience, how much love and voluntary poverty and virtue and perfection. Consider then all the other things that took place on the cross, beneath the cross and around it, and with all your strength think diligently upon them, as if you stood beneath the cross, gazing upon and seeing each particular. Incline your ears and hear what he cries out to you from the cross. "You have wounded my heart, my sister and spouse" (Sg 4:9). Respond to him with enflamed desire. "Draw me after you," O most beautiful among the sons of men (Sg 1:3). Look into the face of your Christ and see his whole body livid, covered with blood and his five open wounds. Enter them in your heart and have your sins washed in the blood flowing from them. Join your heart to his and be kindled with the fire of his love; taste how sweet is your lord, your spouse and lover. Hear and chew upon his seven words from the cross, drawing out their inner kernel, most worthy of all sweetness, imitation, and mystery.

Betake yourself next to all the holy confessors. Examine their many and difficult labors. See how perfectly they offered to God friends, acquaintances, and possessions, temporal goods and worldly honors, how they left all the delights of their own nature for God and followed him in great poverty. Implore them with great diligence that they by their holy intercession deign to grant you perseverance in the holy cross of penance which you undertook in love of him.

On SATURDAY, remember how Jesus, that youthful and almighty king who could reduce all creatures to nothing in a moment, in a dark and lonely night fled into Egypt, and in what poverty he lived seven years in a foreign land with his beloved mother Mary. In so doing he offered you and all men a special example that perverse men, no matter how perverse they may be, are better borne with patience than persuaded by reason.

On that same day turn especially to the blessed Virgin Mary and carefully consider her great sorrow, and how on that day she alone remained constant in faith. Therefore, holy Church preserves her memory specially on that day throughout the whole year. Spend this day accordingly with her and plead urgently with her for chastity in heart and body. Consider as well her holy life and her modest conduct: Imitate her example, for she is the perfect exemplar of all virtue and purity. Meditate as well upon the deposition of Christ from the cross, his burial and lying in the tomb, the descent of his soul into hell and visitation of the holy fathers in limbo, who had looked expectantly and continuously there for the glory of his divinity until the day of resurrection.

Then put before the eyes of your mind the life of the holy virgins, who left behind all the delights of their own bodies for the sake of God and conquered their own natures through penance, extinguishing the fire of carnal desire with the fire of divine love. Taking them as an example, pray for purity of heart and body, constantly imploring them for aid in your infirmity.

On SUNDAY, you must observe how humbly our Lord Jesus came to the baptism of John and wished to be baptized by him, he who wiped away the crimes of the whole world with his holy blood, who alone was born and died without sin. Note how at that time the heavens were opened and the Holy Spirit descended upon him in the form of a dove and the voice of the Father was heard saying, "This is my beloved son in whom I am well pleased. Listen to him" (Mk 1:11).

Then recall again everything from this time to his last meal, his whole life including his temptations while fasting, his hard labor while preaching, his holy prayer practiced frequently through the night, his laborious steps going from place to place, the loving signs of his love demonstrated to mankind, his great thirst, his extreme and voluntary poverty, extraordinary heat and cold, his drinking at the well, temptation by Satan in the desert where he fasted for forty days while living with beasts, his lying down and sleeping upon the ground, and his tears flowing in great compassion for the blindness of mankind. Note each and every one of these points in his life and most holy passion, and reflect upon his great and incomprehensible love shown to you and to all men, as well as his great humility and patience.

Then meditate upon the resurrection of our Lord Jesus Christ who on the last day will raise all the dead, how he liberated his friends from hell and showed himself to Mary Magdalene and his other disciples. Go on to his ascension into heaven and the coming and work of the Holy Spirit, with whom he filled the disciples and friends who in prayer and secrecy had looked for his coming. Then break out into jubilation and ask the Holy Spirit, the comforter of the world, to come into you, singing the hymn, "Come Holy Spirit."

On this same day turn to all the saints of God in general, lifting your heart up to pray for their help. Observe their great charity, the salvation they brought to all men, and then place your confidence in them and demand their aid with urgency, because in every time and tribulation they are prepared to help you by their intercession. And if you so turn to them every day, your desire and devotion toward them will be increased and you will obtain special grace from God through their intercession.

My dearest brother, although I have set out three points for you to exercise each day, know that if one of them pleases you more especially than another you should persevere in it. For it is necessary to provide a special measure of exercises in two or three points for unexercised hearts lest they be seduced into a variety of ways by the levity and instability of their souls. Those unable to find rest in one can then, as mentioned, see what delight another holds if that one will not do. But when you try to exercise yourself in this way, many evil desires and scattered thoughts may overtake you, and it will seem hard and laborious at first—but never stop. Call out to heaven for help; seek, ask, knock. Even though heaven seems bronze to you and the earth iron owing to the hardness and insensitivity of your heart, do not turn to some harmful consolation or some other useless thing. Even though it seems a total waste of time and of no profit whatsoever, do not leave the place in which you are sitting. All incidental thoughts—such as "I could be doing this or that now" or "That would be better"—you should not allow to rise up, nor should you give any place to the devil. Lift your heart and your hands to heaven. Rise, devoutly fall to your knees, and rouse your nature, praying aloud, as was said before, if you are not able to pray in your heart.

Dearest brother, keep yourself from impatience, even when you remain hard and without devotion in prayer and discover no taste for it. Ask God humbly, and persevere in peace; ask him not what pleases you but that his will be done. And look out above all not to do yourself any irrational violence and thus lose your mind. Images which you do not wish to have and from which you wish to be freed, you must allow to come and go. And if what you propose comes to no effect, simply go through the points of the day literally for a time until it goes better for you. Never put the whole off because of hardness or insensibility, but ask God that he would deign to supply, because without him you cannot see it through. Know too that it may be more acceptable to him that you persist in such insensibility and resignation, always careful lest through any faults of your own you give it cause, rather than if you were to have great devotion and sweetness in your exercises. When a man has great sweetness and delight in his devotion, he sometimes ends up in a measure of self-complacency; it seems to him that no one matches him in sanctity and that God cares for no one but him. That is totally deceiving, nothing but evil pride; and through it men sometimes come to eternal harm, wandering wholly away from God. Frequently God even allows such men to fall into terrible temptations, whether in shameful or public vices, so they may learn to know and humble themselves. Those, however, who through no fault of their own, that is, where the cause does not lie in their own defects, remain in great insensibility, will make greater progress because in their long-suffering they take possession of their souls and serve their creator God beyond their own merits, thus making, though they do not feel it, maximal progress.

Evenings, my beloved brother, always call to mind how you have lived over the preceding day. In whatever point or way you transgressed in word or thought, in manner or deed, in commission or omission, recognize it before God and confess it in true contrition. Ask God that he deign to spare his poor creature who daily offends so flippantly and frequently. Consider as well, what you were, what you are, and what you will shortly be. Where are now the men and women who were once lords and princes of the land? Where is all their delight and whatever they possessed in this temporal world, their vanities and riches, youth, beauty, manifold delights and precious ornaments, all the things with which they pleased the world and the devil while they lost the friendship of God and all his saints? Carefully note that every evil work, so delightful to the flesh, brings the loss and privation of eternal life. I ask that you always put this point to men when they come to you from the world, so that your heart and theirs might first be pricked before you discuss any other business with them. For with these kinds of words it is necessary to shape and arouse cold hearts so they will diligently pay attention and afterward be instructed.

Dearest brother, be mature and not light in your manner, especially around secular folk, because foolish manners and too many words about useless things ill become spiritual men. Today everything is called spiritual bliss and re-creation of the soul, when most of it is damnable dissolution. Observe the manner of our Lord Jesus Christ, in whom there was never known to appear anything secular, vain, or pompous, dissolute or inordinate. When men of the world visit you, do not permit them to speak with you of their wives and daughters or jewels or homes or worldly power, lest you take from them harmful images that will hinder your prayers. And if you hear new gossip, do not pass it on among your brothers, even if it seems good. Learn to keep quiet about good things so you may better hold your peace on useless things. For he who uses many words weakens his soul.

Whatever you ask of others, whether in your own name or someone else's, do it with modest words, piously asking "My dearest brother, could you do this or that for the sake of God?" Except in real need never keep anyone from his exercises for conversation, lest you become for both of you an occasion of damnation, which you could thereby draw down upon yourself.

Beloved brother, always remember the holy words of blessed Gregory, "Those whom God delights to hold, he will keep far removed from external affairs." Therefore never aspire to external offices, or desire any command nor become envious of those who hold them, even when they seem faulty in them. Thank and praise God when you find support through them, for it is no small thing to rule other men and provide for them. It is to be feared that there are few of good spirit who seek after this. A good man might well have a good inclination to such things, but he will resist such inclinations by his reason and thus be turned from them by the grace of God. Remember in that connection how many friends of God avoided such things, men who were nonetheless worthy and chosen by God to this end. Know too that abundant evil overtakes many good men just because they were appointed to external offices too quickly and became too occupied in external affairs before they were up to such things or had fully proven themselves.

When you can be, remain willingly alone, that is, if you can bear it.

Be open in your confession. Do not be embarrassed to say all you thought or did that is evil and avoidable because you can drive out the devil in no better way than to reveal his whole counsel. Natural modesty and shyness, at a time when a man ought to be open, has destroyed many.

Constantly think how you might spend the present time more usefully, and always do whatever your conscience or reason dictates as more useful, unless something was specially enjoined upon you under obedience or precept. You will more diligently move toward perfection the less you are inclined toward what you choose by your own will, and learn always to break your own will. It is most harmful to a religious man and most displeasing to God, who came not to do his own will but that of his father.

Try to do everything in such a way that your heart remains free, open, and unchanged except by the exercises of that particular day. And whatever you do, do with a modest and peaceful heart. When you are busy with external matters either within or without, try always to lift your heart upward and turn it toward God, praying with heart or mouth something from a devout author in which you may find rest and with which you may repress perverse thoughts, which will otherwise mightily seize, resist, and block your heart. Do nothing entirely without counsel, and always trust experienced men more than yourself. Learn to submit piously to your fellow religious in all matters good and reasonable, and to humble yourself under your brothers because of him who subjected himself to all men.

Be content to suffer patiently whatever God permits to come over you whether it be from men or even from himself, or whatever other grievous thing may happen to you. Consider that if God had permitted it you would have had to bear eternal damnation and been repaid according to your merits. Many men suffer even more than

you. When it seems to you that someone does you an injury or something contrary, call to mind that you often do things contrary to God
and your neighbor. And when others do not satisfy you or fail to
carry out what you want of them, remember that you often neglected or failed to do what God commanded you. Think: They have
less guilt for not fulfilling their promises to you than you for not carrying out divine commands. When however someone offends or an-
noys you in their frailty, realize that you in your evil state of mind
probably offend more than he who seems to offend you. Consider
that it is probably your own malice that upsets you rather than another's. Turn your anger and displeasure therefore away from him
and toward yourself; work first to help yourself and then him. Correct first in yourself whatever displeases you in another. Cultivate in
yourself the virtues you see in another, just as you desire that those
virtues should favor you that God has worked in you; then you can
rejoice as if they were your own. Look upon the image of God, his
most holy death, his precious blood, and even upon yourself in other
men because each man is an image of God, redeemed by his bitter
death and precious blood, and they are just as precious to God as
you are.

Be sober and modest in your food and drink, especially when
you do not have it to your liking, either prepared or unprepared; then
especially do not murmur. Conduct yourself patiently, remember
the considerable hunger and want of our Lord Jesus, how often he
ate sparingly in fields and upon the ground from rough and unprepared food.

Dear and beloved brother, be pure in heart and thought. Lust
is a terrible enemy to good men. When lustful and perverse thoughts
come upon you, make the sign of the cross over your heart and say
a Hail Mary. Reflect on the purity of the holy mother of God and of
all the saints and the great merit of chastity. Resist manfully, and the
Lord will be your helper, because no one will receive a crown who
has not truly fought.

Vigorously resist avarice, the inclination to desire or to have
anything you do not need. Have before your eyes that eternal good,
a good far better than anything you might acquire here. Wholly
avoid receiving pay for anything, even if it might seem necessary to
you. For things are often possessed in ownership and a man then
thinks himself free; but he only experiences that when he is forced
to give them up.

Be humble in heart and appearance. Do not make too much of

yourself or presume too easily on your own strength. O my dearest brothers, how much I have fallen in this. And would that I did not have so many companions. For it is often far different than what we think about ourselves, but only when we are touched by someone do we and others experience what we really are. Have before your eyes as an example the humility of our Lord Jesus Christ, his blessed mother, all his saints. See their humility, how poor and abject they were in the world.

After holy communion guard yourself from too many words and other external affairs. Try to spend that time especially on good things, lest you impede the holy sacrament in its work. For just as any good man who guards and exercises himself as he should will then receive from God and sense special grace, so whoever neglects to exercise himself and turn toward God will become even further hardened and alienated from God. I would prefer that, after you undertook these exercises, you would, with the consent of your superiors, go to communion every week, because you would thus receive a wondrous grace and special fortitude against all the temptations of the enemy, and I would hope that this would prove very acceptable to God.

Never refuse your brothers what they ask of you if it is within your disposition. For God's sake be ready to serve each one, the lesser as well as the greater, and especially the infirm and those suffering tribulation and anxiety. Do not fail to serve them and to act as a consoler to them, because that is as acceptable to God as if you did it to him.

Do not condemn or judge any living man, whatever his condition or way of life, but do to all men what you would have them do to you. Hold all men in reverence, especially those who are spiritual and seem to draw nearer to God.

Love to be unknown and prefer rejection by others. Bear patiently everything others, as it seems, do to you. Forgive those who wrong you with heart and mouth before God, and pray for those who offend you. When anyone offends or upsets you, whether or not it be your fault, constantly seek forgiveness, recognizing your own fault and showing him all humility until you placate him. When you are reproached for your faults, immediately and humbly admit them without contradiction, and in all things straight or crooked learn to break your own will.

Keep yourself very simple and separate from others. Put all your hope in God, and learn to bring before him all evil and adver-

sity. See what passions move you in all things, and resist them manfully. Commit your heart to God in complete confidence, and be
ever grateful to him in the midst of whatever happens to you.

While lying in bed keep your heart from impure thoughts, because your nature is then especially inclined toward them. Think of
something good and do not play with yourself for any devilish or
carnal delight. Read a psalm or hymn until you fall asleep, if thinking
something good offers no delight.

At table turn your heart toward God at least three times, or
more, in some brief and devotional prayer.

Have particular reverence for the blessed Virgin Mary, frequently invoking her and holding her before your eyes, for she is
accustomed above all to intercede and grant grace.

Also make a general confession once a day, and recognize before
God all the faults in which you daily transgress, in brief or in detail
as time permits, thus sitting in honest judgment upon yourself. And
when you recognize them, note as well the root from which they
come forth. Placing them before God, call down violence upon yourself and upon all these enemies who daily overcome you, seeking
God as helper for you his own creature.

Examine strictly how much in the day you have progressed or
fallen back. If you were lukewarm or unfaithful in prayer and the
hours, if you were impatient with your exercises because of preoc-
cupation, humble yourself before God and seek forgiveness, because
humility is most acceptable to God. This last point in particular you
should never neglect, because when you recognize how much you
have advanced in knowledge of your faults, you will advance equally
in knowledge of God. Knowledge of faults makes a man unhappy
with himself; the more a man is displeasing to himself, the more he
is pleasing to God. You should therefore be taught far more by your
own experience than by what all the books could teach you apart
from self-examination. And when you thus exercise and come to an
inward knowledge of yourself, then the whole of Scripture will become your servant, as if you had put down those things yourself or
it was written just for you. And when you withdraw your senses
thus into yourself, that is, toward self-knowledge, you will acquire
a tenacious memory.

Lastly, I ask you, brother, so far as possible never to neglect
your exercises in the points concerning the Lord's passion as assigned
to the various days. Exercise those especially, and frequently draw
them to your heart. And if they simply have no taste for you, then
take the "one hundred articles"[9] in memory of the Lord's passion

which you can read inwardly with the heart or outwardly with the mouth, as it best suits you to arouse within yourself the passion of Christ. Do not worry how much of them you read, but work to experience their taste in your heart. Read article one or two, then close the book and recall what bitter things the sweet Lord bore for you, such a vile and negligent creature. Next open the book again and again until your stony heart is softened and you are content with the devotional prayers there. Then close the book and with an open heart pray them according to their sense, thanking God for the grace and devotion granted you in your exercises. And if none of this profits at all, then humbly recognize your own guilt and seek forgiveness. But, dearest brother, this cannot happen without abundant divine grace. If you so exercise yourself, you will sense its singular fruit, though at the beginning it may seem less tasty to you.

O beloved brother, what is sweeter, what more secure, more pleasing to God, and more consoling to a simple dove than devoutly to tarry in the cleft of the rock, that is, in the wounds of our Lord Jesus Christ? The sweet Lord, your loving spouse, allows you not only to tarry daily in them, to find delight and rest, but also with that charity by which he was wounded and died, to live each day unto death.

Though I quickly noted down for you this rule or rather this material for entering quickly into certain holy exercises, recognize that it is not equally suitable for all men. The gifts of the Holy Spirit are of many kinds and granted to men according to their qualities, to one this and to another that. The Lord our God, though mighty and powerful, wants to be served in various ways. Therefore a man should vigorously cry out with David and reflect upon what he said: "I will listen to what the Lord God says in me" (Ps 84:9/85:8). For one rests in the wounds of Christ, by far the more secure; another rejoices jubilantly in his unspeakable and marvelous works; a third, exercised in the future goods, hopes and rejoices in the expectation of heavenly things; a fourth bows his head to the ground groaning and beseeching because of the magnitude of his sins and he dares not look up toward heaven; a fifth is frightened by the terrible judgment and torments of the damned and by such fear is kept in the path of God's commands, as a boat is preserved among the breakers by its rudder.

Test the points described, dearest brother, as to whether they suit your inner inspiration, and since the materials are various, take up only those which suit you best. If anything is lacking for you in these, the Holy Spirit will teach it to you more perfectly than anyone could write it to you, if you prepare for Him so far as possible a pure and open heart. May God grant you that. Amen.

On the Times When These Exercises Are to Be Meditated Upon

The three points of the described exercises are to be ruminated upon each day because they look immediately and objectively to God and they bring a man quickly to the knowledge and love of him. No one comes to the Father except through Christ (cf. Jn 14:6). Before mealtime, review: The first point is to be thought upon at night or in the morning when you rise, the second while hearing mass, especially during the canon when Christ is present before you, and the third when the refectory bell rings for the meal. For then you are better able to think back over the virtues, holiness, and labors of the saints known to you after completing the points prescribed for the day. Turn over some hymn or sequence, some response or antiphon concerning those same saints, which may wonderfully illumine a man's heart and lead toward the knowledge and imitation of them. Upon completing the meal, as you have time, take up this additional exercise to induce fear and to whip your back, as it were, into progress: on Monday the last judgment, on Tuesday all the benefits of God, on Wednesday death, on Thursday the pains of hell, on Friday the Lord's passion, on Saturday sinfulness, and on the Lord's Day the kingdom of Heaven. You find material for that in *The Spiritual Ascents.*

This is the way brothers from the congregations of the devout are accustomed to exercise themselves.

CHAPTER FOUR

The Humble Exercise and Resolution of John Kessel, Once Cook in the Lord Florens House in Deventer[10]

"What shall I render to you, God eternal, for all you have given me?" O dear John, take pity on yourself and with great diligence and all your strength think back on your past life, what you were in the world, what you still are, what you promised to become. Think of the inestimable goodness of our Lord Jesus Christ, shown to you more than to many others. Think how much more stringently he will judge you than them, if you do not make amends. Stand in fear, and think that he who has so kindly spared you will perhaps not be willing to spare you any longer.

Set it in your heart that today, or at the latest tomorrow, you will die, and consider where you will go then. "Woe is me, God eternal, where shall I flee from the face of your anger, because my sins are more than the sands of the sea." Yet I know most truly that nothing displeases you so much as despairing and that you seek not the death but the repentance of sinners.

Say to him therefore with a groan from your heart: May the immense pity of God look upon me, a miserable sinner; may his evident mercy be turned upon me, a sinful man. Behold, desolated I come to the Almighty, wounded I run to the Physician. Keep your customary piety, you who held the sword of vengeance suspended for so long. Wipe out the number of my iniquities with the multitude of your mercies.

You can think of the mercy of God in many other ways, as in David, St. Peter, St. Paul, Mary Magdalene, the publicans, and many other sinners. The whole life of Christ shows how merciful he was toward those who repented and came to him. He did not consider how much they had sinned but how much they loved. If I am to come to such love, I must see my own frailty, in truth perceive that of myself I can do nothing good, and constantly hold before my eyes God's greatness and fidelity and my own smallness and infidelity. Here much else is to be considered. If I rightly looked into these things, they would reduce me to a state of subjection toward all men and contempt for myself such that I would desire to be condemned. But this must be exercised truly and by way of constant thought, calling frequently upon God from whom it must come.

If then I am to arrive at such humility and love, I must have a daily exercise and rule to bring me there. According to the sayings of the saints, I must look back upon my past sins, holding them ever before my eyes and trying to reflect often on them. This will deeply oppress and humble me so that I will not make much of my brothers' and other men's faults nor make hasty judgments about them but rather with compassion draw them toward the better. It is good for me to work toward this. I should beware of digging into the deeds or curious talk of others and should altogether flee distraction and try to excuse anything I might hear and put it entirely behind me.

It will help me a good deal to consider the virtues of my brothers, whom, I judge, have in large part never committed mortal sin. By contrast, I should censor the greatness of my own sins and should find that I am not worthy to live among them or to serve them. I should rather hold them in reverence and hope that through their good works and prayers I may come to life eternal.

I must also at all times have the presence of God before my eyes, and each day in my work I should strive from within to think some good thought. I wish especially to follow that most worthy mirror, the life of our Lord Jesus Christ, his humility, his piety, his patience, his contemptibility and poverty, and especially his love. I will try hard to look upon each man as the image of God and to carry out all my work as if I did it for Christ. That will greatly ease my work and render me of good will to all individuals. I will try also to read my prayers attentively and without hurrying and will frequently genuflect in the course of my labors and work, and I will pray moderately and briefly with attentiveness.

When you hear the bell each morning at three you ought to rise without delay and immediately think something good with thanksgiving for the mercies of God. Think too of your own miserable state, that God is present here with the angels and the saints, and look to what you read and to whom you talk. Bend your knees or sit properly without laziness or stretching out one way or the other, and so conduct yourself always in prayer. After matins and prime study

Holy Scripture, and if you become drowsy write a little something down from your reading.

When the fifth hour sounds reflect whether there is anything you have to do in the kitchen, and if you think there is nothing there to do, close the kitchen and bind books or whatever else might be assigned to you instead until the time comes to enter the kitchen. When the bell strikes for mass, begin to read terce on bended knees in the house, up to the psalms. And read the rest through as you are walking along the way to church. In church sit upright on your knees in some corner through the whole mass, and think about the life and passion of our Lord Jesus Christ, as you are accustomed to do. When mass is finished begin to read sext and read up to the psalms in church, then the rest while walking home.

When you have returned from the church to the kitchen, first pray a little and resolve in your heart how you wish to conduct yourself through the day and in what points you must make amends. Try hard to achieve this, holding before your eyes, as was said, the divine mirror of the life and ways of our beloved Lord Jesus Christ, and the fact that you minister to him and not to men.

In the course of your efforts and work, you ought frequently to pray briefly on bent knees with attentiveness, especially at the sound of the bell and when the church bell is struck upon the elevation of the sacred body of our Lord Jesus Christ. Force yourself frequently to think some good thought in the midst of your work, for instance, something about the benefits of God, the kingdom of heaven, the judgment, death. And when someone knocks before the kitchen work is done, force yourself to give a good response. And if you have time, study a little in your collection of excerpts.

Whenever you see one of the brothers inside or outside the house, look upon him as Christ, especially those who bear responsibility for the house. And if any of them wants something from you, do it quickly and with a happy face.

Before you begin to eat, read the "Benedicite" and be zealous to read or meditate on something good during the meal. Beware that you not eat too quickly or from food or drink more delicate than that of the brothers in the dining room, and rise quickly when someone during the meal rings the bell to be served at table. After the meal provide the reader with a warm meal the same as the brothers. Meanwhile read a grace and put back the remaining food, together with the vessels from the kitchen in their proper places, so far as you are able.

When you return to your room after the meal, immediately read nones and then do your work until you hear the second bell for vespers in the church of the friars minor [the nearby Franciscan church], unless you have something else to do in the house or outside, and then read your vespers. And if there is any time left over, think or study something good until the fourth hour has been sounded, and then enter the kitchen to prepare the evening meal for the brothers.

After the evening meal, consider what the infirm and the brothers will eat the next day. If the necessary things are already in the kitchen, go to your room and read your complines and afterward you can study and do something good until the eighth hour sounds.

After the eighth hour, you ought to write down your faults, think something good based on holy materials, and pray something with the invocation of the saints—and with all that go to sleep about the ninth hour, trying to fall asleep in the midst of holy meditation. And if at any time you are suddenly awakened, begin to think immediately on the holy matters with which you may again seek to fall asleep.

Above all these other things I must resolve obedience, so that whatever the rectors of the house order or advise differently from what I had thought, I might at once abandon myself to their counsel and do at once what they want. I should also try to possess no thing and be about no work with any inordinate love, and thus I may the more easily abandon myself. I must try also to hold those in reverence and honor who are the keepers and procurators of the house, and be very careful lest I acquire any hard thoughts or suspicions about them, but rather do simply and piously what they want without judging or scrutinizing why this or that. I should hold ever before my eyes my own simplicity and that I am not wise and should hold their wisdom for great. And I should always hold before my eyes that I resigned myself over to them in the place of God and am not my own. This, however, I did with no binding vow but a free and simple will, a resolve that I hope will prove salutary in allowing me to stand thus and not to act upon my own vision and will. Therefore I want to think hard about myself and ask them often to put me down.

I must try, moreover, in all my works, words, and thoughts to fear God more than men, so that whatever I do be done purely to honor God and to please him alone. In whatever matters I might transgress, I should fear to offend God more than men. And at all times I should keep myself from boasting, from any yearning for display and the praise of men. I should try especially to maintain si-

208

lence, which will greatly help in many ways. I should speak in a provident way, and read one Ave Maria before I speak or make some response, and I should not make of things more than they are. Especially in the kitchen I should beware of falling and of using too many high-sounding words. I should also warn any others who do any of these things.

I should try whenever possible to be alone and armed from within, and in particular I should never be idle and always on guard against hearing or saying detracting things.

Be diligent in the office entrusted to you; keep good watch over these external matters. Be obedient in this, and appear kindly to all, especially in procuring food for the infirm, particularly for Lord Florens himself who is weak and infirm almost daily. Be kindly toward all guests, receiving them as Christ himself, but do not speak much with them. I should also look well upon the poor, and in all these matters I should do only what is charged to me to the best of my ability. Thus I can hold all of them in reverence, show them all kindness, and keep good charge of the things assigned to me.

When I go out on business, I should try to keep watch over my eyes, to read or think something good while in the public square, and to return home as quickly as possible.

I should try often to disclose my temptations and at least once in eight days lament to someone about my faults, thus to receive some remedy, while always trying to show myself guilty and arguing with no one. If I should break or neglect something, I want freely to beg forgiveness for it.

I want also to keep myself from too much tasting of food beforehand without necessity and from drinking anytime outside mealtime apart from the permission of superiors. I should not do anything behind their backs which I would not dare to do in their presence.

I must make a special effort to do humble and despised works and thus whenever possible to lighten the load of our brothers Matthew and John, to hold them in reverence, to show them kindness, and to be always ready to help them in some humble work.

I will watch myself so that complaint about clothing, food, and the like is never heard from me. I will try rather to feel that I am not worthy of whatever things I lack.

I ought also to try to study those books that will help me in these things and indeed to point my whole study in this direction. I will try to conduct myself somberly in going, standing, sitting, and the like.

It is good for me to value the exercises of our house above all others, and to have a good affection for my work in the kitchen and a good resolve to die in this state. No adventure and no thing whatsoever should separate me from this, saving always obedience.

In this I have great confidence in our most loving Lord that he wishes thus to forgive me all my sins and to grant me a special reward for all my labors, however small. Even though many other good works are greater and holier, I will nonetheless not leave my work. I will remain firmly in place and trust that no work is more salutary and useful for me than that to which the Lord has called me.

I want additionally each day after the eighth hour to examine myself fully according to this program, to see wherein I have transgressed, and then, I hope, strongly to resolve in that to make full amends in future.

CHAPTER FIVE

Certain Exercises of
Lord Dirk of Herxen
Found after His Death[11]

The stability of our way of life cannot be provided by any human arrangement or any support men can procure, but we must pray God to bear us up so that we become worthy workers in his vineyard and so that he not take from us the kingdom of God and hand it over to another people who will bring forth his fruit. We must also ask that anyone about to ruin our way of life through his lukewarm ways remove himself in good time before he ruins others; indeed the mother congregation should throw him up and cast him forth as an abortive child.

May the good Lord not suffer me to be defrauded of the fruit of this way of life before I bring it to completion, that is, bear my cross before him, tolerate happily his reproaches, and satiate my mind with the sacred senses of Scripture, which is to draw from the words of Holy Scripture their hidden manna and then to offer that to others for their salvation.

What heavy burdens and perplexities are borne through trust in God, who will never desert those who hope in him. If you wish to possess this, flee pride and presumption in yourself. The proud man relies on himself and therefore stands in a precarious state, for he is borne up by that which is nothing. The humble man relies on God and therefore stands firm.

If you could obtain only one petition from God for your advancement, then seek first contempt of yourself.

A man condemns those who do injury to him; yet who does more injury to us than we do to ourselves? A man condemns anyone who gravely offends and irritates God, but who does that more than you?

He who is to spend time in conversation with other men must be very circumspect in his words. He must take care not to flatter nor to disparage, not to confound or to denigrate, not to lie, not to speak presumptuously or boastfully or with vainglory, nor to offend

211

by any disordered carrying on. He who does not guard against these will suffer a heavy conscience, disquiet in his heart, and strife. With grief he will have to say, "As often as I was among men, I returned a lesser man."

He is in good shape who says (as we put it in Dutch)[12], "I am at peace with whatever God does"; better who says, "With God I cannot be driven wholly to ruin"; and best who says, "God could do no better with me than what he is doing."

If you wish to acquire a heart at rest, try not to take too severely corporal punishment, injury, reproach, and contempt.

Pray God that he forgive your sins, that he drive away adversaries who tempt you, that he wipe away evil images from the face of your mind, that he so order things around you as to change for the better that which you fear, that he visit you with his presence, that he quieten you by imposing silence on the tumult of your vices and cares, that he sanctify you by gracing your interior person with the gifts of purity and virtue, that he beatify you by granting you a place in the heavenly homeland.

A person lives in God when he is forgetful of himself and seeks not his own but the things of God, taking his delight in God himself.

In a time of evil and misfortune, give thanks to God, saying: "May it so please you, Lord God," or "My sins require this, Lord God," or "This is necessary for my salvation," or "Dear Lord God, give me patience to discern what I should be doing," or "Beloved, give me three loaves of bread, that I might understand, might love, and might always do your will," or "Teach me goodness and discipline and learning," or "Teach me to do your will because you are my God."

Anxious concerns arise mostly from a lack of confidence in God. Through love I will be bent back to him.

In adverse and difficult times, show a broad back through patient strength and tranquillity of soul. Preserve a good heart through trust in God. He will have great peace of heart who despises the prosperity of this world and fears none of its adversities, nor indeed is there anything there to be feared.

You ought to love those who injure and harm you, and forgive them from the heart, so that our debts may be forgiven us. They make crowns for us.

To repress murmuring of the heart, as well as suspicion and impatience, and to have instead a good and sweet heart, think thus: God is good, the brothers are good, mankind is good, the works of God are good—and no less the adverse than the prosperous. For those who oppose us do so with God permitting or ordering it. A good God disposes all things well. You alone are bad who abuse the good and the gifts of God.

The benefits of God shown to you were and are such that you should rightly ever seek him, worship him, love him, bless him, praise him, rejoice in him, confide in him, submit to him, obey him in all things, and give yourself over totally to him. But alas, in evil you turn back toward yourself through love of yourself. My soul is disturbed within me, therefore I will remember you.

Beware of entertaining any thoughts of changing or enlarging the buildings. Fear the threats of the Prophet: "Woe to those who join field to field, house to house" (Is 5:8). Fear the sentence of the Lord upon the rich man, saying, "I will destroy your barns," and "Fool, in this night they will require your soul," and so on (Lk 12:30). Again, "Do not put your treasure in the earth" (Mt 6:19), or "Beware that your hearts are not weighed down with the excesses and drunkenness of the cares of this world, and that day come suddenly over you" (Lk 21:24). Again, "May your conduct be free of avarice, and you content with your present situation" (Heb 13:5). Again, "Do not be concerned about tomorrow" (Mt 6:35). Thus all the saints concentrated upon amending their ways, not erecting walls. May God convert the hearts of the fathers toward those of their sons who take no thought about temporal things but await the city with foundations whose maker and creator is God himself.

He will undoubtedly obtain grace for every good who says and knows from the resolve of his own heart: "Dear Lord, even if you will not give me your grace, I will yet ascribe to you all good, all virtue, all honor, and all things pleasing, and to myself nothing other than uselessness and faults." "I will sing your strength, and I will exalt your mercy every morning, because you have become my fortress and my refuge in a day of trouble. My help, I will sing psalms to you because God is my fortress, my God is my mercy" (Is 58/59:17–18/16–17)

Free yourself from cares to which you are not called by the spirit of God. Too much concern about the present life empties out the faith, drives out hope, knows no love, returns no thanks, withdraws itself from divine providence, trusts in itself rather than God, disturbs the head, shortens life, and does not lift itself in prayer to God. Notions about temporal matters are often all the more vain and empty because through the instigation of the devil they are conceived during prayer.

Do not become deeply disturbed over such matters as charges made, damages incurred, a lack of circumspection, improvidence in earthly affairs, and the like since we should not be counted among the prudent of this world but as simple servants of God, especially when these have not arisen from any vice nor caused any quarrels or reproaches among the brothers. Let those who may deceive us look to themselves.

The three principal goods are patience, trust, and sufficiency. Patience produces tranquillity; trust, happiness; and sufficiency or contentment, the work of grace. He who has these three will lead a happy life on earth. Knowledge of his sin makes a man patient, since everything that God sends against us is, as it were, necessary for the uprooting of our vices. We should believe these things happen by the providence of God, lest we stray from the right path, since he is as a father and always zealous for our salvation. Memory of the benefits of God produces patience, because he has granted so many good things even though he could rightly send whatever he wanted: "If we receive good from the hand of the Lord" and so on (Jb 2:10). To reflect on the immense goodness of God generates a confidence which will never leave those hoping in him. And he who showed us such unheard-of and such unexpected things will not deny us in little things. Thinking about the greatness of the things he has granted up to now and has promised for heaven will bring about contentment. All disquiet in the heart, distraction, disturbance, and anxiety seem to proceed from a lack of one of these three, patience, trust, or contentment.

This we owe God: We should know him, fear him, worship him, love him, praise him, preach and bless him, exalt him, glorify him, magnify him, sanctify him, give thanks to him, submit ourselves and all our things to him, be glorified through and take delight in him, rejoice in him, trust in him and obey, and resign ourselves to him.

He who wishes to be seen by God should look upon him. In prayer give shape to one of these attitudes: modesty, weeping, affection, love, pleasantness, or wonder.

No one can praise God from his heart unless God pleases him. God will not be pleasing to him unless he has conquered his desires.

Guard against and fear only sin; otherwise be without fear, because no adversity will harm you if no iniquity rules over you. No hatred of man, no disparagement, no persecution, no evil of any kind, no infirmity or even death, no defects in anything you have done, can harm you or ought to make you anxious or concerned. Only be subject to the Lord and pray to Him. "Reveal to the Lord your way and hope in Him, and he will do it" (Ps 36/37:5).

The highest thing to be desired from God is that by divine grace he open your eyes now, lest he open them later in punishment, as will happen to all sinners. That you may know your sins now, think deeply about them, accuse yourself of them, wash them in weeping and penitence, and then await death as a penitent, because alas you cannot do it as an innocent.

Do not complain about anyone doing injury to you, because complaint generates impatience, turning it into distraction and finally making you more guilty than the one you pointed out and accused. This evil creeps in easily like a scorpion, and then it damages and punctures the conscience. Say often with sighs: Lord my God, make me trustful, continent, and humble.

Anxiety of heart, concern for external matters, and imagining carnal things will weaken the flesh, injure the head, and burden the nature more than any spiritual exercises such as moderate fasting, vigils, prayers, or spiritual meditations.

These things disquiet the heart and permit the body no rest: The presumption with which someone thrusts himself into all things as if what he did not himself teach or do was not rightly said or done. Thus he pleases and confides in himself and does not trust others.

Every morning you will need to set yourself for future battles, injuries, vexations, evil, disquiet, and temptations.

Would that, as soon as some evil occurred, you would know to look to the Lord God, lifting your eyes to him who disposes and ordains all things and provides occasions for gaining favor. May you know to think and say: "Dear Lord, my God, may you be blessed in this prayer, and grant patience with wisdom so we can discern with a tranquil soul what should be done in this matter." May you always know to hope for the better and not exaggerate things, for many things terrify more than they actually oppress. As the saying goes in Dutch, "Hope for the best, the evil will surely come of itself."

If everything were considered to its very depths, all who know you thoroughly should rightly wonder why our brothers placed such a beast, such a monster, over them, when indeed they have men who are prudent, know how to speak, are bold in appearance, virtuous, and of good reputation.

This the venerable father used to say: It is good for a man always to be somewhat fearful, for he never knows in what pit he may chance to fall. He also said: When someone shows no advance or decline, or is abandoned by God, that often happens because a man has kept to himself some secret sin, not yet purged, which he does not strive to correct or for which he does not grieve or has not taken care to acknowledge or to humble himself when it becomes known.

CHAPTER SIX

Gerlach Peter's First Letter to His Sister Lubbe[13]

This is true spirituality: Ever to offer our dear Lord a pure and peaceful heart and so to live all the days of our misery that we could freely meet him if he suddenly ordered us to depart from here.

Dear and beloved sister. In this life we are all wretched pilgrims, cast out from the fatherland and aching to return to our Father. But if we wish truly to return there, we must exercise ourselves in great earnestness by way of good works and thoughts and holy desires. We must daily gather up inner beauty, ornamentation, and wealth, together with all purity of heart, desire for poverty and things common, humility, obedience, denial of your own will, and right thinking in all things, so that we are not found idle within but rather full and decorated with all virtue and with our lamps burning. I desire and ask you therefore zealously to progress in the virtues and never to become weary of the work required, for the virtues are to be gained and held with work. And if we should not strive constantly to make progress in the virtues, a person could lose in a short time what had been gathered over many years. If the things were imposed upon you from without, you should be all the more careful to preserve them both within and without, for a person easily goes backward into all kinds of hardness of heart if you do not carefully watch out for all that external busyness, thus finally coming to grief in your spiritual exercises. Guard yourself against this. Take pains faithfully to do what has been charged to you, but never forget your own ultimate concerns. Strive to remain tranquil and quiet within in the midst of your external busyness and cares; look upon all temporal and transient things with a simple eye as matters foreign to you, which neither concern nor belong to you. Take care particularly that your desires and inclinations not be caught up in love for transient things small or great. For she will long remain small within who treats as worthy of great desire something that is not lasting. For that reason, according to the measure of our own smallness, we should hold and consider all things even so great as the Lord God holds and considers them.

In all that you use and are busy with, be satisfied with holy poverty, for it is a noble treasure that has proved enduring and remains so, for God and the saints. Insofar as you can bring your feelings to it, then, choose always the lowliest place, the poorest and most outcast clothing, and the most contemptible, according to the example of Jesus Christ. Moreover, when it is time to pray or read, try to drive all external busyness out of your heart, so far as you can. As for things with which you are charged, try to keep watch over them in such a way that you never face an emergency or your heart never gets unsettled by them because you have done something in this way or that way. In keeping watch it should help you to know that you can do nothing of yourself.

When you come into contact with worldly people, conduct yourself maturely and gravely, and look out for fashionable display in your behavior. All your movements and manners should cry out and say with Christ, "My kingdom is not of this world." But when you are back with your sisters, conduct yourself lovingly and personably toward them in word and facial gesture, in your general attitude and all you do. Strive especially to keep peace with all your sisters, which you can gain no better than by humbling yourself around all of them. But to achieve that, practice looking upon and honoring your sisters and all people as thrones of glory and of the holy Trinity in whom God himself dwells. Yield to each one in your heart as if in the coming time and the blessedness of eternal life they will be raised immeasurably above you; you should judge and look upon yourself as the very lowest, as a creature whose position you could not even measure.

You must also practice not looking much at the externals of people, their great or common status, their beauty or plainness, their clothing and ornaments, the largeness or smallness of their bodies, their health or illness, and all the rest. For the Lord God also does not really look at these things, which he does not consider very important. Practice instead looking at a person as someone created in her inner person by God and redeemed by his Son's precious blood. If you see virtues and progress in your sisters or in other people, which you yourself do not have, love that in other people as if they were your own, and then all envy and disfavor will be excluded.

A chaste lover is one who loves God purely for God himself and loves herself for God's sake and for that to which God created her, namely, to praise him in all eternity according to his holy image. She should also reflect on the common love that God has for all mankind without distinction, and she should similarly love herself, simply as herself and no more than any others. When she hears therefore that the image of God has been restored in some other people and they have given themselves over to love the highest good, she should rejoice in her own heart and be all the more encouraged; and the more often this happens, the more joyful and overflowing in love and milder in nature she should herself become. For she will count it all as her own gain. And if she should observe something in others that she does not have in herself, because she does not love herself more than others she will be just as happy and satisfied as if she had it herself. With a chaste love she will desire that our dear Lord should increase and fulfill what he once began.

We all have one Father and we all live from one nourishment, which is love. We all have one nobility, which is that we are the children of God en route toward our fatherland. We are all together one body; each is a special limb and the glory of one is the glory of the other. Therefore we should be most loving among ourselves and wholly united in all things, in our suffering and compassion, in our joy and sorrow. No one should seek her own, but each should be most pleased to see her fellow sister at peace and progressing in virtue as much as she. If you feel out of sorts toward one of your sisters, try to show her more love and courtesy in your behavior, and try to have an especially loving attitude in your heart toward those who do you injustice, gossiping about you, causing difficulties or bringing grief. For it is through them that you will earn your bread, providing you with the broad and wide way along which to stretch out your love. No way is wider and more pleasant than to stand together in suffering and tribulation, so that you never show or feel anything toward those who were difficult to you other than how you can be of help to their progress, inwardly in the desires, outwardly in their service. Then all ill feeling and all that upsets are excluded from the heart. For if you are good and pure, you should not draw near someone else's evil and imperfection but it should rather make you more desirous to become like Christ. Here too you should gladly accept blame, even where you have none, taking upon yourself someone else's guilt, scolding, reproach, and suffering, which she had earned—if thereby you can put her at rest and lighten her load. Your thought will always be on what the other is doing and how it is going with her.

Take pains to keep silence, to be yielding and flexible, and in all things show only the most loving attitude. If it is indeed so from your side, you will enjoy great peace within. Strive to be very gentle with your sisters in all points and matters that have not transpired perfectly and in love, both within and without, for each of us has difficulty enough with the imperfection under which we suffer. In the same way whatever surprising, serious, or unmannerly things you encounter, practice forgiving, softening, and adjusting to them with a humble and lowly heart.

In all your ways try ever to show yourself lively and awake, in your rising each morning, in saying your prayers, or in your work. Try to do all without self-seeking; then you will find great peace. Take stock of where you are, for the holy angels are constantly with us, in our prayers, in church, and in all places, and they note with desire how purely and how totally we offer up and guard our hearts for the Lord. They rejoice when all our works are honest, even when no one is looking on. Let us try in some way to emulate their purity and love.

Make a suitable place for Jesus in your heart and he will gladly come live with you. Pray frequently for all sorts of things: for your sisters who are tempted; for their continued progress in the virtues; for your friends among the living; for your departed friends; and so on. Whatever men do or whatever happens, take it as your benefit and be at peace with yourself. Likewise, do not set yourself upon something that may fall away, for as St. Gregory says: "He who lies or rests upon something that falls away, will necessarily fall with it."

Think often about how you should conduct yourself so that no one will be troubled by or take an evil example from your ways, especially any who follow you. Watch out that you never come to a state of presumed security or evil freedom, for that has destroyed many. But hold all of those with whom you associate in great esteem from your heart, as a temple and as an image of God. Because you hold them so high, from this point you will not likely presume evil or unworthiness or take it poorly from them when they admonish you.

In distress and tribulation do not become too dejected in heart, but think that it will soon go better for you and that so long as we are here in this misery we must be visited by both. Our dear Lord Jesus Christ did not hasten into his glory but first tasted all tribulation, bitterness, and the abandonment of nearly all mankind in this world. For thirty-three years he remained patient and long-suffering, receiving during that time nothing sweet, nothing happy, nothing gentle, nothing easy, nothing for which the flesh has a taste. Feel how it was in him, how as the very lowliest of all men he served all mankind, and received in turn for his love from mankind shame, trouble, belittling, rejection, and finally the most bitter death. See how he indicated these things to us, doing them himself in his very life, and he has clothed us with his example so we may take up his example willingly, just as all the saints resolved to do. For it is by way of much tribulation that we must enter the kingdom of heaven and become like our Lord: In our own patient suffering we will take possession of our souls.

The most trouble a person has comes from herself. If she has conquered herself and her passions from within, she will easily conquer whatever troubles distress her from without. If a person has become so united within to her Lord God that her spirit is no longer subject to her passions but she enjoys much peace with her Lord in an inner tranquillity of heart, what more could a person still desire here? And if it is not well with her Lord, what exterior good could be conferred that would be worth asking for? In all your inner and outer troubles and anxieties, therefore, strive always to keep a secure and constant approach to your mild Father, your lord and your bridegroom. Pray humbly that he will not abandon you in evil times, such as come with hardness of heart and inner darkness. Cast all your hope and cares upon him, and do not be unduly concerned about the things that may come your way in the future, so as not to be hindered in your present progress by such useless concerns. For your mild heavenly Father will take care of you, granting all that is necessary both within and without, and in his time, in the midst of trouble and strife or whatever it may be, will provide as if it were a very small matter. And when he thinks it useful, he will give you inner comfort that you never presumed to have, and in the same way provide you with all things in their time, because he cares for his children. Our dear Lord and God, who has so loved us in all eternity and has shown us such great signs of his love, who constantly watches over us and never abandons us but rather helps us the more, how could he abandon you and still be concerned about you? How should he allow some evil to overtake us and at the same time provide for our spiritual progress for his will's sake?

Strive therefore to seek our dear Lord purely and not by way of your own doings or confidence but so as to bring the most honor to God. Seek him then in this way, whether in busywork or not, in confidence or not, within or without, and thus be altogether satisfied and at peace. In time of trouble and distress, say from the depths of a pure heart: "Lord, you know my heart very well, and you know that I will as gladly suffer trouble, distress, inner darkness, or hardness of heart as great confidence and inner illumination, so long as it brings you the greatest honor. You see, Lord, that I, the very least, the lowliest in all your house, have offered up to you a gift, namely, all that I am and all that I ever may do, none of it used for self-seeking or my own glory. I pray you therefore, from my most inward desires, that you not abandon me in the time of my old age or tribulation, in the time when I will be looked upon as abandoned by nearly all people. But bring my feet fully in your paths so that those who oppress me may understand that you have not wholly abandoned me but rather tested me for a time to see if I would be found faithful." Give yourself over to our dear Lord frequently in this way, and then what overtakes you accept as the very best that might happen to you—and exercise yourself in this.

Never forget that you are in a pilgrim and pitiable state and locked in constant strife, and that you are not where you ought to be. It makes very little difference, therefore, just where and in what manner you are maintained and nourished in the little time of your pitiable wanderings here.

Persecute with all determination your evil desires until they no longer increase but die out. Consider often that a person must mortify and never yield to her external sensibility if the spirit is to live within. For the life of the spirit depends upon the mortifying of the flesh, so that it no longer lives, and then through its death we will have conquered.

Be especially open in the midst of your troubles, passions, and temptations. Let the devil make no nest in you, so far as you can guard against it. Say whatever weighs specially upon your heart to any you judge might find it useful. Likewise, in all those things that move and unsettle you, examine yourself and look to the end, as if you were called to stand at the feet of the Lord: Reflect how then you would stand and feel in the business that now moves you.

Consider often too that it is not those who flee their passions and bear them poorly, but those who courageously conquer them and powerfully bear the discomfort, they will be given a hidden heavenly bread and a new name which no one has or possesses other than she who receives it, something which no one can sense whose ways are all exterior and who looks upon the things that trouble her exterior person only from below and not from above. But the wise person tastes all things for what they are and as God made them, and therefore she will never be shocked or transformed in the highest part of her spirit according to the variations and uncertainties of the things that trouble her. She sees through them with a sharp inner glance, even when at times she has no experiential desire or inwardness for God. But the time will certainly come when the bridegroom, feelingly desired, will be received by us. Blessed is she who is prepared for her Lord and continues to taste him after he has departed, just as earlier she did in full anticipatory desire.

For our dear Lord to be loved by us is to show ourselves pure and unblemished by all other things here in this time, a love shown toward him in all places, times, and deeds. Of other spiritual exercises you may read and hear enough in Holy Scripture, but you will never know and feel it better than in a pure heart, if you will only give yourself over to it. But these things are not to be gained in laziness, in saying our prayers and doing our work in a perfunctory way. But you must bring great industry to bear, first gaining victory over larger faults and thus coming nearer every day. If you come into any suffering, never forget to look upon your king who suffered for you and in suffering was crowned with glory and honor. Think how much persecution and opposition he suffered from the evil ones for us. And if God suffered for mankind, should not men suffer for themselves? It is only a little and over a short time that you must suffer, but what you thereby earn is unmeasured. You suffer and that is but a moment, but it works in you an eternal weight of eternal blessedness. Think that eternal damnation must be suffered if God were to apportion it, and that your suffering is nothing but a moment in comparison with eternity. Think of the greatness of the glory that you will receive and have for it, and you will be relieved of any sorrow that produces such a reward. As you suffer, so will you be crowned and thus acquire the crowns with which you will be crowned on the great feast day that will appear when you come to part with your body.

Guard yourself ever against judging others, gossip, and all useless and idle words. Never give ear to any gossipers, and strive always to conduct all your ways not only without complaint but with grace. [The letter appears to end abruptly at this point.]

CHAPTER SEVEN

John Brinckerinck on Conversion[14]

Mary Magdalene sought the Lord early in the morning, and she found him as a gardener. So those who turn to our dear Lord in their youth find him easily and rightly as a gardener, for he plants all kinds of good herbs in their hearts, all kinds of virtues. The heart of a younger person is still totally blank, and if good things are not written there, the devil will write his, thus worldly, carnal, and idle thoughts, or instill an itch to speak unbecomingly with parents or to hear from older folks about worldly things. Just as this is a very bad sign, so it is a good sign when a young woman is upset to hear such things out of fear that she might thus be harmed or troubled inwardly with wicked images. If we do not take pains in our youth to imprint upon our hearts the virtues, inwardness, and good thoughts, we will never come to it in our old age. We will never have any peace then because we gathered no good in our youth on which to rest. For the same reason we should prepare a great book full of the virtues and holy exercises from which we can read in our old age. So too in the book of our heart we should now gather holy exercises and good thoughts so plentifully that the whole world would prove too small. The longer the "lessons" or exercises become, the more that book increases. For the time will come when we will bitterly rue the day we did not pay more attention when it was said to us what we should think or do. For that reason let us now in our youth give ourselves over ardently to our dear Lord and earnestly take hold upon the virtues, when they are still being told to us.

If we do not try to find our dear Lord here by way of the virtues, on the excuse that we expect to find him in eternity, then we shall also not find him in heaven. Whoever would possess him in heaven must seek him here on earth. We should do as the bees who gather so much honey in the summer that they have enough for the winter too. We should now be gathering humility, obedience, and all the other virtues, on which to live when we are no longer in a position to be gathering.

A person genuinely moved to remorse will find and lament in

herself many infirmities. She will pay little attention to honor, flattery, gossip, or contempt, but have only her dear Lord before her eyes and think only of his things. We should therefore always be in a state of goodly desire and not despair when we cannot readily call up desire, for many good exercises will produce holy desire. A good will or good desire for spiritual progress is the beginning of all good things. But if we cool from good desire we will remain stuck in our passions. And when we remain in our passions, we should note at once that our will is not perfect because the works do not follow from it. That in us which is contrary to our will is thus neither harmful nor profitable. Whatever impulses, whatever thoughts, whatever temptations, however bad or evil or impure or strong they may be, if they are contrary to our will, constitute in themselves no barrier or leave-taking from our dear Lord. But in resisting them we will find profit, for thereby we are sorely pained and tested.

If we were to do many good works outwardly, but not truly with our wills and without any real love, they would not prove very profitable to us and we would not be saved by them. Before we take up our work, and again in the midst of work, we should make a good resolution and say, "Dear Lord, I desire to seek you alone in this work, and if something else should interfere, dear Lord, that is not my will or intention, for if I seek myself or others more than you I lose everything." The same holds not only for this work but also in eating and drinking and in sleeping and in all things: "I desire to seek you and your honor so I may find you in all eternity and so I and all mankind may please you and seek to increase your honor."

We should restrain ourselves from all the sensuality of our evil inclinations as well as from all the confidence and flattery of men, for our dear Lord led his bride into the wilderness, there to speak to her heart to heart. Whenever he leads us there, we should turn to him with goodly desire and say: "Your good spirit will lead me into that just land"; or "God, think upon me in my distress. O Lord, to you have I fled, teach me to do your will and draw me after you"; or "God create in me a clean heart"; and the like.

We should also be most careful to sense the visitations and grace of God. St. Bernard considered it very bad when we fail to mark the presence of the grace of God. In the presence of his grace we should make a firm resolve and do our very best not to receive that grace idly or indifferently. With Jacob, and with humble sorrow, we should say, "I will not let you go until you bless me." And as the bride says in the book of love, "I have found him and I will not let him go"; and "Do not take it evil of me to speak to you so freely, for I do it not in reliance on my merits but on your goodness alone."

We should set ourselves down frequently, placing before our dear Lord and lamenting to him all our darkness and shortcomings and passions, and plead with him for wisdom and strength with which to resist our faults, for in him is overflowing redemption. If we could submit ourselves to him as we ought, we would receive much grace from him. And after we have turned to our dear Lord and asked him humbly and ardently for help against our passions, we should set ourselves vigorously against them all. For if we do not put our good will to work, we will in the end become hardened in our passions. But we should bring force to bear on ourselves and grapple with them, as Jacob did with the holy angel, not letting him go until he blesses us and we limp along on one leg, meaning that all the pleasures of this world and what is sweet to our natures has become contrary to us. Those who persist and endure to the end in faith will finally gain what they desire. But those who make no effort to work at it, who remain lying in their laziness and follow the movements of the flesh without any resistance from reason, are in a bad way. For all in this state will surely go to hell, even if such people are now more pleasing to the world and have more leisure and more pleasure in eating and sleeping and in their clothes, more freedom and curiosity, and stand ready to give themselves over to many other faults if there were opportunity. Even if human pressure and shame kept such persons from the sins they were prepared to do, they would nonetheless be rightly condemned for their will's preference. But on the other hand those who are more pleasing to the world and yet desire it not or make use of certain pleasures and freedoms but will them not—who would rather be more pressured and frightened, would rather go more out of themselves and become more pleasing to the saints and devout persons through the work of the virtues, who would rather do more of God's work but are not strong enough in body to carry out what they wish to do—such people have in God's eyes already done it and will find a sympathetic judge.

Since we are to order our wills and our work toward the will of God, we should ask counsel of our dear Lord, saying: "Dear Lord, how do you want me to do this work?" Our dear Lord answers us through the reason: "Work in such a way that you never forget me." So when we go to eat we think: How shall I conduct myself now? St. Augustine answers us that we should approach eating as medicine. We are to strengthen the body so it may persist in the service of God, and we should not desire more than is necessary. When we go to speak with someone, we should think: "Dear Lord how should I conduct myself in this situation?" And so whatever we do, whether thinking or speaking, keeping silent or working, going or standing, sitting or rising, going to bed or going to church, reading or praying, we should say: Dear Lord, how am I to do this? Shall I do it this way?

Our Lord placed in each man's soul a little spark, a kind of confession that says and indicates to us what is good and what is bad, and thus our Lord speaks to our soul through the reason: That good you should do, and that evil you should not do.

This is true inwardness: a humble and ardent desire for God and all the things of God. It is the mark of an inward person that she has our dear Lord present in all her thoughts, words, and deeds, and in all her activities. She who does not try with inner exercises and good thoughts to guard her heart will pour it out upon every fault and infirmity. Whenever we, trusting in the help of God, offer ourselves to him and say: "Dear Lord, I wish that I could at all times offer and give you myself and my heart so totally as St. Augustine or some other person did; this is my whole desire and will. And if I cannot put this perfectly into practice, please come to my aid, for I am sick"—whenever we stand thus, we are not far from the right way.

We should frequently turn to our dear Lord with goodly desire, because we would gain much from great desire for our Lord. This would be fitting sacrifice to our Lord, to die to your own nature and not to preserve your own self but at all times to deny your own strength and arrogance and to seek and to see our dear Lord in all things, to desire nothing else, and to exercise only those things in which you and other persons will appear small and vile. Depending upon how near or far from such exercises you are, and whether you already exercise yourself in this way, especially if you are still far off from this, lament and confess all to our dear Lord so that he knows you recognize your distance from God. The less you confess your distance and faults, the more foolish you are, and the less open, the more blinded you will become and the more arrogant. And when we confess that we have gone astray in arrogance, crookedness, impatience, or whatever else it might be, we should turn to our dear Lord, confess humbly our transgressions, and pray to him that he will forgive us and in future give us the foresight and strength to overcome them, offering him then our whole will and resolving thereafter to will or to do nothing other than his dearest will. Whenever we offer our hearts thus to our dear Lord, he will gladly receive our desires because he takes pleasure in such sacrifices. For he desires to be among the children of men, and he says, "Daughter, give me your heart." We should make such an offer repeatedly to our Lord, because if we do not offer up small things of whatever sort, we can expect instead a hundred or rather an unspeakable hundred thousand faults to creep in. The saints in general, thus St. Bernard, St. Francis, St. Augustine, and many others who left the desires of this world, had such great pleasure within that all the pleasures of this world could not compare. Our dear Lord assumed such dimensions in the heart of St. Agnes that anything the world had to offer seemed much too small. There was such a fire of love in her heart that she avoided neither sword nor any other torture. This world has no such love. She who would choose this bridegroom must learn to know what obstacles prevent her from coming to or following through on this choice. Once we have been able to confess and testify to them, they will then be taken away from us.

No sacrifice is so pleasing to our dear Lord as to put to death our faults and to give ourselves over to the virtues, to conduct ourselves worthily and to make ourselves suitable for the reception of his grace and teachings. And if we do not feel any desire for this, we should fall on our knees, make confession to the Lord, and pray for the bread of grace. And no matter how early we prepare ourselves, our Lord is already there, ready to pour his grace into us. You should therefore press yourself on our dear Lord with force and say, "Dear Lord, I want ever to be bound to you; I will always do what you will, no matter what men try or how difficult it becomes for me." Those who stand in such a state earn far more than those who find what they do altogether sweet. If idle or evil thoughts or a weak spirit or some such fault comes upon us, we should come so to ourselves as to say, "Dear Lord, help me so I do not fail; I want not to consent to these evil faults that come upon me; but, dear Lord, if you will that I should suffer these difficulties, then grant me the power to suffer them humbly. Your dearest will must decide how necessary it is for me to suffer these things." So long we feel thus, we will never be overcome.

We are called to the service of God, but if we make no effort to fulfill our calling it will be turned more to our damnation. The ears must hear what God speaks into them, for he speaks into them if we will but hear it. As often as we follow our sensuality or inclinations in hearing or seeing or one of the other senses, we send up a dark cloud between God and us so that we cannot hear what God says to us. For she who does not respond to that first address made properly to her will have less power to follow him in future; and the more a person is addressed and pays no attention, the more blinded she will become. Once she rejects the grace of God, she will gain it never again. And if we are abandoned by the grace of our dear Lord, it would be better for us to go through life as a frog or a snake or the least desirable animal.

It is not the gray habit that our dear Lord seeks, but just as he is a spirit, so he seeks the spiritual and inner virtues. Therefore those who give themselves over to reading the Our Father indifferently and then depart to please themselves and follow their own will and think they can go as they wish and need make no further effort, they stand in a frightful position, as the saints have often said. If we do not make use of this great opportunity as we should, a great chastisement will follow. And if we use it as we should, then we will become illumined servants of Christ.

There are no worse persons to be found than those who have gone to the school of the Holy Spirit and afterward do not stick to the things they have learned but negligently let them go, assuming arrogant airs as if they knew enough and had no need to listen to or be set right by others. They who make no effort to be taught by the Holy Spirit will remain unlearned for a long time. Poor people, that we make such bad use of this good. There is many a good person in the world who, if they had had the opportunity, would certainly have made good use of it.

We may possess two heavenly kingdoms if we strive inwardly in prayer and outwardly in good exercises and deeds to turn toward God; then our exercises may become so satisfying that we can say with David, "Your righteousness has made me sing." All that men do to us and that comes over us we should accept with humble goodwill from within and without, with gentle and resigned words, while thinking upon the gentleness of our dear Lord. Once we come to grasp something of the humility and gentleness of our dear Lord we will be amazed to see how distant we still were ourselves. I have never yet seen persons fully matured in the service of the Lord who were not also given over to peace of heart. A person who gives herself over inwardly to peace will also radiate peace in all her works. But those who make no effort to keep peace in themselves or among others are in reality still not seeking our dear Lord and will never come to true wisdom.

A person who wishes a peaceful conscience must have a steady vision within and with constant care keep God ever before her eyes so as not to stray from him in words, deeds, or thoughts. And if for some time she fails God, a bitter feeling should well up within her, as when she fails by way of idle listening, idle speech, taking up of worldly things, or—to name a few more—evil suspicions about another for no good reason, or becoming disturbed over little things, or murmuring under your breath, or spending your time in distracted thoughts. All such things and their like infect a pure conscience, and waste the time. A good person should therefore guard herself against such things, because the enemy is always there, inducing people to waste their time and killing in them all their good resolve toward the virtues. But if a person takes counsel with herself thus, she may hope in a short time to gain a virtuous way of life. When however she spends much time still in her old habits—for to fall is human—she should humble herself all the more for her infirmity and nurture a heart compassionate toward her own failures. This may mean to bear her cross, to do battle with bitter determination, and to fight against the sins and impurity of her heart. But if a person makes no effort to guard herself and to protect her conscience from all such little things, she will remain through all her days fundamentally crude and cold, and it is to fear that she will suffer hard and unspeakable times in purgatory after this life.

If someone here knew that her father was in purgatory, she would gladly do penance for him; how much more should we not do penance for ourselves? Unfortunately, you find here so little good feeling among people, even when they are of goodwill. They make no effort to avoid small faults but are more interested in satisfying their senses, and therefore they do not sense God in the uttermost and sweetest depths of their hearts. A person must try to leave behind all her sins, so far as she can, for all sins are contrary to God. Even if in this life we cannot live so purely in thought, words, and deed as we ought, we should nevertheless strive for it, as best we can, and what we still lack the dear Lord will fill with his efforts, made in our behalf through his suffering.

All our works and deeds should be done in an effort to die more and more to ourselves, for the sake of our dear Lord, and if we cannot bear this we will never become truly spiritual persons. Therefore in all our work and activity we should be specially at pains to die to ourselves. When a person does what is called an exterior work, she should think: "Dear Lord, may I do this in such a way that it pleases you; I will gladly do this because I do not readily turn myself to interior things and other sisters give themselves far better to interior exercises"; or "Dear Lord, would that I could take part in this good that the other sisters do"; or "If I have lost you in solitude, may I find you again in work." Those who thus humble and judge themselves will frequently gain far more grace from God than those who are ever praying.

If we find ourselves flat in church, we should say, "Dear Lord, now I have nothing but to read this outwardly. How high must all our sisters' thoughts now be before you? O dear Lord, if they would only pray for me." Such humility will prove more helpful than many good thoughts. Those who seek and see our Lord in all their work have the very presence of our dear Lord among them, and will be rewarded according to this reflection. If therefore in all our works we examine our intentions, we will also soon see our reward.

CHAPTER EIGHT

John Brinckerinck on
The Holy Sacrament[15]

We receive our dear Lord in two ways, spiritually and sacramentally. When we receive him sacramentally, we do so in great danger whenever we approach him without any inwardness. We approach without inwardness when we do not confess our faults nor wish to and have for that no remorse, or again when we stand firm in certain serious faults and do not wish to turn away. But the more we are ready to confess our faults and make a firm resolution to better ourselves, the more inwardly we approach the holy sacrament. The other reception is spiritual and just as salutary. It happens whenever, to the praise of God and to his honor, we give ourselves over to patience in suffering, to obedience, to purity, to the bettering of our way, and to more loving service toward one another.

Therefore, whenever we are to do or to suffer something contrary to our wills, we should think: O holy work in which we may receive Christ. And even if we were to offer ourselves to God in every moment, should that be possible, we should still offer ourselves specially when we approach the holy sacrament and then make an especially humble confession before our dear Lord. For with humble confession a person comes to remorse of heart. And the sacrament is of as much service to us as we receive it with remorse and inwardness.

I have no doubt that those who have offered themselves in obedience to our dear Lord in life and death receive incomparably more grace than those who make no effort to offer themselves. And the more often they approach the sacrament who have not taken pains to offer themselves and to set themselves against their faults and the infirmity in which they still stand, the blinder and harder, the prouder, more confused, and more unsuitable they become.

If we wish to go to the holy sacrament we should always first reflect on what our life has been. When we have done that, and we find ourselves no more loving or inclined to obedience or remorse or the things of God, we should be anxious that we have approached it badly. Any worldly person that wishes to approach the holy sacrament should have sorrowful regret for her sins and be prepared to do penance for them all. She should want to shun the causes of her sin with all her might, and she should wish to guard herself from all disturbances, stubbornness, and self-indulgence and from all that will break down the love between God and herself and also between herself and her fellowman.

We should often think how St. Augustine or St. Agnes would conduct themselves if they went with us to our dear Lord and said: Dear Lord, I wish that I could receive you with such flaming love and sweetness in my heart and submission of myself as you received from your holy people—but that is all too far off. Dear Lord, may I only be granted the will for it! If a person gives herself over in obedience to do and to accept for God's sake all that men prepare for her, she has most truly gone to our dear Lord from within and she may also approach him with praise from without, for she has already received him inwardly.

If we do not receive our dear Lord spiritually, we may also never receive him sacramentally to our salvation. This is what it is to receive our dear Lord spiritually: to persist in all those things that our dear Lord would have us do, carefully to note whether or not all that we do is born of God, always to see our dear Lord in them and to resist all those faults that create a barrier between God and us, and then to say, "Dear Lord, these are the faults found in me: disobedience, arrogance, impatience, making excuses, unworthy behavior toward others, and evil desires in the form of greed, vainglory, and idle curiosity; but I will ever seek to progress and to strive with all my might to overcome." Whoever is steady and zealous in this work and thus receives our dear Lord every day spiritually will receive special grace when she receives our dear Lord sacramentally and may go freely to the holy sacrament, even if on occasion she does not feel as desirous as she herself would desire.

Those who make every effort and take pains daily to exercise themselves in humble obedience, and daily to die to themselves, and to abandon their own wisdom, and are happy to have people tell them their faults—even when it is difficult for them and they feel themselves inclined to many faults, who still try steadily to work against them and ask how they should work against them and believe others better than themselves—such sisters daily receive our dear Lord spiritually in their souls, even if they never again go to church. They may approach the holy sacrament in freedom and security, even if at all times they do not feel themselves so inwardly inclined as they would wish.

Those who do not strive to receive our dear Lord daily in this way must pay very careful attention that they do not become blinded, if they still go regularly to the holy sacrament, as often happens. It would have been far better for them to have stayed home and humbled themselves in the knowledge of their unworthiness. They should stand there in all openness and say, "I have confessed all the points that I know, I shall now say my prayer, and I shall thus go to our dear Lord, I who still sin against him all too much." I have thought that such people will become blinded, going so often in this way to our dear Lord, one day confessing and the third day or shortly thereafter coming again to bring the same thing to confession. Is that the life of a Christian person? We should really be ashamed that we have outlived so many passovers and yet have not passed over. Therefore, we enter congregations such as this in order to pass over, and those who have truly passed over are blessed, but woe to those who have not truly passed over. I would far rather die among worldly men than among those who lead worldly lives in congregations. But for those who wish still to make a passover, obedience should lead them to it.

These are the fruits of the holy sacrament received by those who go to it in a salutary way: regaining grace that was lost, a growing desire for our dear Lord and a yearning instilled to receive him more, a greater taste for the virtues of humility, obedience, and all the others. A person becomes livelier in her soul, readier and more enflamed to take up all the good works that seemed hard before. Holy Scripture becomes tastier and sweeter to read. A person becomes more willing to confess faults humbly, both inside and outside the confessional. Those who feel themselves so turned toward God and their wills so firmly committed that for all the world's sake they would not do anything contrary to the will of God, such should not be timid about receiving our dear Lord, even if they should not feel any of these fruits in themselves.

On those days when you have been to the holy sacrament, you should not speak much but sit alone and speak to your bridegroom: See what he desires and consider what good he has done for you, because he gave his whole life to you as an example. Reflect on how like and unlike your bridegroom you are, try to fix your thoughts upon God, see what he desires from you, think back over your whole life and all your failures, and make of it a humble confession to our dear Lord, for if you take a good look at yourself, you will find plenty to confess. And if you do not know what to confess, you should confess your blindness, because those who do not know what to confess have still many faults. The person who thinks she has nothing to cut away [lit. circumcise] has in reality more than enough still to cut away. Those who, after they have gone to the holy sacrament, find themselves more cautious and inward and wise and understanding have evidence that they truly prepared themselves properly in advance.

CHAPTER NINE

Rector Peter Dieburg of Hildesheim on the Schism of 1443[16]

In a case such as this [an interdict, with the sacraments restricted or suspended], for a brother to return to his heart, to examine himself, to recognize that he is himself the temple of God, to seek the essence of the sacraments and not the sacraments as such, to eat and drink spiritually and thus to communicate with the passion of Christ—in all this, if done with a salutary zeal, the soul is more fruitfully exercised, the affections purged, and the intellect illumined than when someone is bodily in church and busies himself only with the sacramental mysteries. It sometimes happens that in those places where holy things abound with richer relics of the saints and more frequent solemn masses, hearts are found dry and inwardly empty, especially in places frequently and customarily visited. When we worship in such places, vaguely content and busied with the visible mysteries and sacraments, we fail to grasp how empty and dry we remain at heart, how deprived inwardly of spiritual good. For there are some who so hinge the advancement of their hearts upon the sacraments, seeing the mysteries as a final end in themselves, that unless they celebrate or otherwise busy themselves with the mysteries they feel defrauded of the ceremonial mysteries and seek nothing else with the mind. Alienated from things truly divine, they seek to remain in choir or in church only so long as they superficially run through their hours. They do not seek with a divine mind what is at work there or what riches are set before them at the table of Christ.

The more devoutly and intently a brother sets himself free to focus upon things in his mind, the less suited that hour will seem for things sacramental. Yet a devout mind full of the soul's desire will always embrace the divine mysteries, whether celebrated by himself or another, because it is necessary repeatedly to converse with your lover. If on some occasion he finds himself unable to pursue these divine matters, deprived for a time by the authority of an interdict or on some ground of charity or obedience, he should not immediately think of himself either as free or as weighed down with a great burden but rather as given a holiday and acquiring an opportune time for meditation. He should rejoice in heart and seek out the great secret, as if uncertain of one or both its parts, that is, the essence of the sacrament, and then return from it as visited and consoled.

To that end, then, the solemnities of the mass are nevertheless to be continued, even though it sometimes happens that those intent on ceremony taste less of the fruit of the sacrament. For at times the soul flatters itself for its association with the divine offices, even though it may remain empty of their fruit. What is so holy about chalices and other vessels of the church if their effect is not greater upon the soul than the body? For the effect of a sacrament comes from its contents and is not caused only by the external thing containing that effect; this contained essence, moreover, is perceived only by a pure and focused mind. When both (the external solemnity and interior mystery) cannot be had, it is better, all other things being equal, to be distant from the church or the sacrament in body rather than in mind. We should not share the view of those who accommodate the flesh more than faith and say: "Lord, come down before my son dies" (Jn 4:49). We hear how such faith was praised or rather reproached when the Lord said, "Unless you see signs and prodigies you do not believe" (Jn 4:48), but we can observe another person in the Gospel genuinely praised when the Lord said, "Amen, I say to you I have not found such faith in Israel" (Mt 8:10). And what did he say? "I am not worthy that you should enter under my roof, but only say the word and he will be healed" (Mt 8:8), and so on. Indeed for a mere doer and perhaps no hearer of the word, "The hour comes and now is when they will worship neither in Jerusalem nor on the mountain; for the Father is a Spirit and they who worship him must worship him in spirit and in truth" (Jn 4:21, 24). He who loses the material temple, therefore, transfers himself undoubtedly to the spiritual. For it is the Spirit that gives life, and the flesh or other infirm elements profit absolutely nothing. We must therefore rise up from things visible and compare the spiritual to things spiritual, so that according to the Apostle we not only live in the Spirit but also walk in the spirit thus becoming truly spiritual and not carnal (see Gal 5:25, 1 Cor 3:1).

We should say with the bride, "Draw me after you" and "Deliver me Lord and set me beside you, and let any hand be raised against me" (Sg 1:3; Jb 17:3 *Vulg.*). For what can oppose anyone positioned there, whether he be banned from the church, excommunicated, deprived of communion, or finally denied Christian burial, if only he gave no just cause for it and never neglected any of these rites out of contempt. (Yet, even though it is impossible to be constrained by such a human judgment or deprived of the essence or fruit of the sacraments by any such sentence, the binding and loosing of prelates is nonetheless not to be regarded lightly but embraced with fear, since no one knows whether it is worthy of fear or hatred.) Thus even though there are many sacred places, many churches and temples, many and daily masses, as well as many cemeteries, all these nonetheless come back to one, in One we have all. Each singly refers to one, just as we signify only one, follow one, and in the manner of eagles gathering round a body congregate around one: For the mediator between God and man, the man Christ Jesus, is beyond all sacraments and signifying mysteries. He is our Temple, as Scripture says, "Destroy this temple" (Jn 2:19); he is our cemetery, as in, "In him I will lie down and sleep in peace" (Ps 4:8–9); in the Apocalypse he is the one signed with the name of the altar, under which are heard the voices of those cut down, saying, "How long, O Lord, until you avenge our blood," and so on. Under that land, under that altar, are buried all the blessed "who have died in the Lord" (Apoc 14:13). And even if one of the righteous is never buried physically in a cemetery, since he is nonetheless "buried with Christ through his death" (Rom 6:4), he will not be deprived of communion with all the good rituals done throughout the world in behalf of those buried in cemeteries.

For the thing signified and the thing signifying are two different things; whoever is not buried under this land, under this Altar, not only will receive nothing good from an ecclesiastical burial but will also bear greater punishment. Indeed according to Augustine these solemnities do no good for the dead but take place rather for the sake of the living. This may all be deduced clearly enough from the corpses of the martyred saints, whether their relics remain unburied, drowned in water, given over to the flames, devoured by beasts, or whatever. When someone ends their life in the true temple, how can they be deprived of the mystical or signified cemetery? No one who is to be saved dies outside this Temple. He is our Temple, and all who would remain in him, who would not be excluded or damned, must walk just as he walked.

And, if you wish to be found in Christ, there is no other place under heaven in which we must worship except in him or in this holy Temple. No one is included or excluded against his will, this place is banned to no one, no one is excommunicated here except by his own will, since "the gates of this temple are closed neither by day nor by night" (Is 60:11), meaning, neither in adversity nor in prosperity. Wherever we go, wherever we were, this Temple, unless we so will, we shall never lose. Whoever is guilty and flees to this Temple will find refuge, no matter what the crime of which he was found guilty. Oh, how many were once excluded or excommunicated in the earthly temple here below and have been admitted to the spiritual Temple in honor. How many are brought in here who were in truth found excommunicate and reprobate. Oh, how many in this Temple here are among the best known, indeed its most familiar lords and friends, close to this altar and its truest husbands, who nonetheless are there above judged as unknown, the least, or even enemies to be cast far from his face. If according to the Apostle "we know Christ the power of God, the wisdom of God, his righteousness, peace, and sanctification" (1 Cor 1:30), who would dare or presume—to the detriment of the manifold mercies of the Lord—to circumscribe or constrain this Temple and this place with the ecclesiastical sacraments, and indifferently to exclude from the church or even within the church to exclude individually as sinners all those who in faith and in outlook have been made righteous, peaceful, virtuous, wise in doing good, merciful, and so on. We set apart, however, all those who not only out of ignorance but also out of contempt refuse to see or to enter the kingdom of heaven, that is, the church militant, for as the Lord said, "Unless you are reborn by water and the Spirit, you cannot enter the kingdom of heaven" (Jn 3:5). To all those addressed, who hear the precept and are obliged so to be reborn, if there is opportunity, the Lord says, "If I had not come and spoken to them, they would have no sin" (Jn 15:22).

This is amazing, if not wondrous, but only to our eyes and not to those of him who said, "I think the thoughts of peace" (Jer 29:11). In a book on true religion Anselm said that an adult is saved and sanctified only through penance. For penance together with faith and the desire for baptism can take the place of baptism with respect to the remission of guilt and its perfect correction; thus he who has faith and the desire is not to be regarded as without baptism, whence the holy doctors are accustomed to call baptism an inner penance and a baptism through fire. He also says there that God despises or neglects no one from the nations except the person who neglects himself, and so on. Also, that this is hidden in the heart of God; thus the Lord said to Moses of this place of which we now speak, "There is a place near me," and so on (Ex 33:21). Did not the Prophet also sing it aloud? Before the Lord there is mercy in plenty, before him redemption, not before us; for if he was before us, why did he exclaim,

"Where are your ancient mercies, O Lord" (88/89:50/49)? If before us, which sinner ever perished in desperation? Therefore each one of us should cry out, "Let your mercies come upon me that I may live" (Ps 118/119:77). This is not contradicted by the saying of the Apostle, "Those who sin outside the law will perish outside the law," if we exclude those who are a law to themselves, as is to be gathered from the same passage: "For through law comes the knowledge of sin" (Rom 3:20). Otherwise how would God judge this world as a just judge? How would he show mercy toward all and hate none of what he did? For he did not establish all the sons of men in vain, those whose care he also bears, and before him it is hardly a sin simply that we are born, live, and die. For when he said to Moses, "I will take mercy" not just on the seed of Abraham but "on whom I will take mercy" (Rom 9:15), who doubts that he sought to remove any excuse for vain boasting, saying, "They are Jews and I too, they Christians and I too" (2 Cor 11:22, 23)?

When therefore Christians enter into the place of this specially chosen people of the Lord, and he says, "Others have labored and you will enter into their labors" (Jn 4:38), and the Prophet says, "Your sons are born to take the place of your fathers" (Ps 44/45:17/16), we must reflect on that with great fear lest we hear it said of us that we are "an olive branch engrafted contrary to nature" (Rom 11:24), as in many places in the Gospel, now in parables, now openly, it is said of the natural olive branch: "And the first shall be last and the last shall be first" (Mt. 19:30). Since according to the Apostle "all of these things happened to them in figures and were written for us" (1 Cor 10:11), not only for Jews or pagans but also for all the faithful of Christ, "this is an awesome and truly terrible place, the home or temple of God and gate of heaven" (Gn 28:17). The Lord knows who stands in the gate of his house. For if blindness came over the natural olive branch so that the wild one was engrafted, that wild one should tremble terribly if it does not itself stand in humility and fear. But, as the Apostle said, the Gentiles honor God for his mercy and if these others refuse to believe that the Gentiles gain mercy, see whether in these last days, with iniquity abounding, the love of many is not cooled by the mercy shown those others.

For love thrives only among a few any more; there is so little of devotion or the true religion, of a humble and simple walking in Christ. We are nearly all outsiders, nearly all temporal goods, few are mental inhabiters of the true Temple. Do we not see abroad the fulfillment of that so long expected of which the Apostle said:

"Blindness has occurred in part in Israel until the fullness of the Gentiles has entered and thus all Israel will be saved" (Rom 11:25, 26). The fullness of time coming wonderfully, the crown of the Jews fell to the son sent from God when the fullness of the nations entered: "Nation will rise against nation and kingdom against kingdom and there will be earthquakes, pestilence, and famine" (Lk 21:10, 11) and nothing will be heard or told but battles, conflicts, and the rumors of war, and then salvation will return also for the Jews. These things, expressed here as an opinion and not as definitive, should suffice on the true temple and place of God.

The same can be argued for sacramental communion so long as spiritual exercise does not cease, for the Lord said, "It is the Spirit that gives life, the flesh profits nothing" (Jn 6:63). It is food and drink for the soul: Desire is required and blessed are those who hunger and thirst after this bread and this drink. It is good then that the soul should focus its meditation and reflections on some part of the Lord's passion or life or be occupied in some other useful exercise, and thus become enflamed even with desire to eat this passover before passing from this world. When someone does this in hope and with a resolve to improve his life, informed by the example, life, and passion of Jesus Christ, it is piously believed that he is visited here with a grace more salutary than if he had omitted all this and aimed only at sacramental communion. For that reason, I think, the Lord did not wish to end his life by being crushed under the roll of stones or some other such sudden and unexpected death, lest he deny us abundant and more than abundant material for anyone wishing devoutly to meditate on his passion. For in this life such an incident, such a miserable business, could hardly happen to anyone easily, while in the Lord's passion he finds material that is suitable, accessible, healing, and comforting.

Step up securely whenever and wherever you wish, you minister, deacon, or priest of this spiritual communion, even if you are a layman, for according to Chrysostom every holy person is a priest but not every priest holy. Here is revealed no place of fear or feigned excuses unless, as I confess, it be someone who offers no true praise, seeking not to please God but man and doing all his works, as the Lord said, for appearances before men. For we find many thrusting themselves upon the sacerdotal office who understand little of it or who even are derisive of this inner and principle devotion, sometimes dismissing such piety as that of an ass. Together with all such priests we project outward and pretend to a great show of sanctity, and in a remarkable kind of commerce we are busy nourishing and saving others while starving ourselves. We serve and work for others, while others invade and carry off our labors. The whole world is full of priests, churches are filled with altars, and they increase still by leaps and bounds. Whoever can found an altar for, as they say, some poor priest—not to say for some friend, son, or nephew—glories in it as in the certain salvation and redemption of his soul. Thus from a multitude of altars arises the need for a plentitude of priests, of whom not a few lack the uprightness required of clerics and some even display a disordered and abounding immorality. When so few men are found worthy of approbation, how finally are so many altars to be filled with worthy priests? But there is hardly any altar so slight or obscure (in its goods, that is) but that it acquires its man—would that he were suitable and sought out rather than thrust upon it by force or simoniacally! From this there often arises anxious scrupulosity or shameful pressure in the miserable conscience of a man compelled to say polluted masses with a desperate soul, not to speak of all else that he neglects. And just as the family of Christ would be better served by fewer and worthier priests, so perhaps it would not be absurd to draw the same conclusion about saying fewer masses. Think with what earnestness and devotion mass might be attended if there were only one. Even as the value of things is judged by their rarity, are not the apostolic see and its legates treated more devoutly in Germany than by the Italians in the Roman curia? And see if this is not the reason why the Gentiles worship the Holy Land.

All these things were not said to detract from the divine office or any of those saying mass or expanding divine worship, but rather to the consolation of the humble and of those who, within ecclesiastical obedience, find the secrets of the heart more pleasing. These were thought out and said in the expectation that "for those who love God all things work together for good" (Rom 8:28).

PART FOUR

Gerard Zerbolt of Zutphen

The Spiritual Ascents

1. *Five Points Necessary to Make Progress in the Spiritual Life*[1]

"Blessed is the man whose help is from you, who has set his heart to ascend from the valley of tears to the place he has appointed" (Ps 83/84:6–7).

I know, O man, that you wish to make your ascent and ardently desire to reach the heights. For you are a noble and rational creature endowed with a capacious soul, and you have therefore a natural desire for ascent and the heights. This natural appetite is surely not to be despised, if it is well ordered, that is, if your desire is to ascend toward the heights of your original dignity, or your longing is to depart from this valley of tears and misery. But to leave from here and ascend there is possible only if you advance in your heart by way of the ascents and steps of the virtues. For you ascend only so much as you advance in your heart. You must therefore dispose your heart to these ascents, not trusting to make the climb on the strength of your own virtue but resting constantly upon the aid of the Almighty and the protection of the God of heaven. If you ascend in this way, your ascent will be praiseworthy. For you are blessed: The name of "man," as one proceeding "manfully," is not inappropriate to you, and you will eventually receive as your reward eternal blessedness and a glory that never ceases.

Here are proposed to you, as you set yourself for your ascent, five points found in these prophetic words, brief and in reverse order but full of meaning. First, where you ought to ascend, that is, the place which the Lord has appointed. This we should rightly understand as the state of natural rectitude in which the Lord once created and placed you. Set your heart, then, to ascend to that place from which it earlier willed to descend.

Second, the place whence you ought to begin your ascent, a

place called the "valley of tears." That "valley" should be construed as the overthrowing and impoverishment of your natural dignity. At the bottom now, you ought to return and ascend the mount from which you fell.

Third, how you ought to prepare yourself for the ascent, for you must set your heart for these ascents. Before you begin to ascend, carefully review in your heart the means and exercises needed to reach back. Think through and set your heart upon the best exercises for recovering its lost dignity.

Because this ascent is truly not in the power of the one walking or ascending but in the gift of God, you are advised, fourth, to request the aid and counsel of God, for unless you are accompanied in all things by divine grace you will have no energy of your own.

But lest you be frightened by the difficulty of this ascent or defeated by its labor and resist again, the reward is promised you when it says "Blessed is the man." If you advance in these ascents of the heart, you will be blessed, here in hope, afterward in fact, here gaining the blessings of the way which consist in the virtues and righteousness, there dwelling in the blessedness of your homeland. Moreover, when you possess the virtues and righteousness, you already have in a certain sense that future blessedness in its, as I should say, source. For just as natural things contain in themselves certain generative and seminal reasons productive of certain effects, so future blessedness and eternal happiness accompany virtue and righteousness.

Briefly recall then whence, how, and why you ought to make this ascent. Once you were established on the high mountain of your natural and primordial dignity, but you willingly fell headlong into a certain low valley. You must therefore leave this valley and ascend once again the mountain from which you fell. But before you begin to climb, erect a ladder in your heart, arrange a certain means of advancing, by which you may better climb out. And while still on the foot or some lower rung of the ladder, about to lose heart as you look up to the top, raise your arms on high to the Lord, who is leaning down over the highest rung of the ladder, and cry out: "Pull me up after you!" Thus you will become blessed and enjoy everlasting beatitude. Now each of these points must be treated individually.

2. *The State of Natural and Primordial Dignity in Which God Placed Man at Creation, and the Many Gifts He Conferred upon Him*

If therefore the Lord has set your heart toward these ascents and called you to make this spiritual climb, if you are able to take up this mental exercise, come to a knowledge first of your descent and fall; then you will know to ascend from the place where you see yourself to have fallen headlong. To perceive how necessary it is for you to turn from this valley of tears and return to the place appointed and ordained for you, carefully note that the Lord God, who created you in his image and likeness, once placed you in such a sublime dignity, on such a high mountain of natural gifts and spiritual graces, that unless you advance toward the essential vision of God, you will hardly be able to ascend at all. Indeed you were placed in a paradise of delights filled inwardly and outwardly with every good thing. Outwardly you enjoyed a pleasant place sweet with delights; inwardly you possessed a full knowledge of things and affections, all in a quiet and peaceful harmony. For our God endowed you most generously with intellectual and cognitive powers, intellect, reason, and sense, so that through your intellect you might know God and perceive immaterial realities, through your reason rightly discern inferior things and refer all to the praise of God, through your exterior senses grasp the presence and particularity of material things, and through your interior sense be attracted by the images and likenesses of things—even in their absence—as an aid to reason.

He also gave the appetitive powers, that is the will, so that you might love God above all and all other things for his sake and in loving refer all things properly to him. He gave the power of concupiscence so that you might hunger for all that is good and desire the highest good above all. In that concupiscent power he placed various delightful affections: the affection of love that might move you of itself and incline you to the good; an affection of joy, through which you might take the highest delight in God and rejoice in a glimpse of his benefits and in reflecting on his works and wonders; and so on. He gave also an irascible power so you might cling the more firmly to God and through which you might indignantly drive away anything that would separate you. Here he also placed your delightful affections, hope and courage, so that you might manfully advance toward the good and proceed in hope.

Behold how much good he bestowed upon you, on what a sublime peak he placed you. Your intellect was illumined like your first parent, and although, as we believe, it did not see God in his essence, it nonetheless gazed upon him with the pure intuition of the mind and at the limits of contemplation. He endowed you with no evil passion or affection, meaning, any that has evil as its object such as hatred, sadness, or some other inner movement, lest there be something that disturbed you from within. Nor were those faculties,

247

powers, or affections ever at odds with themselves; the law of the flesh never assailed the law of the mind. For there was still no corrupted body and therefore no weighed-down soul. He ordered all these faculties in the best possible way; the inferior obeyed the superior without contradiction or even any desire to do otherwise. For sense obeyed reason, and reason the mind; the mind, however, was subject to God alone. The sensible appetites, that is, the concupiscent and irascible faculties, instantly obeyed the will and the rational appetite. There was in the inner man therefore great concord, and whatever the will willed found obedient response in the other powers and lesser affections. The will however did all according to the counsels of the intellect or the dictates of reason. The intellect, in turn, illumined from above by the light of the face of God, knew fully by this natural and gracious illumination what it should do and what it should repudiate. And this kind of peaceful concord and obedient harmony of the powers and affections is called by the saints our original righteousness.

Behold, man, this is your place, the place in which your Lord God placed you. This is the state of rectitude in which he created you and toward which he inclined your heart to climb. Look now upon this state of rectitude, still represented in the erect state of your body, even though in your heart, it must be added at once, you have wandered very far away, and must now say with tears: "Our feet are standing with affection in your forecourts, O Jerusalem" (Ps 121/122:2).

3. *The Valley of Tears to Which Man Descended through the Fall of the First Man, and the Consequent Loss and Disordering of the Powers of the Soul—the First Fall from Our State of Rectitude*

You heard, O man, about the place in which the Lord placed you and to which you ought to ascend. See now the valley of tears into which you fell headlong. Alas, our first and proto-parent, raised up with so much glory and honor, failed to understand that he was in a state of honor, and turning away from the precepts of his Creator he transgressed the divine command. He thereby fell grievously, and we in him, for we were all in him by a certain generative force or seminal reason. All of us therefore fell, and as Bernard said, "We fell at once into the slime and landed on rough stones." Thus we became polluted with original guilt, bruised and battered and gravely wounded in all the faculties and powers of a soul once so well disposed. Through that fall and by the just judgment of God, original righteousness was lost, and those powers and affections, fallen from their former state, became at once diminished and disordered, though not altogether destroyed. Inclined now in the very opposite direction, they opposed and fought each other in their every movement and impulse. Thus daily, not to say continuously, you experience—if you are not a totally insensitive creature—that sensuality, that is, the concupiscent and irascible appetites rebel against the will, and the will repeatedly in turn, though not always, against reason.

Those powers and affections consequently now move quite differently from the way in which they were instituted by God, prone to evil and inclined always to the desire for something illicit. Reason itself, made blind, erroneous, and obtuse, often holds the false for true and frequently involves itself in the useless and merely curious. The will has been bent and often chooses for the worst, loving the carnal while despising the spiritual and heavenly. The concupiscent force is impoverished and inclined rather toward the carnal, the lust of the eyes and the desires of the flesh, gluttony, lust, and avarice. The irascible faculty is disordered and inclined toward the pride of life and worldly glory. Hope no longer hopes in God but in riches and personal merit and always to a degree more or less than is right: Thus we are saddened by the loss of riches or the disdain of the world, rejoice in gluttony and lust, become irritated with our brother. In short, with the loss of original righteousness all our affections are prone to evil from adolescence, or rather from conception, for a soul conceived concupiscently from the flesh contracts a certain pollution and an inclination of the desires toward evil. Even though Christ's most precious death redeemed us from original guilt, so the destitution of these faculties and the law of the flesh are not now sinful in themselves (since we are not obliged not to have it) and there is no damnation for those who are in Christ Jesus, yet he in no way restored us to our pristine state of rectitude, nor did he reform the powers of our souls, but for the sake of our own exercise and merit he left those for us to reform through holy exercises. Behold this is the valley of tears, the state of the miserable, to which we fell and from which we should ascend, rising up and disposing our heart for the climb.

4. *Man, Descended from the State of Rectitude in the Fall of the First Man, Is Lured by Concupiscent Desires and Strays Still Further into Impurity of Heart. Impurity of Heart: The Second Fall*
Great and indeed too great is the distance between the valley of tears where you now are and the place where God once placed you, that is, the state of rectitude. Therefore a great ascent is necessary,

or rather many difficult ascents, and it will require great labor if you wish to return there. Would that you had remained here at least, that you had been at rest and not wandered still further. But alas, you prodigal son, drawn away by certain prostitutes—meaning, the allure of concupiscent desires—you departed into still more remote regions, or as the holy Gospel says, going into the most distant region in pursuit of your desires and there lying with the prostitutes, meaning, your illicit desires. For as often as we have concupiscent desires, so often, according to Jerome, we fornicate. Thus you consumed the whole portion of natural goods and spiritual graces which was coming to you. In the fall of the first man, as noted already, we contracted an inclination of our concupiscent desires to the lowest things, so that unless we constantly resist them we are forced by their impetus to descend to the depths. You, however, have not only not resisted them, but given in: You descend with them, you cling to carnal desires and affections and worldly things, and thereby lose whatever remained in you of natural good and spiritual gifts inclined toward the right.

By clinging to such vile things with desire and affection, moreover, you are in a certain sense made similar and of a like nature to them. You contract a certain sliminess and ooziness in your desires and faculties, and are kept bound down as it were by a sticky glue; and this is properly called impurity of heart. In the natural order things are called and made impure when mixed with viler things— gold, for instance, mixed with silver, or silver with lead. So, dear man, your rational soul, worthier than all other temporal creatures, becomes impure and unclean when subjected to temporal things by its love of them or affixed, habituated, and stuck to them by affection and desire. And if it adheres to carnal things with a carnal affection, it takes upon itself a certain sliminess called carnality from which a man is made carnal. If it clings to the things and vanities of this world with a worldly affection, that impurity is called vanity and a man is made secular. Thus it is that Holy Scripture distinguishes between carnal and secular men.

So now you see what is meant by impurity of heart, which you have read about in Scripture and perhaps not understood. It is clearly that affection by which you are inclined and cling to the lower things, be it gluttony, lust, vainglory, pride, or praise accorded you for such things. You acquired that impurity in the fall of the first man, but you added much of your own through habit and clinging, so that what was already unclean festered still more. Behold this is your second step downward, and the further you descend, the more ascents you must make to return to the state of rectitude from which you fell.

5. *Man's Third Step Downward: Mortal Sin by Which He Departs Furthest into the Region of Dissimilitude*

Yet the prodigal son goes farther and loses still more, for the further he goes the more he loses when departing from God. What more? Once he has consumed everything with the prostitutes, he enters the region of dissimilitude where he subjects himself to one of the citizens of that region, who sets him to feeding pigs. In short, he subjects himself to the devil through mortal sin and gratifies with his behavior every concupiscent desire. In the region of dissimilitude where you have now come, dear man, there is no longer any vestige of virtue. These are then the three descents downward into the region of dissimilitude.

6. *Three Examinations, and How a Man May Recover His Sense through Memory of His Sins, Especially That of His Last Step into Mortal Sin*

After you have come to see your descent, it is right to prepare for your ascent. But blindness and insensitivity frequently accompany sin. A person weighed down with sin fails to perceive himself a sinner. He remains stupid, acquiring the face of a whore and hardness of heart, and he neither fears God nor respects man. Before you begin your ascent, therefore, you must carefully examine yourself and seek in every way possible to recover your good sense, recognize your descent, and deplore your sin. So as to know how badly you fell in committing mortal sin in your last descent, diligently look into and strictly examine yourself, so you may finally open your eyes and see where you lie fallen.

Strictly call yourself into judgment, if not continuously, at least frequently. Call to mind and consider first of all how much God is displeased by every little sin, how much he detests and is horrified by it. So as to sense this still better, diligently reflect and review until you grasp in your own emotions how pride so displeased God that he spared not his noblest creature but cast Lucifer from heaven. Consider whether he might spare you as better or nobler. Think that he drove Adam out of Paradise for disobedience, and despoiled the whole human race of its original righteousness. For lustfulness he overthrew Sodom and Gomorrah and drowned nearly the whole world in a flood. Scripture recounts many such things for you. Think how displeasing sin was to God, so displeasing that in his justice he preferred to make satisfaction for Adam's sin by dying himself rather than dismissing it unpunished. If you are so hard-hearted as still not to fear your fall, form your meditation around the thought that divine justice cannot judge your works other than as they deserve. For God is a kind of intelligible equity, capable neither of change nor of decline, no less in the punishing of evil than in the glorifying of good. You may be certain, therefore, that he will render to you according to your works, nor will he leave any evil in you unpunished. If you turn this around within you for awhile, you will not be so much shaken with fear, I think, as stupefied with horror.

Then, in the third place, memory should enter and place before you all your past sins, especially the most serious. Think how many sins you have committed, how grievously you erred almost every day and every hour prior to your conversion. Who could number the sins you committed in heart, mouth, and deed? Next, review each one and see how grievously you offended at once the terrible Judge and the sweet and kindly Father, who did and bore so much for you, and whom you in a certain sense crucified again. Then review how shameful some of these were, especially in matters of the flesh—though you should move on quickly lest any impure delight creep in again.

Though converted now to the Lord, you should not dismiss the memory of your sins, but go on to consider with great diligence the sins committed after conversion. Think of the individual vices with which you are still stained. Think especially how great your pride is, how you desire honor and praise, and to what status you aspire. Think how lukewarmly and unfruitfully you have spent so many years in divine service, how little progress you are able to discover in yourself, and how God may punish you even more severely, as an ingrate, for sins committed after conversion. After you have examined all this, diligently consider how little satisfaction you have made for it all, how little was your contrition, how small and unsatisfactory your work—knowing all the while that either here or in the future you will most certainly pay for everything down to the last penny. But in the future, according to Bernard, you will render a hundredfold for what you could have paid straight-out here. When a sinner has turned these and similar thoughts over in his mind and senses himself struck with fear and filled with an inner grief, he should turn his heart most humbly and in deepest sorrow directly to God, saying his prayers and imploring upon his goodness and mercy with deepest yearning, promising to change and correct his ways and to fulfill his promise with the help of God. This formula for meditation, or one similar to it, you ought to follow, not falling into desperation, but rather so as to be warmed thereby to satisfaction and emendation, making yourself ready for every labor and patient in every adversity.

7. The Second Examination, Encompassing a Man's Whole Inner and Outer Status, through Which He Comes to Perceive His First Descent and the Impoverishment of His Soul's Faculties

That you may better know your first fall and descent through Adam and the consequent impoverishment of your soul's powers, or rather that you may clearly sense all the vices and passions, undertake at some convenient time a diligent examination of yourself and your entire condition. Begin with your inner man, and what moves the powers of your soul, how near or far they are from what they ought to be and from that for which God endowed you.

Examine your reason. Think whether it is not in error on many things, whether it is not idle and preoccupied with vain things, departing from that which brings salvation. Is it not deceived, trusting in its own definitions, unyielding to the humble, and thus obstreperous? Is it not proud, thinking itself something when it is nothing, preferring itself to the good, and refusing to learn from anyone? Unspeakable, and unteachable, and incapable of good counsel?

Next examine your memory. See what meditations come forward most frequently, for you think on that which you most love or fear.

Then examine your appetites. Think what saddens you, what disturbs, what gladdens, what brings hope, what you hate; and then you will see clearly how far you have fallen. See what beasts are accustomed to mount your concupiscent power, be they gluttony, lust, or avarice. See what wild animals are transported by your irascible power, be it the lion of pride, or the dog of anger, or the basilisk of envy.

Then examine the exterior man. For the disordered movements of the outer man are the indicators of an inner disorder. See how often you use excessive language, hard, reproachful, flattering, mocking, vain, or superfluous. Look especially whether you show charity to all, or rather sometimes injure the consciences of others with your scandal, restlessness, or presumption of novelty. So too whether you burn with zeal to admonish others charitably and to reproach them humbly, whether you carry out faithfully your assigned work. Examine yourself in your reading, meditation, prayer, and the like as to how you customarily order them.

8. The Third Examination, a Review Each Day of That Day's Excesses, through Which a Man May Learn to Sense the Impurity of His Heart and to Disclose His Passions

To sense your second step downward, how drawn by your own concupiscence you contracted impurity, you ought to conduct still a third self-examination, this one daily and especially, as Bernard preferred, after compline. Each day at that time review diligently and examine strictly how often evil custom drew you toward illicit things, especially how often in that day your slimy and sticky impurity overthrew you: How, for instance, you were drawn to illicit thoughts, dawdled over vain things during prayer, gave expression to idle or harmful words, or idly neglected holy meditation, or conquered by impurity were that day wholly without affection for the good; or again how drawn by engrained custom you offered an occasion for temptations which you failed to repudiate or resist.

If you proved a diligent workman in these three inner examinations and as a just judge judged yourself, tearing away the veil of self-love or self-indulgence and in no way flattered or stroked yourself, you will doubtless advance greatly in self-knowledge. But who has ever held himself in contempt? Love perverts good judgment and zeal has no wisdom. To strengthen your own sentences, seek and take care frequently to have your vices made known to you by others. For another eye often sees us far better, insofar as it judges freely and without prejudice. Following these self-examinations you ought therefore to discuss, seek advice, and frequently bemoan with others your temptations, passions, and evil inclinations. Thus you may be better informed by their counsel, the more humbled when they know you as you are, and the more struck with remorse when you hear from them that you are evil, just as you yourself discovered through these examinations—so long as they who hear what you are, are not thereby themselves made worse but rather edified by your humbling.

There is one thing still to note about the second and third examinations. Through them you should learn to recognize your inner vices, to see disordered desires and affections, and to reflect upon the disordered state of your soul's powers. But you will never perceive fully and perfectly how strong, how rooted, how much a part of your nature they really are until you lay a hand on them, and seek with all your strength to uproot them. Then you will experience firsthand their strength and resistance.

9. Order Your Exercises in Your Heart and Discuss Them with a Spiritual Man before Beginning Ascent, and Do Not Lightly Change but Persist in Holy Exercises to the End

"Dispose your ascents in your heart." Before you ascend, that is, begin to advance spiritually, your heart must be well disposed to reach its end, which is purity of heart and love. Carefully examine and consider what suits you, what is most useful, and if you do not know, ask others, or rather have others order your ascent. Set a certain end in your heart toward which by grace you may come to complete all your works and exercises. Then order the steps, exercises, and means by which to reach that end, and fix both the end and the means firmly in your heart. And this, it seems, is to set your heart upon the ascent: to seize upon certain means and exercises through discrete and diligent conversation with yourself and others, then to imprint and fix them firmly upon your heart, whence they will be of manifold utility to you.

First, do everything as you have ordered it in your heart and not casually like one of those inconstant types who does this exercise today and that tomorrow, grabbing at everything and advancing in nothing, trying everything and finishing nothing, doing whatever comes up since he has nothing ordered or fixed in his heart. You should not be so, but do everything just as you ordered your ascent in your heart, so that you may advance in that way and arrive at the goal you set. Do everything, the Lord said to Moses, according to the exemplar which was shown you on the mountain. You, thus, seek to complete everything according to the exemplar which you discreetly ordered in your heart. If a craftsman does not first order in his heart the form and disposition of the home he is to build by way of some model, he will never produce a proper home in reality or one built in its proper dimensions. Similarly it is necessary for you first to erect a ladder in your heart, according to which model you will do everything externally. So also God, the first cause of all things, would not have brought forth all things in reality in their proper disposition and form without first having the essential exemplar and idea of all things.

Second, you will be kept from deception by this predisposing of your heart. For those who do not set in advance a certain exercise or spiritual means will receive from their exercises as many impressions as they see others at work; they will believe in every spirit, remain stable in and fixed upon nothing, but rather wander about in everything. You ought therefore first to dispose the steps in your heart with diligent examination so that you may regulate your life by them all the way to the end, praising the life and exercises of others but not adopting them, just as Abbot Nestor taught.

You ought similarly to order your exercises in your heart with discreet moderation so as to keep yourself stable within a certain variation. Do not persist immoderately in one certain work or ignore all others and dismiss them as slight, lest tedium or infirmity or something similar overcome you. For anything that lacks an occasional pause will not last. Read therefore from time to time and afterward you will be stronger for prayer; first meditate and then work so these might reinforce one another, and all together may then preserve you whole, passing from one to the other without tedium. The disposition of these ascents in your heart should be in conformity with Holy Scripture and be approved in discussion with a spiritual man.

10. A Man Should Order His Heart Differently with Respect to the End and the Means to the End

You ought to dispose your heart differently toward the end and the means to the end. Your end, purity of heart and love, should be so fixed and immovably imprinted upon your heart that you never depart from it by any accident, advice, or order from another, nor indeed from its inner virtuous act or love. But every deed and every exercise should be directed to this end, and your eyes ever focused upon it. Just as sailors who do not have their port in sight will sail here and there, first to the east and then to the west, just as the wind carries them, and never know whether they are coming closer or going farther away, so he who does good works and knows not the end of purity may permit vices to master him and will not know how much he is advancing or declining in the true spiritual life.

The means we ought so to order in our hearts as will best serve to advance us toward the end of purity and love; when they obstruct this end, they are to be abandoned. For we should not be so insistent upon reading and meditation that, should charity be required, we leave them only with murmuring and sadness, thus incurring the impurity of sadness or some other evil which was supposed rather to be uprooted by sacred reading or meditation. We should never be so totally fixated upon such exercises as we are upon their end. When charity is required or obedience, the exercises are humbly to be deserted for a time. As Bernard says, what was instituted for charity should not militate against charity.

11. *The Three Ascents, Counter to the Three Previous Descents, Which Will Restore Us Again to the State of Rectitude*

. . . The first ascent is that which returns you to your heart. For through sin you departed far from your heart, nor will any spiritual exercise advance you in your heart unless you return to it. Whence the Prophet warned, "Return, you liars, to your hearts" (Is 46:8). The second step, after returning to your heart, is to ascend from a heart impure with concupiscence to a pure heart. Purity of heart and love mark this ascent away from the opposite descent. The third step lies also in the heart. By it you ascend from the disordered affections inborn since Adam and now engrained in you by custom, and this is principally directed against the first descent.

12. *The First Ascent Upward from Mortal Sin, the Three Steps of This Ascent, and Contrition*

Rise up, then, and ascend on high, begin the journey toward your heart. Just as you incurred mortal sin in a threefold descent—for you turned away from your Creator in pride (the formal cause of sin), turned toward the creation in love, and transgressed in deed the divine law commanded by your God—so it is necessary for you to ascend by three contrary steps. First, turn your heart away from creatures and sin, and fix such an aversion firmly in your heart together with a firm intention of serving your God and never subjecting yourself to creatures through any illicit desire, even if it became necessary to die a thousand deaths. Resolve this in general, but do not examine yourself too much in particular on this, for you will grieve mightily to have departed so far from God, to have offended him so deeply, and in a certain sense to have crucified him again.

This aversion marks one step upward called contrition, by which your heart is in a sense broken from its hardness. Just as in nature hard things are said to be "ground up" when they are broken and reduced to small pieces, so metaphorically the heart is said to be ground up when it is softened from its hardness. Earlier it was turned away from God, hard and stubborn in its sin, not yielding to any divine movements, not admitting any impulses from the Holy Spirit, but always turning a deaf ear lest it hear. Or, as Bernard says in *De consideratione*, the heart is said to be hard when it is not torn by remorse, nor softened by piety, nor moved by prayers, and so on. It is ground down, however, when it is liquified by remorse and softened by piety.

13. *Confession, the Second Step in This First Ascent*

Because through pride you were contemptuous of God in your sinful state you must humbly submit yourself to a man, a vicar of God holding the keys, and to him, as to the Lord Christ sitting as your judge, humbly, contritely, and mournfully confess your sins. Humbly: knowing your own sins, accuse yourself in all things, your ways, deeds, words, answers, and all particulars, as if sitting in judgment on yourself. Look out that you do not, as some, confess a great crime and seek therefore praise when you deserve instead reproach from God—as some do when, for instance, they confess to sharp arguing in the schools. Do not seek to excuse your sins or intentions, but say simply and humbly what gnaws upon your conscience. Confess contritely and mournfully, exercising yourself beforehand in the remorse you will have afterward so as to approach confession contritely and mournfully. If you do this rightly—not as some, telling their sins like a tale, or reciting sins straightforwardly without grief as if speaking about some other secular matter, but in a true spirit of compunction—it will become difficult, or rather impossible, to hold back the tears. You should also hold it for certain that your sins will be forgiven you in confession according to the measure of your contrite intention and human modesty. If possible, choose for yourself a confessor who knows how to bind and loose discreetly and prudently, to whom you are able confidently to commit your soul, your estate, and your life, to whom you can also trustingly lay out all your exercises, and from whom you may expect counsel on particulars. And if you find such a confessor, do not lightly seek another. For different doctors apply different medicines, and changing medicines often aggravates rather than heals the disease. In everything, however, always respect the law and the obedience of the Church and your superior.

You should also know that good works enjoined by a priest have more satisfactory value than those undertaken of your own will, primarily owing to the power of the Church's keys and the humble obedience of the penitent. When you expose your wounds to your priest, therefore, and he—as is only right—wants to use lighter medicines, insist from time to time that he not spare you but boldly lay on what best suits your estate and improvement, and show yourself ready to bear it. This is the second step in the first ascent, called confession with the mouth.

14. *Satisfaction, the Third Step of the First Ascent*
The third step in this first ascent is this: Just as you once showed your members arms of iniquity in various sins and evil deeds, so now make them arms of righteousness through satisfaction. Thus just as you cure with contrary antidotes, so do battle with all those crimes you committed, especially all those vices and passions, by applying yourself to fasts, vigils, labors, and other devout exercises—and this especially, as was said, at the injunction of your confessor because these will prove especially meritorious. This is the last step in the first ascent, called satisfaction. With these three steps the first ascent is finished, for with these three parts of penance you both return to your heart and are reconciled to God.

15. *The Second Ascent, the Return to Purity of Heart, and the Three Steps Required to Advance beyond the Three Steps Downward*
Behold, you have been healed and reconciled to God. Go, advance farther, and seek to sin no more, but only to advance from virtue to virtue. Do not think it is enough to be reconciled to God through penance and to be received into his good graces in perfect charity. Or do you forget that Absalom, though reconciled to his father, did not deserve to see his face until he had stayed for a time in his home? So too, if you wish to see the face of God with a pure heart, do not presume upon this at once. Seek first to ascend gradually in your heart, to exercise yourself for a long time in the ascents of the heart, and thus to arrive at purity of heart, proving yourself three times over, purging yourself seven times over, and emptying yourself to the point where all refuse and impurity is removed. For as we said above, when a man returns to his heart from wandering abroad in concupiscence, though he be reconciled and purged by grace from guilt, the remains and refuse of sin are still in his soul. Those harmful and impure affections, that sliminess acquired through sin and engrained through custom, must be removed and left behind step by step. This is what it means to advance from an impure heart to purity of heart and to counteract the second descent.
To counter this descent it is necessary to dispose the heart toward three ascents, since the impurity of your heart and affections seems to consist in three things. First, you cling to lower things with an inordinate affection and a disordered inclination, to vainglory, honor, praise, gluttony, lust—in short, loving what ought not to be loved. Second, you do not love what ought to be loved: Your affections and appetite are so immoral, impure, and infected with evil humors that they have no taste for spiritual and heavenly things but are

rather made nauseous by heavenly manna, left unmoved by the thought of the kingdom of heaven, and so on. Such impurity might be called a hatred of what ought not to be hated, meaning you have no appetite for what you ought to find appetizing. Impurity of heart is, third, a certain infirmity of the heart or inability of the mind: Thus a person purged in his affections and even to some degree restored in hope is still unsuited for or incapable of clinging to God with an ardent affection of perfect love, for the full vigor of charity is somehow lacking.

Against these impurities of the heart, you must make three successive ascents, advancing in three steps of virtue. For we make the first ascent through fear of the Lord who, as it were, violently shakes the heart and breaks it loose from its harmful affection for and adherence to things lower. We advance against the second impurity through hope because hope lifts our hearts and restores its taste for the heavenly, instilling it with an affection for acquiring things celestial. We ascend from the third impurity through love, by which we are united to God and cling to him.

16. *Fear, the First Step in This Ascent, and How It Removes Our Heart from Harmful Affections*

When evil desires so weigh down your heart, so affix and imprint it that it can hardly be pulled free, when you are suckling upon the honey of evil desire and the milk of harmful nourishment, you must sprinkle these with something bitter, much as women suckling infants are accustomed to sprinkle their breasts with something bitter so that children will taste the bitterness, turn away from the sweetness of the breast, and finally forget it altogether. Fear of the Lord must thus fill your heart with bitterness. For example, when you are full of this world's desires and carnal vices, yearn mightily for high station and the world's glory, cannot forgo delicate foods, find it hard to be looked down upon, and so on, the fear of the Lord should come into your heart and sprinkle all these sweet things with something bitter: showing you how quickly all earthly delights will pass, terrifying you with the great and unspeakable punishments for such disordered delight, and representing to you how severely and terribly the just judge will punish you for the little bit you gain. By these and similar considerations, your heart must be turned to bitterness, shaken with fear, confused with terror, and so violently pulled away from its delights that it forgets them. Do not neglect therefore to make a kind of elixir from these and similar meditations, which, though it be bitter, is wonderfully purgative of all evil humors, meaning, evil desires. With it you must oil and water every delight of this world and so spread these with bitterness that you will come to spew out and loathe them. So that you may prepare such an elixir, called "remorse arising from fear," as often as you like, I will describe a way of making it.

17. *Remorse Arising from Fear May Be Adopted Variously in Exercises and Meditation.*

Remorse born of fear arises in several ways. First, when someone calls to memory his past sins and the degree to which he has offended God and the great punishment he therefore deserves, he will become shaken and frightened and be brought to bitter tears. Second, when someone diligently examines his own defects, the passions of the soul and harmful desires still agitating and stirring in him even if not dominant, and sees how little progress he makes in fighting them, the thought will bring him to cry out in grief. Third, when someone recalls the sins he has perpetrated since his conversion, doubtless offensive to God every day even if they are not criminal, he will deplore himself in mourning and fear. These three were noted already in the discussion of self-examination. Fourth, let a man consider that the judgments of God are inscrutable so that a man never knows whether he is worthy of love or hatred. Though he knows himself to have repented, he does not know whether he was moved toward remorse and contrition by fear alone or by infused grace, and thus he will become totally shaken with horror, uncertain what will become of him in the future, whether he will be saved or damned. Fifth, let a man diligently attend to the brevity of his life and recognize how little as yet he has advanced, and then he will be set afire with fear and consumed inwardly with remorse. Sixth, let him remember the strict examination coming and that the judge will render to each according to his works, and then he will be struck with fear at the cognizance of his own sins. Seventh, let a man reflect on the magnitude and variety of punishment in hell and recognize himself worthy of it, and then he will begin to grieve and to fear deeply.

18. *The Usefulness of Remorse, and How It Purifies the Heart*

If you carefully reflect on all this in your heart and frequently fill it with some or all of these considerations, everything sweet will turn bitter, the world and its desires will pass from your heart, and then the desires of the flesh and of the eyes will also disappear, and you will sense no bitterness without, saturated as you are with bitterness within. And thus your heart will begin to spew out all the sweetness and affection and allegiance to this world, and to loathe vainglory, honor, popular favor, gluttony, and lust. To prepare this sort of remorse readily, I will also describe the art and means of concocting it.

19. *A General Way of Preparing Meditations on Death*

A person must therefore meditate on the fact, never to pass from before his eyes, that after a little while he will pass from this life into another unknown region. You will leave everything behind, all the glory and honor and whatever else delights you in this world. With every hour of every day you draw nearer to your final hour. Consider therefore and, so far as you are able, form within you the affections of a dying man. Dispose yourself and your meditation as if you were about to die, with this now the moment, which doubtless would still be a living moment for you. See how much fear there is in you when so affected, how much remorse of conscience and internal clamor over your evil delights, how much you grieve not to have made amends, not to have pulled yourself away from such delights, to have transgressed God's commandments. For in that hour you will see what you did and what you deserve. Then bring before your eyes the individual delights: See the particular vices and passions in which you now find sweet delight. Think how bitter it will be to become separated from those delights, and how much you will regret not to have died to desire while still alive.

Then think and shape in yourself such an affection as if your soul had suddenly to depart: How freely you would leave all delight behind, how gratefully you would take up every labor and penance, if you were able still to have your life. Think how brief will seem in that hour the whole of your life and your delights. You will see then your whole time pass away as a dream or a shadow, especially when you begin to weigh in eternity, which never ends. Think next how sorrowful you will be that for so little delight in such a short time you lost everlasting delight, happiness, and glory. Think too that all those delights will confer nothing more upon you than to make the bitterness of death still more bitter. The more you were bound to so many things by disordered desires, the more difficult it will be to leave them behind. Hence the wise man: "O death, how bitter is your memory to a healthy man who has peace in his being" (Eccl 41:1).

When you sense that you have formed such an affection within you and impressed it upon your heart, then proceed further to the thought that that hour will most certainly come and is unavoidable.

For all men die and a thousand generations have perished since the beginning of time, and so will you. Think next that you are not able to know the exact hour in advance. It will come unexpectedly, perhaps this year, this month, or this week, because it will come as a thief in the night, just when you are thinking nothing of it but much about what you are planning to do.

From time to time, so that fear may crucify and purge your desires the more, turn over in your mind the way in which you will come to die. Very serious illness commonly precedes death. Think how great will be your illness, how serious your infirmity, when your heart will nearly break from an excess of grief. Think how depressed your heart will be then, as if the whole world weighed down upon it, owing partly to the gravity of your illness, partly to a natural inclination toward such a marvelous horror, and partly to fear for its own sins and the coming judgment—and then finally death will follow.

On another occasion, place before your eyes the image of some dying man, and carefully note the form, means, and order by which he comes to die. His whole body withers, all its members grow stiff, the eyes turn up, and so on. Then think how the demons will arrive expectantly, like beasts preparing to eat, looking to see if they can discover anything of their own in his soul and whether they might meet any impure spirits leaving it, in short, looking in it for their handiwork so they might drag him along to the depths of hell. Then think how the body leaves the soul and suddenly stands before the Judge's tribunal to receive the sentence which will never again be changed from that moment down through all the ages. Then follow the bier to the burial and see how that poor body, for which so many delights were sought, is given over to the earth, food for the worms consigned to eternal oblivion. From these and similar meditations, see that the joy and delight of this world are like a point that passes, a mere shadow, and man is like a traveling guest who stays but one night.

On the other hand, you ought also at times to assume the affections of a just man dying, well-disposed toward death. Think how happy he will be who repented beforehand, purged himself from such delights, loved nothing in this world of such evils, and so on through the particulars.

20. *General Meditations on the Last Judgment Meant to Instill Fear*
Turn your mental eye next upon the last judgment so that its most bitter recollection may embitter all sweetness. Think of the

great fear, clamor, and wonder that will arise when the Archangel's trump sounds, when lightening flashes so terribly, thunder booms, the sun becomes darkened to the fright of sinners and the moon no longer gives forth its light. Think what kind of heart the sinner will have then, how all the dead will rise, each one turning over in his mind what he did of evil and of good. The good will await the Judge with unspeakable happiness, but the unjust will fear the coming and the face of the Judge with unspeakable terror, saying, "May the mountains fall on us and cover us from the face of the Judge." For the time has passed away, and they can no longer go out and buy the oil of merit.

Step out then and meet him in your meditation. See the Judge coming with great power, with the leaders from among the people and accompanied by all the saints and angels. Consider that bitter divorce when the sheep will be separated from the goats. Now there are two in one house or in one mill, but then one will be taken and the other left, the two never again to be joined together. Form in yourself the affections of those at the left, to whom he will say, "Go you cursed into the fire," and so on, and how they will wail saying, "Behold these are the ones we once held in derision." What grief and mourning will overtake them. Then assume the affection of those at the right: How filled they will be with joy that for such modest labors they merit an eternal reward.

Think how strict will be the examination of all deeds, words, thoughts, and evil affections: All will be bared and revealed, including what was covered over here. For Jerusalem will be scrutinized with lanterns, and some who were thought to be citizens of Jerusalem will be uncovered as citizens of Babylon. The devil will be a witness there, pointing out to us the sins we committed together with their times and places, and he will say, "Most equitable Judge, judge this man to be mine for his guilt; in his pride he never wanted to be yours." Your own conscience will accuse you, and so will the holy angels. Christ will show there the marks of his passion and deny to the evil all its benefits because they were contemptuous and ungrateful. Then the Judge will pronounce the definitive sentence which no one can appeal, contradict, elude, or ward off. Think what bitterness, grief, and horror is contained in that sentence, "Go, you accursed." Think what sweetness, wonder, and joy there is in that voice saying, "Come, you blessed."

Meanwhile think too about your own individual judgment, and shape meditations from the above accordingly.

21. *How to Acquire Fear and Remorse through Recalling the Pains of Hell*

Turn your eyes next to the region of the damned and the prison of the miserable, carefully examining what goes on there, what for a house and place it is. Our blinded minds are better led to a knowledge of the invisible through the visible and material, and so to better sense those pains, take up the images of hell put in writing by the saints.

See therefore hell itself, a most horrible chaos, a subterranean place sunk in the depths, totally dark, the deepest pit and yet totally enflamed, all a great burning furnace with terrible leaping flames, a great city dark and murky, totally alight and burning, full of an infinite multitude of people crying out, giving forth the most miserable sounds, screamed out with grief and ardor, people mutually tearing at one another in envy like mad dogs bound together. Think next of the bitterness of the pains: a heat there greater than any comparable here, but also an intolerable cold without equal here. Think too of the excruciating intensity of the individual punishments, and of their multitude. There is a fire inextinguished, abounding heat, an undying light, an intolerable cold, a rotten stink, a palpable darkness, undying worms. There is punishment for every sense and in every member. The sight will see the wormlike faces of demons horribly afflicting it with their horrible aspect. The hearing will take in nothing but grieving, weeping, and wailing, and voices saying, "Woe, woe that I was ever born or created by God and have not perished; cursed be God and cursed be the Trinity which created us for this punishment." Behold this is the song which they sing there with all its lamentations, and so on.

Think of that most miserable society of demons and their cruel tortures, for they are without mercy. They never tire of torturing and are never moved to mercy but rather increase the pain by every means possible. They are insulting, saying, "Where is your glory now, your sensuous desire, your honor, your high station, your immense riches, your power, your dignity, your influence, your rule? What profit is there now to all these things, so brief, so quickly passing?" Think that whoever erred more with his tongue or in his heart will be punished the more in his members, and the more someone gave himself over to delights, so much graver the punishment that strikes there. Think too of the inner pains, especially exclusion from the divine vision, the greatest of all punishments. Think what it is to be eternally damned and cast out from that heavenly and glorious

Jerusalem above, never to return. Think about the worm of conscience, which will never die, never cease to cry out and to afflict
with the thought that for so little joy in a passing moment it must
now descend to such punishment. Think how the passions of the
soul, anger and envy, will join in the affliction, for impatience, envy,
and the like rule in the world of the damned. Carefully reflect on the
eternity of the punishment, which afflicts more seriously than any
other punishment: There will be no end to the punishment, in hell
there is no redemption. After a thousand years the end will draw no
closer, because there is no end.

By these and similar meditations you should conceive a fear of
God and a salutary remorse so that you may tear your affections
away from the lower things. But you must spend much time in such
exercises and so by these meditations and other virtuous works purge
the affections as a remedy for the vices to be discussed later. Otherwise we will not be able to ascend any higher. For so much as we
repudiate carnal and earthly affections, we gain spiritual; if a little,
then a little; and if much, then much. Therefore, according to the
Prophet, from the fear of the Lord we must give birth to a spirit of
salvation. The fear of the Lord is the beginning of wisdom, and we
must studiously exercise ourselves in it and purge our heart so that
we may come to love. As the Wise Man said, they are to begin with
fear if they are to come to charity. See therefore how appropriately
Holy Scripture ascribes purity of heart to faith, as it says, "purifying
their hearts by faith" (Acts 15:9), because fear, which is the first affection of faith, tears and extracts the heart from impure affections
and vicious stains. Faith or fear, which is its effect, is therefore the
first step of the second ascent, tending toward purity of heart.

22. *The Second Step of the Second Ascent: The Hope and Desire for
Celestial and Spiritual Things That Purges a Man and Heals Him from
the Second Impurity of Heart*
Just as faith, fearing future judgment and punishment, causes
the disease of the vices to diminish by thoroughly shaking, as it were,
the whole inner being and removing it from its affectionate clinging
to the lower vices, so hope subsequently calls our mind—removed
from such vices but not yet elevated, even depressed still by the
weight of present evils—and raises it on high. In expectation of celestial reward it repudiates all the delights of the body and vanities of
this world. It begins to yearn for that above, and the mind aspires
toward that supreme joy which hope represents to the inner being.
If therefore you sense that your heart has now been pulled away

from the lower things by fear, do not stand still or think yourself in the clear, for if you begin to stand, you will again descend. Indeed your heart cannot be wholly empty of affections. If therefore it is empty of harmful ones, fill it with celestial and holy affections; otherwise it will again descend to the place whence you purged it by fear. It is important that in the meantime you find solace in hope. But he who has spent some time advancing and purging his heart by fear will ascend to hope in quite another way.

The second impurity of heart consists in affections so infected by desires or weighed down and weakened by the vestige of desires that it has no taste for celestial things, and the way to ascend above that is through hope. For hope inculcates a taste for things eternal and restores an affection for things above. Just as a person, as noted, became impure through adherence to, contact with, and affection for things below, so he becomes pure through adherence to and affection for things above, for the spiritual and celestial, and this happens through hope. Therefore, O man, imagine above you a place wholly quiet, pure, and clean, and below you a place wholly restless and turbulent, in continuous motion, turbid and impure—and you yourself in the middle. The more you descend to the place below the more restless you are made by concupiscence, unstable with various desires, impure with immoral affection and the admixture of the unclean. The more you ascend on high through constant meditation, continuous affection, desire and hope, and admixture of the celestial, the more restful and stable you will become in the one, desiring only that one thing, to be in the courts of Jerusalem. And through it all you will yourself become all the purer.

23. *Remorse Exercised through Love*
When you began first to ascend, compelled by fright and fear, we gave a medicinal dose of bad humors, a purgative by which you might be driven to ascend. But because some weakness and bad taste remains from these humors, and you cannot ascend very high with so little taste for the spiritual, you must receive another medicinal dose made up of the hope of forgiveness, that is, compunction arising from love. For if you desire to ascend through hope, you must exercise yourself much in this.

This remorse is stirred up primarily in two ways, though many other ways are possible. First, when you have ascended a good while through the exercise of fear and its horrors, you should have completed many good works and devotional exercises, been purified of many harmful desires, and so far ascended as to have arrived at hope.

When you stand in hope, you can begin to see Jerusalem from afar, which in fear was not possible. You can glance at her often, admire her wonderful beauty, and drawn by that beauty, begin to yearn, groan, and complain because you are still so far distant. You may now wish to be dissolved and united with Christ, and cry out, "Who will free me from this body of death?" Seeing that you are still wandering far from that heavenly Jerusalem, you will begin sweetly to weep and often to complain that you cannot reach it.

This remorse arises, second, when you diligently look into your heart, and count the benefits of God which he has bestowed out of such great and manifold affection. Begin to consider your own ingratitude, and to expand and reach out with a certain internal desire toward the God who gave you so many benefits. This is the compunction of piety, arising from the wellspring of charity, which wonderfully overcomes the second impurity of heart.

That you may have something from these two ways which will easily serve to stir up remorse, there follows a way to shape and construct your meditations around celestial bliss.

24. *A General Way of Shaping Meditations on the Kingdom of Heaven, to Stir Up Remorse and Desire for the Kingdom*

You can find in the saints material images of that celestial homeland adjusted to suit our capacities. That city is therefore most glorious in breadth, of the purest gold and wonderfully constructed out of the most precious gems with pearls for each of its gates. It is a spacious field abloom with all the most beautiful flowers. There is always most pleasant air, the most fragrant scents, and a plenty of every delight. Think, gather up your whole strength to consider, what joy it will be to gaze forever on God in his essence, to look upon the great and only Trinity with the pure eye of the heart. There is the splendor of all beauty and all delight, the essential exemplar of all goodness. In that vision you will see all; all that you desire you will know; and you will be filled by it with all goodness, joy, and happiness. In it you will be blessed, and will enjoy fully the most blessed bliss, which is God himself.

Think what joy it will bring to be seated forever near the Lord Jesus Christ, and to gaze unceasingly upon his most holy and glorious humanity, seeing him, as Peter did, transfigured and wishing to remain this way forever. What great joy to see him exalted and glorious in his kingdom, he who once became a pauper, exile, and pilgrim for us in this pilgrimage. Think what joy to join the celestial court, what happiness to look upon the queen of heaven, the mother of God with all the other virgins, what happiness and exaltation to be among the angelic ranks, to rejoice with the patriarchs, prophets, apostles, martyrs, and confessors.

Think about the endowments bestowed upon your beatified body, its immortality, impassibility, great agility, and most glorious luminosity. Think of the endowments that will fill your beatified soul, the fullness of learning for the rational faculty, the fullness of justice for the concupiscent faculty, the abundance of happiness for the irascible. Think how many other great and unspeakable gifts will flow from these principle endowments: security, so you need not fear to be cast out, or to be overcome by the flesh, Satan, or the world; freedom to do what you wish; all the purest and most pleasurable desires for body and soul; friendship, love, honor, harmony, and perfect charity; in sum, whatever you wish, or do not wish.

25. *How Memory of the Benefits of God Kindles a Person to Devotion and Remorse*

That you may have greater confidence in your hope of obtaining true glory, carefully consider from time to time the signs of love God has shown. Reflect diligently on his benefits, and be enkindled as by a stimulus to love again. Think first of the greatest sign of your God's love. However many times you offend him, turn your back on him, leave him, and sin most gravely, he nonetheless receives you back whenever you wish to return, forgives you grieving your sin, and helps you toward correction and emendation.

Count up the natural benefits he has conferred on you, if you are able. He created you, giving you being from nothing, a being that is beautiful and handsome, sensible, alive, and adorned with five senses. He gave you understanding beyond all the other lower creatures, setting you above all animate being. You can know your God, understand the truth; and the light of his face is poured out upon your understanding, providing a great brightness of natural light. He gave you memory with which you can put together the likeness of similar things so as to recall something. He also gave you an impressionable understanding where you can gather up the species of intelligible things. He endowed your soul with such dignity and nobility that nothing can fill it, or indeed flow into it, except the one God, the holy and glorious Trinity in whose image and likeness he created you. What more? He gave you the sun to light you by day, the moon by night, and he made every lower creature subordinate to you and subject to your will.

Think next about the gifts of grace bestowed on you. For he

gave you contrition and grief for your sin, recalled you from unrighteousness, and infused you with righteousness—all of which came only from God, though he denied many others. He gave and inspired a will such that you wanted to make correction, he ordained a time and place where you could, and all this he did not give to many far better than you. Think of the truly extraordinary gifts conferred on you, for instance, that he gave you his most beloved son: first in the incarnation, for he was born for you and crucified for you; then in the sacrament of the altar in its food and drink. He sent the Holy Spirit as a little pledge of his acceptance, a privilege of love, an engagement ring.

To raise still more your love, devotion, and remorse in piety, think how many things that great Lord went through for your salvation. He spoke with the fathers, appeared in figures, addressed the prophets, led them out of Egypt, brought them into the promised land, and performed an infinite number of miracles and wonders. Why else did he do all this except out of love and desire for you, that you might earn the kingdom of heaven and eternal bliss, that your understanding might be illumined with the knowledge of the celestial, and your affections purged from the lower things? All this should raise your hope and affection upward in love of your God.

That these and similar meditations on the benefits of God might move you the more, keep to this way and then form such an affection in meditating that you diligently seek out the greatness and power of the benefactor who conferred all this on you. For he is all-powerful, as you can see in the creation of things; all-wise, as appears in his governance of them; and most provident in his disposition of them, which you may consider greatest of all if he grants you any little thing.

Second, note and consider with what great solicitude and desire he confers these benefits on you. From eternity he had arranged to give them to you, from eternity he had prearranged it. From eternity, with never any pause, he thought about you directly, and preordained to benefit you. He always was and is as solicitous about you as about an entire city or globe, so intensely solicitous about you as if to be free of all the others.

Third, look upon all the divine benefits conferred generally on the human race as if they were to be bestowed on you alone, and think: Behold for me he created the whole world and everything in it, for me he was crucified, and so on. And that will stir you no little to love, charity, and gratitude, rendering you liable for still more such benefits. But then note and marvel at yourself, that on such a vile, unworthy, lukewarm, and ungrateful creature he granted such benefits with so much affection and love.

26. *The Third Step of This Ascent toward Charity and Purity of Heart, and How a Person May Know That He Has Made the Step*

All the efforts thus far of both beginners and the more advanced have focused upon the preceding ascents and their steps. To come this far they have expended great labor and grief in vigils, fasts, readings, meditations, manual labor, and other devout exercises. No lukewarm, negligent, remiss, soft, or lazy person could ascend this high. Nor is it a small matter in the first ascent to dismiss, deplore, and repent of your previous life and to perform worthy fruits of penitence. But it is a far greater labor, or at least a longer one, to overcome engrained custom, disordered affections, and the inclination to lower things, to desert uncleaness and impurity, to purge the acquired affections, to extinguish all gluttonous desire, to repress lust, to stifle anger, to war against pride, and so through all the other evil affections which pertain to purgation by fear. Yet it is still more difficult, or rather a steeper climb, to raise your whole soul with all its affections to the celestial regions and to dwell there in hope. See how great is the ascent from one to another, from fear to hope; so great also is the distance within this ascent and the work of climbing. But he who has advanced well thus far is drawing nearer to purity and charity, though he still has some steps to ascend. For he must exercise himself a long while in these two steps, ascending and descending in fear and hope, trying to fight back the evil affections of pride, anger, gluttony, and so on, while making humility, chastity, and all the other virtues a part of his own nature.

There are two things in which the perfection of this third step, this purity and charity, consists. First, a man should now put on the virtuous affection, making it in a certain sense into his own nature, so that he will not perform the virtues as one driven by the fear of punishment or enticed by the hope of reward but rather as one delighted simply with an affection for goodness. That same affection for purity and charity, now become a love and desire inwardly habituated, will then stand in horror of evil and impurity. Consequently he will perform those virtues, not while fighting off other inducements, but with an affection for them lodged at the very core of his being. His heart will not only refuse to accept but also positively detest anything contrary to that affection for the virtues. He becomes one who does good for the sake of the good, drawn by an affection for it. Once he has won the battle against the vices, he will enjoy the security of peace and pass over into an affection for virtue itself. He will assume the condition of someone totally conscious of the good, for he will consider nothing more harmful than damage to that inner purity. He will judge nothing dearer and more precious than that present purity, so that some evil transgression brings the most serious pain. For him the reverence for a human presence will add nothing of moral well-being, nor will solitude diminish it, but he will bear about with him everywhere and at all times a conscience that judges his thoughts as well as his acts and will allow no impurity into the mind.

Second, just as affection for virtue becomes habituated into him, so through ardent love that affection will be inflamed, fervently ready at all times to please the divine will and to rise toward the divine vision. There it clings in fervent love and through its gaze stands in horror of all vice and sin, ever aflame with love and zealous in its gaze, everywhere intent upon the truth, fervent in the study of wisdom. Holiness of life and disciplined morals are its friend so that it is embarrassed by the boastful, abhorrent of distraction, ignorant of envy, hateful of pride. It flees and condemns as weariness all human glory, aggresively seeks out and despises all its own impurities of flesh and heart. In sum, as if by nature, he rejects all that is evil and embraces all that is good. This is the lush mountain on which all who ascend, coming and going, will find pasture. Entering by way of the concupiscent faculty, he will find joy in the Holy Spirit, long-suffering, kindness, modesty, and so on; by way of the irascible faculty, fortitude, constancy, perseverance, patience, and so on; by way of the intellect, frequent ascent beyond itself toward glimpses of the divine vision, even though in a mirror darkly. Upon leaving, he will be enkindled to love of the Creator through the knowledge and beauty of his creatures. Compare this condition to that with which Adam was originally constituted to see how much they differ. This is the condition of perfection, the mount of purity, and the perfect ascent toward true charity. He who is able to climb and capture it should ascend and seize it, but let the lazy depart and flee from the labor. Though this step of perfection is granted only by the special grace of God, that grace is not given to the negligent, the sleeping, and those who do not actively cooperate. That love is a kind of knightly service. Depart, you lazy. You can eventually find it and draw nearer only by constant exercise.

27. *The Three Steps Upward from the Third Impurity, Disposing a Man Progressively toward Ever More Perfect Adherence to God*

The third impurity of heart, as noted, consists in a certain inability or inaptitude for adhering to and knowing God. Even after the affections have been purged and hope instilled, a man may still not be suited for and capable of clinging to God or of resting quietly in him through the affections. . . . You must therefore set your heart upon new ascents, learning and growing accustomed to clinging to God constantly in love. To this end you should know that the God-man, Jesus Christ, himself God and man and mediator between God and man, is the way to ascend at once to knowledge and love of divinity, as Augustine taught in his *Confessions*. Christ took flesh particularly to this end, so that we who could not grasp God spiritually might ascend to spiritual love and knowledge through him, the Word made flesh. Establish for yourself therefore a threefold ascent through devout exercises in the life and death of Christ.

The first is when you cling to Christ with a certain sweet affection and heartfelt desire, even if it is still somewhat carnal. Accompany him emotionally through all his life and death. Take delight through your exercises in his presence and memory. In this first ascent or first affection, you can vary your exercises in different ways just as many different people with various affections followed Christ in his life. For the apostles followed him initially drawn only by his corporeal presence, refreshed by his talk, and enticed by his sweetness and affability. So too you might first follow Christ, join his band, in this same way. Think how sweet would be his presence, the elegance and beauty of his body. For it is a figure shapely beyond all the other sons of men. Note the sweetness of his words and teaching, the way in which he conducts himself with others, how sweetly and kindly he proffers his honeyed words. Note too his inner manner, the mildness, kindness, and sweetness from within. Observe his mature stride, his handsome appearance. Think of the profound wisdom that lies in Christ's heart, the most ornate eloquence in his mouth, the finest disposition of his external manner. This is the way the apostles followed him.

Others followed him because Christ healed their infirmities. Follow him for awhile in this way too. Bow down and adore him saying, "Lord, if you wish you could heal me," or "Jesus, son of David, have mercy on me" (Mt 7:2; Mark 10:47). Some followed him for his miracles, and you should marvel as well at the power in his miracles: He alters nature, transforms the elements, puts demons to flight, and heals every infirmity. Learn from this that he is the God who first endowed natural things with their effects, which remain ever obedient to him in all things, even to producing supernatural effects.

In these ways you can vary your exercises and affections in this first ascent. But know that while this exercise is very useful in such spiritual matters as focusing upon the ways and deeds of Jesus Christ our Lord, it will not suffice for ascent to the love of Christ, indeed will produce little to that end. What did it profit Judas, Pilate, Herod, or the Pharisees that they saw Christ's ways or deeds or physical presence when they did not want to follow him? Therefore the end of this first ascent, according to Bernard, is that drawn like the apostles by this affection you too will leave all things, the riches of this world, and so on. Then you too will persevere in this step: Its sweetness will occupy your heart and rescue you totally from the love of the flesh and of fleshly delights. In sum, a man should so extend his heart in such exercises toward the love of Christ's humanity that all his affections and desires are transferred to its sweetness.

The second ascent focuses upon the life and passion of Christ. This is to climb a little higher and requires exercise not only in Christ's humanity but aims as well, as Bernard says, to discover God himself in the man Christ. You must grasp neither the man nor God alone, but Christ as both God and man, and must love and adore him as both God and man. Exercise in the life and passion of Christ the Lord bears much fruit, if, so often as you read or think about something Christ did or suffered, you can shape it into a concept that lucidly represents both the God and the man. One person should signify both at once. Thus, when you read or think about him rising from the dead or performing miracles you should never doubt that Christ the man did so; when you read that Christ suffered the piercing of his hands or the binding of his feet, you must believe without doubt that God suffered this—all because of the unity of his person in which divinity and humanity subsist together without any mixture of their natures.

Every true Christian believes this, but the more lucidly a devout man can conceive of it, so much richer his affection for the life, passion, and miracles of Christ. If you think on Christ the man, it will instill sweet affection and great trust because he is the mildest, kindest, noblest, sweetest, most decorous and gracious man; thence you will conceive the more easily confidence to approach and adore him. For knowledge of his humanity is easier, as something imprinted on the mind, than that of God, which is far from our minds. But if you think on Christ as God, all his words, deeds, miracles, and acts will seem all the more awesome, terrible, and marvelous. And thus if you understand and conceive both in Christ, great devotion, love, and trust will be born in you together with fear and reverence.

The third step is to rise through the humanity of Christ to a spiritual affection, and to gaze with mental eyes upon God himself through a mirror darkly, and thus to come through the humanity to a knowledge and love of the divinity. Here especially, through adherence to God, the third impurity of the mind is cast off. Through such gazing, clinging, and transforming of the mind, a man begins to become in a certain sense one spirit with God, to go beyond himself, to gaze upon the very truth, and thus to grow accustomed to union and adherence. . . . This, as Augustine described it in his *Confessions*, is the last ascent in this pilgrim state prior to our ascent into the essential vision of God. But let the animal in us beware lest it touch this mountain, let the impure still not approach, for the beast that touches this mountain will be stoned. So that you may have a means of exercising this ascent, we will note down another way of meditating on the life and passion of Christ Jesus.

28. *The Figures, Prophecies, and Scriptural Passages Dealing with Christ's Incarnation*

The whole of Holy Scripture and everything in it revolves around the work of our redemption. The Old Testament heralded the New, and the New showed it fulfilled. Think then how many figures, deeds, prophecies, and apparitions by way of kings, prophets, and priests preceded that work. Grasp its magnitude, which demands thanksgiving. Think of your own ingratitude and lack of affection in comparison with the longing of the ancients. Consider their desire, and marvel at the lukewarmness of yourself and many others.

29. *Our Lord's Annunciation*

When the fullness of time brought about the fulfillment of those figures and it pleased Christ to fulfill the longing of the ancients, the angel Gabriel was sent to announce the Lord's incarnation to the Virgin. The desires and prophecies of the fathers was about to be fulfilled. Note the angel's reverence toward Mary, and marvel at God's humility. Reflect on the exaltation of the Virgin, but note too her humility, chastity, and other virtues. See now her happiness, exaltation, and pleasing devotion. Nor should you forget Elizabeth's ministry.

30. *A Brief Review of the Life of Christ Down to the Last Supper*
Thus the Son of God, of whose greatness there is no end, became a tiny infant. Think how God the infant journeyed into this
world and cried out in his manger. See the poverty there, the humility. Marvel at the gathering of angels, and gaze at the worship of
the shepherds. Hear the conversation between the angels and the
shepherds. See an amazed Joseph, a jubilant Mary. Note the face
and most beautiful disposition of the boy—but also the inner greatness of that little one. Marvel at the wisdom of it all, and reverently
kiss the boy's manger.
    On the eighth day he was circumcised and called Jesus. Though
without sin he took upon his own body the cure for sin. Have compassion upon such a tender infant wounded and pouring out his
blood for you. Consider how he cried out loud while inwardly taking
compassion on man. Think of the sweet name of Jesus. Take upon
yourself the example of circumcision.
    A bright star then appeared and led the Magi to Christ. Think
of their devotion. Follow them, and with them offer whatever you
have to Christ, that is, your soul. Consider the meanness and poverty
those Magi found, nor did Christ change anything because of their
arrival. Note here the threefold testimony to Christ's birth: the star,
the Magi, and the Jews', lest you waver in your own faith. Mary then
offered up Christ, and by that offering redeemed this poor little one
as her firstborn. Think of the procession of Mary, Ann, Simeon, and
Joseph. Devoutly look on and sweetly take in their conversation and
devotion. Note the humility of Christ and mother Mary. Still a
child, Christ had to flee from Herod. See his patience and learn to
suffer yourself. Follow the pilgrims, hear their conversation, and
from it all learn poverty and humility.
    From his twelfth to his thirtieth year that king of glory remained
hidden among the people. He did not teach, he did no miracles, and
yet so long as he kept quiet he taught and performed more than ever
just by keeping silent and doing nothing—he taught you not to rise
quickly to teach until you have first remained seated for a time and
humbled yourself.
    In his thirtieth year he was baptized by John. Think of John's
reverence, how he trembled at Christ's touch. Think of Christ's humility in subjecting himself to John, and of how he fulfilled all righteousness in perfect humility. Note too how all three persons of the
Trinity showed themselves, how the Father sent Christ out to
preach, saying, "Listen to him," and so on.
    Then he fasted in the desert for forty days and forty nights, and

was afterward tempted by the devil. Think of Christ's conduct in the desert, what he did there, his devout prayer and contemplation. Note his humility there, for he was with beasts according to Mark. Think on Christ's amazing patience, how he was tempted repeatedly by devils and bore it all. Think how wisely he resisted Satan, and take it as a model of resistance for yourself. Marvel at his dignity as the angels ministered to him.

Then he chose some low-class fishermen to take up the sword of preaching with him, and he began to do battle with the whole world. Note his life in common with the apostles, and his sweet conversation with them. Reflect upon their secret dialogue together at home and along the way. Think about how he was among them, as one who ministered to them, who ate with them at a common table and common plate, not as one having a special privilege, and so on.

And then he was seen throughout the land conversing with men, that is, walking among men and everywhere sowing the word of God. He performed many miracles that could not have been done except by God: He restored sight to the blind and hearing to the dumb, he put devils to flight, he cleansed lepers, in short he healed all and did so many miracles that they can hardly be written up. He forgave the sins of those pleading with him. He preached everywhere. He told mystical parables, in one of which he called himself the pastor sent to recover the lost sheep. Note carefully here how often great multitudes followed Christ, even four and five thousand people out into the wilderness. You follow too, and become part of his circle so that you can hear his words, gaze upon the face of Christ and the apostles, and see the discourses and miracles.

Wanting to offer up the sacrifice for which he had come and thus to show himself the paschal lamb, on the fifth day before the passover, astride the donkey fetched by the disciples, the Lord of heaven and earth ascended and entered his own Jerusalem, with great triumph and Hebrew children shouting out his praises, "Hosanna in the highest." Note the humility of the seated King Christ, how he sits, how he was dressed up, what kind of royal entourage accompanied him. As he approaches and sees Jerusalem, see how he weeps over it, but especially over any sinful soul.

31. *The Last Supper*

When the time of his suffering drew near, he who had always loved his own loved them to the end. About to pass from this world, he held a great and wondrous supper full of mystery and somber with sacraments, to which he invited the apostles. I desire, he said, to eat this passover with you. He did many wonders during this supper, indeed he instituted a certain memorial to and summary of all his wonders, providing those who fear him with food in memory of those miracles. This, he said, you must do in memory of me. . . . When therefore we receive this from the priests we are reminded that it is the body and blood of Christ so that we do not become ungrateful for so many benefits.

In this supper there are many things to be considered with devotion and reverence and to be worshiped in all piety. Meditate upon the way in which at this supper the great and praiseworthy Lord himself washed the feet of his disciples and his traitor, bowing to the ground and taking up a towel, so as to instruct us by example in humility. Think of the way in which he conducted himself inwardly and outwardly at this washing, for outwardly he washed most humbly and lovingly while inwardly he completed his work in the highest humility and devotion. Look upon the pious master and lord sitting at one table and eating out of one dish with the disciples. Think how abundantly Christ nourished the hearts of his disciples with this meal, pouring out his teachings. Finally he addressed them in words individually aflame, alight as it were with the torch of love, which John the evangelist saw more sharply than the others and, flying higher, he alone described more fully. Think how he ate the lamb as a figure, thereby prefiguring how you ought to eat the true lamb and eucharistic sacrament.

Above all you ought always to see with mental eyes and to desire most devoutly and take to your own heart that most excellent of all the sacraments which he instituted there. Wonder at the munificence of Christ and the profound dignity of this sacrament. When you recall this most worthy sacrament, all that Christ did for you in the flesh ought also to come before your mind. . . . Indeed because a long way and a steep ascent still lies before anyone making such a difficult and arduous climb, this food is of the greatest necessity along the way that you walk—whence its name, as it is called the "viaticum." . . .

That you might partake worthily, you ought to exercise yourself in three things necessary to worthy eating: corporeal cleanliness, purity of conscience, and sincere devotion. Corporeal cleanliness is sometimes preferable and sometimes necessary, since corporeal uncleanness has various causes and origins. But purity of conscience is particularly necessary for you, and therefore prior to partaking of communion you ought especially to examine yourself in the first and second ways given above, thereby bringing yourself to contrition and compunction so that you may grieve for sins committed in heart, word, or deed and for sins of omission. Then go to confession and confess your sins, especially the more serious ones, though you may also confess the well-known, commonplace, and forgotten ones.

Third, you ought to exercise yourself toward sincere devotion, which with reference to this sacrament consists in two things, that you have both fear and reverence for it, and that you be moved by a genuine love and desire for union with Christ. Fear induces reverence, provoking within an attitude of profound respect and awe. That you may understand the reverent dignity of this sacrament and not approach it thoughtlessly and without fear, diligently note whom it is you are about to take and of whom you are about to partake. For you are partaking of him whom John the Baptist feared to touch; him whom the prince of the apostles drove away in fear of approaching him with the words, "Go away from me, Lord, for I am a sinful man"; him whom the dominations adore and the powers fear; him whom you take will be your judge and you will stand before his tribunal to be judged. He is the one into whose hands your soul will go at its departure to receive what it deserves. See therefore how reverently you should approach. Observe that nothing so offends God as presumption and brash irreverence.

Think next who you are, a negligent and lukewarm man, full of vices. Recall what you know of yourself from the three previous examinations. Consider then that even if you prepared yourself for a thousand years, it would never suffice for a worthy partaking of this sacrament, even if you enjoyed the merits of all the saints and flourished in the purity of all the angels and men. How, then, dare you approach without fear and reverence, you who in so little time can hardly set your heart in order? Fear then lest it be said: "Behold the hand of him who will betray me is at the table"; or as Bernard puts it, lest you betray the Christ you have taken to the vices of pride, envy, and so on. Fear to partake unworthily, lest you eat and drink judgment to yourself.

But fear should not be so great as wholly to exclude desire and to raise up devotion. For that bread, as Augustine puts it, wants a man inwardly hungering. So you must have desire and love. You can inflame your desire for this sacrament in many ways. Sometimes love for union with Christ should enkindle you to have Christ come to you more often, thus to embrace him in the affection of your mind and desire of your heart. Sometimes a desire for internal healing should draw your affection: When you see yourself so full of desire and passion and so deficient and imperfect, introduce the Lord Jesus as a most pious physician, for his very name *Jesus* means savior. Sometimes consciousness of your faults should spark desire: When you feel yourself to have offended God in serious sin and you read that Christ instituted this sacrament for forgiveness of sin, it is no wonder you should become inflamed to receive it. Likewise, love and compassion for your neighbor might draw your affection, so that you might succor the living and the dead through his sacrifice.

To inflame and exercise your desire still more, carefully unfold before you how Christ bore the grief and infirmities of all those desiring, adoring, and believing in him. Thus, for instance, the woman approaching him from behind and humbly but confidently touching his hem was healed; the sinful woman kissing his feet was cleansed; the Canaanite woman who persistently followed him was healed; lepers coming up to him were cured; demoniacs, paralytics, and all other monsters of nature approaching in belief found healing. For power went out from him and healed all. The publicans and sinners who approached him gained forgiveness, and he did not refuse to eat with them.

When therefore you have done what is in you, approach him with reverence and fear as well as with desire and love, hoping upon the infinite piety of God. When you set yourself to receive this sacrament, you ought diligently to exercise yourself in recalling the passion of Christ. Among the devout, the mind and the exercises fluctuate between these two, between fear and love. Some yearn for and come frequently to this sacrament with ardent desire, while others tremble in fear and reverence. Considering the sacrament's dignity and their own vileness as well as the danger of eating unworthily, they pull back in fear and wish to distance themselves from communicating. Both affections are in fact recommended, and it is praiseworthy sometimes to approach with desire and other times to withdraw in fear, according to the time and place. According to Augustine, it should be left to each person's conscience to do what seems best. One thing however is certain for all: We should not exclude desire and hope out of fear, nor in turn should we abandon reverence and fear out of hope and desire, but we should alternate moderately between both, one time having more of the one and another time of the other.

32. *The Lord's Passion, and Three Ways in Which a Man Should Exercise Himself in It*

"I will go to the mountain of myrrh" (Sg 4:6). If, O man of devotion, you wish to attempt this mountain, that is, this bitter penance by way of mortifying the flesh, and thus to ascend through fear and hope up the mount of purity, there is nothing more useful than to gather the first myrrh from the death of your Savior. For when you see your Lord ascend the mountain of myrrh, the mount of Calvary, to bear the greatest of all punishment for your sins, the bitter myrrh of fear will preserve you from the rot of depraved love. Consequently, hope and devotion and the most precious scent of fear, love, gratitude, and compassion will emanate from you. That the labor may not terrify you or the bitterness repel, that the hope may draw and devotion entice, and that gratitude, love, and compunction may compel you to ascend the mount of purity, go first to look carefully at Christ, who may quite aptly himself be called the mount of myrrh for his most bitter passion.

You must first go to him yourself, animatedly gathering and devoutly impressing his passion on your heart as the first myrrh. This will happen when you devoutly, thoughtfully, and sadly reflect on Christ's passion, scrupulously imagining it literally or according to the first meaning of the words. Second, you must go to Christ's passion as a kind of myrrh and draw from it something useful to yourself, either medicine against your festering passions or an example of virtue. Third, you must go to it and from that first myrrh anoint your mind with devotion, inflame it with love, and make yourself ready to bear all tribulation.

That you may devoutly read Christ's passion literally and focus upon it thoughtfully, you must know that such meditation on the passion according to the letter alone, the simple deeds and acts and punishments, quite especially induces compassion for and devotion to Christ. To elicit compassion and devotion still more, try hard to conceive of Christ as one person, not doubting that he was and is both God and man. When therefore you read that Christ bore a certain punishment and responded to this a certain way or held his peace, think of it always and so conceive of it that the name *Jesus* conveys to you the God and the man; then you may look upon him more devotedly and with greater reverence, and have all the greater compassion upon him. For if you show human compassion toward a brute animal severely afflicted, how much more Christ himself, if you conceive of him and represent him to your mental eyes not only as a most pious, sweet, mild, noble, loving, and gracious man but also as omnipotent God, to be reverenced, feared, and adored as your creator and judge.

Second, to have greater compassion upon Christ and to have his punishments cut through the very marrow of your soul with the

sword of grief, you must not only look upon him suffering some punishment but more especially must discern his inner self filled with
grief and satiated with the awful bitterness of the whole world.
When you read that Christ suffered some punishment or mockery,
do not think of it as just any man bearing it but as something un-
speakably beyond every other man. And you ought diligently to
gather its causes into your heart, for they are great stimulants to compassion. Knowing how much someone can be tortured and afflicted
by a certain punishment, you must consider how much more he felt
it as something unfitting. Moreover, the more lively the sensibility
of a man, the more he will suffer from a punishment and in turn be
tortured by his sensitivity. But Christ's was the most lively and
nobly dignified of all natures, and therefore suffered those punishments more than any other. See if there is any sorrow like unto his
sorrow. Think therefore how intolerable for you or some other
tender person would be some punishment such as having the head
punctured with spines, the whole body brutally whipped, and so on,
and how much more awful that punishment was for Jesus Christ,
man and god, with his noble and delicate nature.

Second, Christ suffered as much as he willed. For according to
the evangelist Jesus undid himself, not the passion. He was likewise
offered up because he so willed. He undertook his passion for the
satisfaction of original sin, which had despoiled the whole human
race of its original righteousness, infecting human nature and spoil-
ing its eternal bliss. He also took on the passion and death so that he
would be the sufficient sacrifice for all men, and because the works
of God are perfect it seems that Christ assumed the most bitter of all
deaths. . . . Indeed the doctors say that his death was the most bitter
and aggravated, exceeding the grief of all men ever to have suffered
death since the beginning of the world.

Third, it increased Christ's grief no little that he suffered this
passion at the hands of people upon whom he had conferred so many
benefits, to whom he could rightly say: "You are my people because
I am your God; what could I have done for you that I have not
done?" But how could you have repaid me worse than to have in-
flicted such a death? . . . The passion of Christ was also in every
member, in every sense—the hands perforated, the head spiked with
thorns, the whole body whipped, and so on. Go through and study
each. There was in his passion as well the most shameful derision,
confusion, scandal, spitting, and covering of his head such as you
never read elsewhere, and this primarily out of the Pharisees' envy.

To sense still better the bitterness of Christ's passion, take this for your rule: Whenever the evangelist ascribes some punishment to Christ in plain language, you add in your heart the word "very" or "severely." For instance, "The servant of the high priest struck him," and you think "very hard," as no doubt he did, though you cannot know exactly how hard or how much pain it caused.

Now bring together in your heart carefully all the causes for that affliction and inner grief of Christ which probably far exceeded any external pain. This internal affliction arose first of all from his fervent zeal to save the human race. Moreover, though more than sufficient for all, he saw his passion as largely unfruitful and useless owing to the evil of so many. He also had great compassion on his blessed mother, who was filled with all bitterness. Christ's inner pain was also heightened by his misery for the Jews as well as by his grief for the disciples and especially for the sins of Judas, and not least by our blindness and ingratitude, as when he wept over Jerusalem. Now look upon Christ in his passion with pious eyes. Read his passion and see him afflicted not only outwardly but full of affliction and most bitter sorrow inwardly and outwardly. It would be wondrous indeed if you could look on the God-man so afflicted and overwhelmed with tribulation, and not be moved yourself with an affectionate compassion.

The second point is to apply Christ's passion usefully and fruitfully to yourself, in imitation of his virtues and in flight from the vices. To this end you must direct your whole intellect and affections toward sensing how Christ conducted himself inwardly and outwardly in all his deeds, words, and responses as recorded in the text of the Gospel, that is, how he acted inwardly and outwardly in different places and times, as well as the Jews, Pilate and Herod, his mother Mary and Mary Magdalene, and so on. This way you will find in his passion a plenitude of every virtue and the best medicine against every vice. For instance, when you read that "Jesus stood before Pontius Pilate," think first how he stood, how he conducted himself outwardly, with what inclination of the head, casting down of the eyes, and other signs of humility. Think too of his response, his way of expressing himself, how humbly, how gently and piously. Think of how he conducted himself inwardly in all things, and you will find him without rancor, envy, or impatience, truly humble and gentle of heart. . . .

The third point is to fuel your mind from the bitter passion of the Lord's passion with a rich devotion and so enkindle your affections to love. Think that you, dear man, were the cause of so much grief, so much bitterness. Seize then upon this benefit: Think of

Christ as dying for you alone. Thence will arise gratitude, for he suffered to effect your illumination, redemption, justification, and glorification. For your illumination, that you might follow his example and illumine your intellect with knowledge of the truth. Thus whatever you read that Christ did, apply to yourself as if he did it for you alone. Think always that it was as if Christ had said to you, "I did this that you might follow me." For your redemption, because you were forever damned by original sin. Think how grave your sin was to require the pouring out of such a medicine, the paying of such a price; then a fear or horror of sinning will arise in you—and so with all the others. For your justification: Gratitude should arise because he wanted to suffer only so that you might be worthy of receiving God's justification. For your glorification: Great love should spring up from the fact that he, who had no need of you or your good works, wanted to suffer so much for your glory.

Because, dear man, you are not able to gather or hold in your heart all at once this mountain of myrrh, this magnitude of bitterness, you must gather it progressively through this exercise and put it in place gradually. Therefore I have added a section which apportions the passion of Christ into brief sections and particulars, for an easier administration of your exercises and greater profit in your meditations.

[Chapters 33–37 break down meditation on the passion into shorter articles according to traditional schemes, and Chapter 38 links the passion to the opening of the seven seals and the revelation of God in the seven gifts of the Holy Spirit.]

39. *The Lord's Resurrection*

On the third day Christ rose a victor over death and showed that we too would rise. If you suffered with Christ's passion, rejoice now with the resurrection. Think devoutly on how Christ's soul descended to hell, what he did there, the joy of the holy fathers, the sadness of the demons, and the fear of the guards. Think of the angels' watch over the grave, of whom we are told that one sat alone, then stood, then sat upon a stone, then was in the tomb, and then of two in various positions—all of which shows a multitude of angels around the tomb and several visits of the women. Think what love and desire compelled Mary Magdalene and the other women to run frequently to visit the Lord's tomb.

Think of Christ's various appearances, his sweet conversations with his disciples. Think why Christ wanted to appear in Galilee, namely to show that you too should move beyond your vices, whence "pasch" [= Easter] means a transition. In Galilee we see the passing over and changing of our bodies, like Christ's, after the general resurrection.

40. *Christ's Glorious Ascension*

Forty days after the resurrection Christ ascended on high, taking captive the captivity of the holy fathers. Meditate on their glorious ascension, rising on high in procession with Christ, for the saints followed, the angels came to meet them, and then they put questions among themselves, as in Isaiah, "Who is this who ascends," and so on.

Think of the apostles' sadness and joy, of the angels returning to console them. Learn that you too will ascend to Christ, through the ascensions here set forth, as you leave vice behind, for no vice ascends with the Savior, as Augustine said.

41. *The Sending of the Holy Spirit*

Then the Lord sent the Holy Spirit from heaven in tongues of fire. See how the apostles were comforted then and troubled in love. Meditate on why the Holy Spirit appeared in fire, why in tongues, why in both at once, and why in other creatures. Seek to acquire the properties of each within yourself. Think of the effects and gifts of the Spirit, and many other such things concerning his mission.

42. *None of the Preceeding Three Steps Can Be Completed Perfectly in This Life*

By these three steps we ascend to purity of heart and love. In the first, through fervent love, we seek God but do not find. In the second, we are going about the squares of the heavenly Jerusalem and offering sacrifice in his tabernacle with a loud cry of desire, and the watchmen who guard this city, the holy angels whom we contemplate in hope and desire, discover us. But we are not to rest there, but to ascend higher. Gradually, he says, as I pass them by, that is, climb the third step, I discover what my soul loves. Thus in the first desire for the world is abandoned, in the second the mind is raised on high, and in the third it rests quietly in God.

But you should not think that we are able to climb any of these steps completely or perfectly in this life. Nor are we able in this life to purge all evil desire, since even Paul himself could not reach perfection, which according to Augustine is to know no evil desire. For as long as we live, we will never be able to raise all our affections on high; something will ever remain on the earth. The corrupting body weighs down the soul, and dwelling on earth oppresses the senses of those thinking. We are still less able to become so pure and apt as to cling continuously to God. For as long as we are in the body we are alienated from God. But these are the steps and the progress over which our frail selves should order its ascent and, so far as possible, progressively make its climb.

43. *The Three Steps Which Sustain and Advance Spiritual Ascent: Reading, Meditation, and Prayer*

Human frailty cannot be constant in its pursuit of purity of heart, nor in its various ascents, spiritual affections, and exercises, and therefore it is hard for someone ascending never to descend unless he has a place where, fatigued, he can rest, and, hungry, he has food to sustain him. Therefore, just as above we offered a threefold discussion to inculcate fuller knowledge of the three descents, so here, with the ladder of ascent now erected, we offer three forms of nourishment so the fatigued soul may find rest and be refreshed along the way when it begins to fail. These three are reading, meditation, and prayer. Every spiritual exercise begins and ends in these three. These are, as it were, the food along the way. Just as God gave bread, wine, and the like to sustain the body, so he conferred these three to sustain the soul in its pilgrimage, as Augustine says.

Reading pertains more to the first step of the ascent which ends in fear. For, according to Hugh, reading pertains to beginners who always conceive first in fear but give birth to a spirit of salvation. Meditation looks more to the second step, the more advanced who have been instructed through the readings and know how to make their way about in their hearts. Prayer, though appropriate to every ascent, suits especially those on the third step of the ascent who have begun to cling to God. For prayer is man's inclination to or desire for God, a certain familiar and pious conversing. But let us see how these three, rightly directed, may advance, help, and sustain us in these ascents.

44. *How Sacred Reading Aids and Sustains Those Ascending, and How It Is Ordered toward Spiritual Progress*

Struck by fear and depressed with remorse, therefore, yet also inflamed with affection and desire for the ascent, take up some reading apt to spiritual progress, one that admonishes toward constant ascent and exhorts to progress. What you choose to read should speed your ascent toward purity and charity, show you the way through holy exercises and works, warm your affections for the ascent, instill fear, or raise hope. Therefore, as someone said, reading should be a form of admonishment for a Christian philosopher and not just busywork. This will easily happen if, following the teaching of Augustine, you begin your reading in the fear of the Lord, and it regulates your intention and affections so you seek nothing but spiritual advance toward purity of heart. Like that holy Anthony of whom Gregory speaks in the fourth book of the *Dialogues*, you should not seek knowledge of words but the tears of compunction, for thereby your mind will be aroused to ardor, turning away from things below to seek things in heaven.

If that reading is to be fruitful to your spiritual ascent, you must consider what you read, when, how, and to what purpose. What: for not all things, however useful, are equally profitable for the ascent. You ought therefore to concentrate upon reading what will inflame your affections toward spiritual progress and ascent rather than obscure or enticing matters that illuminate the intellect or sharpen curiosity, as in disputations. Reading more difficult writings does nothing to refresh the more tender souls and may even crush their good intentions. Read those writings especially that will instruct you in morals, that is, in the nature and uprooting of the vices and in the exercising and spiritual advance of the virtues, together with those that increase your devotion and inflame your affections toward Christ and celestial matters. Even if for some reason you occasionally read something else, return at once to devotional material. For the more continuously you study Scripture, the more you will shape your affections and your sense of things accordingly, and thus your meditations as well.

Note, second, when you read. Reading, to be fruitful, should not be done on the spur of the moment and by chance but at a fixed time. A man must attentively refresh his soul through sacred readings, thus to provide his memory with material for his exercises when nothing better occurs to him. Therefore reading should not become an occupation unto itself but should rather direct us toward devout meditation and spiritual prayer, and these in turn by their sweetness should further guide our work and keep us in pleasure during work.

Note, third, how you read. There are those who skim through a whole book before they begin it; others study one folio at the beginning, then abruptly another in the middle or at the end, and proceed in this casual fashion. For a fastidious stomach, as someone said, there is much to taste which in its great variety pollutes rather than nourishes. Choose for yourself a whole book that will suit your purposes, inform your morals, and increase your devotion, and study it from beginning to end in the fear of God with suitable devotion and reverence.

Note, fourth, to what end you read. Certainly your principle intention, as in all your exercises, ought to be purity of heart, not vanity or the pursuit of knowledge alone. The point is not so much that you learn something but rather that it profit you and others through you. That you might refer your reading directly to purity, always extract something from it appropriate to your purpose which may fill your memory and spur your progress, like a clean animal chewing its cud.

To draw further fruit from your reading, vary things, now reading, now praying, now doing your exercises, so as to avoid tedium and keep your stability. In all your regular exercises, find some special delight, for delight keeps a worker at his work. Always fear tedium of the mind. This alone should be your end: to persevere with delight in your works and exercises. So that you may order your reading immediately toward purity, frequently interrupt your reading with prayer; form an affection shaped by reading and thus rise to prayer.

45. *Meditation*

Meditation is the means by which you studiously turn over in your heart what you have read or heard and thereby stir up your affections or illuminate your intellect. Therefore as you ascend and advance in hope, frequently reflect in your heart upon those things which aid your progress in purity, instill fear, or increase love.

That your meditations might prove fruitful to you and you may easily grow accustomed to good meditation, two things must be carefully considered.

First, provide your soul with useful material which will serve to advance and fruitfully occupy your intention. As the saints say, your soul is like a mill that grinds whatever is put into it; but if nothing is put in, it grinds away at vain and idle things. If you do not determine upon something fixed, lest nothing better should occur to you, whatever comes along will necessarily gain entry. For your heart will easily cling to whatever is happening if it is not intently fixed upon something. But even if you should have something to fall back on, it can happen often enough that you propose to meditate devoutly on a particular matter and before it takes full shape, your proposal slips away, your will slackens, and idleness once again overtakes your heart. You have already heard what materials are useful to meditation and will profit your ascent: recollection of your sins, of your death, the last judgment, the pains of hell, heavenly glory, the benefits of God, the passion of our Lord, and so on. These meditations can be varied in time, taking up what is most appropriate and will most serve your devotion at a given time. Thus, when the church recalls or performs the Lord's passion, you conform yourself and form meditations around the bitter passion of our Lord. Do the same for all the other major feasts of the Church, shaping your exercises around the matter of that feast, as Bernard recommends.

Second, so far as his fragile nature will bear it, a man should strive at all times and in every hour to fill his soul with holy meditations together with spiritual and devout affections. But, as Jerome recommends, a man must set aside certain hours specially to exercise his soul, focusing his spirit and enkindling his spiritual desire. Jerome believes the hour of matins [early morning] especially good for this, for then a man is more sober and better disposed toward spiritual exercise, not yet caught up in the worldly tumults of the day. In this hour therefore a man should strive especially to exercise himself in some devotion, because frequently a man will then persist through the whole day in the desire aroused that morning. For then particularly a man should make every effort to seek some devotion from the Lord or through devout exercises to induce his heart toward meditation by exercising and preparing himself for the readings and chant at matins. He should do something similar at vespers before retiring for sleep. Then, in fear of nightmares, when sleep has overtaken other men, he should carefully listen for some divine whisper, praying to the Lord after his daily self-examination—which should also take place then—that he forgive what he did wrong, even while giving thanks for what he had accomplished that was praiseworthy. Then he should arm himself fiercely against nocturnal fears with pure affections and devout prayers. If you read Holy Scripture at that time, your reading should focus particularly on devotional material, not, for instance, the Old Testament histories—as Saint Benedict also recommends. What was said about performing meditations at certain times applies to all exercises, so you may know when to take them up and when to turn to other things, thus having a time for praying and a time for reading, and all of it in good order.

46. *On Prayer and the Manner of Praying*

Be in prayer wherever you go and wherever you are, in the house or in the field. Always have recourse to prayer and find refuge in it. With prayer you must take note of four things: First, the affect of prayer, that is, what manner of prayer you take up; second, what kind of prayer, short or long; third, for whom you pray; and fourth, your attitude and mental concentration in prayer.

First, the vigor and virtue of prayer proceeds from the intent of the person praying: God hears the desire of the heart more than the noise of the voice. Therefore, always assume an intention and desire like that of the exercises and meditations with which you are occupied, so that your prayer may proceed from the roots of your heart, and not just from the lips of your mouth, always from a feeling of fear or sadness or love or wonder or gratitude. For instance, if in your first examination you discover your sins multiplied beyond the sands of the sea, assume an attitude of humility or grief and take on the person of the servant who offended his Lord. In such a frame of mind, shape a prayer, saying: According to the multitude of your mercies wipe away my iniquity. If in the second and third examination you find your heart full of evil lust and vicious desire, assume again an attitude of humility and take on the person of a sick man calling upon a doctor and saying: Heal my soul, O Lord, because I have sinned against you. Or again, there is no health in my flesh in the face of your anger, nor is there peace in my bones, because my iniquities have multiplied over my head, and so on. If in the second ascent you exercise yourself in fear through meditation on death, the judgment, or hell, assume the attitude of fear and take on the person of someone standing before a judge with fear and trembling as one convicted, against whom by law a sentence must be handed down, and say: Do not condemn in your anger, Lord, and so on. But if you exercise yourself in hope through recollection of the kingdom of heaven, assume an attitude of love and pray with a fervent heart, saying: One thing I ask of you, O Lord, this I require, that I may dwell in the house of the Lord. Or: As a hart pants for the water streams, so my heart desires you, Lord. Do the same with all the other affections which you may form, just as your exercises and meditations require.

Second, form some long prayers and some short ones. By longer ones we mean the canonical hours or anything similar to which you are obligated or which you voluntarily assume. Before these prayers you must always do what the Prophet admonished, saying "I have focused my spirit," and so on, until your spirit is warmed with devout meditation and conceives an affection and desire of fear or sadness or love or whatever. This applies especially to matins and vespers when you take up meditations on the last judgment, your sins, the hour of your death, the pains of hell, the benefits of God, the passion of Christ, or whatever else is suitable. The others are short prayers which in his *Letter to Proba* Augustine called exclamatory. Just like the holy Fathers before us, we must always have these ready to exclaim when our desires and affections have been ignited from the reading, so we say: "May declaration of your words give understanding," and so on. Similarly prayer may interrupt meditation or work. But here no great preparation of mind is needed; it suffices to raise the mind a little toward God from the devout meditation then in progress.

Third, while bodily necessities are also to be sought from God, we must pray more and more often for divine grace, remission of sins, entrance to the kingdom of heaven, the uprooting of the vices, and the acquisition of the virtues. But especially and most often we must pray with ardent desire for the destruction of that vice against which we are principally at war. Nor should you pray only for yourself. Like the whole Church, you should pray for the departed in purgatory and for all your friends who are tempted, troubled, sick, or on pilgrimage.

Fourth, in the short prayers that you utter most frequently, it is good to conduct yourself with an affection conceived or a meditation formed as if you were conversing with God in your very presence. Seek some grace from him or deliverance from temptation, seizing upon words composed and shaped on the spot, suited to your affection or that will serve that affection. This mode is more difficult in longer prayers and a serious burden on the head to sustain. You must therefore attend devoutly to what you are reading and from it form a sensible affection suitable to prayer, guarding your heart from wandering. Furthermore, when your conscience troubles you and you fear to praise Christ in trust, turn like Job to one of the saints, pleading with him to pray for you—a type of prayer called postulatory. Cry out: "Mary, pray for me," and so on. Have fixed times for both the short and the long prayers. Make short prayers especially when temptation grips you, lest it overwhelm you and also when you leave the house, that the Lord watch over your coming and going, just as the holy Fathers did according to Jerome, and again whenever you become conscious of a sin through admonition or self-examination.

47. *The Third Ascent*

In the third ascent we do war against the vices, ascending from virtue to virtue, and reforming again the powers of the soul. The Prophet well described the heart of man as "high," a summit or high peak reached only after many ascents. Indeed its upper part, if well ordered, reaches directly up to God and is subject only to him, so that if you stand in the upper part of your soul you can see so high as to discern God himself, though not yet in his essence owing to your unsuitability and the impurity and weakness still of your eyes. Therefore the human mind is a high mountain to whose ascent we have ordered the heart. But would that the labor lay only in the ascent to the heights and the multitude of ascending steps. Oh, that the way were otherwise safe from enemies and straight and level for walking.

Two things particularly impede and obstruct this ascent: the many enemies that ambush it and the ignorance of the wayfarers. The way that leads to life is narrow, surrounded by enemies on the right and the left who shoot flaming arrows against the climbers and gravely wound them. Lying in wait, those enemies bend their bows and take aim at those advancing toward pure and spotless hearts. They throw out chains, that is, affection for the lower things, to catch the feet and thus drag them down or cast them over the edge of the royal way; thus you may see a thousand falling to the left of this way, and ten thousand to its right. Those enemies talk at the same time to hide their traps and so conceal them that they say, "Who will see them?" The way itself has many digressions. All round the way to the right and left are numerous paths that seem good but in the end lead to hell. The enemies seek to deceive still more by enticing the wayfarers and then overwhelming them with powerful temptations. They frequently clothe their vices in the splendor and beauty of the virtues and join themselves to the climbers as if they came from elsewhere and not from the enemy party, just as the Gibeonites deceived the people of God.

48. *How the Vices Take Over the Powers of the Soul and Impede Spiritual Ascent*

As explained earlier, the faculties and powers of the soul with which God endowed man are concupiscent, irascible, and affectionate so that he may quietly ascend beyond himself or descend below without labor or fear of enemies. In the fall of the first man, however, those powers were rendered destitute by their opposites, the enemies who have pitched camp against them. Pride is the queen of the vices and the firstborn of Satan; she now lives supreme among these powers, and has dispatched seven dukes, that is, the seven chief vices, to guard the way by which the other affections, powers, and appetites are to make their ascent and to catch the feet of the climbers.

Because the ascent leads through their camp, you must take up battle against each of them in turn, to fight continuously against the evil desires rising up in us from the first descent. Thus the third ascent, where we now find ourselves, is in a sense directed against the first descent in Adam. But this ascent is not steeper than the others, but similar, or rather one and the same ascent exercised in various respects and modes. It promotes, aids, rectifies, and prepares the previous ascents; without it no one could even begin to climb.

49. *On Those Who Abandon the Uprooting of the Vices and Turn to Other Spiritual Activities, and on the Origin of Affection*
There are some who err and do not find the direct route to the heavenly dwelling. Once they have removed their reigning vices, they begin to ascend with great devotions, steep and arduous spiritual exercises. Then in the hour when they least expect to be caught in the enemy's plots, they learn too late that it is not safe to commune with the serpents of evil desire and the habituated motions of the vices. . . .

This is the safest way, here the most secure devotion, the sweetest and purest affection: With all disordered affections driven from the soul, we take delight in the inner working of the virtues, for this is truly to take delight in the Lord, that is, in charity, chastity, and humility; indeed all other devotions can be deceptive. So that there may be some discernment here, it should be understood that this devotion is a certain sweet affection or affectionate inclination toward the good, a certain sweet arousal drawing the affections. Such delight or affection can be twofold or have a twofold origin. Sometimes it comes and goes quickly, though perhaps striking home penetratingly, and this seems to arise from some appetitive or loving desire. For instance, when a man is confronted with something delightful, whether from without through hearing or from within through suggestion, the affection of love is immediately drawn toward it, followed by the motion to pursue it called "desire," or flight from it called "hatred." In this way beginners often have a devotion toward the good or away from the evil, a sweet inclination frequently infused from above as a gift of God. Indeed in this way the most secular of men sometimes, though lost in mortal sin, have such affections, especially tender or weak men and women easily moved and agitated in their appetites. When they hear of the kingdom of heaven, such people are frequently moved with desire, wishing to dissolve and be with Christ. But then vainglory forcefully imposes a strong desire, always sweet and almost like honey but laced with poison. Thus, for instance, men are rendered vain by hearing something read out about some mighty warrior, to which their love is inclined by forceful reading. When afterward they hear that he has been captured or killed, they are moved with mercy and sometimes weep most ridiculously. Many conceive some momentary and sudden affection for the good, and then just as quickly another affection for the world or the flesh in gluttony or lust. Thus many are deceived, extolling variously such affections as some great devotion. In fact if such an affection were conceived for the glorious flesh of Christ, it could never be judged worthy of charity or true devotion in itself. It is only useful and to be taken up insofar as we thereby uproot and extinguish inordinate affections and passions.

Yet such an affection is not to be repudiated but rather brought under rein and applied as an aid to charity and against vicious affections, though it does not itself contain the merit of charity and true devotion. . . . Many are deceived in this, seeking merit and perfection in this delight or affectionate inclination. But such an affectionate delight or sweet inclination, even for the body of Christ or the like, may also affect the less loving and the less perfect. For someone does not love so much as he senses this delight and find himself in a state of delight but rather insofar as he is grounded in the virtues, in humility, patience, charity, and all the rest, and is found faithful in keeping the commandments. For that other sweet affection toward God is sometimes in fact carnal and erring, more of humanity than of grace, of the heart than of the spirit, of sensuousness than of reason, and thus may kindle more of the less good, and less of the greatest, more what tastes good to him.

But there is another kind of devotion which comes when after long battles and many exercises, with the help of divine grace, those vices are subjugated to the rule of reason, clothed with a certain natural affection for the good, and he sweetly takes delight and finds rest in it. This is not something transient but in a sense infused into the very marrow of the soul. There it becomes rooted through the habituated virtues, and is always ready to fulfill God's will, to do or to suffer all things. If this happens with sweet affection and delight, it is true devotion, a continuous and permanent quality of the will, which can virtually be judged love. So much as you suppress the vices and progress in the virtues, so much you advance as well in this devotion, unless it is withdrawn by God, its giver.

50. *The Three Things Necessary for Those Who Would Do Proper Battle with the Vices: Strenuousness, Severity, and Kindness*

Do not deceive yourself; do not think you can ascend without working to uproot the vices. You find no good in yourself, that is, in your flesh, only those vices which have pitched camp within and over against you in the concupiscent and irascible powers. Only your will is left to you, and therefore it is necessary to arm it on the right and on the left against every kind of vice. These are the arms: strenuousness, severity, and kindness. Bonaventure defines strenuousness as a vigor of the soul which shakes off all negligence and disposes it to do good works vigilantly, confidently, and gracefully. Severity is a certain vigor of the soul which restrains all evil desire, making it fervent instead and capable of embracing harshness, poverty, and rejection. Kindness is a certain sweetness of the soul which excludes all evil and enables it to exercise benevolence, tolerance, and inner happiness.

These three are your arms. Be strenuous in casting off negligence and taking up work, however hard and difficult. Be severe so that when you take up the fight against the vices and first experience just how tough they are you will not give way or take flight but manfully persist in what you have begun and pursue evil desire with all severity to its destruction. Third, be kind so that when you frequently get wounded and dejected you not let your soul fall into confusion, grief, dejection, or despair. If you have these three arms you will have no reason to worry that their number is small in the face of such a gang of vices. For victory comes from heaven and to the Lord it is all the same to conquer with many or with few. Take note of Jonathan, the son of Saul, who slew so many with his arm-bearer, of the Maccabee brothers Judas, Jonathan, and Simon, as well as of Gideon and many other strenuous soldiers who with few helpers slew many, all the while putting their hope in the Lord and not in themselves.

51. *Anyone Progressing in Spiritual Exercises Will Find It Useful and Even Necessary to Have a Spiritual Man as a Guide*

Because there are many paths on this ascent and the way leading to life is not easily recognized, do not climb without a guide; do not even set out without a guide who knows both the way and the treachery of the adversaries. God often teaches men through other men and thus admonishes them in the correct ascent and the true path. Woe to those who confide in themselves and set out without a guide, for they will easily fall into the traps of the hunters and when they fall in will have no one to lift them out. Therefore, also for the sake of humbling us, he wants us to follow guides. Thus he led the whole people of Israel to the promised land through the guide Moses; the people did everything by his counsel and acquiesced in his admonitions. Thus Lot was compelled to leave Sodom and ascend the mount, not through himself but by an angelic guide. Thus Christ did not instruct Cornelius himself but sent Peter to that end. So also he sent Ananias to Paul. And this is what a certain devout eunuch said, reading Isaiah in his chariot: "How will I be able to understand unless someone teaches me?" And you can find many similar things in Scripture. When you order your heart toward the ascent into heaven, therefore, choose a guide, a spiritual man, through whose admonition, erudition, and examination you may carry out and perfect all your exercises. This is the safest teaching, a view approved long ago by the holy Fathers.

52. *To Take Up Battle against the Eight Capital Vices Is in a Sense to Fight All Disordered Affections*

If you have taken up arms, therefore, and found a guide to lead with counsel and direction, the time has come to begin the fight. You are to do battle against all the disordered affections which arise primarily from the loss of the soul's powers in your first descent away from original righteousness. Though there are many evil affections restraining your soul from its ascent, all the evil passions in fact arise from one queen and seven dukes. Once they are conquered and the opposing virtues put in their place, all disordered desire will quiet down, and the battle against those eight will in some way restore the powers so that those evil inclinations are reined in by reason. These are the eight vices, sometimes called "principal" as if they were princes of all evil, and other times "capital," as if all others found their origin in them. Other vices which proceed casually from them are called their daughters. Sometimes they are also called the mortal sins because they kill with guilt and separate from the life of grace as well as from God, who is the true life. But these eight are not always mortal, nor are they by their very nature so. And here they are: pride, vainglory, tedium, envy, anger, greed, lust, and gluttony.

53. *How to Fight Them: Do Not Fight All at Once but First a Single and Principal Vice*

Do not fight all of them at once, just as you cannot make all the ascents at once. As the Lord says, "I will not drive them from your face in one year but slowly lest the earth be turned to waste." In keeping with the traditions of the holy Fathers, take up this fight against the vices in this order.

First and before all else carefully examine yourself according to the form given earlier. Inquire which vices lie hidden and which are open in you, which strongest and which the most festering; next which remedies are the most effective against each vice. Then take up battle against the vice that seems to fester most. Try with all your strength to purge it; focus all your effort and concentration on driving it out. Constantly plead with God, and let it come before your eyes in prayer. Pour out tears without ceasing for its extermination. Devoutly raise up groans and sighs before God. Do not fight the one in such a way as to lose all thought of the others, but fight principally against the one in such a way as to conceive general horror of all the others. Indeed the more strenuously and wisely you do battle with the one, the greater horror you will conceive for all.

In nature different mixtures of four humors, the sanguine, choleric, phlegmatic, and melancholic, produce different natural complexions; so too in different men there are different moral dispositions arising from a mixture of the affections and a corruption of the powers. Thus one is more inclined to lust, another to anger, and frequently a man has a certain basic inclination, a kind of basic specific gravity, from which the other vices, or at least a major part of them, arise, and this might be called a kind of moral complexion. Again, one is sad, another confused, another impulsive, another scrupulous, a fifth querulous, a sixth afflicted in his exercises, a seventh preoccupied. All these seem to arise from a certain inner disorder of the soul or organs, and are in a way not much different from those who suffer melancholy. Another, on the other hand, is happy, cheerful, relaxed, and so on. Each should first carefully examine his own inner being, as described, and order his heart accordingly in its ascent toward the virtues and his exercises as remedies for the vices. He should always hold his own particular evil inclination suspect and seek in every way to restrain it with the rule of reason.

When that one principal vice has been so weakened by devout exercise and vigorous battle that it no longer presumes to rise up and disobey reason, but is instantly restrained by the command of reason and without a fight, then seek out another vice from among the more festering in you and do battle with it in the same careful way. Never think you will be able to uproot a vice so fully that you will no longer have to fight it except by way of some general horror of evil. For, as Bernard says, vices once thought withered grow again, the driven out return, the extinct are rekindled, and the sleeping awakened.

54. *Different Vices Are to Be Fought in Different Ways, and Wherein That Diversity Consists*

Just as the vices are of a different nature, so they are to be fought in different ways. The carnal vices are best overcome by fleeing every occasion for and inducement toward them. But the spiritual are better fought by confronting occasions in which they are aroused and then vigorously resisting them. Consider too the different characters of the vices. Some, such as envy, always arise from others, never from themselves, and then you must do battle primarily with that which caused it. Consider too the varying kinds of their temptations. Some, like lust and anger, openly entice toward evil and seek to overwhelm the soul by force; resist these with effort and sadness. Others deceive by seduction, especially of the appetites, as in temptations arising from an excess of vigils or fasting; here it is less a matter of vigor than of discretion. Here, according to Bernard, to know is to have conquered and to believe is to conquer. Still others draw by their force and appearance of goodness, as in an inordinate affection for preaching; under the guise of a zeal for souls, it is driven by an appetite for praise and for fame. This is the most dangerous kind of temptation. The first point here is to know and to believe that it is a temptation; not to know or to have known is to be conquered, and the real point is to restrain this drive with various labors and exercises.

55. *The Three Ascents Directed against Each Vice and toward Virtue*

With these general admonitions in mind, we can descend into single combat with each of the vices. But you must first know that you dispose your heart toward certain ascents and progressive steps against each vice so that you may judge how much you have ascended in virtue or descended in vice.

There are three steps to be considered with respect to each vice. The first is that of a beginner and belongs to the first step upward, the purity of heart which comes from fear. The second is for the advanced and pertains to the second step upward which is taken in hope. The third is for the perfect and pertains to the final step upward toward purity.

56. *Ascent Directed against the First Vice: Gluttony*

The first battle is against the vice of gluttony. With it the devil tempted the first man and overcame him; with it he also tempted the second and was himself overcome. It is also situated, as it were, at the very boundaries of nature. If therefore we are not able to overcome it, how should we overcome spiritual temptations attacking us beyond the confines of our carnal natures?

We ascend away from this vice by way of sobriety, through which we dispose our heart for its climb. Sobriety is the virtue by which we take bodily nourishment with proper moderation. You must dispose your heart for a triple ascent away from the vice of gluttony so that you may restrain the appetite for gluttony and to this end reform the concupiscent power.

The first step in the virtue of sobriety and away from gluttony is to bear up patiently when exquisite food and drink is not to be had, and not to become annoyed when your desires cannot be completely fulfilled. At this stage a gluttonous man suffers many battles and sharp jabs of desire. So sometimes he must stand up and fight to conquer it.

As you know, it is the nature of gluttony to arouse in the concupiscent faculty an inordinate appetite for food and drink which impedes ascent. This inordinate affection or desire compels some to eat before mealtime, some to eat too much as they fall upon their food with uncontrolled desire, others to seek inordinately for exquisite foods, and still others simply to eat to excess. . . . To purge this impure affection driving us in an evil way toward food, you must understand first the general nature of the soul as it pertains to the purgation of all evils. The soul possesses a threefold motivating force with respect to the body: a natural force derived from the movement of the humors, from which gluttony and lust often arise; a vital force by which a man carries out his vital motions; and an animating force by which a man exercises his imagination, his mind, and so on. The less a man exercises his animating force, the more his natural force is focused and increased. Thus men who are bored, lukewarm, and who take no inner delight in their meditations and spiritual yearnings are especially threatened by carnal vices. As Solomon says, every idle man is prey to desire. . . . By contrast, the more focused the animating power, the less forceful the natural, as is evident in studious men. Wherefore Jerome said to Rusticus: Love the study of Scripture and you will not love the vices of the flesh. In sum, the more a man is delightfully intent upon interior and exterior occupations and concerns, the more he will overcome the carnal vices. The remedy therefore for gluttony and even lust is complete concentration and inner affection for the good, as in remorse which is very powerful against gluttony and lust, but also devotion, sacred reading, and every useful external occupation accompanied by an inner affection.

With these and similar remedies you must do battle with gluttony so that you may proceed to a higher step. This is to progress so willingly and with so little contrary appetite that you are content with simple and common food and can abstain from the more delectable, as in wines, even when readily available. On this step you stand more securely, but not yet without some destructive counterattacks.

To reach the third ascent you must completely suppress gluttonous concupiscence with such remedies as fasts, vigils, readings, and frequent compunction of the heart, recalling perhaps some past defeat, groaning with horror at your vices, and again with desire for perfection and the last step. When the mind is occupied and possessed with such concern and meditations, it will look upon the taking of food not as a concession to delight, but as an imposition of the human condition, and perceive it as something far more necessary for the body than desirable for the soul. And when you have put on such an affection, you will have attained the third step. . . .

When you will have conquered gluttony, put sobriety in its place, which carefully observes quantity and quality in food, quality lest you seek out the delicate and extraordinary, quantity lest you exceed the measure. For however varied the capacity of human beings, all have the same end, namely continence lest someone burdens his proper capacity with gluttonous excess. Sobriety looks out chiefly, however, that a balanced and moderate fast be ever observed.

57. *Ascent to Battle the Vice of Lust*

You must order your ascent, second, toward conquering lust. It also has its seat in the concupiscent forces. Anyone completely possessed by it will not be able to ascend in his heart, but will rather rot in his own dung like a beast. We ascend and battle it through the virtue of chastity, a daughter of sobriety through which it is nourished and increased. Chastity is a great virtue, of heavenly origin. The holy angels learned it from the very beginning and from the Lord himself. Christ brought it from heaven to earth and made his glorious virgin mother its perfect disciple, to be imitated by others.

We conquer lust by way of a triple ascent. The first is a continence from the carnal act itself, with the resolution to hold fast and to deny consent to any illicit impulses. At this point a man is still in the midst of battle and not far removed from the enemy; only his will has chosen for chastity and his affections still resist it. A man on this step must be fiercely armed for battle, for the struggle against this vice is great and longer lasting than any of the others.

To know what you are fighting, carefully note the nature of lust and the means with which you are to battle it. It has a twofold nature, partly of the flesh and partly of the soul. Its fleshly nature stirs up movements in the body and brings about an uprising of its members. In the soul it stirs up an affection for women, an inclination toward them, fostering images of them, familiarity with them, and so on. Its daughters, according to Gregory, are sevenfold: a blinded mind, a lack of regard for death and hell, wandering thoughts and desires, love of self, inclination to sin, hatred of God, attraction to the present age, and indifference to the future. To conquer these impulses and affections, carefully consider that this vice, as Chrysostomus said, is the passion of an idle soul, that is, one without exercise and desire. Thus, the more you fill your heart with fear, concern, and remorse, the less you are tempted. This is why during sleep, when the soul's powers are at rest, this beast rises up all the more.

As regards special remedies for lust, note that this passion is sometimes of the flesh and other times of the soul; and when it lies in the flesh it arouses affections in the soul, and by contrast when it is in the soul it moves the flesh. Remedies specially meant for healing fleshly lust are fasting (perhaps the principle one), then manual labor, vigils, works, tribulation, and so on. Remedies for lust in the soul are contrition of spirit, devout prayer, frequent and holy meditation, mental concentration and spiritual exercise, studious and intent occupation both within and without. Then too, keeping watch over your senses in the public square, at home, and so on; repressing inner imaginations; avoiding familiarity with women and never being alone with them in secret, nor frequenting their homes. Humility and meekness also help considerably. As the wise man said: "When I knew that I was not able to be continent in any other way, I went to the Lord and pleaded with him." Though triumph over vice is never possible without humility, with this vice we especially stand in need of divine grace. After exercising yourself in these ways, you may ascend to the second step of chastity, the second stage of progress against lust.

The second step comes when your affections are so purified and your flesh so subjected to your spirit through disciplining the flesh and all the other exercises that you are rarely tempted, and temptation is then easily overcome, a matter of command rather than of battle. Above this there is a third and higher step reached when, after long exercise and much labor with the help of divine grace, you so subdue the desires of the flesh that you feel them only rarely and gently, and you have put on such an affection and love for chastity that you detest and are horrified by all the motions of the flesh, even to a degree nauseated by them.

58. *Ascent Away from Avarice*

Third, you must order your ascent away from avarice through the virtue of poverty and contempt for wealth. As before, there are three ascents.

The first is never to seek any unjust gain, and from just gain to give alms and never to abuse it for yourself or some other vice. If you wish really to root out this vice entirely, you should have only food and clothing and a covering over your head, and be content. The best remedy is to leave all for Christ and to carry on under the care and provision of another, having no thing, not the least bit of property, for yourself. Then too, to trust in God who will not abandon those who put their hope in him.

In the second ascent, you are not only content with just gain and necessities alone, but with no superfluity in food, clothing, dwelling, and so on. The third step is to possess nothing in this world, to want nothing, and frequently to suffer want in all necessities. The daughters of avarice are six: betrayal, fraud, distraction, perjury, restlessness, and hardness of heart against all mercy.

[Chapter 59 treats anger and emphasizes self-control.]

60. *Ascent Away from Envy and Toward Love of Your Neighbor*

Ascent against envy means taking progressive steps toward love of your neighbor. The first point is to hate no one, to wish to block no one's good, never to withdraw help from any neighbor in need, and—in short—never willingly to do or to wish evil upon anyone but to wish and to do good as he would for himself if he were in need.

Love . . . is the endpoint of the ascent, and therefore just as nothing is to be advanced more than love of God and neighbor, so nothing is to be restrained more than envy. Above all, we must retain unity in peace, the bond of perfection. There is nothing in which the holy angels take greater delight, nothing in which we so expressly represent the heavenly Jerusalem, than when we preserve a unity of hearts in love, all speaking the same, all sensing the same, all guarding against injuring another's conscience by scandal, singularity, or presumption of novelty and the extraordinary. As he departed from us, therefore, Christ pressed this commandment upon us so many times. "In this," he said, "men will know that you are my disciples, if you love one another." We must fight this vice above all, a vice properly ascribed to the devil, for death entered the world by way of his envy, and they follow him who are of his party.

The best remedy against envy is to love none of those things the world loves, its honors, riches, and sensuous delights. Insofar as we love something earthly and are obstructed in our pursuit of it by someone else, just so far we are also roused to envy. . . . The daughters which follow from envy are hatred, whispering, disparagement, rejoicing in your neighbor's adversity, and pain at his success. The second remedy is for a man carefully to consider that even if some person should lack the good of which he is envious, he would himself nonetheless still not have it. So too, fear the vengeance of God, who does not forgive a man his sin unless he forgives his neighbor. And again, a man should strive to be more favorable, affable, and kindly toward a person he hates.

The second ascent against envy and progress in love of neighbor is so to rejoice and to love another's good fortune and so to suffer with him in adversity as if it were your own, and to assign another's gain to him in pious affection. The third ascent is to love your enemies, to foster a sweet affection toward those hating and persecuting you like that you show toward your most beloved friends, and then to be prepared to lay down not only your possessions but even your body for your brothers.

61. *The Ascent and Battle against Tedium*

Just as love of neighbor drives out and destroys envy, so in ascending toward love of God we conquer tedium and depressive sadness. For the love of God works ardently and does great things if it is real; but if it refuses to work, it is not love. The act of love also brings rejoicing in the Holy Spirit against sadness.

The first step in the love of God is to love the things permitted you and so to use them as to avoid what is illicit. In this step you do only what is necessary for salvation and you avoid being so cast down in tedium that you neglect what must be done or even what has been ordered. This is a very small ascent and it is not good to stay here long. You must, therefore, break yourself through constant exercise in good works, resisting tedium and stirring up affection for good works and devout exercises. Then you will not only do what is necessary for salvation but with full and fervent affection and the tedium partly conquered you will begin to do all the things of God, become zealous to do them, and even fulfill the counsels.

Here you ascend the second step in the love of God and against mental tedium. So long as you are attacked by tedium and have not yet reached this step, however, realize that the best remedy for tedium is never to yield but always vigorously to resist. That you may recognize the nature of this beast, note that its impulses and agitation aim principally at two things, change of place and variation in the exercises. It obtains a change of place in this way: It weighs down and depresses your mind with an initial tedium that removes all delight in things spiritual. But a soul cannot exist without some kind of love or delight. Therefore it begins at once to aspire toward bodily recreation and wishes to leave this place in which it finds no recreation. It therefore brings upon you a horror of the place, boredom with your cell, and boredom with all good things, especially spiritual. In the meantime it gladly seizes upon things carnal so as to be less occupied with the spiritual. Finally it begins to extol remote places, to beatify the brothers living there, and to conceive a certain hardness toward your present brothers as somehow less spiritual. When a soul so affected by tedium finds no consolation, it immediately leaves the place or falls into dreaminess and decadence. Seeking some kind of solace for a time, it quietly and secretly introduces the fresh guise of changing exercises. For when the soul is weighed down with exercises of a certain kind, it concocts some other lighter ones, highly extolling them and imagining them much more meritorious, for instance, to visit the sick or certainly to build a new house—in which an evil and bored disciple will make an even worse master and rector.

If you wish to conquer tedium legitimately, above all never desert your place. For the more you change places, the more your mind will wander to other things, bored with things spiritual. . . . The daughters of tedium are six, according to Gregory, namely malice or the will to concoct something evil, desperation, weak-heartedness, rancor or inveterate hatred, sluggishness toward the commandments of God, and wandering of the mind toward things illicit. Remorse, if someone suffering tedium is able to rouse it, helps mightily in countering this disease. . . . Again, variety in action can also help in combating tedium of the heart. A man should first pray and then read until he conceives some affection, and then force himself to do those works which most bore him. Truly if a man is severe and strenuous and yet gentle in his devout exercises and holy works and if he persists in them, he will finally begin to have some hope; the affection of love will begin to increase and to draw him toward God, so that in the end without him he could not live, caught up as he is in

304

the desire to dissolve and be with Christ. This is the third step of love in which tedium is overcome.

Depressive sadness is twofold. There is a certain general sadness surrounding all passion and it can be very difficult to discern its origins. But there is also a certain heaviness and bored sluggishness in things spiritual which is an aspect of tedium and from which you ascend through steps upward in the love of God. For the act of love is joy. The remedy for sadness is, if it arises from desperation, the recollection of God's kindness and mercy and the gazing upon his benefits. Another approach is to join willingly in human society where men speak of God and of matters spiritual. So too that verse of James: "If anyone among you is sad, let him pray and sing psalms."

[Chapter 62 treats of vainglory and teaches self-denial.]

63. *The Ascent to Battle against Pride*

Now, at last, you must order your ascent toward the throne where pride is seated and overthrow that proud queen of the vices like queen Jezebel. You must make your ascent by way of the steps of humility.

The first is that a man truly recognize himself infirm, incapable of good, full of vice, as well as all his other defects, and therefore not elevate himself above what he is. If on occasion, yielding to temptation, he does that, he should reproach and chastise himself. But two kinds of pride, carnal and spiritual, will attempt to pull him back from this ascent. For the carnal deceives a man, suggesting to him that he is better than what he really is—because of his learning or his riches or the dignity of his parents or whatever else—and thus does not allow a man to see himself truly and to recognize his own vileness. Cassian provided a long list of the signs of this kind of pride. . . . To repress it and reach the first step of humility, you must first show true humility to your brothers with the most intimate affection of heart, allowing yourself in no way to harm or grieve them. Constantly exercise yourself in humble works and despicable jobs, as, for instance, in kitchen duty or such basic necessities as cleaning the house, washing dishes, wearing the vile garb of a pauper, and so on. Be humble in your ways and words, choose the last place, avoid marks of vainglory such as to be called "rabbi" or "lord," and never boast in any way. Always have your hour of death before your eyes. When these and similar things become customary, they will incline you to humility and repress any swelling up on your part.

There is also spiritual pride, which causes the mind to expand and rise above itself by, for instance, attributing to itself many virtues and great merit, or glorying in its own special gifts, or judging these as given by God for its own merit. This is much more dangerous than carnal pride. There is no other vice that so drains the virtues, so despoils and denudes a man of all justice and righteousness, as this evil of pride. Climbers at the very peak of virtue are often cast down by it to the most serious ruin or even death.

To repress this internal swelling up and to ascend to the steps of humility, you must look upon all your virtue, all your progress, all your good works, and then say and feel with your whole heart and mind: "It is not I but the grace of God in me"; or "I am what I am by the grace of God"; or "It is God who works to will and to perfect his good pleasure." Carefully consider your own vileness and reflect that the good of your mind is not yours but a gift of God and for it you will have to give account. But the evils are yours and they are purely evil, serious in all their particulars and worthy of the most serious punishment. Our goods, however, are not purely good but imperfect in many ways. Negligence, lukewarmness, hypocrisy, vainglory, and the rest often so taint our good deeds that they are of little merit to us and hardly acceptable to God. Be attentive as well to those higher and better than you, humans as well as the Lord Jesus Christ himself who said: "Learn from me because I am mild and humble of heart," and thus you will better know your own vileness in comparison with others.

When a person has done this for a long time and regularly exercised himself, he will begin to know himself as he truly is. Indeed if he exercises himself with feeling and with perseverance, he will begin to acquire the affection that the vileness and poverty he recognized during his first ascent should be evident to others, seeing him as he is, who ought to count him worse rather than better, were it not to give scandal to a neighbor. This is then the second ascent and the second step in humility.

The third step and ascent comes when through humble exercises and knowledge of himself a man gains such an affection of humility that he receives no praise even for great virtues and sublime gifts and never flatters himself, but rather restores and redirects everything to him from whom he received all his good. Such was the humility of Christ; such is also the humility of the angels and the saints in glory.

[PART IV: SPIRITUAL DESCENT]

64. *Two Forms of Spiritual Descent, to Yourself and Your Neighbor*

. . . Scripture says of all these ascents at one point, "Jacob saw a ladder, and the angels of God ascending and descending on it." You may well wonder how angels, beings completely holy, descend, for that they ascend is not surprising. But this can be sensibly understood. Even holy men, so long as they are still pilgrims and weighed down by bodies that corrupt, cannot ascend continuously and without interruption. Sometimes, burdened by the weight of corruptibility, they slacken in their ascent and descend for a time when they let up on their spiritual exercises.

But there are also useful descents, more appropriate to our purpose. Even true climbers and spiritual men sometimes interrupt their ascent for a time and make useful descents. Briefly put, there are two, one by which a man descends into himself and a second by which he descends to his neighbor, each of which has three steps.

65. *The First Descent by Which a Man Descends from a Higher to a Lower Stage with Respect to Himself*

First, a man descends into himself when, for instance, someone at a higher ascent and lifted to a elevated stage descends for a time to exercise himself more perfectly in a lower grade, lest always climbing higher he become negligent and lose what he acquired at a lower stage. For in his ascending a man should not so exert himself toward what lies ahead as if there were no purpose in looking at what lies behind, but should rather so exert himself and advance from virtue to virtue as not to neglect the stages through which he climbed, striving rather always to keep that which he has obtained.

An example. Through fear you first knew remorse, and through meditation on death, the last judgment, and the pains of hell you did good works, and then you reached hope, the memory of heavenly glory, and the benefits of God, roused more sweetly still to the remorse of love. But should you now leave fear? Should you forever forsake meditation on death and judgment? No, sometimes you ought to climb higher through hope to gaze on heavenly glory and be enticed by its beauty to climb higher still. But another time you should descend in fear and carefully contemplate the vanity of the world, the brevity of life, and the bitterness of the pains of hell so as to be frightened away from descending any lower. In this way you may be drawn by hope, or really fear, and compelled, as if by a sharp stick, to advance and ascend. You should be thus ever ascending and descending in your exercises between fear and hope and love until that love becomes perfected, casting out all fear. The danger otherwise is that you fall into laziness or false security or even presumption.

So too the angels, that is, the holy men, ascend into heaven through affection and desire and descend into the abyss to live in hell through careful examination of themselves. It is a matter of discernment to determine at which stage a person should exercise himself further, differing according to the progress, status, and condition of a person. By ascending and descending you embrace both feet of Christ with Mary the sinner. With the Prophet you sing both mercy and judgment to the Lord. According to Augustine everything in Scripture refers finally to these two, this ascent and descent, so that you may love mercy and fear force. So too the holy Prophet in his divine address says that he heard only these two: "The Lord spoke once and I heard these two things, for the Lord is merciful to you, and you render to each according to his works." All the prophets and all of Scripture turn on these two. . . .

66. *The Second Descent, to the Disciplining of External Morals and Actions*

Sometimes, dear man, you must descend into yourself and order rightly your outer person so your inner devotion and sanctity may radiate outward in external morals and actions. Rule your exterior conduct, then; be your own watchman; be an example to others; be loving to all. This you will do best if you strive to observe three things in your exterior morality, that it be mature, humble, and kindly. Maturity will make you an example to others, humility a guardian over yourself, and kindness will render you loving to others.

Maturity consists in this, that a man be not too quick to run or too ready to laugh, not curious or talkative or always joking. This maturity rules the head, composes the mind within, and guards the entire body from insolence without. The head rules lest it be blown lightly about here and there, lest the eyes wander, the ears listen too curiously, and so on through the rest. Humility in conduct bows your head, shapes humble responses, smooths out your actions, loves simple clothing, puts itself at the end, avoids ostentation or standing out, is prompt and ready to show favor to others. Kindness shows affability and compassion to the pained, is flexible and approachable in matters of counsel, communicative of itself and others in matters of the good, happy and modest, pleasant, loyal and sociable, grateful and thankful.

So far as certain outward signs of kindness which the Philosopher calls "friendship," this kindness is necessary to social well-being. No one, as he says, can survive a day with only sadness and without delight. You are bound therefore by a certain debt to nature and goodness to dwell with others lovingly and in kindness. When you are among other men, therefore, you ought especially to show kindness and delight, even to cover over sadness of mind with happiness of expression. But an effusive display is to be avoided, lest the vice of vanity be nurtured under the pretext of piety. Therefore, as Hugh says, when you are with others and taking delight in mutual conversation, let your talk turn to morality and the Scriptures. Let us groan with the miseries of this world, rejoice with the hope of future joy, refresh ourselves with the disclosure of mutual secrets, and then sigh together for the vision of Jesus and heavenly delight. If it is sometimes useful for us to relax our tense spirits with certain lower pleasant matters, let that relaxation be full of goodness, devoid of frivolousness, and let it not lack edification even if it lacks great weight. In these three, then, maturity, humility, and kindness, are found the entire outer discipline of our moral conduct. Humility, however, should temper maturity lest it become too stuffy, as should kindness lest it become too austere and full of indignity.

67. The Third Descent to Yourself: A Man Unable to Persist Long in Spiritual Matters May Need to Exercise Himself for a Time in Manual Labor

Third, you ought frequently to climb down and take up some manual or corporeal labor. You must in any case so order your exercises that each day you exercise yourself for a certain time in work of the hands and at another time make progress in the ascents of the heart. But work of the hands should not obstruct progress of the heart, for during your work you can pray, meditate, and exercise yourself in fear and desire. Our holy Fathers had the rule of hand that the more faithfully someone applied himself to manual labor, the higher they expected him to go in his ascent toward purity and love and in his spiritual progress. Frail man that you are, never think yourself an angel that can live only on spiritual food.

You should exercise yourself in manual labor at fixed times for a variety of reasons. First, lest you be conquered by tedium and altogether leave off with your spiritual exercises. Do not imagine yourself more fervent and spiritual than the great Anthony, who would have been overcome by tedium and returned to the world had he not learned from an angel the ascent and descent between spiritual and manual labor. Cassian wished it for the same reason: Whoever is not content to do some work with his hands each day will not finally persevere in his cell.

Second, though manual labor will for a time take you away from your contemplative solitude, on returning afterward you will be even stronger. For, as you already heard, you cannot ascend with evil desires; they are what obstruct ascent. You must therefore conquer those evil desires, and chiefly with manual labor, for every idle person is full of desire. Manual labor thus often serves spiritual ascent by removing its impediments.

Third, your heart is highly instable, and, tossed around like a ship on the waves of the sea, is shaken by various affections and thoughts. Therefore, as Cassian says, you must affix your heart with some kind of anchor, that is, with the weight and occupation of manual labor.

Fourth, because the enemy finds far more opportunities to tempt us if we are idle than if we are occupied. The busy, as they say, are tempted by one demon, the idle overwhelmed by innumerable demons.

Fifth, if you carefully pay attention to that manual labor, it will usefully admonish you towards ascent. First, it reminds you of the place in which the Lord placed you and from which you fell, for if you were still established there in all tranquillity you would not need to work. And if Adam was put to work in Paradise, as Scripture says, that was not labor but worship with the highest delight, seeing in the lesser creatures the power, wisdom, and goodness of the Creator and applying that to his praise. Manual labor is therefore, as Bernard says, a kind of bandaged wound, which reproaches and admonishes you about your guilt. In the aftermath of your guilt, this command of the natural law was given: In the sweat of your face you will eat your bread. So often as you work with your hands, therefore, you should stand admonished on the guilt of your transgression. Through work of the hands you are also admonished that for six days, that is, your whole earthly life, you must work, for it is the time for working. On the seventh day, the close of this present life, the Spirit says that you will rest from your labors. By manual labor you are thus admonished to work toward that, toward the place where you need not labor but only rest and see how sweet the Lord is.

Sixth, work of the hands will render you free, so that you need not go about flattering others and seeking support from them, as the Apostle wrote to the Thessalonians.

Seventh, according to Bernard, work of the hands often depresses, as the body does by its weight, thus expressing remorse more sweetly and more purely. For these and many other reasons, then, our Fathers, especially those in Egypt, always worked faithfully and are so sublimely praised by the saints for their labors.

Lest, however, you depart too far from the ascent of the heart, you must always, so far as it lies within you, choose corporeal works that seem more apt for things spiritual, such as the copying of sacred books, which little obstructs ascent and is spiritually much more fruitful. For each sacred book you copy is another herald to the truth you have made, and as many people as are thereby brought to remorse and to progress will be added to your share in the reward. For that reason St. Bernard strongly approved of copying books, many of the holy Fathers were copyists, many brothers and disciples in the monastery of St. Martin copied books, and—among others—the blessed Jerome specially admonished the monk Rusticus on the work of copying. Many of the saints wrote books with their own hands partly out of humility and partly to avoid idleness, as is written of Ambrose and Jerome.

While you work with your hands, you ought not to have an idle mind but to exercise yourself in a pious heart by praying or meditating or at least reflecting pleasantly on what you are copying. Indeed according to St. Augustine, in his book on the work of monks, you can even sing something devoutly during work. Work of the hands hinders this no more than it does worldly folks from singing their songs while working with their hands. You must always work faithfully and not like the worldly folk who receive only a transient reward, for you receive not only a temporal reward but also an incorruptible crown in heaven. Note that holy angels announced the birth of Christ the Lord to shepherds busy about their work. Do not work to excess or too impulsively, but with moderation and discretion. Especially during manual labor you must keep silent. For silence is our strength, and though to be observed always and everywhere unless necessity or utility requires otherwise, it must be maintained especially during manual labor, as the Apostle says, "We ask you in the Lord Jesus, that you eat your bread in silence."

68. *Descent to or for Your Neighbor, the First at Your Superior's Command*
It is likewise often necessary to climb down from these ascents—that is, to cease for a time, not to desert the climb alto-

gether—for your neighbor, and this in three ways: for your superior, for a colleague, for some below you.

You seek with all your might the contemplative life, to weep for your sins with Lazarus and to stir up remorse through recollection of your sins or of the last judgment, or you sit with Mary at the feet of Jesus while he preaches, meaning, mentally to exercise yourself in the life and passion of Christ, or some other such great ascent. But then you must descend for your superior because he comes and calls you, ordering you to go out, commands you to climb down, without delay like Martha to throw yourself at the feet of the vicar of Jesus (your superior). That is to say, you must descend promptly and devoutly, and withdraw from your inner exercises. But if Mary remains within the house and so busies herself still with the inner life that she is unwilling to be pulled away, and Martha murmurs at her sitting at the feet of Jesus or even reproaches some brother, then Martha must enter that home, meaning, the inner man, and speak there under silence. That is to say, you must secretly reprove yourself, saying to your Mary: The Lord is here, and is calling you. He to whom you entrusted yourself in discipleship is present; your superior is calling to you, and orders you out; will you still remain seated? On hearing this, your Mary should rise and throw herself at the feet of Jesus, saying: My heart is ready, ready and waiting upon your command, ready also when you order me to minister in external matters. It is not only the command of your father but also sometimes the need to exhort a brother in love that may oblige you. The holy Fathers freely set aside all exercises in order to maintain inviolable obedience. Moreover, this they valued more than all else: not to carry out their own will but that of another. Then too, while obedience in response to some command or need is necessary, you should not even consider whether you are obliged to something, for obedience born of love is often more meritorious and itself increases love; therefore devoutly do it.

69. The Second Descent to a Neighbor, Supporting Him with Aid, Counsel, Admonition, or Reproach

You ought, second, to descend to a neighbor when moved by compassion and piety to support with aid and counsel, for instance, to help and succor those bodily afflicted. Still more, when you see the spiritually afflicted, you should aid them as much as possible by admonishing, reproaching, and drawing them in and by comforting and consoling them in their trials and temptations. Unless Paul had descended from the third heaven and lowered himself from this high state of mind to those beneath him, he would have drawn in no one; but he descended and he did all things for all people: To carnal men he preached Jesus and Christ crucified, to the spiritual however he compared things spiritual; so too you should be all things and aid each person, as necessity requires. If there is bodily infirmity, have compassion from the heart and willingly minister to them so far as you can, especially to those in your own house. If there is poverty, give if you can and support them, even suffering need for a time yourself, offering like the widow not from your superfluity but from your necessities, bringing support in food and clothing and other necessities from your own poverty and the needs you suffer. If you cannot help with things, then with pious admonition. For a good word is the greatest gift, and spiritual alms are greater than corporeal.

Particularly when perched upon some ascent in your heart you see beneath you people wandering from the yoke of Christ, descend quickly, leaving your ascent (if it seems that for a time it could help), and draw them in, admonish and reproach them. Never say in your heart: My own salvation suffices for me; I wish to be concerned only for me, not for others. Am I his superior? Am I his keeper? Certainly the zeal of God did not produce such an evil thought. But, as the Blessed Gregory said, insofar as you accept the grace of the highest inbreathing, recall your neighbor from evil, proclaim to the erring one the eternal kingdom and eternal punishment, so that you might deserve to be called an angel. Dispense thus a word of admonition to everyone, as it seems wise and useful. Think that, according to Bede, among men there cannot be any way higher and more pleasing to God than to chastise ourselves over the vices, to subject our souls to the school of virtue, and in addition by daily exercise to strive to convert others to the author of all grace and ever to increase the joy of the heavenly homeland. This we do not understand of public preaching but of private admonition and fraternal exhortation, of which it is said, "The lord has given a commandment to each concerning his neighbor."

Public preaching should be taken up only with the greatest reluctance, expecially by youth, unless they are in some way full of grace and virtue, like a shell that has not burst and that has first been filled, as Bernard says on the Song of Songs. It is truly hard and dangerous for someone with only a moderate amount of oil, as the explanation continues, except for those with the mandate of a prophet, lest contrary to the law of love the person seems to love others more than himself.

You ought similarly to descend with a spirit of gentleness and compassion for a brother whom you see sinning or ruling himself in a disordered way, however you may perceive this, so that by piously descending to him in fraternal correction you may draw him up again and lead him to make amends. So far as it lies in you, you should not allow vice to reign in anyone. Proceeding in compassion and humility, you ought to consume your zeal in moderation and discretion, never ceasing to presume to reproach where amends are to be made, but watching over yourself lest you also be tempted. May that zeal burn in us, as Bernard says, that love of justice and hatred of iniquity. No one, brothers, should flatter vice, no one should cover for sin. Let no one say: Am I my brother's keeper? No one, if he can, should bear in good spirit order being destroyed or discipline diminished. Thus you must bring aid to your neighbor: If he has corporeal needs, succor him with corporeal alms; but if he has spiritual needs, freely dispense spiritual mercy and spiritual aid.

You ought secondly to aid your neighbor with counsel, instructing and directing the errant, especially those erring in temptation and in their spiritual exercises. But look out that you not teach others what you do not know yourself. It is better humbly to profess ignorance than presumptuously to want to teach. Let your counsel therefore always be consonant with Scripture. Anything you hear in offering counsel or discussing counsel in another case, if it be a confidential matter, watch out that you not publish it abroad, especially what concerns another's temptations. Many dangers arise from this, as it says in the second collation of the Fathers. In giving counsel, be careful lest you simply follow your own passions or inclinations, for they pervert judgment even as zeal knows no wisdom. So too, before you give counsel, especially in a hard case, deliberate for a long time, and do not say what first occurs to you but only what you have reflected upon. Submit your counsel to the good sense of others, lest you be found stubborn, and be willing to give consent to the humble rather than make them consent to you. Never disparage anyone's counsel. God often reveals to little ones what he keeps hidden from the wise. Give heed to everyone's counsel, but not in simply taking it up. Test it, as the Apostle says, to see what is really good. Hold to that, humbly granting your assent in the end.

70. *The Third Descent, in Which a Superior Must Descend to Care for His Subjects*

If you have people below you, it is necessary to climb down frequently, indeed to desert the ascents often in order to be free for the care and discipline of those subjected to you: for their care, so that you may preserve in uprightness those who are now living worthily; for their discipline, so that you may correct those who err and live less properly. Otherwise the Lord will require of your hands the blood of their souls, for unless you carry with you, so far as you are able, the least of your brothers, you will not see the face of Joseph, your true Savior.

See then how dangerous is the position of a superior, who as a man must desert himself and thereby, in neglecting himself, often loses all. For when a man is much occupied externally and is inwardly idle, he sometimes neglects his ascents, descending to hardness of heart and insensitivity: He perceives only exterior matters and has no taste for the spiritual, as the blessed Bernard showed very well in his first book *On Consideration*. Therefore, as the saints counsel, so far as it lies in you, avoid the position of a superior and too much external occupation—while always maintaining humble and prompt obedience to your own superior.

When therefore someone is compelled to serve in external affairs, he should be very concerned to return to his inner life and to be free for himself whenever he has the time, lest, as it is said, he is rendered insensitive. As the holy Gregory said: Holy men who are forced by their offices to serve in external ministries should studiously take refuge in their hearts, there to ascend the heights of intimate thought, to perceive the law of God as upon a mountain, to cast aside the tumults of temporal action, and upon the peak to examine the judgments of the divine will. For to serve in external offices without offense, a person must constantly take care to return to the secret places of his heart.

Notes

INTRODUCTION

1. Henricus Pomerius, *Opuscula de Viridivalle* 2.8, in *Analecta Bollandiana* 4 (1885): 288.

2. "Epistola de prima institutione monasterii in Windeshem," in J. G. R. Acquoy, *Het Klooster te Windesheim en zijn invloed* (Utrecht, 1880), 3.237–38.

3. Thomas à Kempis, *Dialogus noviciorum*, in his *Opera Omnia*, ed. Michael Joseph Pohl (Freiburg, 1922), 7.30.

4. Johannes Busch, *Chronicon Windeshemense-Liber de Reformatione Monasteriorum*, ed. Karl Grube (Halle, 1886), pp. 251–56.

5. For general orientation, see A. Ampe, *L'imitation de Jésus Christ et son auteur* (Rome, 1973); *Thomas à Kempis en de moderne devotie* (Brussels, 1971); Stephanus G. Axters, *De imitatione Christi: een handschrifteninventaris bij het vijfhonderdste verjaren van Thomas Hemerken van Kempen* (Kempen-Niederrhein, 1971); and (still basic) L. M. J. Delaissé, *Le manuscrit autographe de Thomas à Kempis et "L'imitation de Jésus Christ"* (Brussels, 1956). The dispute between the "Dutch" and "Italian" schools over authorship has proved so contentious down almost to this day that objective accounts, based on a careful assessment of all the manuscript evidence, hardly exist. Despite certain very real ambiguities in the evidence, most scholars still accept Thomas as author or compiler.

6. The best historiographical account is to be found in W. Jappe Alberts, "Zur Historiographie der *Devotio Moderna*," *Westfälische Forschungen* 11 (1958): 51–67; R. R. Post, *The Modern Devotion* (Leiden, 1968), pp. 1–49; A. G. Weiler, "Recent Historiography on the Modern Devotion: Some Debated Questions," *Archief voor de geschiedenis van de Katholieke Kerk in Nederland* 27 (1985): 161–75; and Kaspar Elm, "Die Brüderschaft vom gemeinsamen Leben: eine geistliche Lebensform zwischen Kloster und Welt, Mittelalter und Neuzeit," *Ons geestelijk erf* 59 (1985): 470–96, esp. 470–74. Perhaps the most influential earlier work in America and also elsewhere—to which Post's book responded some forty years later—was Albert Hyma's *The Christian Renaissance: A History of the Devotio Moderna* (Grand Rapids, Mich., 1924), later ex-

panded into two volumes, *The Brethren of the Common Life* (Grand Rapids, Mich., 1950) and *The Christian Renaissance* (1965). The most recent assessment of this age-old tension between "Catholic" and "Protestant" interpretations of the movement may be found in Elm (pp. 492–96); Reinhold Mokrosch, in the *Theologische Realenzyklopädie* 8.609–16; and Heiko A. Oberman, *Masters of the Reformation: The Emergence of a New Intellectual Climate in Europe* (Cambridge, 1981), pp. 45–56.

7. The best discussion in English, with extensive summaries of letters, chronicles, and other historical evidence, is to be found in Post, *Modern Devotion*. Those able to read other languages will find additional help (and further literature) in Willem Lourdaux, "De Broeders van het Gemene Leven," *Bijdragen: Tijdschrift voor filosofie en theologie* 33 (1972): 372–416, an extended version of his "Les Frères de la Vie Commune," in the *Dictionnaire d'histoire et de géographie ecclésiastique* 18 (1977): 1438–54; Pierre Debongnie, "Devotion moderne," in the *Dictionnaire de la Spiritualité* 3 (1957): 727–47; C. C. de Bruin, E. Persoons, and A. G. Weiler, *Geert Grote en de moderne devotie* (Zutphen, 1984); *Moderne Devotie: Figuren en Facetten* (Utrecht-Deventer, 1984), the catalogue of an exhibition in origin, now one of the best guides to the subject; C. van der Wansem, *Het ontstaan en de geschiedenis der Broederschaap van het Gemene Leven* (Louvain, 1958); and Emile Brouette, "Devotio Moderna," *Theologische Realenzyklopädie* 8.605–09. There is an excellent guide to the sources and literature for each individual house (except the still missing Dutch volume) in *Monasticon fratrum vitae communis* (2 vols., Brussels, 1977/1979). For the German sisters there is now an excellent work by Gerhard Rehm, *Die Schwestern vom gemeinsamen Leben im nordwestlichen Deutschland* (Berlin, 1985) (available to me only as I completed this introduction). For Dutch houses of sisters and brothers, scholars must still use M. Schoengen, *Monasticon Batavum 2: De Augustijnsche Orden benevens de Broeders en Zusters van het Gemeene Leven* (Amsterdam, 1941). There are running bibliographies in *Ons geestelijk erf* and the *Archief voor de geschiedenis van de Katholieke Kerk in Nederland*.

8. This lay opposition to new religious orders, although little studied as yet, was a common feature of late medieval towns. It has been well presented for the New Devout (probably those in Zwolle) by Willem Lourdaux, "Dirk of Herxen's Tract *De utilitate monachorum*: A Defense of the Lifestyle of the Brethren and Sisters of the Common Life," in *Pascua Mediaevalia: Studies voor Prof. Dr. J.M. de Smet* (Louvain, 1983), pp. 312–36. Lourdaux and Marc Haverhals will soon publish an edition of this text. Elm, "Die Brüderschaft," p. 487 n. 40, will publish a similar defense, probably written for the brothers in Emmerich.

9. Gerard Zerbolt's defense was first published by Albert Hyma,

NOTES

"Het traktaat *Super modo vivendi devotorum hominum simul commorantium* door Gerard Zerbolt van Zutphen," *Archief voor de geschiedenis van het aartsbisdom Utrecht* 52 (1926): 1–100. See also L. Korth, "Die ältesten Gutachten über die Brüderschaft des gemeinsamen Lebens," *Mittheilungen aus dem Stadtarchiv Köln* 5 (1887): 1–27. See now the important chapter by Rehm, *Die Schwestern*, pp. 148–61; there is a summary of older literature in Post, *Modern Devotion*, pp. 273–92, but more study of the brothers' legal defense is needed: Elm, "Die Brüderschaft," pp. 386ff.

10. Lourdaux, "De Broeders," has emphasized the importance and similarity of these descriptions, and provides a number of the Latin originals in the body of his essay.

11. This is the central theme of Elm, "Die Brüderschaft."

12. Except for Lourdaux's "De Broeders," scholars have not sufficiently appreciated this point. In most extant archives or cartularies, a legal agreement reached with the local curate or authorities is among the first documents to be found.

13. The part of Gerard Zerbolt's defense that concerned this issue traveled independently and was also edited separately: Carl J. Jellouschek, "Ein mittelalterliches Gutachten über das Lesen der Bibel und sonstiger religiöser Bücher in der Volkssprache," in *Aus der Geisteswelt des Mittelalters*, ed. A. Lang, J. Lechner, and M. Schmaus (Münster, 1935), pp. 1181–99. It was also translated into the vernacular: J. Deschamps, "Middelnederlands vertalingen van *Super modo vivendi* (7de hoofdstuk) en *De libris teutonicalibus* van Gerard Zerbolt van Zutphen," *Handelingen der koninklijke Zuidnederlandse Maatschappij voor Taal-en Letterkunde en Geschiedenis* 14 (1960): 67–108, 15 (1961): 176–220.

14. See C. C. de Bruin, "De moderne devotie en de verspreiding van de volkstaalbijbel," *Ons geestelijk erf* 59 (1985): 344–56 (with further bibliography).

15. Rehm, *Die Schwestern*, is now essential, together with Schoengen for the Dutch houses. There are useful overviews in Post, *Modern Devotion*, pp. 259–72, and by Persoons in *Geert Grote*, pp. 60–63.

16. This development is traced in Post, *Modern Devotion*, pp. 259–64, who also edited the statutes: "De statuten van de Mr. Geertshuis te Deventer," *Archief voor de geschiedenis van het aartsbisdom Utrecht* 71 (1952): 1–46; cf. *Moderne Devotie*, pp. 128–30.

17. See F. W. J. Koorn, "Ongebonden vrouwen: Overeenkomsten en verschillen tussen begijnen en zusters des Gemenen Levens," *Ons geestelijk erf* 59 (1985): 393–402.

18. Post, *Modern Devotion*, pp. 494–95; Schoengen, *Monasticon Batavum 2*, passim; and Rehm, *Die Schwestern*, pp. 59–113, an excellent and

exemplary account (which I could no longer fully exploit for this Introduction).

19. For the brothers, see Post, *Modern Devotion*, pp. 197–272, 343–468; Persoons, in *Geert Grote*, pp. 65–78; the *Monasticon* for Belgium and Germany; Schoengen, *Monasticon Batavum 2*, for the Netherlands; van der Wansem, *Het ontstaan*, passim, on the problem of origins; *Moderne Devotie*, pp. 121–39; Robert Stupperich, "Brüder vom gemeinsamen Leben," *Theologische Realenzyklopädie* 7.220–25; and Scott Hendrix, "Brethren of the Common Life," *Dictionary of the Middle Ages* 2.366–70,

20. There is an excellent edition of these materials by M. Schoengen, *Jacobus Traiecti alias de Voecht, Narratio de inchoatione domus clericorum in Zwollis* (Amsterdam, 1908).

21. Summarized schematically by Persoons, in *Geert Grote*, pp. 66–67.

22. Acquoy, *Het Klooster*, is still basic, but the fundamental approach is now through the *Monasticon Windeshemense*, ed. W. Kohl, E. Persoons, and A. G. Weiler (Brussels, 3 vols., 1976–80). Useful overviews may be found in Post, *Modern Devotion*, pp. 293–313, 502–20; Persoons, in *Geert Grote*, pp. 79–100; *Moderne Devotie*, pp. 174–85.

23. The basic work on the statutes was done by E. Persoons and W. Lourdaux, "De statuten van de Windesheimse mannenkloosters in handschrift en druk," and "De statuten van de vrouwenkloosters aangesloten bij het Kapittel van Windesheim," *Archief voor de geschiedenis van de Katholieke Kerk in Nederland* 6 (1964): 180–224 and 9 (1967): 231–44.

24. L. Jocqué, "De Victorijnse wetgeving als inspiratiebron voor de constituties van Windesheim," *Ons geestelijk erf* 59 (1985): 211–23, and *Moderne Devotie*, pp. 177–78.

25. Relatively little has been done by way of serious study into the social origins of brothers and sisters, but see A. G. Weiler, "De intrede van rijke weduwen en arme meisjes in de leefgemeenschappen van de Moderne Devotie," *Ons geestelijk erf* 59 (1985): 403–19, and especially Rehm, *Die Schwestern*, pp. 212–24, with additional sections on the sisters' work and relations to late medieval cities (pp. 225–45).

26. Post, *Modern Devotion*, pp. 362–65. This was a point Post considered important and tended at times to overstate in reaction to Hyma and other "Protestant" interpretations.

27. See Robert Stupperich, "Luther and das Fraterhaus in Herford," in *Geist und Geschichte der Reformation, Festgabe H. Rückert zum 65. Geburtstag* (Berlin, 1966), pp. 19–38, for a full review of the documentation and the incident dated 1 January 1532 (WABr 6, Nr. 1900, 1901). Reformation historians have inevitably sought thematic or even doctrinal links between Luther and the brothers he was willing to "recommend"

at Herford in 1532, thus saving them from the closure required of other religious houses. It seems to me that what Luther saw in them was not Reformed teachings in any special sense but a reformed way of life that he and they considered grounded in the Gospel; as exemplary Christians and clergymen, they were not subject to the laws made against institutionalized monastic houses, and that was the operative point in the context of this letter.

28. The essential work for Louvain is Willem Lourdaux, *Moderne Devotie en christelijk humanisme* (Louvain, 1968), and for Tübingen, Oberman, *Masters of the Reformation*.

29. On the spirituality of the Modern Devotion, in addition to the general literature in note 7 above (especially the very useful dictionary article by Debongie), see F. Vandenbroucke, in J. Leclercq et al., *La spiritualité au moyen âge* (Paris, 1961), pp. 487–533, esp. 512–25; C. Egger, "Devozione moderna," in *Dizionario degli Istituti di Perfezione* (Rome, 1976), 3.456–63; R. Farcia-Villoslada, "Devotio Moderna," *New Catholic Encyclopedia* 4.831–32; Stephanus Axters, *Geschiedenis van de vroomheid in de Nederlanden:* vol. 3, *De Moderne Devotie 1380–1550* (Antwerp, 1956); K. C. L. M. de Beer, *Studie over de spiritualiteit van Geert Grote* (Brussels, 1938); L. A. M. Goosens, *De meditatie in de eerste tijd van de Moderne Devotie* (Antwerp-Amsterdam, 1952); C. C. de Bruin, "De spiritualiteit der Moderne Devotie," in *Geert Grote*, pp. 102–44; Otto Gründler, *"Devotio moderna atque antiqua:* The Modern Devotion and Carthusian Spirituality," in E. Rozanne Elder, ed., *The Roots of the Modern Christian Tradition* (Kalamazoo, Mich., 1984), pp. 27–45; Francis Oakley, *The Western Church in the Later Middle Ages* (Ithaca, N.Y., 1978), pp. 100–13; R. W. Southern, *Western Society and the Church in the Middle Ages* (Harmondswoth, 1970), pp. 331–58; Lucien Joseph Richard, *The Spirituality of John Calvin* (Atlanta, 1974), pp. 12–77.

30. J. J. Mak, "Christus bij de moderne devoten," *Ons geestelijk erf* 9 (1935): 105–64, offers useful detail on a theme often treated as a commonplace.

31. A masterful account of the way this tradition reached the Modern Devotion is offered by C. C. de Bruin, "Middeleeuwse levens van Jesus als leidsraad voor meditatie en contemplatie," *Nederlands archief voor kerkgeschiedenis* 58 (1977–1978): 129–55, 60 (1980): 162–81, 63 (1983): 129–73.

32. A first attempt at a systematic computerized analysis of the language of the Modern Devotion has been made by Leen Breure, "Het devote sterven als menselijke ervaring," *Ons geestelijk erf* 59 (1985): 435–55. Older works that deal with the spirituality of the Modern Devotion in part by way of its characteristic vocabulary and conceptions include

de Beer, *Studie*, and the introductions to D. de Man, ed., *Hier beginnen sommige stichtige punten van onsen oelden zusteren* ('s-Gravenhage, 1919), and D. A. Brinkerink, ed. *Van den doechden der vuriger ende stichtiger susteren van Diepen veen* (Groningen, 1904).

33. Discussion of this issue has not evolved significantly beyond that found in P. Debongnie, *Jean Mombaer* (Louvain-Toulouse, 1928), and M. Smits van Waesberghe, "Origine and developpement des Exercices spirituels avant saint Ignace," *Revue d'ascetique et de mystique* 33 (1957): 264–72, and summarized by Debongnie in "Exercices spirituels," in the *Dictionnaire de Spiritualité* 4. 1923–34.

34. The lives of Geert Grote: a *"dictamen rigmicum"* in 238 verses from 1421 and an *"aliud dictamen"* from ca. 1430 edited by Titus Brandsma, "Twee berijmde levens van Geert Grote," *Ons geestelijk erf* 16 (1942): 5–51; Thomas à Kempis's *Vita Gerardi Magni*, a part of his *Dialogus noviciorum*, 7.31–115; a *Vita magistri Gherardi* by Peter Hoorn, written probably before 1450 and edited by William J. Kühler, *Nederlands archief voor kerkgeschiedenis* n.s. 6 (1909): 325–70; and Rudolf Dier de Muiden, *Scriptum de magistro Gerardo* from about 1458 and edited by G. Dumbar in his *Analecta seu vetera aliquot scripta inedita* (Deventer, 1719), pp. 1–12. Manuscripts and further bibliography are listed in M. Carasso-Kok, *Repertorium van verhalende historische bronnen uit de middeleeuwen* ('s-Gravenhage, 1982) under nn. 215, 216, 371, 347, 361 respectively.

35. While nearly every treatment of the Modern Devotion begins with some remarks on Geert Grote, see Post, *Modern Devotion*, pp. 51–196; Theodore van Zijl, *Gerard Groote, Ascetic and Reformer (1340–1384)* (Washington, D.C., 1963); Georgette Epiney-Burgard, *Gérard Grote (1340–84) et les débuts de la devotion moderne* (Wiesbaden, 1970); A. G. Weiler's contribution to *Geert Grote*, pp. 9–55; and *Moderne Devotie*, pp. 78–117. His name (lit. "Gerrit the Great") has been spelled in a variety of ways. I have adopted the form closest to medieval usage and contemporary Dutch: Master Geert Grote. The "great," by the way, was an early family name coming from "the elder" (de Groot) in contrast with "the younger" (de Jong), and should not be misconstrued as a personal epithet, although Master Geert's medieval disciples already put such interpretations on it.

36. Letter 23, ed. W. Mulder, *Gerardi magni Epistolae* (Antwerp, 1933), pp. 105–06.

37. The best introduction to these translations is in A. G. Weiler, *Getijden van de eeuwige wijsheid naar de vertaling van Geert Grote* (Baarn, 1984), and *Moderne Devotie*, pp. 93–117, while the only reasonably complete edition is found in N. van Wijk, *Het getijdenboek van Geert Grote, naar het Haagse handschrift 133 E 21 uitgegeven* (Leiden, 1940).

38. The importance of this document for Grote's biography has been recognized: Epiney-Burgard, *Gérard Grote*, pp. 44–50; van Zijl, *Gerard Groote*, pp. 95–111; and especially Southern, *Western Society*, pp. 334–37.

39. How these sayings came to be preserved and passed down has yet to be sorted out in the manuscript tradition. Beyond that translated, the other main set of sayings, which mixes Master Geert's with those of Florens Radewijns, has been edited by J. F. Vregt, "Aliqua verba notabilia domini Florentii et magistri Gerardi magni," *Archief voor de geschiedenis van het aartsbisdom Utrecht* 10 (1882): 421–42.

40. The circumstances of this letter were noted by Johannes Busch, ed. Karl Grube, *Des Augustinerpropstes Iohanes Busch Chronicon Windeshemense und Liber de reformatione monasteriorum* (Halle, 1886) 149.

41. The exact circumstances remain unknown; A. G. Weiler, in *Geert Grote*, p. 51, tentatively suggests the man was a canon regular at Eemstein or Groenendael.

42. J. Busch, *Liber de reformatione monasteriorum* 22, ed. Grube 702–03 (see reference 40 above).

43. This sermon-treatise, no easy work, has received very little treatment to date. Compare Epiney-Burgard, *Gérard Grote*, pp. 258–65. There is now a critical edition with an Italian translation and extensive notes by Ilario Tolomio, *Gerardo Groote, Il trattato "De quattuor generibus meditabilium"* (Padua, 1975).

44. See note 34 above for the lives of Geert Grote. There is no single scholarly work that analyzes the interest shown in this movement for the lives of individual brothers and sisters.

45. In both Thomas à Kempis's *Dialogus noviciorum* and Rudolph Dier de Muiden's *Scriptum*, Florens Radewijns received the lengthiest treatment, and he was always remembered with genuine affection. The *Vita Johannis Brinkerinck* was edited by D. A. Brinckerinck, *Nederlands archief voor kerkgeschiedenis* n.s. 1 (1902): 323–54.

46. This is the oft-noted *Dialogus noviciorum*, followed much later by a chronicle of his house on the Agnietenberg; see H. J. Jedin, "Thomas von Kempen als Biograph und Chronist," in *Universitas: Festschrift Dr. A. Stohr* (Mainz, 1960), 2.69–77.

47. Deventer: Rudolph Dier de Muiden and others, of which the only edition is G. Dumbar's from 1719 (see note 34 above), pp. 1–223. For Zwolle, see the edition of Jacobus Traiecti de Voecht by Schoengen in note 20 above, pp. 1–215.

48. For Master Geert's house, the main source is the collection of lives edited by de Man.

49. The essential chronicler of Windesheim was John Busch; his *Chronicon* is also organized essentially in terms of "lives."

50. For the canonesses at Diepenveen, there are slightly varying accounts, of which one has been edited: Brinckerinck, *Van den doechden*. A brief account of these differing manuscripts (with further literature) appears in *Moderne Devotie*, pp. 211–13.

51. The concluding chapter of his "Liber de viris illustribus" published in the *Chronicon Windesheimense*, ed. Grube, pp. 222–26.

52. The standard edition is de Man, *Hier beginnen*, and his introduction (pp. xi–xciv) remains basic. Recent work on this text includes Weiler, "De intrede van rijke," and Breure, "Het devote sterven."

53. W. Jappe-Alberts and M. Ditsche, *Fontes historiam domus fratrum Embricensis aperientes* (Groningen, 1969). See the *Monasticon fratrum vitae communis: Deutschland* (Brussels, 1979), pp. 63–68, for further sources and literature, and compare the overview of Emmerich's history in Post, *Modern Devotion*, pp. 415–21.

54. There is an overview of these *rapiaria* in Axters, *Geschiedenis*, pp. 84–87, and in *Moderne Devotie*, pp. 153–60. For Florens Radewijns, see M. van Woerkum, "Het Libellus *Omnes inquit artes*, een rapiarium van Florentius Radwijns," *Ons geestelijk erf* 25 (1951): 133–58, 225–68; and Goosens, *De meditatie*, pp. 209–54. On Dirk of Herxen, see *Moderne Devotie*, pp. 139–43.

55. For an introduction to these customaries, see van der Wansem, *Het ontstaan*, pp. 25–47; and W. Jappe Alberts, *Consuetudines fratrum vitae communis* (Fontes minores medii aevi 8, Groningen, 1959), pp. vii–xii, which includes the edition of two texts. The customary of Zwolle, translated in this book, is printed in Schoengen, *Jacobus Traiecti*, pp. 239–73, and taken from Jacobus Phillipi, *Reformatorium vitae clericorum* (Basel, 1494). There are two interrelated sets from 's-Hertogenbosch, printed in G. van der Elzen-W. Hovenaars, *Analecta Gijsberti Coeverinx* (Den Bosch, 1905), pp. 93–115, another almost certainly from the Lord Florens house in Deventer and edited as Appendix C in Hyma, *Christian Renaissance*, pp. 440–74; that from Emmerich in Alberts and Ditsche, *Fontes historium*; others from German houses in A. Miraeus, *Regulae et constitutiones clericorum in congregatione viventium* (Antwerp, 1638), pp. 144–50; and especially Robert Stupperich, *Das Fraterhaus zu Herford*, vol. 2: *Statuten, Bekenntnisse, Briefwechsel* (Münster, 1984), pp. 55–132.

56. On the date and origin of this text, see Schoengen, *Jacobus Traiecti*, pp. cxxvi–cxlix, and van der Wansem, *Het ontstaan*, pp. 26–30. Beyond the links to Deventer and other Dutch houses, the parallels to the customary of Herford, dated to 1437, are also considerable.

57. See Rehm, *Die Schwestern*, pp. 180–89, together with his presentation of the offices and "inner ordering" of the sisters' houses, pp. 190–

211; cf. Post, *Modern Devotion*, pp. 259–65, and his edition of the statutes (see note 16 above).

58. The basic work remains W. J. Kühler, *Johannes Brinckerinck en zijn klooster te Diepenveen* (Leiden, 1914), with a full discussion on pp. 202–27. There is a life of Salome in Middle Dutch in the collection edited by Brinckerinck (*Van den doechden*), and a Latin version in Brussels, Royal Library 8849–59, ff. 149r–164v.

59. General information in André Rayez, "Exercices spirituels," *Dictionnaire de Spiritualité* (Paris, 1960), 4.1902–23; and Debongnie, "Devotion moderne"; cf. *Moderne Devotie*, pp. 297–300.

60. The essential critical study and edition of the Latin text is Monica Hedlund's *Epistola de vita et passione Domini nostri: Der lateinische Text mit Einleitung und Kommentar* (Leiden, 1975).

61. Johannes Busch, *Chronicon Windeshemense*, ed. Grube, 32, 244.

62. C. C. de Bruin, "De dietse oertekst van de anonieme *Epistola de vita et passione Domini nostri Ihesu Christi et aliis devotis exerciciis*," *Nederlands archief voor kerkgeschiedenis* 34 (1944–1945): 1–23.

63. Nearly all that is known about John Kessel derives from Thomas à Kempis's *Dialogus noviciorum* 4, ed. Pohl 7.292–306, with the text of his personal meditations or exercises following on pp. 306–17. The quotations in the text are from Thomas à Kempis.

64. The basic work on Dirc of Herxen remains the dissertation by P. H. J. Knierim, *Dirc van Herxen (1381–1457) rector van het Zwolse fraterhuis* (Amsterdam, 1926). Compare Post, *Modern Devotion*, pp. 360–82, and *Moderne Devotie*, pp. 139–44.

65. There is no single work on the origins and developing tradition of collations within the Modern Devotion. General information and some literature may be found in de Bruin, in *Geert Grote*, pp. 102–44; *Moderne Devotie*, pp. 161–67; and G. C. Zieleman, *De preek bij de moderne devoten: een verkenning* (Deventer, 1984).

66. Despite his importance, Gerlach Peters has received relatively little scholarly attention. The basic study of his life and edition of his works remains Willem Moll, "Gerlach Peters en zijn schriften: Eene bijdrage tot de kennis van de letter-arbeid der school van Geert Groote en Florens Radewijns," *Kerkhistorisch archief* 2 (1859): 145–246. Compare Post, *Modern Devotion*, pp. 337–42; *Moderne Devotie*, pp. 185–89.

67. The literature on Brinckerinck and his collations is much more extensive: basic are Kühler, *Johannes Brinckerinck*, passim; Willem Moll, "Acht collacien van Johannes Brinckerinck, een bijdrage tot de kennis van den kanselarbeid der Broeders van het Gemene Leven," *Kerkhistorisch archief* 4 (1866): 97–166; Post, *Modern Devotion*, pp. 330–31; and the newest effort to resolve complicated questions of authorship, Pieter F.

NOTES

J. Obbema, "Brinckerinck en Jan van Schoonhoven," in *Codex in Context: Studies . . . aangeboden aan Prof. Dr. A. Gruijs* (Nijmegen/Grave, 1985), pp. 277–87 (with more literature).

68. The materials concerning Hildesheim, including Peter of Dieburg's chronicle, were edited by Richard Doebner, *Annalen und Akten der Brüder des gemeinsamen Lebens im Lüchtenhofe zu Hildesheim* (Hannover-Leipzig, 1903). General information and complete bibliography in the *Monasticon fratrum communis vitae: Deutschland*, pp. 83–93.

69. For a full discussion of manuscripts and editions down to the mid-1930s, see J. van Rooi, *Gerard Zerbolt van Zutphen: Leven en Geschriften* (Nijmegen, 1936), pp. 287–322, 358–85. Not yet available to me was a new work by G. H. Gerrits, *Inter Timorem et Spem: A Study of the Theological Thought of Gerard Zerbolt of Zutphen (1367–98)* (Leiden, 1986). For the Dutch-Latin text, see H. Mahieu, *Gerardi a Zutphania, De spirtualibus ascensionibus* (Bruges, 1941). The English translation was that of J. P. Arthur, *The Spiritual Ascent: A Devotional Treatise by Gerard of Zutphen* (London, 1908). It was done in an archaizing English characteristic of some Victorian religious writing ("Here beginneth the devout treatise" . . . etc.), and I have deliberately avoided using it.

70. Albert Hyma, "Is Gerard Zerbolt of Zutphen the author of the *Super modo vivendi?*" *Nederlands archief voor kerkgeschiedenis* n.s. 16 (1921): 107–28. For newer literature on Gerard Zerbolt, beyond van Rooi and in expectation of Gerrits, see Post, *Modern Devotion*, pp. 325–30, and *Moderne Devotie*, pp. 144–51.

71. For general information on the Observant Movement, now widely regarded as the essential religious context for the Modern Devotion, see Kaspar Elm, "Verfall und Erneuerung des Ordenswesens im Spätmittelalter: Forschungen und Forschungsaufgaben," in *Untersuchungen zu Kloster und Stift* (Veröffentlichungen des Max-Planck-Instituts für Geschichte 68, Göttingen, 1980), pp. 188–238.

PART I

1. This translation follows the Latin text in Michael Joseph Pohl, *Thomas Hemerken à Kempis, Opera Omnia* (Freiburg, 1922), 7.87–107. The subtitles in brackets were provided by me, except those on pp. 70, 71, and 73, which almost certainly came from a medieval editor and not Grote himself. It is quite possible that these *Resolutions* were left in fragments by Grote.

2. Vergil, *Georgica*, 2.501–02.

3. A full treatment of these books and their influence on Grote in Epiney-Burgard, *Gérard Grote*, pp. 51–103.

NOTES

4. In the Late Middle Ages the *pax* was a board passed around to be kissed at mass, which came to be regarded as a kind of spiritual communion at a time when actual communion was infrequent among the laity.

5. This translation follows the Latin text provided by Pohl, *Opera Omnia*, 7.107–09.

6. This translation follows the edition by Willelmus Mulder, *Gerardi Magni Epistolae* (Antwerp, 1933), pp. 124–31.

7. Ovid, *Remedia amoris*, 91.

8. *Horologium Sapientiae* 2.2, ed. P. Künzle (III n. 9 below) 526ff.

9. A reference to Ruusbroec's *Vanden kerstenen ghelove* (On Christian Faith).

10. This translation follows the edition by Mulder, *Gerardi Magni Epistolae*, pp. 232–43.

11. Augustine, *Confessions*, 9.12.

12. The Middle Dutch text was edited by J. van Vloten, "Zedelijke toespraak van Geert Groete," *Nieuw archief voor kerkgeschiedenis* 2 (1854): 299–307.

13. See Thomas, *Summa Theologiae*, II/II q. 62.

14. This translation follows the text provided by Ilario Tolomio, *Il trattato "De quattuor generibus meditabilium"* (Padua, 1975). Scholars should consult his introduction, notes, and Italian translation.

15. *De celesti ierarchia* 2: *PL* 122.1040. The preceding three paragraphs have echoed this chapter at several points.

16. This was borrowed from the *Life of Nicholas* found in James of Voragine's *Golden Legend*.

17. Augustine, *Confessions*, 7.1, and *On True Religion*, 55, 108.

18. There follows here a lengthy quotation (omitted in my translation) from Augustine, *On the Trinity*, 8.45.

19. Here and in the paragraphs that follow Master Geert draws on a number of points he would have learned and developed at university while studying Aristotle's *On Sense and Sensation*.

20. Compare Aristotle, *De sen. et sens.*, I.437 a 14–15 (see Tolomio, *Il trattato*, p. 90 n. 76).

21. Compare Thomas, *Summa Theologiae* I. q. 35 a. (this noted by Tolomio, *Il trattato*, p. 95).

22. Ps-Dionysius, *De celesti hierarchia*, 1: *PL* 122.1038.

23. Compare William of St. Thierry, *De natura et dignitate amoris* 35, 24, and the commentary by Tolomio, *Il trattato*, pp. 104–05, n. 89.

24. Ps-Dionysius, *De celesti hierarchia*, 1: *PL* 122.1039; and earlier Aristotle, *On Sense and Sensation*, II.438ff, IV.443.

NOTES

25. Ps-Dionysius, *De divinis nominibus: PL* 122.1133; and *Epistola IX ad Titum*.
26. In fact, William of St. Thierry, *De natura et dignitate amoris*, 5.
27. Jerome, *In Epistolam ad Galat.* 3.5: *PL* 26.450.
28. Thomas of Cantimpré, *Bonum universale de apibus*, 2.35.

PART II

1. The Dutch text is found in D. de Man, *Hier beginnen sommige stichtige punten van onsen oelden zusteren* ('s-Gravenhage, 1919), pp. 3–25, 245–53.
2. An allusion to Ps 117/118:24, used in the Easter morning liturgy.
3. The Latin text is found in Jappe-Alberts and Ditsche, *Fontes historiam*, pp. 28–37, 58–66.
4. This is the opening sentence in Gerard Zerbolt's *Spiritual Ascensions* (Part IV, below), another indication of how widely read this work was among the New Devout.

PART III

1. The Latin text may be found in Schoengen, *Jacobus Traiecti*, pp. 239–73.
2. These were two of the most influential religious guides for the brothers and sisters: John Cassian's *Collations*, and David of Augsburg's *De profectu religiosorum*, 1.3, in *Opera Omnia sancti Bonaventurae* (Paris, 1898), 12.332–35.
3. This is another text well known among the brothers and sisters, William of St.-Thierry's *Golden Epistle* (frequently attributed to Bernard during the Middle Ages); see *Guillaume de Saint-Thierry, Lettre aux Frères du Mont-Dieu* (Sources chrétiennes 223, Paris, 1975), pp. 266ff.
4. "Schoolboys" and "men of goodwill" (lay folk) were, beyond sisters, the two main categories of people for whom the brothers felt a religious and quasi-pastoral responsibility.
5. A reference to the brothers' contested legal status; see Introduction, note 9.
6. These were among the earliest houses of the movement, respectively the canons at Windesheim (1387), at the Agnietenberg (1398), and at Bethlehem (ca. 1400), all in or near Zwolle, and the brothers in Deventer (mid 1380s), in Hulsberghen (1407), and in Alberghen (1406). By the early 1420s all were established and recognized houses.

NOTES

7. The Latin text may be found in Kühler, *Johannes Brinckerinck*, pp. 360–80.

8. The best edition of the Latin text may be found in Hedlund, *Epistola de vita et passione*, pp. 89–110.

9. On this work, another of the texts well known in the movement of the Modern Devotion, see Pius Künzle, *Heinrich Seuses Horologium Sapientiae* (Spicilegium Friburgense 23, Freiburg/Sch., 1977), pp. 28ff.

10. The Latin text may be found in Thomas à Kempis's *Dialogus noviciorum*, in the *Opera Omnia*, 7.306–17.

11. The Latin text may be found in Knierim, *Dirc van Herxen*, pp. 160–66.

12. Dirk of Herxen used three Dutch sayings in the midst of his Latin text, another indication of the importance of these short sayings as guides to their religious lives.

13. The Middle Dutch text may be found in Moll, "Gerlach Peters," pp. 202–15.

14. The Middle Dutch text may be found in Moll, "Acht collacien," pp. 111–21.

15. The Middle Dutch text may be found in ibid., pp. 143–47.

16. The Latin text may be found in Doebner, *Annalen und Akten*, pp. 144–50.

PART IV

1. This translation follows the Latin and Dutch texts provided by Mahieu, *Gerardi a Zutphania, De spiritualibus ascenionibus*. His Dutch text is a slightly modernized version of the original Middle Dutch translation. Zerbolt's text becomes repetitive at a few points, as many of these devotional treatises did, and I have abbreviated or summarized a few sections in the interest of saving space.

Index to Texts

Other Volumes in this Series